STUDIES IN BAPTIST HISTORY AND THOUGHT

Analogous Uses of Language, Eucharistic Identity, and the 'baptist' Vision

STUDIES IN BAPTIST HISTORY AND THOUGHT

STUDIES IN BAPTIST HISTORY AND THOUGHT

Analogous Uses of Language, Eucharistic Identity, and the 'baptist' Vision

Aaron B. James

WIPF & STOCK · Eugene, Oregon

Wipf and Stock Publishers
199 W 8th Ave, Suite 3
Eugene, OR 97401

Analogous Uses of Language, Eucharistic Identity, and the 'baptist' Vision
By James, Aaron

ISBN 13: 978-1-62564-840-2
Publication date 4/15/2014
Previously published by Paternoster, 2014

STUDIES IN BAPTIST HISTORY AND THOUGHT

Series Preface

Baptists form one of the largest Christian communities in the world, and while they hold the historic faith in common with other mainstream Christian traditions, they nevertheless have important insights which they can offer to the worldwide church. *Studies in Baptist History and Thought* will be one means towards this end. It is an international series of academic studies which includes original monographs, revised dissertations, collections of essays and conference papers, and aims to cover any aspect of Baptist history and thought. While not all the authors are themselves Baptists, they nevertheless share an interest in relating Baptist history and thought to the other branches of the Christian church and to the wider life of the world.

The series includes studies in various aspects of Baptist history from the seventeenth century down to the present day, including biographical works, and Baptist thought is understood as covering the subject-matter of theology (including interdisciplinary studies embracing biblical studies, philosophy, sociology, practical theology, liturgy and women's studies). The diverse streams of Baptist life throughout the world are all within the scope of these volumes.

The series editors and consultants believe that the academic disciplines of history and theology are of vital importance to the spiritual vitality of the churches of the Baptist faith and order. The series sets out to discuss, examine and explore the many dimensions of their tradition and so to contribute to their on-going intellectual vigour.

A brief word of explanation is due for the series identifier on the front cover. The fountains, taken from heraldry, represent the Baptist distinctive of believer's baptism and, at the same time, the source of the water of life. There are three of them because they symbolize the Trinitarian basis of Baptist life and faith. Those who are redeemed by the Lamb, the book of Revelation reminds us, will be led to 'fountains of living waters' (Rev. 7.17).

To:

St. John The Evangelist Catholic Church, McAlester, OK
Immaculate Heart of Mary Catholic Church, Magnolia, AR
Lakewood Christian Church, McAlester, OK
Hopewell Baptist Church, Bethel Acres, OK
University Baptist Church, Shawnee, OK
Calvary Baptist Church, Shawnee, OK
Immanuel Baptist Church, Norman, OK
Far Hills Community Church, Dayton, OH

". . . so that through the church the manifold wisdom of God might now be made known to the rulers and authorities in the heavenly places."
Ephesians 3:10

Contents

Acknowledgements

It is not uncommon for authors to assert that without the help of so and so his book would not have been completed. I always assumed that such a claim was gracious rhetorical overstatement—until, that is, I tried to write a book. So, I join so many past authors in asserting that without the help of many people this book would not have been completed.

First, and most importantly, my wife, Jessica, deserves much credit for suffering through working 'vacations,' blank stares, and forgotten tasks. She labored hard when her husband was absent from so many of the tasks that make marriage and a 'real life' possible. Also, much thanks to Maddie whose exuberant, toddler ballerina dances entertained (and continue to entertain) her father endlessly. Her little sister, Callie, was gracious enough to wait until after the substance of the text was completed before making her beautiful entrance into the world. My parents deserve much credit for supporting my education, both financially and spiritually.

This project originated as my dissertation in completion of the PhD in Theology at the University of Dayton. I could not have asked for better guidance, both on the substance of the project, and on the practical difficulties of writing a dissertation than I received from my friend, mentor, and advisor, Brad Kallenberg. Kelly Johnson, Elizabeth Newman, Matthew Levering, and John Inglis served as fair, probing, and constructive examiners.

Thanks must also go to my friends and colleagues, Shawn Graves, Ryan Peterson, and John White. All of us were hired to full time teaching positions before the completion of our PhD degrees, and so wandered together through the dark and frightful forest of not-yet-completed-dissertations. Thankfully, all of us survived and flourished on the journey. Their encouragement was invaluable.

All of the churches to which this project is dedicated have nurtured my life in Christ in various ways. My own personal convoluted ecclesial history forms the backdrop of the project, and so the project is offered in the hopes that it might serve as one small step toward healing the wounds of division in Christ's body.

CHAPTER 1

Introduction

In the following book, I argue that attention to analogous uses of language reveals there to be an intrinsic relation between Eucharistic identity claims and James Wm. McClendon's articulation of the 'baptist' vision, such that the baptist vision and the identity of Jesus's body in the bread and in the church are not foreign to one another, but in fact share an internal 'logic' that is mutually illuminating of their real (i.e., not merely figural or symbolic) identity.[1] Furthermore, it is the baptist vision itself that baptists ought fruitfully to offer as a constructive contribution to broadly catholic reflection on Eucharistic identity.[2]

---

1 McClendon's use of (lower case 'b') baptist needs to be explained. The baptist vision is not limited to denominational Baptists, and so McClendon prefers to speak of those who inhabit the vision as (lower case 'b') 'baptists.' McClendon says, "Who are these present sharers [of the vision]? Well, I cannot say. There is no single, distinct body of people called 'believers church,' or 'baptists.' Empirically, there are indeed Disciples of Christ and Churches of Christ, Mennonites, Plymouth Brethren, Adventists, Russian Evangelicals, perhaps Quakers, certainly black Baptists (who often go by other names), the (Anderson, Indiana) Church of God, Southern and British and European and American Baptists, the Church of the Brethren, the Assemblies of God and other Pentecostal bodies, assorted intentional communities not self-defined churches, missionary affiliates of all of the above (and . . . hundreds of other bodies even in the United States and Canada alone)." James Wm. McClendon, Jr, *Ethics*, 2nd. ed., vol. 1 of *Systematic Theology* (Nashville: Abingdon Press, 2002), 33-34.

In the course of the book, I will use both 'Baptist' and 'baptist.' My own ecclesial context, and an intended primary audience of this book, is denominational Baptists. So, when referring to these denominational Baptists I will use (capital 'B') Baptist; when referring to the vision that these denominational Baptists share more broadly with others, I will use (lower case 'b') baptist.

2 Through the course of this book I will use (lower case 'c') 'catholic' to refer to the corporate identity of all churches as one church in Christ. 'Catholic' (with a capital 'C') will be reserved for the Roman Catholic Church. Furthermore, I will usually continue to use (lower case 'c') 'church' for both a local church and the church catholic, except when discussing the views of others when I will follow the convention they have adopted. I recognize that there is much substantial disagreement among Christians about

In this first, introductory chapter, I identify the context that situates my claim (a context to be more fully explicated in chapter 2), and the method followed in defending the claim. I also briefly introduce what I mean by 'real' and 'merely symbolic' identity claims. Finally, I offer a brief survey of the chapters to come.

Whither a Claim About Eucharistic Identity and the 'baptist' Vision?

In the synoptic gospels and in Paul's first letter to the Corinthians we are told of the identity claim Jesus utters at the Last Supper, an identity claim that has proved seminally determinative of Christian Eucharistic practice and reflection: this is my body; this is my blood. Furthermore, Paul in the same letter makes explicit the link between Jesus's body and the church, and between the church, Jesus's body, and the bread: "Is not the bread that we break a participation in the body of Christ? Because there is one loaf, we, who are many, are one body, for we all partake of the one loaf" (1 Cor. 10:16-17).

The majority (though importantly, not all) of Baptists have understood these identity claims merely symbolically. That is, this is not *really* Christ's body; it is, rather, nothing but a figure or symbol of Christ's body.[3] Likewise, if the church is one body, it can only be insofar as the bread is nothing but a symbol or figure of the church. Particularly among North American Baptists, this understanding of the sense of the words is so pervasive that Herschel H. Hobbs, the most prominent spokesperson in the mid-20th century for the largest Baptist denomination in the world can say simply without defense or explanation, "Baptists believe that the Lord's Supper is symbolic. The bread and fruit of the vine are but symbols of the broken body and spilled blood of Jesus."[4]

Yet, this majority Baptist impulse is at odds with the broad trajectory of the Christian church. As contemporary British Baptist John Colwell has

---

what constitutes a church, much less the whole church, whether a Baptist can talk intelligibly about the whole church in a way at all analogous to the way a Roman Catholic does, and what and who constitute the catholic church. Still, 'catholic' and 'church' are good theological words, and any practical confusion about the adopted convention is itself a witness to our convoluted ecclesial existences.

3 See below, the section entitled "A Brief Word On 'Real' and 'Merely'" (p. 17-18) for some explication of what I mean by 'real' and 'symbolic' identity.

4 Herschel H. Hobbs, *What Baptists Believe* (Nashville: Broadman Press, 1964), 84. Of course, an affirmation of symbol need not entail *mere* symbol. Yet, this is Hobbs' unmistakable intent. He contrasts this view with three others: Roman Catholic transubstantiation, Lutheran consubstantiation, and the (Calvinist) view that "grace is present with the elements, or that the partakers receives grace thereby which is not available otherwise" (Ibid., 84).

observed, "It is the reality of the Lord's Supper as a participation in Christ's body and blood, in his once-for-all sacrifice, that the overwhelming majority of the Church, for the overwhelming majority of its history, and from its earliest extant confessions, has unequivocally affirmed: the risen Christ is made present here in a unique manner and to a unique degree."[5] Hence, while there are no doubt symbols involved, to reduce the Lord's Supper to *mere* symbolism is strikingly out of step with most of the rest of the Christian church.

Herschel Hobbs and most Baptists have resisted 'realistic' identifications of bread and body as perceived by way of the Reformation disputes, where 'realistic' is set against merely metaphorical or merely symbolic (i.e., illustrative) identifications. Consequently, the Baptist rejection of real identity, though also having in view Lutheranism and variations of Reformed theology, has largely had in its sights Roman Catholic transubstantiation.

Yet, despite Roman Catholic claims to the contrary, it is not at all clear that Roman Catholic transubstantiation is any more in the broad tradition of the catholic church than the Baptist rejection of real identity. Some Eastern Orthodox theologians have raised objections to transubstantiation.[6] The official way of articulating transubstantiation is not even the *only* way of articulating the claim in Roman Catholicism's own history.[7] So, while transubstantiation may be a Catholic teaching, it is disputable whether it is a catholic teaching.[8]

Furthermore, if transubstantiation is not catholic in the sense that it is not shared by all Christians, it furthermore may not be catholic insofar as it appears to be at variance with theologians and traditions Roman Catholicism claims as its own. In particular, Roman Catholic philosopher Garth L. Hallett has noted that the claim that the bread is changed without remainder into the body of Christ, so that after the conversion there is no longer bread but only body,

---

5 John E. Colwell, *Promise and Presence: An Exploration of Sacramental Theology* (Milton Keynes: Paternoster Press, 2005), 162-163.

6 For example, see Alexander Schmemann, *The Eucharist: Sacrament Of the Kingdom*, trans. Paul Kachur (Crestwood, NY: St. Vladimir's Seminary Press, 1987). Schmemann will be considered more fully in chapter 4. For another Eastern Orthodox objection, see Sergius Bulgakov, *The Holy Grail and the Eucharist*, trans. Boris Jakim (Hudson, NY: Lindisfarne Books, 1997).

7 For example, see Gary Macy's discussion of the various officially acceptable understandings of the conversion, and one "blunder" of a version forced upon Berangar, in Macy's *Treasures From the Storeroom: Medieval Religion and the Eucharist* (Collegeville, MN: The Liturgical Press, 1999), 20-35.

8 Unless, of course, one simply defines catholic as co-terminus with Roman Catholic, a point that reminds us that 'catholic' is one of those perennially essentially contested concepts that goes to the heart of Christian identity.

appears to be at variance with, perhaps even in contradiction to, a number of the church fathers.[9]

A brief sampling should be enough to illustrate the point: Ignatius easily refers to the Eucharistic meal as "Bread of God."[10] Justin appears to hold together clearly bread and body: "Not as common bread or as common drink do we receive these, but just as through the Word of God, Jesus Christ, our Savior, became incarnate and took on flesh and blood for our salvation, so . . . the food . . . is both the flesh and blood of that incarnate Jesus."[11] Irenaeus appears to state rather explicitly that the Eucharistic bread is both bread and body: "For as the bread of the earth, receiving the invocation of God, is no longer common bread but Eucharist, *made up of two things*, an earthly and a heavenly, so also our bodies, partaking of the Eucharist are no longer corruptible, having the hope of the resurrection to eternity."[12] Ephraem the Syrian affirmed explicitly the identification of bread with body.[13] Augustine says, "What you see, then, is bread and a cup. This is what your eyes report to you. But your faith has need to be taught that the bread is the body of Christ, the cup the blood of Christ;"[14] and "The bread which you see on the altar, sanctified by God's word, is the body of Christ. The cup, or rather its contents, sanctified by God's word, is the blood of Christ. Through these Christ our Lord wished to bequeath his body and His blood which He shed for us for the forgiveness of sins."[15]

Of course, several of these *may* be consistent with transubstantiation; but they are not obviously so. Furthermore, there are more problematic sayings of the fathers. John of Damascus appears harder to square with transubstantiation: "since it is man's custom to eat bread and drink water and wine, he *joined* his Divinity to these and made them His body and blood;"[16] and "In like manner, the bread of communion is not plain bread, but bread *united to* divinity."[17] Likewise, Theodoret of Cyrus: "for not even after the consecration do the

---

9 See Garth L. Hallett, *Identity and Mystery in Themes of Christian Faith: Late-Wittgensteinian Perspectives* (Aldershot: Ashgate, 2005), 96-97. Hallett will be considered further in chapter 3.

10 Ignatius, "Letter To the Romans," 7.3, in Daniel J. Sheerin, *The Eucharist*, Message of the Church Fathers, vol. 7 (Wilmington, DE: Michael Glazier, 1986), 243.

11 Justin, *First Apology*, 65, in Sheerin, 34.

12 Ireneaus, *Against Heretics* IV, xviii, 5. Cited in Darwell Stone, *A History of the Doctrine Of the Holy Eucharist*, vol. 1 (London: Longmans, Green, and Co., 1909), 35. Emphasis added.

13 Ephraem, *Memra for the Fifth Day of Great Week*, in Sheerin,139.

14 Augustine, Sermon 272, in Sheerin, 94.

15 Augustine, Sermon 227, in Sheerin, 96.

16 John of Damascus, *Exposition of the Orthodox Faith*, 86, Sheerin 170. Emphasis added.

17 Ibid., 171. Emphasis added.

mystical symbols depart from their own nature. *They continue in their former essence*, both in shape and appearance, and are visible, and palpable, as they were beforehand. But they are considered to be what they have become, and are believed to be that, and are adored as truly being those things they are believed to be."[18] Finally, Pope Gelasius: "Yet the substance or nature of the bread and wine does not cease to be. . . . Thus, as the elements pass into this, that is the divine, substance by the operation of the Holy Ghost, and *nonetheless remain in their own proper nature*, so they show that the principle mystery itself . . . consists in this, that the two natures remain each in its own proper being so that there is one Christ because He is whole and real."[19]

Now, of course, there may be ways for Roman Catholics to square these sayings with transubstantiation; or, if not, to understand them in terms of a trajectory or development of doctrine. But, at minimum, following the lead of Hallett, I only mean to note that it is not only conceptually possible, but apparently evidenced in the patristic sources, to affirm a real identity of bread and body (i.e., not merely symbolic) such that both poles of the identity remain without competition.

That such an identification is possible is relevant to the 'baptist' vision as articulated by James William McClendon Jr. McClendon frames his three volume systematic theology around what he calls the 'baptist' vision.[20] McClendon claims that this vision is what organizes baptist practice and theology and animates baptist life. This vision is at heart a strategy for reading Scripture, a vision that "effects a link between the church of the apostles and our own church."[21] It is a hermeneutical principal of a "shared awareness of the present Christian community as the primitive community and the eschatological community."[22] Hence, the baptist vision is fundamentally an identity claim linking *this* church with *that* church.

In fact, it is an identity claim that helpfully illuminates Eucharistic identity, a claim that, I will argue, shares a 'logic' of real identity, without collapsing the poles of the identity into one another. If this proves true, that the baptist vision shares an intrinsic relationship with Eucharistic identity, then it may prove to be the case that, at least in one respect, this dissenting vision is a thoroughly catholic vision. Of course, the dissenters operating by this vision have come to conclusions about disputed matters and disputed practices that in some (though certainly not all) cases are at variance with the broadly catholic church. But, if I am right, the point remains: the vision that animates them is a catholic vision.

---

18 Theodoret of Cyrus, *Eranistes*, Dialogue 2, in Sheerin, 258.

19 Gelasius, *On the Two Natures of Christ*, in Stone, 102.

20 See footnote 1 above for McClendon's use of (little 'b') 'baptist.'

21 McClendon, *Ethics*, 30.

22 Ibid.

This is the claim I mean to pursue. I do not intend to construct a full-blown baptist doctrine of the Lord's Supper, or of the real presence of Christ in the Lord's Supper. Nor do I intend to construct a theory of sacrament that can account for the baptist vision and Eucharistic identity. Nor do I intend a primarily historical investigation of the church fathers, or of Roman Catholic transubstantiation, or of Baptist rejections of real identity. Rather, I intend this as a conceptual investigation, an exploration of the shared linguistic and conceptual contours of the claim 'this is my body' and 'this church is that church.' The fruit of this investigation is, hopefully, the thesis I mean to defend: namely, that attention to the analogous uses of language that constitute Eucharistic identity claims, and that constitute James William McClendon's articulation of the 'baptist' vision, shows there to be an intrinsic relation between the two, such that the 'baptist' vision and the identity of Jesus's body in the bread and in the church are not foreign to one another, but in fact share an internal 'logic' that is mutually illuminating of their real (i.e., not merely figural or symbolic) identity.

Consequently, this book is aimed first at Baptists, and secondarily at the church catholic. In particular, I mean to prod Baptists to reconsider their usual ways of articulating the identities of bread, body and church in light of their own animating vision. As suggested above, this is not a full theology of the Lord's Supper. For Baptists, such a theology must center on Scripture, and while attention will be given to Scripture, it is not the primary goal to fully exegete the relevant Eucharistic passages. Hence, for Baptists, this can remain but a 'working hypothesis,' one that needs further, more complete biblical testing. Even so, as I will suggest later on, the 'working hypothesis,' if right, will *demand* a reconsideration of central biblical texts precisely because it suggests that the conceptual framework within which Baptists have traditionally read those texts has not adequately taken into account analogous uses of language in identity claims.

To the church catholic, I mean this investigation of Eucharistic identity and baptist identity to display the contours of a broadly catholic understanding of the identity of bread, body and church, an understanding that *may* be consistent with transubstantiation (or, a number of other ways of articulating the identity), but need not require it (or, any other particular way of articulating the identity). However, to repeat, there is no pretense of a broadly catholic *theory* of real presence. Rather, I mean to call attention to the conceptual contours of Eucharistic identity claims about bread, body, and the church in light of analogous uses of language. Furthermore, if I am right that there is an intrinsic relation between the baptist vision and Eucharistic identity, then the implicit suggestion is that baptist dissent has something constructive to say to the church catholic.

The sort of claim I mean to make can be illuminated by considering the method adopted for the project. As I indicated above, this project is neither historical, nor exegetical, but rather conceptual. My use of conceptual owes much to Ludwig Wittgenstein. Wittgenstein's mode of doing philosophy turns out to be helpful for a theological project such as this. So, to method I now turn.

Method and Wittgenstein

The model followed in this book is that of Ludwig Wittgenstein's way of doing philosophy. Wittgenstein's writing is not thesis driven in the sense of a series of new proposals set out to solve philosophical problems. Rather, his writing is a series of comparisons, examples, pictures, often by means of pointed aphorisms or implicit dialogue, the purpose of which is to open our eyes to the unnoticed and unexamined pictures by which we operate. Calling attention to these unexamined pictures serves the ultimate purpose of bringing clarity to our ordinary uses of language. This way of writing constitutes a method of doing philosophy which self-consciously illuminates what is already before us in order to help us go on living well.

In what follows, I offer a brief overview of Wittgenstein's method of doing philosophy for the purpose of identifying a pattern to follow throughout this book. First, I explore what Wittgenstein thought progress was in philosophy. What is philosophy aiming at? For Wittgenstein, what philosophy aims at is clarity, not *solving* philosophical problems, but providing the light necessary to avoid them in the first place. Second, if the goal is to dissolve philosophical problems, how does one go about doing that? For Wittgenstein, the method to be followed was not theory construction, but rather the identification and exploration of illuminating comparisons or models, comparisons or models that allow us to get our bearings in the thicket of language so that we are able to 'go on.' Finally, I will describe how it is that this method will shape the following book, including a brief defense of why I appeal to a method of *philosophy* for a book that has as its primary issue a matter of *theology*.

Progress in Philosophy

Wittgenstein's method of philosophy contrasts with the dominant mode of philosophy in his day. When Wittgenstein first began in earnest his philosophical pursuits early in the 20th century, a philosophical idea with real traction was the notion that in order to make progress, what philosophy needed was a pure, ideal language with clear and unambiguous referents. Ordinary language was fine for mundane, everyday tasks, but was too messy to do rigorous philosophical work. Philosophical problems were to be analyzed into their smallest constituent components by means of a symbolic logic as a way of bypassing the vagaries of ordinary language. Bertrand Russell in England, and the Vienna circle (led principally by Moritz Schlick), assumed that philosophical problems were largely logical problems that could be overcome by a unified language of science. Such a language would have to be a philosophical construction in order to get around the inherent sloppiness of ordinary language.

As Wittgenstein saw it, the problem with this approach was that 'progress' in philosophy came to be defined in a way extrinsic to truly *human* life. Wittgenstein found himself out of touch, even repulsed by the overall tone of the project. Wittgenstein thought that this was another instance of what he called "the spirit of the main current of European and American Civilization."[23] This spirit of progress was linked with mechanization. Progress for the logical positivists was pursued by attempting to transcend the given boundaries of ordinary language. So, their 'clarity' was a foreign clarity to the actual ways humans lived. It was a clarity on the model of the machine, a clarity that was in the end instrumental to an abstract philosophical efficiency without reference to any actual human community. Hence, such progress in clarity was indexed to a manufactured language, rather than attending to the languages already in place.

For Wittgenstein, then, the purpose of philosophy was not an instrumental clarity in service of a mechanized 'progress.' He wrote, "for me, on the contrary, clarity, perspicuity are valuable in themselves."[24] They were valuable in themselves because they constituted a better view of the linguistic and lived contexts in which humans in fact find themselves. So, if perspicuity, clarity are valuable in themselves, then unlike the ideal language philosophers, what Wittgenstein sought were not philosophical or theoretical developments, breakthroughs, or anything *new*, but rather a better view of what is banal. He wrote early on, "each of the sentences I write is trying to say the whole thing, i.e., the same thing over and over again; it is as though they were all simply views of one object seen from different angles."[25]

For Wittgenstein philosophy is the modest enterprise of clearing up conceptual difficulties, and we do this not by offering new theories, but by uncovering and displaying the sources of confusion. This is why 'progress' in the sense of 'new' philosophical discoveries cannot be the goal. Unlike modern progress, Wittgenstein seeks to attend to what is old, to language as we use it. This is because progress, in his view, is best measured by the criterion of real human community, not abstract criteria of the philosophers.

The rejection of theorizing in favor of the more modest goal of clarity displays Wittgenstein's pervasive mistrust of generality. Wittgenstein thought that a number of philosophical puzzles were a result of "our craving for

[23] Ludwig Wittgenstein, *Culture and Value*, ed. G.H. Von Wright, with Heikki Numan, trans. Peter Winch (Chicago: University of Chicago Press, 1980), 6.

[24] Wittgenstein, *Culture and Value*, 7.

[25] Ibid.

generality."[26] The result of this craving for generality is that we look for explanations, or principles that hold in all cases, or general laws lying 'behind' the world. Wittgenstein identifies several sources for this craving. For one, we regularly subsume under one general name a variety of objects and activities. But another main source of this craving, according to Wittgenstein, is "our preoccupation with the method of science." Wittgenstein continues,

> I mean the method of reducing the explanation of natural phenomenon to the smallest number of primitive natural laws; and, in mathematics, of unifying the treatment of different topics by using a generalization. Philosophers constantly see the method of science before their eyes, and are irresistibly tempted to ask and answer questions in the way science does.[27]

And yet, such a method while helpful in certain contexts leads the philosopher "into complete darkness."[28] The corollary of our temptation to generality is an embarrassment of the particular. We feel a definition is incomplete if it can only account for a limited number of cases. But, Wittgenstein insists in an aside, "Elegance is *not* what we are trying for."[29] For Wittgenstein, what we are trying for is clarity—but, for Wittgenstein, clarity and elegance are rarely, if ever, found together. Hence, progress will not be found in theorizing about generalities.

Of course, to say that Wittgenstein is opposed to a spirit of progress is not to say that course corrections in our uses of language are always out of place. In his notes from 1931, Wittgenstein remarks that from one perspective philosophy is generally thought not to progress, that we still deal with the same philosophical puzzles as Plato. What Wittgenstein finds remarkable about this general acknowledgment is that *why* we deal with the same philosophical puzzles is generally overlooked. Why do the same puzzles continue to trouble us?

> It is because our language has remained the same and keeps seducing us into asking the same questions. As long as there continues to be a verb 'to be' that looks as if it functions in the same way as 'to eat' and 'to drink', as long as we still have adjectives 'identical', 'true', 'false', 'possible', as long as we continue to talk of a river of time, of an expanse of space, etc. etc., people will keep stumbling over the same puzzling difficulties and

---

[26] Wittgenstein, *The Blue and Brown Books* (New York: Harper Colophon Books, 1958), 17

[27] Ibid., 18.

[28] Ibid.

[29] Ibid., 19.

> find themselves staring at something which no explanation seems capable of clearing up.[30]

The problems of philosophy, for Wittgenstein, are problems of language. For example, that philosophers are befuddled by 'the nature of being' is a result of an examined picture of language—implicitly comparing 'to be' with verbal constructions like 'to drink.' The unexamined model implicitly suggests that if there is some*thing* we drink, then there must be some*thing* that just *is*. The problem, then is not a problem of being, but of 'being'—and even more specifically, of the operative picture frequently at work when we use 'being' in speculative contexts: "The confusions which occupy us arise when language is like an engine idling, not when it is doing work."[31] If the confusion is about *language*, then we do not need a new theory of being, for instance. We need simply to clear up the confusion of the various uses of 'to be,' and often the confusion with language is at heart the dogmatism of a bad picture.

Hence, for Wittgenstein, there is something like progress to be made in philosophy, only it is the sort of progress an addict finds in therapy rather than the sort of progress of science. What we need is not something new, such as a theory of being. What we need is therapy that can show us how we in fact use the language, therapy that confronts us with the bad pictures we have inherited from language (and perhaps from some philosophical reflection on language). Of course, if it is the progress an addict makes in therapy, then there is always the danger, perhaps even the expectation, of regression. As Wittgenstein says, some pictures are more bewitching and harder to excise than others.[32] And yet, progress can be made in the sense that we learn to *see* how our language works. Note again, however, that as we do come to see clearly, progress is made not by replacing the old with the new, but by gaining clarity on what is already there, and hence gaining facility, fluency in the language in which we find ourselves.

> You must say something new and yet it must all be old.
> In fact you must confine yourself to saying old things—and *all the same* it must be something new![33]

Philosophical puzzles are not so much solved, as *dis*solved—and they are not dissolved by a new theory of language, but by paying attention to the rough ground, to the language as we use it: "The real discovery is the one that makes me capable of stopping doing philosophy when I want to.—The one that gives

---

30 Wittgenstein, *Culture and Value*, 15.

31 Ludwig Wittgenstein, *Philosophical Investigations*, trans. G.E.M. Anscombe, 3d ed. (New York: Macmillan Publishing, 1953), § 132.

32 Wittgenstein, *The Blue and Brown Books*, 23.

33 Wittgenstein, *Culture and Value*, 40.

philosophy peace, so that it is no longer tormented by questions which bring *itself* into question."[34]

A Method for Clarity

If clarity is achieved by attending to the unexamined pictures by which we operate, then the method for achieving clarity is offering a series of models for comparison—problems are *dis*solved when we see the root of the problems in misleading pictures by which we are operating. The point of the method of offering models for comparisons is not to propose new theories based on the model. Rather, as Wittgenstein says, "in giving all these examples I am not aiming at some kind of completeness, some classification of psychological concepts. They are only meant to enable the reader to shift for himself when he encounters conceptual difficulties."[35] The pictures enable us to see the problem not from the 'outside' as the scientist sees the dissected rat, but rather to get our bearings 'inside' the uses of language at issue, bearings that make us puzzle at why we ever thought there was a puzzle to begin with. If this is the method, how does one go about doing philosophy without theses? Wittgenstein's writing, especially his later work, is characterized by a series of thought experiments and aphorisms rather than traditional thesis-centered argumentation. Oskari Kuusela argues that the key to grasping how one would do philosophy without theses is to see how in fact Wittgenstein uses these philosophical aphorisms. Wittgenstein wrote:

> for we can avoid the ineptness or emptiness in our assertions only by presenting the model as what it is, as an *object of comparison*—as, so to speak, a measuring-rod; not as a preconceived idea to which reality *must* correspond. (The dogmatism into which we fall so easily in doing philosophy.)[36]

Kuusela argues that a philosophical thesis in the traditional sense is a "thesis concerning an essence."[37] He continues,

> Such theses are thought to concern the necessary features of 'things' in contrast to what is accidental to them. They tell us what something must be in order to be (or count as) whatever it is. In this sense, such theses

---

34 Wittgenstein, *Philosophical Investigations,* § 133.

35 Ibid., § 206.

36 Ibid., § 131. First italics added; second italics original. Kuusela introduces his argument with this quote (see note below for reference).

37 Oskari Kuusela, "Do the Concepts of Grammar and Use in Wittgenstein Articulate a Theory of Language or Meaning?" *Philosophical Investigations* 29 (October 2006): 310.

> bring to view what things *really* are in contrast to what they might happen to be, or appear to be.[38]

But Wittgenstein never intended to offer theses, "preconceived idea[s] to which reality *must* correspond."[39] For Wittgenstein the danger of such theses is that they are frictionless, they spin in the air with no contact to the rough ground, and hence bewitch us—and insofar as we do not recognize them as so we run the danger of dogmatism; that is, the model becomes a necessary truth about the object of inquiry.[40]

Instead, for Wittgenstein, the philosopher is providing *objects of comparison* for the purpose of shedding light on the issue at hand, again not to *solve* it, but to allow us to find our way about. Joseph Incandela notes that what interpreters of Wittgenstein often overlook is the fact that Wittgenstein always says what he does for *particular* purposes.[41] So, for example, Wittgenstein's famous use of 'language games' is not intended as "preparatory studies for a future regularization of language,"[42] but rather, language games are objects of comparison for the purpose of throwing light on what is often invisible to us, and is often the source of our confusion, so that we can 'go on' successfully.

Example 1: Meaning As Use

In order to show what Wittgenstein has in mind with philosophical models as objects of comparison, Kuusela focuses on Wittgenstein's claim that meaning is use and the attendant claim of meaning as constituted by grammar. Wittgenstein says, "'The meaning of a word is what is explained by the explanation of the meaning.' I.e.: if you want to understand the use of the word 'meaning', look for what are called 'explanations of meaning.'"[43] 'Explanation of the meaning,' however, is not "an empirical proposition and not a causal explanation, but a rule, a convention."[44] Hence, as Kuusela says, for Wittgenstein, "meaning . . . can therefore be understood as something

---

38 Kuusela, 310.

39 Wittgenstein, *Philosophical Investigations*, § 131.

40 Kuusela, 311.

41 Joseph M. Incandela, "The Appropriation of Wittgenstein's Work by Philosopher's of Religion: Towards a Re-evaluation and an End," *Religious Studies* 21 (December 1985): 460. Wittgenstein says in *Philosophical Investigations,* § 127: "The work of the philosopher consists in assembling reminders for a particular purpose." The context here is a series of brief reflections on what Wittgenstein takes himself to be doing philosophically, and how it contrasts with the usual method of philosophizing.

42 Wittgenstein, *Philosophical Investigations,* § 130.

43 Ibid., § 560.

44 Wittgenstein, *Philosophical Grammar*, ed. Rush Rhees, trans. Anthony Kenny (Berkeley: University of California Press), 68.

explainable in terms of rules."[45] If we want to know what the meaning of 'knowledge' is, for instance, then we look at the ways we use 'knowledge'; and the ways we use it are not random, but follow settled conventions. It is these settled conventions that give humor, or metaphor their power—for it is in breaking the rules that we find surprise, or new connections.

How are Wittgenstein's statements about meaning and use not just another thesis? For if it is the case that meaning is constituted by rule-governed use, then it looks like Wittgenstein has made a theoretical claim about the essence of meaning.[46] Kuusela argues that we take seriously Wittgenstein's suggestion that his philosophical models are objects of comparison. If this is the case, then what we have with the notion of meaning as use is not an explanation or a theory of meaning, an articulation of what *must* be the case, but a useful model with which we can compare our actual uses of 'meaning'—a comparison that sheds light on those uses by displaying both similarities and dissimilarities between the use and the model, and between uses themselves.[47] The model is to be "set against the manifoldness and blurredness of language use so as to bring order to linguistic relations and to make it possible to perceive them more clearly."[48] Wittgenstein says:

> If we look at the actual use of a word, what we see is something constantly fluctuating.
> In our investigations we set over against this fluctuation something more fixed, just as one paints a stationary picture of a constantly altering landscape.
> When we study language we *envisage* it as a game with fixed rules. We compare it with, and measure it against, a game of that kind.
> If for our purposes we wish to regulate the use of a word by definite rules, then alongside its fluctuating use we set up a different one by codifying a characteristic aspect of the first one in rules.[49]

Significantly, in the project of comparing no claim need be made about what *must* be the case, for where we are confused is in our language use—and what we need is clarity on how we use those philosophically puzzling expressions like "I know that . . ." or "This word means . . .".

Kuusela's argument suggests that those who want to find Wittgenstein's theory of language, meaning, or the like are on a wild goose chase—

---

45 Kuusela, 314.

46 Kuusela, 316. Specifically, Kuusela has in mind G.P. Baker and P.M.S. Hacker, *Wittgenstein, Understanding, and Meaning: An Analytical Commentary on the* Philosophical Investigations (Oxford: Basil Blackwell, 1980).

47 Kuusela, 319.

48 Ibid.

49 Wittgenstein, *Philosophical Grammar,* 77.

Wittgenstein simply does not have a theory of anything. Theories are a source of the problem, something that leads to confusion, because theories, though they purport to account for so much, in fact miss what is most important, that *pictures* are at the heart of the way we conceive of and articulate knowledge, meaning, understanding, and the like. Theorizing simply does not account for the fact that our confusions are not a lack of information, or of explanations of the information, but bad pictures that seduce how we organize our thoughts, and the sorts of 'solutions' we think we need.[50] So what Wittgenstein offers us is not alternative theories, but a series of exercises, the purposes of which are to display to us the pictures that give rise to various kinds of explanations and conceptions, and consequently to that which puzzles us.

Example 2: Understanding

Consider another example of this method at work: Wittgenstein considers the philosophical problem of understanding. What, exactly, is meant when we say that someone understands something? In the section of *Philosophical Investigations* in which this consideration appears, Wittgenstein addresses a series of examples about what it means to say that someone has understood a notation.[51] The point of the examples is to challenge the prevalent theory that understanding is a *mental process* of bringing before the mind a picture or image or idea of whatever the object of understanding is. For instance, on the prevalent view, when someone says the word "cube," what it means to understand the word is to have before the mind an image of a cube and not, say, an image of a triangle. This process constitutes a mental state, the state of understanding.

Wittgenstein tackles this philosophical question with a series of examples, or 'games' as he often calls them. The purpose of the games is to suggest an alternative picture for conceptualizing 'understanding.' He addresses this alternative picture to an imaginary interlocutor who operates on the picture of understanding as a mental picture (Wittgenstein regularly uses interlocutors as a device in his writing). Wittgenstein writes, "I wanted to put that picture before him [the interlocutor], and his *acceptance* of the picture consists in his now being inclined to regard a given case differently: that is, to compare it with *this* rather than *that* set of pictures. I have changed his *way of looking at things*." If Kuusela is correct, then Wittgenstein is challenging the notion of understanding as a mental state not by offering a counter thesis (e.g.,

---

[50] One might worry that the claim that "*pictures* are at the heart of the way we conceive of and articulate knowledge . . . and the like" is itself a theory. However, there is no need to take the claim as anything other than yet another object of comparison that sheds light on what we are doing when we use phrases like "I know that . . . " in some ways and not others. However, it is not the purpose of this book to pursue that.

[51] See Wittgenstein, *Philosophical Investigations,* §§ 143-155.

"understanding is not a mental state but a . . ."), but by calling attention to the particular *model* of understanding at issue. So, Wittgenstein offers a series of examples to challenge the dogmatism of the model.

The immediate thought-experiment that Wittgenstein offers is a teacher trying to teach a pupil a notation that consists of a series of signs, say 0 through 9 ordered numerically.[52] How would we know that the pupil truly understands the series, and is not, for instance, merely mimicking us when we write down the numbers 0-9? On the accepted model of understanding as mental process, we might say something like this: the pupil understands the notion when, on an occasion when we ask him to write out the series, he brings before his mind the series and then writes out the series for us.

Imagine, Wittgenstein suggests, how we might teach him the series 0-9: perhaps we guide his hand writing out the series; perhaps we flash cards at him; perhaps we make him recite out loud the series: "but then the *possibility of getting him to understand* will depend on his going on to write it down independently."[53] Furthermore, imagine that when writing independently, the pupil makes mistakes: perhaps he slips up and randomly puts numbers out of order; or perhaps he systematically puts numbers out of order, or only writes every other number, etc. He does not appear to understand. But what then? Well, maybe with enough practice he will start to write the order correctly. Or, Wittgenstein suggests, perhaps we can teach him the order as a derivative of his order. Of course, it may also be the case that "our pupil's capacity to learn may come to an end."[54]

How does this example challenge the prevalent notion of understanding as mental state? By offering another model for comparison. Wittgenstein is saying something like this: imagine understanding as something more akin to *training* than to a *mental state* of picturing the object. Wittgenstein's example turns on the fact that in the ordinary course of things, a teacher judges that a student understands the series when the student can go on and perform successfully with the series. Wittgenstein wants to suggest that such a model simply avoids all the problems of the mental process theory of understanding (e.g., how closely must the picture in the mind match the object? What criteria are used to determine whether the picture in the mind is in fact a picture of the object?) without needing to speculate about an essence of 'understanding.'

The philosopher of course may not be satisfied: "Yes, but does the child *understand*?" But at this point this seems to be the philosopher's problem, not ours, insofar as the philosopher would appear to be asking for a theoretical account of understanding that can take account of the child's success or failure. Rather, given the whole series of examples that occur throughout the section it

---

52 Wittgenstein, *Philosophical Investigations*, § 144.

53 Ibid., § 143.

54 Ibid.

seems clear that what Wittgenstein wants his interlocutor to see is that he is blind to the *picture* of understanding that captures his conception of it. If the philosopher can accept an alternative model as illuminating, then the puzzle about what it really means to understand simply disappears, not because we have the proper theory of 'understanding' to inform us, but because we can stop demanding a theory and go on. The child and the teacher can go on successfully, and that is enough. Wittgenstein's point is not that it *must* be the case that understanding is nothing but being successfully trained, but rather that this is a useful picture, a picture that helps clarify some of the confusion surrounding 'understanding.'

The Method and this Book

In an academic book there are expectations that must be met, expectations that may not fit well with a rejection of *theses*. A series of aphorisms will likely not pass muster for most readers. So, I must spell out the way in which Wittgenstein's method informs this project.

First, like Wittgenstein, I hope to achieve a measure of clarity in what follows, in particular about Eucharistic identity and the baptist vision. I mean to set clarity against 'progress' in the sense that what I hope to achieve is not a new *theory* of Eucharistic identity based on the baptist vision, or of Jesus's presence, or of a notion of sacrament. Rather, I hope to achieve perspicuity on the way in which language is used to constitute the identity claims at issue, and what that suggests about the baptist vision itself. Gaining clarity, it is hoped, will help baptists 'go on' in felicitous Eucharistic practice and reflection.

Second, while like Wittgenstein I hope to avoid *theses* in the sense given above, this need not entail the adoption of aphorism over against argumentation. I do have claims to make, and hence arguments to offer in order to defend those claims. The arguments are subject to all the usual ways of evaluating arguments (plausibility, logical validity, etc.). However, the *style* of argumentation here in view, including its aims and purposes, is not that of the theoretician. If a theory (of anything) is an all-encompassing account of the thing (its essence, its justification, its causes and effects, and so on—an account necessarily 'from above'), then the mode of argumentation (that is, the way in claims are defended, and the directedness of the claims and defense) will be so shaped. In theory construction, the 'shape' of the argument is to establish the theory, and as such the unity of the argument comes fundamentally from how the systematic 'inter-locking' of the parts serve ultimately as a justification for the theory.

In contrast, I mean the arguments I make as themselves something like objects of comparison. The arguments in chapter 3 about language use, in particular identity and analogous uses of language, link with the other chapters not as the first rung on the theoretical ladder, but as illuminating models of comparison for what follows. Chapter 3 is programmatic insofar it is the orienting model for this book, but it does not (emphatically) attempt to establish a theory of language use or of analogy. Similarly, my claim about the baptist vision and Eucharistic identity is not, strictly speaking, defended or constituted by the claims I make about Thomas Aquinas and Balthasar Hubmaier. Rather they are *illuminated* by the claims I make about Thomas and Hubmaier, though I intend to show (by argumentation) the fruits of that illumination

But still, *why* this method? What justifies its adoption over against theory construction? Put succinctly, what justifies it is its fruits. If it succeeds in shedding light in such a way that aids Baptists (and the church catholic) 'going on,' then it is a worthy method. This claim runs incredible risk, and of course borders on hubris. Still, I know of no other more fundamental way to argue for the method's adoption. Of course, if this is so, then its justification cannot be established upfront.

Still, I can make a couple of preliminary remarks. First, this method is especially suited to those who acknowledge that they always find themselves in the middle of things. As suggested above, one of the things that so repulsed Wittgenstein about the philosophers of his day was their methodical disregard for actual human communities. For them, progress took them out of ordinary ways of living and speaking and into an artificial world. If progress is indexed to our ability to 'go on,' then what facilitates progress is not abstract theoretical reflection, but keeping one's nose to the ground in hopes of avoiding being tripped up by unnoticed obstacles. Wittgenstein's method of philosophy is especially suited to this because, as indicated above, it calls our attention to the unexamined pictures by which we are operating. As I will suggest in chapter 3, there are at least two unexamined pictures that appear to be operating in Eucharistic identity: the notion of identity as *one* thing only; and relatedly, language as fundamentally univocal, and hence analogical only 'decoratively.'

Second, it is more or less the method adopted by the two programmatic wise guides of chapter 3, Garth L. Hallett and David B. Burrell. Without making precisely the claims that Kuusela makes, they both operate on the model of rejecting theses in the sense identified above. That is, their writing is structured more like pedagogy than theory building. For instance, we will find Hallett offering no theory of language, but clarifying remarks about the uses of language in philosophy, particularly in identity statements. We will find Burrell explicitly rejecting a theory of analogy, and rather drawing our attention (largely through Aquinas) to the ways in which analogous uses of language seem to be working.

Up to this point, I have said nothing about *theology*, only philosophy. So, is this a book in philosophy or theology? Another way to put the question: what about the above method is theological? Here, I simply want to suggest that, if we drop pretenses to theory, we can dissolve this question and go on. The line between theology and philosophy can and has been variously drawn, and sometimes to useful purposes. However, outside of theory, there is no *necessary* reason to draw any line at all, much less in any particular place. Of course, confusion is always possible, and if confusion is present then some conceptual distinctions might need to be drawn. However, I want to suggest that for my purposes, the line is of no consequence. There is no evident reason why talk about God and the church cannot make use of a method like Wittgenstein's. Whether in the end it is theology (because of the content) or philosophy (because of the method) appears to be a theoretical question with no bearing on the fruit sought. Of course, this again is a claim that can only be defended in the doing of it.

A Brief Word on 'Real' and 'Merely'

Throughout the book I will contrast 'real' identity claims with 'merely symbolic' or 'metaphorical' identity claims. It will help the progress of the book to briefly introduce what I mean by these uses and the contrast I mean to identify between them. Introducing them here might appear out of place. I will be explicating how the Baptists in chapter 2 articulate theologies of the Lord's Supper that do not reduce to merely symbolic accounts of the bread and the body; and chapter 3 as the programmatic chapter will employ Hallett and Burrell as guides for an extensive discussion of identity claims and analogous uses of language. Either of those places might be more natural to address the issue.

However, aside from avoiding further cluttering already long chapters later, the value in introducing this contrast here is the opportunity to emphasize what I do *not* mean to be attempting, namely a theory of identity or analogous use that can account for the difference between real and merely symbolic identity claims. Insofar as Wittgenstein is the methodological guide, it is appropriate, then, to address the issue here. In short, whatever the contrast I mean to make between real identity claims and merely metaphorical or symbolic ones, the contrast does not rest on a theory, but rather on a sensibility that can be indicated, if not defined, by a few examples. Here, then, I mean to attempt straightforwardly what Wittgenstein suggested in a different context: "I cannot characterize the point better than by saying that it is opposed to that which Socrates represents in the Platonic dialogues. For if asked what knowledge is I would list examples of knowledge, and add the words 'and the like.'"[55] So, what will do the work here is not some theory of the essence of real (or merely symbolic) identity, but a brief list of perspicuous examples.

By 'real identity' I have in mind these (though, of course, not only these) sorts of identity claims: Barak Obama is the 44th president of the United States; Jesus is God; This book (pointing at a Bible) is the Bible; and so on. By

---

[55] Wittgenstein, Manuscript 302, 14. Cited in Garth L Hallett, *A Companion to Wittgenstein's "Philosophical Investigations"* (Ithaca: Cornell University Press, 1977), 34.

'merely symbolic or metaphorical identity,' I mean these sorts of identity claims: Barak Obama is a machine on the basketball court; God is a lion; The Bible is my best friend.

In ordinary English, the first examples of identity claims would likely occasion a positive answer to the question, "but is X *really* Y?" Barak Obama really is the 44th president, Jesus really is God, and this book really is the Bible (presuming, of course, that a Bible is the book at issue and not a cookbook). The latter cluster would likely occasion a negative response to the same question (though, as indicated momentarily, with more explanation): Barak Obama is not *really* a machine on the basketball court (owing to the fact that he is a human and not a robot), God is not *really* a lion (since, among other reasons, God is spirit), and the Bible is not *really* my best friend (since, in ordinary English usage, only living things can be friends).

Of course, denying a positive response to the "what is it *really*" question for the latter cluster in no way denies the possible usefulness, even truthfulness of the claims. Surely 'Barak Obama is a machine on the basketball court' is a more apt, useful, even 'true' claim than Barak Obama is a wilting flower; surely 'God is a lion' is better than 'God is an inch worm'; and the 'Bible is my best friend' is more appropriate than 'the Bible is my sworn enemy', assuming a Christian and not a zealous atheist is making the claim. (Of course, these denials need not entail that there is *never* any usefulness for even these odd claims, perhaps in poetry, for example).

In the other direction, cataloguing a claim as 'real identity' does not necessarily entail its truthfulness. 'Barak Obama is the 44th president of the United States' is a claim of real identity, but if historians uncover a long forgotten president somewhere in the early 19th century, then the claim would be false. 'Jesus is God' is a claim of real identity made by Christians, but of course it is at least possible that Christians are wrong about this.[56] Still, both instances are examples of what I mean by real identity, even if they both turn out to be making claims of real identity that are false. Furthermore, each cluster of claims need not presume any univocal identity (indicated by univocal uses of 'is') within the clusters. For example, just because 'Barak Obama is the 44th president' is grouped with 'Jesus is God' as both being real identity claims, it need not follow that they are both real identities in precisely the same way. This will be explored more fully in chapter 3.

---

[56] Of course, there are identity claims that might not fit neatly in either category: is 'God is love' more like 'Jesus is God' or 'God is a lion'? Is 'I am the vine' more like 'Barak Obama is the 44th president of the United States' or like 'Barak Obama is a machine on the basketball court'? As I am not articulating a theory of identity, there is no need to settle those debatable claims here, only to note that, if the offered perspicuous examples have done their work, *what* is being asked ought to be clear enough to fruitfully pursue the questions.

Of course, the usefulness of the "but is X *really* Y?" question can only be affirmed along with the acknowledgment that the question itself depends upon a sensibility or facility with shifting contexts in order to be useful. For example, that Barak Obama is a machine is more apt than he is a wilting flower indicates the context-bound characteristic of any "what is it *really*?" question (this will be explored further in chapter 3). If the dispute is over whether or not Obama's basketball skills are more machine or wilting flower, then the answer to the *really* question would indeed be machine, insofar as if the two options are machine or wilting flower, Obama *really* is a machine. This acknowledgment indicates that even here, with uses of 'really' we are already in the domain of analogous uses of language.

Still, established English usage has at its disposal words like 'metaphor' and 'symbol' to suggest the different ways in which Obama *really* is the 44th president and a machine. Without presuming any theoretical account of metaphor, it would occasion little if any resistance to say that Obama is metaphorically a machine and really the 44th president. This is all I mean to indicate by the difference between real identity and merely metaphorical or symbolic identity.

For my purposes, if Eucharistic identity is at issue, then the question might be this: Is "This [bread] is my body" more like the first cluster of identity claims, or more like the second? The majority of Christians throughout history have understood it as more like the first (without needing to presume that it is *exactly* like any of the claims in the first grouping); the majority of Baptists (though, importantly not all) have understood it as the second. A central purpose of this book is to suggest why the baptist vision would (surprisingly to some Baptists) side with the majority of Christians throughout history.

The Plan of the Book

The book will proceed as follows. In chapter 2 I situate the claim I make in the context of a lively stream of contemporary Baptist theology. There are a number of Baptists, in both North America and Europe who, while identifiably and convictionaly Baptist, have returned to catholic sources for constructive theology. One fruit of this turn is reinvigorated reflection on the sacramental aspects of baptism and the Lord's Supper. So, in chapter 2 I will survey a few of the important North American voices (and one British Baptist voice), paying special attention to the Lord's Supper, with the goal of showing both the continuity of my claim with contemporary Baptist conversations, and how my claim is a constructive contribution to those conversations.

Chapter 3 is, as indicated above, a paradigmatic chapter for the book, insofar as it calls attention to analogous uses of language in identity claims. Two main guides will lead us through the conceptual and linguistic thicket of analogous uses of language and identity. First, I will employ Garth L. Hallett to suggest why attention to language use is important, why it is so often overlooked, and how attention to actual uses of language displays the in-use boundaries, or grammar, of analogous uses of language. Furthermore, attention to actual use will display how pervasive (if often overlooked) analogous uses of language are. In the second part, I will turn to the work of David Burrell as the primary guide for fleshing out the uses identified in the first part. Burrell's work on analogy has repeatedly, though not exclusively, centered on Thomas Aquinas, and so Aquinas will serve as something of a perspicuous example that will ultimately shed light on analogous uses of language in Eucharistic reflection.

Having set the paradigm, I will turn to two case studies of theological reflection on Eucharistic identity. First, in chapter 4 I will argue that attention to analogous uses of language suggests that Thomas reached a wrong conclusion in his account of transubstantiation, that analogous uses of language allow us to trace the contours of a claim about bread *as* body, rather than the claim that bread is converted into, without remainder, body. The purpose of this argument is not directly to contribute a theoretical 'peg' in the argument I mean to make about the baptist vision. Rather, the purpose is to indicate the fruit that can come of analogous uses of language. In particular, I will argue that Thomas's account of transubstantiation, rather than an 'explanation' of the conversion, is what Matthew Levering calls metaphysical *ascesis,* the exercise of bending language towards Eucharistic identity by means of tracing out the contours of the limits of what can be said about Christ's body. Furthermore, the argument I make about Thomas will recur throughout the last two chapters as a perspicuous object of comparison, a model that sheds light on the particular identities at issue.

In chapter 5 I turn to Balthasar Hubmaier, a sixteenth century Anabaptist theologian. There, I argue that, like Thomas, attention to analogous uses of language suggests that rather than a simple denial of Christ's body in the Lord's Supper, Hubmaier rather traces out the limits of what can be said about Christ's body. In the case of Hubmaier, he makes explicit how the identity of bread and body is necessarily linked to the identity of the church. I will suggest that Hubmaier, like Thomas, skillfully makes use of analogous uses of language, though he appears to be thematically less reflective than Thomas is about *how* he makes the claims he does. What we will see is that Hubmaier affirms the presence of Christ's body, but preeminently in the mode of the suffering church. If Thomas undertakes metaphysical *ascesis* in order to bend human language toward prayer and contemplation in Eucharistic identity, for Hubmaier, language must be reworked, bent towards the habits of speech fitting of a church of martyrs, and these habits of speech must include ways of articulating the reality of Christ's body in the church. For Hubmaier, then, the Lord's Supper provides the conceptual 'vocabulary' by which the church articulates its identity as a *suffering* church on the way to martyrdom. As I will suggest, this conceptual vocabulary makes prolific, if relatively unreflective use of analogous language. Again, like Thomas, this chapter is not a theoretical 'peg' in the argument I mean to make about the baptist vision. Rather, like Thomas, its purpose is to bring to the surface the sorts of grammatical remarks required to bring order to analogous uses of language in Eucharistic identity, an order that facilitates the real identification of bread, body, and church, without collapsing the poles of the identity into one another.

These grammatical remarks will be brought to bear on McClendon's articulation of the baptist vision in chapter 6. I want to suggest that these two previous examples of tracing the contours of analogous uses of language serve as illuminating parallels for McClendon's baptist vision in such a way as to show the intrinsic relationship between the baptist vision and Eucharistic identity. Specifically, the two are intrinsically related insofar as the shape of the baptist vision itself is generative of just such an identity claim. Chapter 6 will argue that the identity claim that constitutes McClendon's baptist vision is one of real identity that holds together without collapsing the poles of the identity, namely 'this church' and 'that church.' In turn, the baptist vision will prove constructive for Eucharistic identity insofar as McClendon's baptist vision will suggest that the 'logic' that orders the varied uses of 'is' is fundamentally a logic shaped by the narrative reading strategy baptists bring to their readings of Scripture. Furthermore, bringing McClendon's baptist vision to bear on Eucharistic identity will bring to the fore the intrinsic relationship between the two. In other words, the 'logic' at work in Eucharistic identity that is fleshed out by narrative is a logic constituting the articulation of the vision itself. Hence, I will suggest that Eucharistic identity and the baptist vision ought not be foreign to one another. They are organically related to, and even generative of one another. This suggestion will provide a modest contribution to the Baptist conversation identified in chapter 2, as well as to catholic Eucharistic theology more broadly.

CHAPTER 2

Baptist Catholicity and the Lord's Supper

Introduction

The claim I mean to defend, that Eucharistic identity is intrinsically related to the baptist vision as articulated by McClendon, would likely be met by quick dismissal from most Baptists. For Baptists, the nature of Christ's presence in the Lord's Supper was settled long ago, and it was settled in favor of a bodily *absence*. The Lord's Supper is a memorial of Christ's suffering and death, and though Christ is of course present in spirit (as he is always present with his church in spirit), his body is in heaven awaiting his return and is in no sense present in the celebration of the Lord's Supper. Furthermore, so the Baptist objection might go, Baptists have never affirmed anything like the bodily presence of Christ, considering it to be a component of a manipulative sacramental system that Baptists have always rejected. Finally, so the dismissal might say, Baptists reject claims about Christ's presence on the basis of Scripture only. That other Christians have affirmed Christ's bodily presence is of no real concern for Baptists. So the claim that an affirmation of Christ's bodily presence in the Lord's Supper is of a piece with Baptist life and thought is a claim from academic left field, so to speak, a claim with no real traction for Baptists.

However, such a quick dismissal would be to display ignorance of sacramental reflection present in the writing of a significant number of contemporary Baptists, and to display a serious "mis-remembering" of Baptists' own past.[1] My contention that an affirmation of real identity between Christ's body and bread in the Lord's Supper is an organic fit with Baptist life and practice is intended to be a contribution to a contemporary and lively stream of Baptist theological reflection on the ordinances. This contemporary Baptist conversation on the ordinances is rooted in some contemporary Baptist re-investigations of Baptists' own history and identity in intentional

---

[1] Mis-remembering is Philip E. Thompson's description. See, his "'As It Was In the Beginning'(?): The Myth of Changelessness In Baptist Life and Belief," in *Recycling the Past or Researching History: Studies in Baptist Historiography and Myths*, ed. by Anthony R. Cross and Philip E. Thompson, Studies in Baptist History and Thought (Milton Keynes: Paternoster Press, 2005), 198-205.

conversation with wider catholic Christianity. It has been variously called Bapto-Catholic,[2] Catholic Baptist,[3] or Baptist Catholicity.[4] It is a way of engaging important themes in Baptist life and thought in distinctively Baptist ways, yet with an eye to participation in the broader catholic tradition.

These Baptist theologians, while interested in theological reflection in a catholic mode, are explicitly and identifiably Baptist. For these theologians, this is important. Baptist Catholicity is not just another attempt at 'ecumenism' under a clever name. Clearly these Baptists are ecumenical in the sense of wanting to speak to and in the church catholic. But they are distinctively and unapologetically Baptist. There is no attempt to 'water down' Baptist identity for the sake of being catholic; nor an attempt to reduce all Christians to some thin common denominator.[5] That is, the catholic thrust of the work is not a diminution of Baptist identity, but a way of constructively bringing to bear their Baptist identity on behalf of broader Christianity.

So, in order to situate my claim I need to survey this contemporary Baptist conversation with respect to the Lord's Supper. The method adopted suggests such a move. If, rather than theory, I mean to offer clarifying remarks 'on the way' for the purposes of helping Baptists 'go on,' then giving a survey of the landscape serves to locate the investigation. To that end, while not a book *on* Baptist Catholicity, it is a book *from* Baptist Catholicity and a survey of relevant themes in Baptist Catholicity will situate the proposal within the context of the Catholic Baptist conversation.

In so reviewing Baptist Catholicity, I have two broad goals. First, the survey will help identify the broad contours of Baptist Catholicity, including some of the key voices and important themes. This brief survey will, second, allow me to show how one of the emerging themes, reflections on the

---

2 Cameron Jorgenson credits Ralph Wood with the appellation, while noting that its "genesis in print is rather difficult to establish." Cameron Jorgenson, "Bapto-Catholicism: Recovering Tradition and Reconsidering the Baptist Identity" (Ph.D. diss., Baylor University, 2008), 3, footnote 4.

3 See, for instance Curtis Freeman, "A Confession for Catholic Baptists," in *Ties that Bind: Life Together in the Baptist Vision*, ed. by Gary A. Furr and Curtis W. Freeman (Macon, GA: Smyth and Helwys, 1994); and Barry Harvey, *Can These Bones Live: A Catholic Baptist Engagement With Ecclesiology, Hermeneutics, and Social Theory* (Grand Rapids: Brazos Press, 2008).

4 See Steven R. Harmon, *Towards Baptist Catholicity: Essays On Tradition and the Baptist Vision*, Studies in Baptist History and Thought (Milton Keynes: Paternoster, 2006). I will usually refer to the movement using Harmon's title, Baptist Catholicity, and refer to particular participants as catholic Baptists.

5 Harmon describes thin ecumenism as an attempt to "overcome difference through a too facile identification of lowest common denominator agreements between traditions." Harmon, 16.

ordinances as having a sacramental dimension, converges with issues surrounding Eucharistic identity. To accomplish these goals, the survey will take the following shape. First, following Steven R. Harmon's work I will briefly describe some of the important marks of Baptist Catholicity. Second, I will survey select contemporary Baptist reflections on the sacraments, paying special attention to the Lord's Supper, with the goal of showing both the continuity of my claim with contemporary conversations, and how my claim is a constructive contribution to that conversation.

Baptist Catholicity

Perhaps the first thing to note about Baptist Catholicity is its diffuse nature. There is no formal organization of Baptist scholars, no denominational authorization or authority. Though, for sake of convenience I will refer to it as a movement, even this may suggest too much of an organized identity.[6] Cameron Jorgenson has helpfully compared it to Radical Orthodoxy with respect to its identity as a diffuse movement. Rather than a clearly defined movement or organization, Radical Orthodoxy is self-described as a "sensibility."[7] While there are some authors who explicitly identify themselves with Radical Orthodoxy, there are many who publish on issues amenable to Radical Orthodoxy without identifying themselves as such. As Jorgenson notes, this is largely true of the catholic Baptists. There are some who self-identify as such. There are others who do not but who are interested in themes and questions clearly related to it.

Still, though diffuse, it is not unidentifiable. It is enough like a movement to enable the identification of some key characteristics of Baptist Catholicity. Steven R. Harmon, in his book *Towards Baptist Catholicity: Essays on Tradition and the Baptist Vision* identifies seven marks of Baptist Catholicity that in his judgment distinguish it from other modes of Baptist theology. There is no need to reinvent the wheel here, so a quick review of those seven marks will suffice to help set the context.[8]

---

6 However, Harmon says that the number of theologians joining in the task of engaging catholic tradition is enough to "constitute an identifiable movement in Baptist Theology." Harmon, 6.

7 Jorgenson, 122. A comparable case is postliberalism. John Webster has noted that postliberal theology is "more a set of projects than a position." John Webster, "Theology After Liberalism?" in *Theology After Liberalism: A Reader*, ed. John Webster and George P. Schner, Blackwell Readings in Modern Theology, ed. L. Gregory Jones and James Buckley (Oxford: Blackwell Publishers, 2000), 54. This could also be said of the catholic Baptists.

8 Harmon's seven marks can be found in his *Towards Baptist Catholicity*, 7-17. Because Harmon helpfully gives each mark its own subheading in the text making them

First, Baptist Catholicity acknowledges tradition as a source of authority. Baptists have often prided themselves on a rejection of tradition for the purposes of submitting only to Scripture. In Baptist life church tradition has most often been seen as an obstacle to full submission to Scripture itself. In continuity with past Baptists, catholic Baptists have consistently maintained Scripture as the highest authority, but have argued that, as Stanley Grenz has said, tradition is "theology's hermeneutical trajectory."[9] So, catholic Baptists explicitly engage with tradition, not as a static deposit of doctrines, but rather by adopting "a dynamic 'retrospective' understanding of tradition as a critical open-ended 'looking back' to the Christian past in configuring continuity for present contexts."[10] Furthermore, they do so with an eye to Baptist's own history, arguing that the earliest Baptists were not nearly as dismissive of tradition as so many contemporary Baptists are.[11]

Second, catholic Baptists acknowledge a place for creeds and confessions in Baptist worship. Creeds and confessions, they argue, are not only testimonies of a peoples' convictions (a common Baptistic way of articulating the nature of a confession of faith in contrast to a creed). Rather the ancient ecumenical, orthodox creeds are faithful retellings of the gospel story, and insofar as they are faithful retellings of the gospel story serve as a normative interpretative grid for Scripture.[12] Creeds are not only markers of Christian orthodoxy. They are also an integral part of the formation of Christian lives. So, catholic Baptists endorse the active use of creeds in Christian worship in order to facilitate faithful readings of Scripture.[13]

---

easy to find, I will refrain from further citations unless specifically quoting from the text.

[9] Harmon is citing Stanley Grenz and John Franke, *Beyond Foundationalism: Shaping Theology in a Postmodern Context* (Louisville: Westminster John Knox, 2001), 93.

[10] These are Harmon's words, but for the point he cites Mark Medley, "Catholics, Baptists, and the Normativity of Tradition: A Review Essay," in *Perspectives in Religious Studies* 55 (Summer, 2001): 126-128.

[11] For example, see Philip Thompson's essay, "A New Question in Baptist History: Seeking a Catholic Spirit Among Early Baptists," *Pro Ecclesia* 8 (Winter, 1999): 51-72.

[12] For example, British Baptist Stephen R. Holmes argues that while Scripture always retains ultimate authority, because of Jesus's promise to send the Spirit who would make clear what God revealed in Jesus, there is a relative authority owed to tradition. See Holmes, *Listening to the Past: The Place of Tradition in Theology* (Grand Rapids: Baker Academic, 2002), 153-164.

[13] Harmon relates how Curtis Freeman, Stephen Harmon, Elizabeth Newman, and Philip Thompson petitioned the 2005 gathering of the Baptist World Alliance to recite the Apostles' Creed. The 1905 Congress in London had recited the creed in

Third, if creeds and confessions are part of the process of forming Christians, catholic Baptists have argued that worship is the primary location of such formation. More specifically, catholic Baptists have argued for worship that is liturgical, worship that is disciplined by regular patterns of worship rooted in the broad tradition of the church. The Baptistic emphasis on gathered worshiping communities is an affirmation that the tradition is made alive, so to speak, not primarily in second (or even third) order academic discourse, but in the church's worship.

Fourth, as the focus on worshiping communities might indicate, catholic Baptists emphasize the life of the community as the locus of authority. Catholic Baptists seek to retain the Baptist emphasis on the worshiping community without allowing Baptist accounts of freedom to, in their judgment, degenerate into an individual exercise of freedom undisciplined by the church. That is, the freedom of individuals is a freedom that is exercised together for the sake of Scripture. In spite of much criticism, catholic Baptists have not suggested that only 'the church,' understood as an institutional, hierarchical teaching body has authority to interpret Scripture. Instead, they claim that only 'the church,' understood as the gathered body of believers has the authority to read and interpret Scripture. Individual readings are offered to and disciplined by the whole reading community.

Fifth, and highly significant for this project, is a recovery of sacramental theology. 'Recovery' here is an important term, for along with catholic Baptist claims of a sacramental dynamic at work in God's relationship to creation is the argument that many early Baptists were in fact highly sacramental, and that the modern tendency of Baptists to reject sacramental theology is a detour from historic Baptist practice. Furthermore, the notion of 'sacramental dynamic' suggests that this is more than a recovery of baptism and the Lord's Supper as sacraments. It is, in the words of Harmon, "a theology that understands the sacraments of baptism and the Eucharist as paradigmatic of the relation of God to the material order that is disclosed in the incarnation."[14]

Sixth, catholic Baptists see tradition as not only a source of authority, but as necessary for faithfully doing theology in ever changing contexts. Harmon compares catholic Baptist appropriations of tradition with the *ressourcement* movement in Roman Catholicism. Tradition becomes a resource for retrieval, which itself is a requirement for moving forward. Harmon cites work on the Trinity, reappropriations of ancient concepts of the church such as *altera civitas*, and Baptist engagement with the patristic concept of divinization as examples.

---

response to Alexander Maclaren's proposal. Harmon, *Towards Baptist Catholicity,* 9. Harmon includes the letter written by the four catholic Baptists as an appendix to *Towards Baptist Catholicity* (225-226).

[14] Harmon, 13.

Finally, catholic Baptists reject a "'thin' ecumenism [which] seeks to overcome difference through a too facile identification of a lowest common denominator," and instead embrace a "'thick' ecumenism [which] proceeds on the basis of a common commitment both to deep exploration of the ancient ecumenical tradition and to a deep exploration of the particularities of the respective denominational traditions . . . . "[15] Citing Paul S. Fiddes, Harmon argues that thick ecumenism seeks "full communion" instead of a "one world church." [16] The difference is important, for it is the difference that allows and accepts diversity within Christian unity. It further helps clarify the logic behind how a group of historic dissenters can constructively contribute 'baptistically' to the broad catholic tradition from which they frequently (though not completely) dissented.

Such are Harmon's seven characteristics. They are descriptive of a number of Baptists from across the spectrum of Baptist life. As Harmon himself acknowledges, given the diffuse nature of the movement, the degree to which each of his seven characteristics is descriptive of any particular Baptist will vary. A full accounting of the varieties is well beyond the scope of this book, and given the diffuse nature of Baptist Catholicity perhaps an undesirable and unworkable project anyway. Furthermore, my claim is not a claim about the catholic Baptists as such, but rather about how a constructive contribution to one element of the wider catholic Baptist conversation, namely a return to the sacraments, can illuminate not only the logic of the claim of real identity in the Lord's Supper, but also the nature of the 'this is that' hermeneutic identified by McClendon as the heart and soul of Baptist life and thought. So, since the purpose of this chapter is simply to set the context, to situate my claim within the sacramental conversation among catholic Baptists, I will limit my attention to a particular sub-set of North American catholic Baptists, with one substantial and necessary British addition. The North American catholic Baptists to which I refer are the principle authors of the document, "Re-Envisioning Baptist Identity: A Manifesto for Baptist Communities in North America" (hereafter referred to as "Manifesto").

Baptist Catholicity and The Lord's Supper

Before turning to the "Manifesto" and the sacramental contribution of its authors, I offer two justifications for limiting the context to this group of catholic Baptists, aside from the already mentioned practical necessity. First, McClendon was a contributing author and so there is an immediate connection

---

15 Harmon, 16.

16 Paul Fiddes, *Tracks and Traces: Baptist Identity in Church and Theology*, Studies in Baptist History and Thought (Milton Keynes: Paternoster, 2003), 194-195. In Harmon, 16.

to his theology. The genesis of the "Manifesto" was a gathering of the Region-at-Large section of the National Association of Baptist Professors of Religion in 1996. This group met as a program unit of the College Theology Society, an organization of mostly (though not exclusively) Roman Catholic university professors.[17] This group has continued to meet regularly in conjunction with the College Theology Society since. At the 1996 meeting Curtis Freeman, Barry Harvey, and Philip Thompson began the process of writing what became the "Manifesto," and were joined by McClendon, Mikael Broadway, and Elizabeth Newman.[18] All of these Baptists have contributed significantly to the catholic Baptist conversation, and the "Manifesto" is an attempt to re-articulate Baptist identity in constructive, catholic and Baptistic terms. The "Manifesto" generated much discussion in the years following its initial publication in the *Baptist Standard,* a major Southern Baptist publication. Furthermore, the document displays several of the themes of catholic Baptists, and includes a substantial section on the sacraments.

Second, though a small subset of catholic Baptists, the authors of the "Manifesto" are fair representatives of the broader catholic Baptist conversation. Any quick survey of footnotes in their writings evidences wide-ranging conversations that are both influenced by and constructively contribute to the broader catholic Baptist conversation. Just as one example, these North American authors have quite clearly learned much from British Baptists who have worked hard to show both the historical presence of a sacramental life in the history of Baptist churches, and the recovery of a largely forgotten or mis-represented sacramentalism in the contemporary life of British Baptists.[19] So, limiting my brief analysis to these North American Baptists will in no way limit or misrepresent the contours of the conversation. Insofar as they have learned from and contributed to wider catholic Baptist conversations, especially with respect to the sacraments, the themes present in their work will be sufficiently reflective of themes present throughout the catholic Baptist conversation on the sacraments.

---

[17] Harmon, 1-2.

[18] Jorgenson makes this claim about the order of participation, though without any given documentation (Jorgenson, 76). But, as Barry Harvey was the advisor for the dissertation in which the claim occurs, it is reasonable to assume its reliability. In any case, the document itself lists those six as the authors without any qualification in terms of participation.

[19] For just two examples related to baptism, see Stanley K. Fowler, *More Than a Symbol: The British Baptist Recovery of Baptismal Sacramentalism*, Studies in Baptist History and Thought (Carslile: Paternoster Press, 2002); and Anthony R. Cross, *Baptism and the Baptists: Theology and Practice in Twentieth-Century Britain*, Studies in Baptist History and Thought (Carlisle: Paternoster, 2000).

As noted above, along with these six representative North American catholic Baptists, I will include in this brief analysis the British Baptist, John Colwell. The inclusion of Colwell here may at first appear somewhat *ad hoc.* To my knowledge, Colwell has not participated directly in the North American catholic Baptist conversation. Furthermore, there are other British Baptists who could serve as apt representatives of sacramental reflection in the British Baptist context, were the goal merely to include a voice outside of North America. However, Colwell has authored perhaps the most thorough contribution to date of a Baptist reappropriation of the notion of sacrament, and the practice of the sacraments.[20] Consequently, his work is important to consider, given my focus on the Lord's Supper.

In what follows, then, I will survey and briefly analyze the sacramental contribution of these catholic Baptists. First, I will describe the theological articulation of the sacraments in the "Manifesto." As noted above, the "Manifesto" serves as a useful focal document as in substance it is the collective product of the six North American representatives. The articulation of the sacraments in the "Manifesto" will serve as a useful introduction to some of the major contours of the catholic Baptist reappropriation of the sacraments.

Then, I will turn to the six American representatives. First, I will consider Thompson's, Freeman's, and Broadway's contributions to the conversation. They articulate a reappropriation of a sacramental understanding of the Lord's Supper in terms of Baptists' own sacramental history. Second, I will consider Elizabeth Newman who, among the six Baptists, has done the most constructive reflection on the nature of Christ's presence in the signs that constitute the Lord's Supper. Then, I will consider Barry Harvey who articulates an account of the sacraments, and the Lord's Supper in particular, in terms of the social and political identity of the church in the context of the church's historic 'Constantinian' compromise. Of the six North American Baptists, I will end with McClendon. McClendon's systematic project as a whole will receive further attention in chapter 6, but in this context he serves as a useful summary of some of the themes present in the North American Baptists. Finally, I will consider Colwell's sacramental contribution, in particular the way in which he articulates a sacramental account of the Lord's Supper in terms of the doctrine of the Trinity.

Following these surveys, I will make explicit how these Baptists display the contours of catholic Baptist reappropriations of sacrament, and how my book will contribute constructively to that reappropriation. I will show that the contours of these catholic Baptist reappropriations of the sacraments with respect to the Lord's Supper may fruitfully be traced along the contours of the traditional affirmation of the threefold articulation of Christ's body: Christ's

---

[20] Harmon, too, judges Colwell's book as a "noteworthy exemplar" of the sacramental dynamic. Harmon, 13.

historical body, his sacramental body, and his ecclesial body. Harvey makes explicit use of this threefold articulation, and it unfolds and displays the inner logic of the Lord's Supper for all of these Baptists. I do not mean to claim that all would articulate this threefold identity in just the same way that a patristic Christian might, and certainly there are differences of emphases even among these Baptists here surveyed. In fact, we will note some ambivalence in these Baptist about how to speak of what the tradition calls Christ's sacramental body. We will, nevertheless, see the unmistakable logic: In the Supper Christ himself nourishes us, he nourishes us with himself, and in so nourishing he makes the church. For these Baptists, Christ himself in his historical bodiliness is the source and defining pattern for the Christian life; the identity of the church is unmistakably given in terms of Christ's body; and Christ offers himself, his own body, as nourishment to the body which is his church. This threefold pattern is unmistakable, and sets the context of my contribution to Baptist reflections on the identity of bread and body in the Lord's Supper.

Before doing so, I should acknowledge that up to this point I have not offered any definition, even a provisional and working one, of 'sacrament' or 'sacramentology.' This is partly because of my attempt to avoid theorizing a concept of sacrament. In this same trajectory, though from a different direction, Christopher J. Ellis, a Baptist whose work displays several of Harmon's characteristics of a catholic Baptist, argues that we should resist the pull to first doctrinally explicate the concept of a sacrament, followed by showing how baptism and the Lord's Supper, for example, fit that concept. Rather, we should look first to the practices themselves and use their internal logic to explicate a notion of sacrament.[21] Having said that, Ellis concedes that one may fruitfully "distinguish between a pre-existent definition of 'sacrament' . . . and the notion of 'sacramentality' which is the principle underlying the use by God of material media—or 'embodied grace.'" [22] Following Ellis's lead, it is enough for the purposes here to note that catholic Baptists accept the claim that God uses material media to interact with his people. This is a claim that is accepted by all the Baptists below.

"Manifesto"

The primary authors of the "Manifesto" explicitly offer it as a proposal for re-envisioning Baptist identity for North American Baptists, and the issues and the

---

[21] Christopher J. Ellis, "Embodied Grace: Exploring the Sacraments and Sacramentality," in *Baptist Sacramentalism 2,* ed. by Anthony R. Cross and Philip E. Thompson, Studies in Baptist History and Thought (Milton Keynes: Paternoster, 2008), 4-5. Ellis cites Baptist Neville Clark as the source of the insight. See, Neville Clark, *An Approach to the Theology of the Sacraments* (London: SCM Press, 1956), 71.

[22] Ellis, 4-5.

way the issues are framed clearly indicate this historical and geographic location.[23] Nevertheless, the manner in which the document addresses the issues displays some of the key tendencies of catholic Baptists and as such serves as a useful introduction. Furthermore, the treatment of the sacraments, and the Lord's Supper in particular, in the "Manifesto" displays some of the key themes of the Lord's Supper explored more fully by the Baptists below.[24] So, in what follows I will survey the major affirmations of the "Manifesto," paying the most attention to its affirmation of the sacraments.

The "Manifesto" frames its five central affirmations within a discussion of freedom. The "Manifesto" claims that "Human freedom exists only in relationship to the triune God who lovingly creates, wisely governs, mercifully redeems, and justly judges the world."[25] The freedom of God is entirely a gift, and is the freedom "*from* the domination of selfish human impulses," and the freedom for faithful service and participation in God's new humanity.[26] The earliest Baptists understood this freedom to entail that faith cannot be coerced. Freedom has remained a key theme for Baptists, but Baptists in North America have tended to articulate the notion of freedom in terms of modern liberalism.[27] In rejecting this modern appropriation of freedom, the authors explicitly appeal to a Baptist heritage that "predates the formation of modern democratic societies in North America."[28] Consequently, the authors report that some of their primary sources are from Baptists who have "resisted modern notions of freedom and have practiced a more communal discipleship."[29]

What follows from a rejection of modern notions of freedom and a recovery of other strands in the Baptist heritage? First, the authors affirm that Bible reading is properly a community practice rather than a personal or private practice. The freedom of the gospel is not the freedom of each individual to

---

23 Andrew D. Black helpfully situates the "Manifesto" in the context of the cultural, political, and theological shift in Southern Baptist life, the largest Baptist (and Protestant) denomination in North America. See his "Kingdom Priests or Democracy of Competent Souls? The 'Baptist Manifesto,' John Howard Yoder, and the Question of Baptist Identity" (master's thesis, Baylor University, 2006), 30-54.

24 See Jorgenson, 77, footnote 5 for a textual history of the document. While the body of the document has remained consistent, it has variously appeared in publication with a cover letter and a page of signatories, and at times without these. As I am interested in the body of the text, when citing I shall refer to the page numbers as it appears attached at the end of Curtis Freeman's essay, "Can Baptist Theology be Revisioned?" *Perspectives In Religious Studies* 24 (Fall 1997): 273-310.

25 "Manifesto," 303.

26 Ibid.

27 Ibid., 304

28 Ibid.

29 "Manifesto," 304.

interpret Scripture as he or she sees fit, but is the freedom of the community to discern together God's word. Second, the Christian life is a life of shared discipleship rather than a merely private matter between an individual and God. The authors reject what they consider to be a corrupt account of the priesthood of believers which would claim that "we may do and believe what we want regardless of the counsel and confession of the church."[30]

Third, the authors affirm that the church is gathered and always reforming, rather than merely voluntaristic and "withdrawn."[31] Here, the authors emphasize strongly a key theme in Baptist Catholicity. While affirming the distinctive contribution of the Baptist claim of a "called-out church membership," they confess that Baptists themselves have frequently failed to follow through on their best theological instincts. While regularly condemning the use of infant baptism as a practice that fails to make true disciples, in many Baptist churches baptism is no more disciple-making than in pedo-baptist churches. Consequently, the authors say "Our call for a believers church . . . is not a condescension to other traditions. It is first a summons to close off nominal Christianity in our own ranks." Furthermore, without letting go of the strong Baptist insistence on a church of disciples, owing to the failures of the believers churches, "we look to the church catholic as it appears throughout the world and through history for other examples of faithful communities."[32] The authors affirm that believers churches can and should learn from other churches.

Fourth, the authors affirm baptism, preaching and the Lord's Supper as "powerful signs that seal God's faithfulness in Christ and express our response of awed gratitude rather than as mechanical rituals or mere symbols."[33] The authors affirm that these three practices (without excluding others) have "sustained and nourished" Christians.[34] Furthermore through these practices "God's grace and Christian obedience converge in a visible sign of the new creation;" and in these signs "we learn to see the world as created and redeemed by God." The 'work' that the practices accomplish is a result of God: "The Spirit who proceeds from the Father through the Son makes the performance of these signs effectual so as to seal and nourish the faith and freedom of believers."[35]

Baptism is a sign of fellowship in Christ, of rebirth through the Holy Spirit: "Thus by baptism we enter into a covenant of mutual accountability and

---

30 Ibid., 305.

31 Ibid., 306.

32 Ibid.

33 Ibid.

34 Ibid.

35 "Manifesto," 307.

discipleship with the community of the faithful."[36] Preaching is a powerful sign because "God graciously declares the liberating Word which seals salvation through our proclamation of the gospel."[37] In the celebration of the Lord's Supper "the Spirit thus signifies and seals the covenant that makes us one with Christ and one in Christ with one another."[38] In the meal, "the Lord himself is with us" and in so being with us makes us one body. In the Supper we both "renew our pledge of faith and are renewed by the grace of God as we envision the coming fullness of the new creation."[39] Following immediately after the paragraph on the Lord's Supper, but explicitly related to Baptist reflection on the sacraments as a whole, the authors call for renewed reflection on the practices unshackled from "late medieval and early modern theories."[40] They reject the claim that the presence of Christ is limited "to the performance of the enacted signs as we also reject all accounts that deny the reality of his presence in their enactment."[41] Even so, they reserve their strongest critique not so much for Baptist theological reflections on the practices, but for the neglect of the practices: "Baptism has been superseded by the evangelical invitation. Preaching is being displaced by other media. The Supper is so infrequently observed that Christians starve for lack of nourishment."[42] So, the authors appeal to the freedom of Christ as the freedom for the "communal enactment of the Lord's remembering signs."[43]

Finally the authors affirm the freedom of God's people to renounce coercion. The authors argue that the free church's witness to a disestablished church entails a "distinctive way of living in and engaging the world."[44] Such a way is not identifiable with either so called conservative or liberal views of political engagement, but rather a set of skills that enable the church to challenge the world with the gospel of peace: "The skills we learn in the baptized and remembering community help us to resist these powers that otherwise would determine our lives."[45]

With respect to the threefold articulation of Christ's body in the Supper, we can identify a strong emphasis on Christ's ecclesial body. The logic of the church as the body of Christ is of course internal to the logic of the gospel and is spelled out explicitly by St. Paul. For these Baptists, the emphasis likewise

---

36 Ibid.

37 Ibid.

38 Ibid.

39 Ibid.

40 Ibid.

41 Ibid., 308.

42 Ibid.

43 Ibid.

44 Ibid.

45 "Manifesto," 309.

has its roots in their desire to contest the modern emphasis on the individual defined in terms of modern accounts of freedom. The source and goal of the church is Christ himself. The account of the sacraments as "powerful signs" likewise affirms their effectiveness as "nourishment" for the making of the church. While the "Manifesto" lacks an explicit affirmation of Christ's sacramental body as such, it does affirm that in the Supper Christ is present in the signs (though not limited to the signs) in a way that effects the unity of the church as Christ's body. So, the logic of the threefold articulation of Christ's body is here, if not explicit: Christ nourishes us, he nourishes us with himself, and he nourishes us into his body, the church.

Philip Thompson, Mikael Broadway, and Curtis Freeman

Philip Thompson, Mikael Broadway, and Curtis Freeman are important to the conversation because, among American participants in catholic Baptist conversations, they have provided some of the more trenchant arguments for understanding and reinvisioning Baptist identity in light of Baptist's own history. A central part of their work is a recovery of an identifiable (though appropriately diverse) Baptist tradition of the sacraments. Though there are important differences of emphases among them, differences that in another context undoubtedly warrant separate treatments, I want to focus for the purposes of this book on two complimentary themes that they develop. Thompson, Broadway, and Freeman all contribute to the two themes, but for sake of space and simplicity I will emphasize just one aspect of each of their work to illustrate the themes. First, Thompson in particular has shown that there is a strong tradition in Baptist life of sacramentality, and that this tradition includes a realism about the Lord's Supper that most contemporary Baptists would find surprising. Along similar lines, Broadway has shown that within the African American Baptist tradition of North America there is a clear emphasis on the communal nature of the Lord's Supper that moves beyond the more usual reductively individualist and memorialist strands present in much of Baptist theology. I will highlight just a few examples of these traditions, and draw out the significance of them in order to better show why the claim I am making is in continuity with historic Baptists. Finally, Freeman in particular offers constructive proposals for a contemporary reappropriation of a Baptist sacramental dynamic in light of Baptist history on the sacraments that contributes significantly to the catholic Baptist conversation on the Lord's Supper.

Philip Thompson. Thompson has argued that there is in Baptist history a strong current of Baptist reflection on and practice of the Sacraments. Joining a chorus of works on baptism, for instance, Thompson notes that earlier Baptists frequently understood baptism in sacramental terms, even when designating it as an 'ordinance.'[46] For instance, the Midlands General Baptists, in their "Orthodox Confession," stated of the sacraments: "And as [Israel] had the manna to nourish them in the wilderness to Canaan; so have we the sacraments, to nourish us in the church, and in our wilderness-condition, till we come to heaven."[47] In contrast to contemporary Baptists who most frequently understand sacraments as merely symbolic and testimonial in nature, these Baptists understood the sacraments as having "definite and saving effects in the rites by the presence of the Lord held forth in each."[48] In the late 17th century Thomas Grantham "plainly affirmed the mediation of grace in baptism for the sake of conformity to Christ."[49] Likewise, the 18th century Baptist Andrew Fuller claimed that "Sin is washed away in baptism in the same sense as Christ's flesh is eaten, and his blood drunk in the Lord's Supper: the sign . . . leads to the thing signified."[50] With respect to baptism, 18th century American Baptists would have found much affinity with Grantham: "The theology [that late 18th century American Baptists] sang, prayed and performed ritually was churchly and sacramental (even if sacramental terminology was not widely utilized."[51]

Likewise, many early Baptists held to a sacramental account of the Lord's Supper. It is worth citing several here to get a sense of their sacramental

---

46 Thompson, "As It Was In The Beginning," 203-204. 'Ordinance' and 'sacrament' were often used interchangeably in early Baptist theology, though in North America 'ordinance' has been by far the most common designation. Bill J. Leonard notes that one reason for this was a desire to clearly distinguish the way Baptists practiced and understood baptism and the Lord's Supper from Roman Catholics. See Leonard, *Baptists In America*, Columbia Contemporary American Religion Series (New York: Columbia University Press, 2005), 76-77.

47 Thompson, "A New Question," 66. "Orthodox Confession," along with many other important Baptist confessions of faith can be found in William L. Lumpkin, *Baptist Confessions of Faith* (Philadelphia: Judson Press, 1959).

48 Thompson, "A New Question," 66-67.

49 Ibid, "As It Was In the Beginning," 204.

50 Andrew Fuller, "Circular Letters," in *The Complete Works of the Rev. Andrew Fuller With a Memoir of His Life by Andrew Gunton Fuller* (2 vols; Boston, MA: Lincoln, Edmans, & Co., 1833), II, p. 469. Quoted in Thompson, "As It Was In the Beginning," 204.

51 Thompson, "Re-Envisioning Baptist Identity: Historical, Theological, and Liturgical Analysis," *Perspectives in Religious Studies* 27 (Fall 2000): 290. Thompson references Morgan Edwards, *The Customs of Primitive Churches –or- A Set of Propositions Relative to the Name, Materials, Constitution, Power, Officers, Ordinances, Rites, Business, Worship, Discipline, Government, & c. of a Church; to Which are Added Their Proofs from Scripture, and Historical Narratives of the Manner in Which Most of Them Have been Reduced to Practice* (Philadelphia: n.p., 1774).

realism. Andrew Fuller's above quotation ("Sin is washed away in baptism in the same sense as Christ's flesh is eaten, and his blood drunk in the Lord's Supper: the sign . . . leads to the thing signified") is by no means out of the ordinary. Early Baptists confessed that the Lord's Supper, along with being a remembrance of Christ's sacrifice, was to be observed

> for the confirmation of the faithful believers in all the benefits of his death and resurrection, and spiritual nourishment and growth in him; sealing unto them their continuance in the covenant of grace, and to be a band and pledge of communion with him, . . . as also of our communion and union with one another, in the participation of this holy sacrament.[52]

Thomas Grantham, along with a sacramental view of baptism, affirmed a sacramental account of the Lord's Supper within the Reformed tradition: "Sure in this Ordinance we have as real an offer made of the Flesh and Blood of Christ for us to feed upon by faith, as in any other part of the Gospel of God."[53] Grantham connected the celebration of the ordinance with Christian nourishment to the degree that, as Thompson says, "the sacrament could be said to form the church itself."[54] Early 18th century Baptists claimed that in the Lord's Supper participants were made "verily Partakers of his body and Blood through the working of the Holy Ghost;" and that "the Supper is a Spiritual participation of the Body and Blood of Christ by Faith."[55] In the 19th century, Baptist Robert Hall claimed that the supper was "a spiritual participation of the blood . . . and body of the crucified Savior."[56] Hall also argued that the Lord's Supper "is a feast upon a sacrifice, by which we become partakers at the altar, not less really, though in a manner more elevated and spiritual, than those who under the ancient economy presented their offerings in the temple. In this ordinance, the cup is a spiritual participation of the blood, the bread of the body

---

52 Thompson, "As It Was In the Beginning," 68, citing the "Orthodox Creed" from Lumpkin, 321.

53 Thompson, "As It Was In the Beginning," 68.

54 Ibid., 69.

55 These examples are respectively from Hercules Collins, a London Baptist who died in 1702, and William Kiffin, who died in 1710. Both citations are from Michael A.G. Haykin, "'His Soul-Refreshing Presence': The Lord's Supper in Calvinistic Baptist Thought and Experience in the 'Long' Eighteenth Century," in *Baptist Sacramentalism*, ed. by Anthony R. Cross and Philip E. Thompson, Studies in Baptist History and Thought (Milton Keynes: Paternoster, 2003), 181.

56 Hall, *Terms of Communion*, I.III, in O. Gregory (ed.), *The Works of Robert Hall* (6 vols; London: Henrey G. Bohn, 1851-1853), 45. Cited in Curtis Freeman, "'To Feed Upon by Faith,': Nourishment From the Lord's Table," in *Baptist Sacramentalism*, 204.

of the crucified savior."[57] No less a Baptist than Charles H. Spurgeon claimed of the Supper, "As surely as the Lord Jesus came really as to His flesh to Bethlehem and Calvary, so surely does He come really by His Spirit to His people in the hours of their communion with Him."[58]

The sacramental theology of these early Baptists usually had an explicitly churchly thrust. That is, the purpose of the sacrament was to nourish the church, and in so doing both effected and exhibited the unity of the church. Already noted is Thompson's claim that for Grantham one could say that the Lord's Supper forms the church. In the same vein, conjoined with his reformed sacramental understand of the Lord's Supper, Grantham claimed that the presence of Christ in the "ordinance" was the occasion by which Christians "must hereby testify true unity with the Church."[59] And, as noted above, for Grantham the sacrament was in some sense implicated in the formation of the church itself. Again speaking of 18th century Baptists in America, Thompson, following Barry Alan Shain, notes that these Baptists had a "basic orientation toward the whole rather than the individual."[60]

But, of course, the sacramentalism of early Baptists has not survived, not at least in the majority of Baptist churches. This anti-sacramental trajectory is largely in place by the end of the 19th century. However, though beyond the scope of what can be accomplished here, it is important to note that the sacramental trajectory does not vanish entirely. Thompson claims that even when a majority of Baptists had abandoned a sacramental understanding, there has always remained "what we might call a residual liturgical presence of sacramentality."[61] For instance, Sean A. White surveys (American) Southern Baptists in the middle of the twentieth century who articulated 'sacramental' accounts of the Lord's Supper. Fred D. Howard published *Interpreting the Lord's Supper* in 1966, and a series of engagements followed in *Review and Expositor* in 1969.[62] Howard affirms a presence of Christ in the Lord's Supper

---

57 Cited in Ellis, 1. Ellis is citing Ernest A. Payne, *The Fellowship Of Believers: Baptist Thought and Practice Yesterday and Today*, enlarged ed. (London: The Carey Kingsgate Press, 1954), 67.

58 Charles H. Spurgeon, "Mysterious Visions," in *Till He Come* (London: Passmore & Alabaster, 1894), 17; cited in Freeman, "To Feed Upon," 204-205.

59 Thompson, "As It Was In the Beginning," 68.

60 Thompson, "Re-Invisioning," 293. Thompson is commenting on Barry Alan Shain's *The Myth of American Individualism: The Protestant Origins of American Political Thought* (Princeton: Princeton University Press, 1994), 23-28.

61 Thompson, "Introduction: Practicing Sacramentality in Baptist Modality," in *Baptist Sacramentalism 2*, xx.

62 Fred D. Howard, *Interpreting the Lord's Supper* (Nashville: Broadman Press, 1966); Frank Stagg, "Lord's Supper In the New Testament," *Review and Expositor* 66 (Winter 1969): 5-14; Eric C. Rust, "Theology Of the Lord's Supper," *Review and*

distinct from the way in which Christ is present in other occasions of worship. Working with Marcus Barth's claim that the Word is event rather than substance, he takes *soma* to refer to the full reality of Christ, not merely his physical body. Furthermore, this "'hypostatized symbol' is substantive of the unity between Christ and the church."[63] All of the respondents, while noting nuances, claim that the Supper is more than a mere remembrance and that in some form or fashion, Christ is present to believers in a special way.[64]

Mikael Broadway. Mikael Broadway's research shows that this near dearth of sacramental language in modern Baptist reflections on the Lord's Supper is less pronounced in African American Baptist writing and preaching on the Lord's Supper. While retaining some distinctive Baptist hesitations about sacramental language in general, African American Baptists have much more clearly and forcefully reflected the corporate nature of the practice. Broadway argues, "The combination of Baptist liturgical freedom and ecumenical openness [more characteristic of African American Baptists than white Baptists] has contributed to black Baptists developing a more complex language and theological understanding of the Supper than is often observed among other Baptists."[65] For instance, Gordon C. Taylor's sermons on the Lord's Supper stress "the communal aspects of the Supper, drawing implications for transformed life that extends the loving community of the church into the structures of social life that struggle against the good of humanity."[66] In a similar fashion Broadway holds up Samuel D. Proctor's sermons as examples of how black Baptists articulate the formative influence of the celebration on the church.[67] Of his survey of black Baptist sermons, Broadway concludes, "Apparent in all is a strong witness to many dimensions of communion. The Supper brings people together as one body of Christ, providing them strength to face with sacrifice the challenges of life, and reminding them that Jesus, who has been through trials, is present with them in their struggles."[68] Of more explicit theological articulations of black Baptists, Broadway notes that for James H. Evans, while eschewing arguments about the

---

Expositor 66 (Winter 1969): 35-44; Lewis E. Rhodes, "Sacrament of Wholeness," *Review and Expositor* 66 (Winter 1969): 59-65; John W. Carlton, "Lord's Supper In Worship," *Review and Expositor* 66 (Winter 1969): 67-74.

63 Sean A. White, "Southern Baptists, Sacramentalism, and Soul Competency," in *Baptist Sacramentalism* 2, 202.

64 See White's engagement with the authors, p. 202-208.

65 Mikael Broadway, "Is It Not Communion Of the Body Of Christ?" *Review and Expositor* 100 (Summer 2003): 426.

66 Ibid., 428.

67 Broadway, 430.

68 Ibid., 431-432.

presence of Christ in the elements, Evans "affirms the presence in the event through a reconstituting act of memory which unites the past and present."[69]

What one finds in Broadway's survey is a clear counter-emphasis to much of North American white Baptist reflection on and practice of the Lord's Supper. Rather than the prevalent trend of articulating the celebration in terms of individual acts of remembering, the black Baptist church has a strong emphasis on the communal nature of the Supper, such that it can in no way be conceived of as a *mere* remembering, since the remembering celebration is both community constituting and community sustaining. While not often using the traditional language of sacrament, the sacramental dimensions of the black Baptist church are clear.

Curtis Freeman. Despite the exceptions noted above, the thrust of modern Baptist reflection on the sacraments is decidedly anti-sacramental. Recall the quote in chapter 1 from Hershel H. Hobbs, perhaps the central practical spokesperson for Southern Baptist theology in the mid-20th century. Along with the above citation, Hobbs wrote in the introduction to the *Baptist Faith and Message*, the confessional statement of the Southern Baptist Convention, "Baptists believe the elements merely symbolize the body and blood of Jesus with no saving effect in partaking them."[70] This is an apt example of what Stanley Grenz has noted: "Baptists, especially in the USA, have stood at the vanguard in upholding the idea that baptism and the Lord's Supper are ordinances and not sacraments."[71] It is simply no stretch to say that in theology and practice, Baptists in American are almost exclusively anti-sacramental. The reasons for the near total absence of sacramentalism in contemporary Baptist life and thought are certainly complex. What is important for my purposes is attending to the Baptist attempts at reinvigorating a Baptist sacramentalism. Freeman, in particular, has offered an account of what such a recovery might look like and its positive contribution to contemporary Baptist life and thought.

Freeman, along with several catholic Baptists has contributed a great deal to the contemporary conversation about Baptist identity and has done so by returning to sources often ignored or misinterpreted in Baptist's own history. In

---

[69] Ibid., 437.

[70] Herschel H. Hobbs, *The Baptist Faith and Message* (Nashville: Convention Press, 1971), 88, cited in Anthony R. Cross and Philip E. Thompson, "Introduction: Baptist Sacramentalism," in *Baptist Sacramentalism*, 4. In an earlier exposition of the Baptist Faith and Message, Hobbs said essentially the same thing. He contrasts the Baptist view with Catholic transubstantiation, Lutheran Consubstantiation, Calvinistic Spiritual presence, and says "Baptists believe that the Lord's Supper is symbolic. The bread and fruit of the vine are but symbols of the broken body and spilled blood of Jesus." Hobbs, *What Baptists Believe* (Nashville: Broadman Press, 1964), 84.

[71] Stanley J. Grenz, "Baptism and the Lord's Supper as Community Acts: Toward a Sacramental Understanding of the Ordinances," *Baptist Sacramentalism*, 77.

his own reflections on the Lord's Supper Freeman invokes a central theme that is axiomatic to his writing on Baptist identity: the relationship between modern, and often peculiarly American accounts of individual freedom, and modern Baptist accounts of identity. With respect to the sacraments, Freeman contends that Baptists in North America have been characterized by a practice closer to Spiritualism than anything else.[72] In the vast majority of contemporary Baptist churches, "the Lord's Supper has become an empty relic as the spirituality of unmediated and individualistic piety reigns supreme in American religion."[73] This is lamentable because the result is that the Lord's Supper is relegated to an infrequent tack-on to most Baptist services, and as a result "many Christians are spiritually starved."[74] Freeman, rather, wants to suggest ways of recovering an account of the Lord's Supper that will provide "spiritual nourishment from the Lord's Table," and, as is clear from his constructive contribution to a theology of the Lord's Supper, the nourishment of the Supper is an antidote to the starvation caused by American individualism.[75] So, I want briefly to outline Freeman's account of the relation of Baptist identity and American individualism in order to more clearly articulate how the trajectories Freeman identifies facilitate a necessary cleansing of the Baptist anti-sacramental diet.

In his writing on Baptist identity, Freeman consistently argues that contemporary Baptists have not taken sufficient account of the degree to which their functional understanding of Baptist identity is dependent not upon Scripture, nor even upon the best of Reformation insights, but upon an account of the freedom of the individual where freedom is defined in terms of a libertarian notion of autonomy—the refusal of any external authority over the person. Baptist articulations of soul competency or the priesthood of believers takes the form of a rugged individualism for both so-called conservatives and so-called moderates.[76] For contemporary Baptists in America, John Leland, an early American Baptist is an important figure in the setting of this trajectory. In contrast to earlier Baptists who articulated the freedom of believers and the freedom of the church in terms of the freedom of God in Christ (which entailed the restriction on ecclesial and civil authorities from coercing faithful belief and practice),[77] Leland articulated the freedom in terms of natural rights and voluntary associations taken from Locke and Madison.[78] The trajectory that Leland accelerates is so successful that "in time, the democratic language of

72 Freeman, "To Feed Upon," 196-197.

73 Ibid., 197.

74 Ibid., 196-197.

75 Ibid.

76 See in particular Freeman, "Can Baptist Theology Be Revisioned."

77 Ibid., 279-281; see also Thompson, "Sacraments and Religious Liberty: From Critical Practice to Rejected Infringement," in *Baptist Sacramentalism*, 43-49.

78 Freeman, "Can Baptist Theology Be Revisioned," 281.

rights became so identified with the religious convictions and practices that subsequent generations of Baptists failed to distinguish between the two."[79]

With respect to the Lord's Supper, Freeman identifies two related and damaging consequences. First, the Lord's Supper transitioned from the community forming practice of earlier Baptists, to "a private experience of remembrance and a personal matter of obedience."[80] He identifies Leland as a representative. Leland, owing to his libertarian view of freedom, rejected the corporate, ritual elements of the Lord's Supper as obstacles that came between God and the individual.[81] Second, the Lord's Supper was reduced to a personal memorial because of Baptist accounts of ordinances which explicitly rejected sacramental dynamics.[82] That is, Baptists affirmed the rationale for the Supper as obedience to Christ's commands. While, as Freeman acknowledges, there is certainly nothing wrong with affirming their practice out of obedience, it rendered the rationale for the Supper as ultimately arbitrary. A related reason for the lack of a rationale for the Lord's Supper can be found in Baptist reactions against accounts of real presence, accounts which resulted in a functional "real absence."[83] This real absence is likewise related to the common Baptist affirmation of a strong disjunction between a symbol and that which the symbol symbolizes. Such a functional real absence "reduce[s] all things sacramental to merely outward signs of inward experience."[84] That is, because there is no 'objective' reality to the symbols, their purpose is reduced to individual expressions of meaning in the supper. What does the work of the Supper is not God's initiation, but individuals' mental experiences.

This confluence of American individualism and Baptist anti-sacramentalism has, as already noted, the consequence of rendering the Lord's Supper as at best a superfluous, merely obligatory action, and at worst an outright annoyance for Baptist congregations. Freeman suggests that such a rendering of the Lord's Supper is dangerous not only because it ironically tends toward disobedience of the ordinance command ("Do this," when in fact it is rarely actually done), but because it tends toward what can only be called the *un*making of the church. That is, the degree to which Baptist self-understanding is co-opted by America notions of individualism, is precisely the degree to which the church loses its ability to meaningfully form Christian lives after the pattern of the gospel. This is because what counts in one's Christian life is ultimately what one personally finds meaningful rather than that which God uses to shape and form.

---

79 Ibid., 283.

80 Freeman, "To Feed Upon," 196.

81 Ibid., 197

82 Ibid., 200-203.

83 Ibid., 203.

84 Ibid., 204.

So, Freeman suggests counter-trajectories to the Leland/Individualism trajectories, trajectories which Freeman hopes can move Baptists "to a renewal of a higher and holier understanding of the Supper."[85] First, Freeman suggests that Baptists recover an understanding of the Lord's Supper as an act of common prayer.[86] Using the work of Max Thurian, Freeman argues that remembrance in the Lord's Supper is not primarily a subjective calling to mind of something that happened in the past, but a corporate act of recalling "as a memorial before the Father the unique sacrifice of the Son and invoke[ing] God's abiding and eschatological presence through the Spirit."[87] Second, Freeman argues for conceiving of the Lord's Supper in terms of a practice, whereby the Lord's Supper is a complex, socially embodied activity that aims at socially embodied goods.[88] Third, Freeman argues that Baptists need to recover a sense of real presence in the Lord's Supper. Freeman appeals to Hall and Spurgeon who both understood Christ as being really, spiritually present. He follows John Rempel in a description of the Radical Reformer Pilgram Marpeck, whose Christological reflections on the Lord's Supper articulated the practice as an extension of the incarnation. Marpeck argued that Christ's physical presence was in heaven, but that his real spiritual presence in the practice (rather than in the inward parts of the participant) had as a consequence nourishment for the church.[89] Finally, Freeman advocates overcoming the disjunction between mere signs and the reality that they signify.[90] Rather than conceiving the elements of the supper as mere symbols, they should be conceived of as "powerful signs." Here, Freeman invokes McClendon's account of the sacraments whereby "God acts so as to make them effectual like God originally acted in the great historic signs of salvation."[91]

Conclusion. Freeman, Thompson, and Broadway then, together argue for a recovery of Baptist sacramentalism, especially with respect to the Lord's Supper. The argument is simply that Baptist anti-sacramental affirmations are a product of Baptists' uncritical appropriation of modern accounts of individualism, and a lack of attention to Baptist history. So, a recovery of a

---

85 Freeman, "To Feed Upon," 197.

86 Ibid., 199.

87 Ibid., 200. Citing Max Thurian, *The Eucharistic Memorial,* vol. 2, translated by J.G.Davies (Richmond: John Knox Press, 1961), 33.

88 Freeman, "To Feed Upon," 202.

89 Ibid., 205-206. John D. Rempel, *The Lord's Supper In Anabaptism: A Study in the Christology Of Balthasar Hubmaier, Pilgram Marpeck, and Dirk Philips,* Studies in Anabaptist and Mennonite History, no. 33, ed. Cornelius J. Dyck, *et al*. (Waterloo, Ontario: Herald Press, 1993).

90 Freeman, "To Feed Upon," 206-210.

91 Ibid., 209. See James William McClendon, Jr., *Doctrine*, vol. 2 of *Systematic Theology* (Nashville: Abingdon Press, 1994), 382, and below.

sacramental understanding of the Lord's Supper is in fact a true and faithful carrying forward of the Baptist tradition. Furthermore, it is a recovery that contributes to the catholic Baptist project of articulating Baptist convictions for the benefit of the church catholic, and in a way so as to recognize historic dependence of Baptists on the church catholic. Such a turn to the catholicity of the sacraments, even granting continued differences between Baptists and other Christians, can only strengthen the life of the church, even the Baptist church.

The threefold articulation of Christ's body is present in Thompson, Broadway, and Freeman, and their work makes evident that it is present in Baptists' own past reflections on the Lord's Supper. Christ's historical body is clearly the source and pattern of the sacrament. The goal, as for the *"Manifesto,"* is the making of the church. Worthy of special note is the realism of Christ's presence in the Lord's Supper. Quite clearly affirmed as a work of the Spirit, and clearly calling for a response of faith, many Baptists explicitly affirmed that it was Christ's "flesh and blood" that spiritually and by faith nourished the church. Here, it is important to note that for these Baptists, "spiritually" is quite clearly *not* "merely symbolically." Less clear, but still the case, "Spiritually" need not entail the absence of the body of Christ in the sacrament. Rather, as will be explored in later chapters, 'spiritual' names the unique manner in which Christ is bodily present to his people, not the mere absence of his body. This is why the near disappearance of the practice of the Lord's Supper in so many contemporary Baptist congregations is identified by Freeman as a central factor in the *un*making of the church. If the sacraments provided for "spiritual nourishment and growth in him" (to recall the Orthodox creed), then their absence can only lead to malnutrition and atrophy. And so, as Freeman argues, Baptists must recover the practice of the Lord's Supper as a central component of worship, for in doing so Jesus himself is present to the church as both the source of nourishment and as the goal of that nourishment.

Elizabeth Newman

Among North American catholic Baptists, Newman has done some of the most sustained reflection on the Lord's Supper in the context of the broader catholic church's claim of the real presence of Christ. Newman notes that transubstantiation is a *Roman* Catholic account of the Real Presence, an account not shared by most other Christians.[92] So, according to Newman, there

[92] Of course, Roman Catholic theologians recognize that there is a conceptual distinction to be made between transubstantiation and the real presence. For just two examples, see Robert Sokolowski, *Eucharistic Presence: A Study in the Theology of Disclosure* (Washington, D.C.: The Catholic University of America Press, 1993), 98; and James T. O'Connor, *The Hidden Manna: A Theology Of the Eucharist* (San Francisco: Ignatius Press, 1988), 219-220.

is room for a Baptist to affirm the Real Presence of Christ in a fully catholic manner, without necessarily needing to affirm transubstantiation.

For a Baptist to offer such an account will require the rejection of two dualisms that have tended to shape Baptist reflection on the Supper. First, drawing on the work of William Poteat in particular, Newman says that our usual ways of contrasting the present with the past and the future—the present is what is *real,* the past is absent because it is gone, and the future is absent because it is not yet present—are in fact not true to reality. The past informs the present and the present takes shape as it passes into the future. For example, Newman asks us to consider music. The notes not yet played on a score are nonetheless real: "their actuality is present in a different way, as *anticipated*, but this makes their presence no less real."[93] Second, we regularly contrast reality with symbols, words or signs. Yet, this too is untrue to the world. Our words frequently bring about realities; and our words carry with them a reality prior to our uptake of them. Following Poteat, Newman argues that the dichotomy between reality and symbol rests on a "name-relation theory of meaning," where the meaning of a word "derives from the object for which it stands."[94] In contrast, the "'real' is not primarily that which matches an object, but rather that which flows from the way we rely upon and inhabit the world."[95]

The rejection of the dualisms of past and present and word and symbol are biblical as well. They make sense of why later generations of Jews were commanded not merely to *recall* the Passover, but to *participate* in the original by *anamnesis*; it makes sense of the biblical emphasis on covenants, that the contrary of reality is not word or symbol, but false or faithless words. That is, whatever counts as real is defined in terms of faithfulness to one's words; and of course faithfulness is, at least in part, a temporal indicator. One is not faithful in an instant. One is faithful or unfaithful in duration. And so, recognizing the link between words and deeds is likewise to recognize the link between past, present and future; faithful words that *do*, that are real, are words that endure, that carry the past into the present and on to the future in ways that inform the world.

In this sense, then, we can affirm that "as in the word, so also at the table, Christ is really present, offering us his very self: 'This is my body. This is my blood.'" Furthermore, the goal of his presence is made real in the gathered congregation. That is, "the *real presence* of God is manifest in the gathered

---

[93] Elizabeth Newman, *Untamed Hospitality: Welcoming God and Other Strangers* (Grand Rapids: Brazos Press, 2007), 155. Her emphasis. See William H. Poteat, *A Philosophical Daybook: Post-Critical Investigations* (Columbia, MO: University of Missouri Press, 1990).

[94] Newman, "The Lord's Supper: Might Baptists Accept a Theory of Real Presence?" in *Baptist Sacramentalism*, 220.

[95] Ibid., 222.

community as it proclaims the body of Christ for the world."[96] Newman compares it to marriage when the minister proclaims, "I now pronounce you husband and wife." Upon this utterance something new comes into being. The minister's words "are deeds, bringing about a new reality."[97] So, too, "this is my body" brings about a new reality. What is this new reality? Newman says, "in receiving this gift, that is Christ, the church herself becomes Christ's body for the world. The new reality that is brought into being and extended is the body of Christ, as those gathered around word and table are incorporated into Christ's body."[98]

Because it is God's gift that we are incorporated into Christ's body, the celebration of the Lord's Supper does not depend upon the feelings or intentions of the participants, nor does its reality depend upon the 'meaning' an individual may or may not find in the Supper. Rather, its reality is the work of God. As a work of God, Newman argues that the criteria for Christians to share together the Supper should not be articulated in terms of doctrinal unity with respect to various understandings of Christ's presence (or absence). For Newman, the purpose of the Eucharist is God's gathering together the church as the prefiguring of the eschatological fulfillment of the promise God makes in Christ to renew all of creation. Hence, the Lord's Supper is a divine means of Christian unity, not merely a celebration bearing testimony to a prior doctrinal unity.

Such a view of the Supper has not often been articulated, both by baptists and others. Newman notes that for Conrad Grebel and Anabaptists, "the liturgical celebration of the meal itself is not unitive or binding but representative of a prior unity. The Lord's Supper is not a participation in the self-offering of Christ but a *symbol* of a unity already achieved."[99] She says this is surprisingly similar to a Roman Catholic account insofar as one must first be in full communion with the Catholic Church in order to celebrate the Eucharist.[100] While not denying the importance of coming to doctrinal unity, Newman argues that this fails to account for the fact that precisely because Christ is really present, the Eucharist itself is a unifying practice. Of course, as Newman admits, such an approach has its problems. But to deny it is to deny that church unity is fundamentally not in the minds of believers, but in the action of God. Newman quotes Bruce Marshall: "God makes the church one by bringing human beings to share in his own unity; Christ through the promised Spirit will draw the church into the unity of being and love he has with the

---

96 Newman, "The Lord's Supper," 224.

97 Ibid.

98 Ibid.

99 Newman, *Untamed Hospitality,* 163. Emphasis hers.

100 Ibid.

Father, assimilating the church to the unique bond that exists between them."[101] Hence, the presence of Christ in the Lord's Supper is what makes the church the church, and as such the performance of the Supper is itself a performance of Christian unity. This is why, in Newman's judgment, the fact that Christians cannot celebrate the Supper across confessional lines is such an affront to the church catholic. It does not merely display a prior disunity on doctrinal issues. It actually makes and embodies that disunity, and as such is a deep wound on the body of Christ.

With respect to the threefold articulation of Christ's body, Newman in keeping with the Baptists so far surveyed displays a clear emphasis on the church as Christ's body. Christ's historical body is determinative for the shape of the church, and Christ himself is present at the meal as the gift which he offers to the church for the purposes of making real his ecclesial body. That Christ offers himself in the meal is akin to the traditional affirmation of Christ's sacramental body—Christ's body offered at the table is the nourishment that results in the making of the church.

Barry Harvey

Barry Harvey's reflections on the Lord's Supper come in the context of his understanding of the church as an alternative social body in the world, which itself depends upon a narrative of the church's unfortunate submission to dismemberment by the powers hostile to the gospel. So, I will briefly offer his narrative in order to then situate his understanding of the Lord's Supper.

Prior to Constantine the church was a minority in the Roman Empire, at best ignored and tolerated, at worst outright persecuted. In this context, the self-identity of the church was centered squarely on faithfully embodying the gospel in a hostile context. The church was a small minority with a way of life that was most frequently seen as a threat to the imperial order.[102] And yet, despite periods of persecution, the church did not 'withdraw' awaiting a future vindication. Rather, it viewed its own way of life as a continual invitation to the world to submit itself to the Lordship of Christ, an invitation that would more frequently incite the world's wrath than the world's acceptance. [103]

However, at the conversion of Constantine, something decisive changed.[104] Now, the church went from being a minority whose self-identity does not depend upon Rome, to being the official religious sponsor of the

---

[101] Bruce D. Marshall, "The Disunity of the Church and the Credibility of the Gospel," *Theology Today* 50 (April 1993), 79.

[102] Barry Harvey, *Another city: An Ecclesiological Primer For a Post-Christian World* (Harrisburg, PA: Trinity Press International, 1999), 67.

[103] Ibid., 64-71.

[104] Ibid., 79.

Roman Empire.[105] That is, the form of the church's engagement with the powers that be went from an embodied, pilgrimage witness to those powers, to a "power-sharing arrangement" with the powers.[106] The problem with this power sharing arrangement is that the church lost "most of the meaningful distinctions that it had formally cultivated between itself and the world as distinct political societies."[107] This had the result that the church came to view successful engagement with the world not primarily in terms of a timefull endurance as a distinct society, but as spatial extension throughout the empire. Of course, the spatial extension of the church is one of its missions: to bring the gospel to *all* nations. But in this instance, the spatial extension takes the form not of the penetration of the timefully enduring habits and practices of the gospel in all nations, but of the conquest of those nations to whom the gospel was to be peaceably offered.

While official Constantinianism is long gone, its habits and dispositions remain. As the above narrative indicates, perhaps the most pernicious bad habit the church picked up was a loss of its missional identity. The loss of this identity was replaced by the habit of seeing itself as a cooperative agent to the coercive powers rather than as a missional, prophetic embodiment of an alternative form of life.[108] Here, Harvey understands the church's missional identity not so much as winning individual converts, but as continually incarnating the good news of the gospel as an alternative, inviting society. In this sense, officially dis-established Christianity is still suffering from the habits of Constantinianism, for the Western church has accepted the modern narrative of religion as something internal to individuals and distinct from politics.

The subordination of religion is of a piece with the narratives and practices that constitute modernity. The Enlightenment was an attempt to arrange social life under the auspices of reason in order to control the whims of fate, and in doing so created the myth of the 'universal man,' the notion that whatever the contingencies and particularities accidental to persons, they are fundamentally units of reason.[109] The result was a set of disciplines that constitute the "individual" by submitting persons to various management techniques (e.g., economics). However, in doing so, those disciplines sunder the deep ties of persons to communities and traditions, the narratives that

---

105 Ibid. While Harvey finds Constantine's adoption of Christianity as a helpful marker, he thinks it can be overplayed. See, for instance, Barry Harvey, *Can These Bones Live?: A Catholic Baptist Engagement with Ecclesiology, Hermeneutics, and Social Theory* (Grand Rapids: Brazos Press, 2008), 99-101.

106 Harvey, *Another City*, 22.

107 Ibid., 72-73.

108 Ibid., 81-82.

109 Harvey, *Another City*, 101-111.

constitute self-identity in community. In the modern project, such particular identities stood in the way of the universal man, encumbering him with demands that prevent him from exercising his innate freedom. As a result,

> the uprooting of personal identity from the daily activities, habits, and allegiances of church, mosque, synagogue, and temple effectively prevents these communities and their intellectual and moral traditions from interfering with the public sphere of power and knowledge—politics, law, economies, and science—that have been reserved solely for the institutions of the modern secular domain.[110]

The irony is that instead of a world free of the risk of fate, there is now a world bound by the unintelligible, undirected lurchings of identity-less units. This, in a sense, is the post-modern condition, really hyper-modernity. The universal man turned out to be a myth, and what is left is no-man. What remains is an "empty self of the modern age," which turns to "'the experience of being continually filled up by consuming goods, calories, experiences, politicians, romantic partners, and empathic therapists in an attempt to combat the growing alienation and fragmentation of its era."[111] Religion itself becomes another one of these commodities consumed by the empty self, and hence cannot provide the sort of narrative to make life intelligible.[112]

So, the task of the church is to recover the practices and habits that constitute it as an alternative social body to the deformed bodies of the modern/post-modern world. There are several dimensions of this recovery, but a central one is the sacraments. On the one hand, the church itself is a sacrament insofar as its very life is a sign, a real and effectual sign, of God's grace in the world.[113] On the other hand, it is the sacraments themselves out of which "God fashions from the resources of this time and place an alternative idiom for creaturely existence over against the sinews of the world's body politic."[114] In the sacraments, the spirit "repeats" the fullness of what has been

---

110 Ibid., 126.

111 Ibid., 160. Harvey is quoting Philip Cushman, "Why the Self Is Empty: Towards a Historically Situated Psychology," *American Psychologist* 45 (May 1990): 600.

112 For an important treatment of the commodification of religion see Vince Miller, *Consuming Religion: Christian Faith and Practice In a Consumer Culture* (New York: Continuum, 2003). See also, Michael Budde, *The (Magic) Kingdom of God: Christianity and Global Cultural Industries* (Boulder, CO: Westview Press, 1997), and Michael L. Budde and Robert W. Brimlow, *Christianity Incorporated: How Big Business Is Buying the Church* (Grand Rapids: Brazos Press, 2002).

113 Harvey, *Can These Bones Live?,* 95.

114 Ibid., "Re-Membering the Body: Baptism, Eucharist and the Politics of Disestablishment," in *Baptist Sacramentalism*, 102.

revealed in Christ, and it does so principally by the "sacramental labor" of baptism and the Lord's Supper (without excluding other sacramental signs). The practice of the sacraments of baptism and the Eucharist forms the "process of recovering the sinews that hold together the members of Christ's body," a process fraught with danger insofar as "that which Jesus intended to serve as signs of our unity," have historically been occasions for disunity.[115] And yet, we are to practice them.

The repetition of the Spirit in the sacraments is no mere mimicry. It is rather the re-presentation, the dramatic re-enactment, or the re-membering of Christ's body in particular times and particular places. To speak of repetition as re-membering rather than mimicry is to point to the way in which God uses the sacraments to re-habilitate (i.e., re-habituate) the church into the form of bodily existence that constitutes it as an alternative body. With respect to the Eucharist, Harvey notes that, following from Paul

> patristic and medieval texts speak of a threefold articulation of Paul's image of Christ's body: the historical body of Jesus; the sacramental body (*corpus mysticum*, mystical body); and the ecclesial body (*corpus verum*, true body). The sacramental body and the ecclesial body are closely linked in these early writings, with a temporal *caesura* or gap between them and the historical body. Together the Eucharist and the church constitute the contemporary performance of Christ's historical body.[116]

This *caesura* is significant, for it prevents a too close identification of the church with a direct continuation of his physical presence. Rather, Christ's mystical (or sacramental) body is the means of joining past and present, such that the church is made present to Christ's unique life and sacrifice. As such, the sacrament of the Lord's Supper is the continuing embodiment of God's work in Christ, the re-membering of the sinews that form the church into an alternative body to the broken bodies of the world. Of course, given its missional identity, the church does not merely stand against those broken bodies. It rather invites them into community, to participate sacramentally in the true body of Christ, broken and raised for broken bodies.

Harvey explicitly appeals to the rubric of the threefold articulation of Christ's body. For Harvey, Christ's historical body is the source and pattern for Christ's ecclesial body as it is the locus of God's action in overturning the

---

[115] Ibid., *Can These Bones Live?,* 201.

[116] Ibid., "The Eucharistic Idiom of the Gospel," *Pro Ecclesia* 9 (Summer 2000): 300. Here Harvey credits William T. Cavanaugh, *Torture and Eucharist: Theology, Politics, and the Body of Christ* (Oxford: Blackwell Publishers, 1998), 212, and Henri de Lubac *Corpus Mysticum: The Eucharist and the Church In the Middle Ages*, translated by Gemma Simmonds with Richard Price and Christopher Stephens, ed. by Laurence Paul Hemming and Susan Frank Parsons (London: SCM Press, 2006).

powers that co-opt the world. God in the Spirit works to constitute the church as the alternative social body to the world of fragmented bodies. Harvey articulates Christ's sacramental body in terms of the alternative disciplines and habits that constitute Christ's ecclesial body. The link with Christ's sacramental body is made insofar as these disciplines and habits are not merely sociological descriptions of the politics of a community, but the gift of God's Spirit making Christ present as the source and goal of the church's social identity. As such, Christ's sacramental body makes the church.

James Wm. McClendon, Jr.

More will be said about McClendon's systematic theological project as a whole below, and so here I want only to continue with the task of summarizing his contribution to Baptist sacramentalism with respect to the Lord's Supper. McClendon's contribution is important because it carefully articulates two complimentary strands present throughout the Baptists so far surveyed: the 'ethical' identity of the Supper as one of the God-ordained and empowered loci of community formation and nourishment, and the 'doctrinal' identity of this 'ethical' practice as one of God's repeatable signs of his very own continuing presence to the church in Christ by the power of the Spirit. These two strands clearly articulate the Lord's Supper in terms that are far from merely symbolic. These two strands correspond to McClendon's reflections on the Lord's Supper (and the "signs" in general) in his *Ethics*, and *Doctrine* respectively, and so my summary will follow this pattern as well.

McClendon articulates the ethical thrust of the Lord's Supper in terms of the life of the Christian community, specifically the formation of the community as the body of Christ. This is in contrast to modern ethical accounts which may see value in the Lord's Supper as a merely instrumental means of instilling certain community values in believers. Such modern "decisionist" understandings of the Lord's Supper illegitimately limit its significance to the individual (and even then, according to McClendon's further reflections on the nature of ethics, misunderstands the ethical identity of persons and communities).[117] But, biblically speaking, the Lord's Supper is a *community* practice, and as such the ethical 'work' that it does is not primarily as instruction for individuals (though it certainly is instructive), nor as a source of inner motivation (though it may well motivate persons to live and behave in certain ways). Rather, the primary 'work' is the work of community formation—by this "powerful practice" God forms the gathered community

[117] For McClendon's account of decisionism in modern ethics, see his *Ethics,* rev. ed., vol. 1 of *Systematic Theology* (Nashville: Abingdon Press, 2002), 73-75.

into Christ's body.[118] This says much about both the relationship of the gathered community to God and to one another: "The rite pledges and performs the *incorporation* of the lives of the gathered disciples not only into their crucified and risen Lord, but also into one another."[119] Hence, the Lord's Supper can be "named" as the "*practice of establishing and maintaining Christian community.*"[120] The biblical warrant for this is most clearly seen in 1 Corinthians 10-12. There, Paul sandwiches his exposition of Jesus's teaching on the Supper in chapter 11 between explicit reflection on the community as the body of Christ. Common in Paul's day was the notion that sharing a meal with someone was communion with them, and Paul uses this to link Christ's sharing of "my body" with the disciples as the logic of the communion—in this body the disciples become Christ's body, and they become Christ's body precisely because Jesus shares with them his own body.[121]

This 'ethical' account of the Lord's Supper certainly does not exhaust the conceptual identity of the Supper—or, perhaps it would be better to say that the 'logic' of the ethical count needs to be articulated in terms of a doctrine of the Lord's Supper, what the church teaches about its identity, purposes and actual practice. Appropriately enough, McClendon's most sustained reflections on the subject are in the context of worship. There he develops two notions that are key to understanding the Lord's Supper: 1) Worship is a dialogue between God and humans, but centrally the human component is divinely enabled; 2) The 'God-language' of this dialogue is the language of God's signs, those occasions of God's self-revelation.

First, McClendon carefully delineates the way in which worship is a "response" to God (a qualification especially necessary given some of the unfortunate trajectories of Baptist worship).[122] Whatever worship is, it is not merely a monologue of humans speaking to God in response to some past

---

[118] For more on the concept of a powerful practice see, Ibid., 172-182. The concept of a "powerful practice" is essentially a combination of a qualified Macynterian notion of practice, and the biblical notion of the principalities and powers. The usefulness of the combination is 1) to account for the way that practices themselves are often institutional practices (McClendon's example is hospital operation—hospitals are basically a collection of related practices), and 2) the way in which those practices can both form and de-form—the powers are not *simply* fallen. They are certainly fallen and as such can destroy, but God continues to use them for his own purposes. Terrence Tilley challenges McClendon's account of powerful practices in his otherwise positive "Review Essay: Why American Catholic Theologians Should Read 'Baptist' Theology," *Horizons* 14 (Spring 1987): 7-8.

[119] McClendon, *Ethics*, 219.

[120] Ibid., 220.

[121] McClendon, *Ethics*, 219.

[122] McClendon, *Doctrine*, 374.

event. It is instead a "two-sided practice" whereby God and humans dialogue. Second, worship is never an attempt to control God, to manipulate God to respond to our prayers and worship.[123] Echoing themes noted from Thompson (and to be seen in Colwell below), one might say that McClendon's qualifications of response are to clearly show how God is freed *from* manipulation and control by humans and freed *for* the faithful fulfillment of his promises to commune with people. The divine initiative and human response are constituted by Jesus Christ as the "*objective* driving force of worship" and the Holy Spirit as the "*subjective* driving force."[124] That is, Christian worship is worship of the triune God—a real meeting of "God-in-Christ-by-the-Spirit."[125] That Christ is the objective driving force is simply to say that the "engine" of Christian worship is the life, death, and resurrection of Jesus. That the Spirit is the subjective force is simply to say that the human response to God's supreme sign in Christ is no *mere* human response. It is a response that is "Spirit-given, Spirit-led, and thus always more (though never less) than human. In this worship, we meet the present Christ; in this worship, that very meeting is the Spirit's gift."[126]

This meeting of Christ is indeed 'real.' But that the two loci of Christian worship of God are Christ and the Spirit makes clear that his real presence is not something conjured up either by liturgical or emotive rituals. That is, McClendon affirms a real meeting with Christ in the Spirit, not merely an inner awareness of Christ. This is significant, for as McClendon says, "the promise is not, 'Where two or three are gathered, you will have such and such *worship experiences*. He only promised to be at hand."[127] As for the mode of Christ's presence, McClendon is content to say that in worship Christ "is present *in a way that matters* . . . . [which] is to say that the one of whom this story tells is present in such a way that *the story continues*, present in a way that makes no sense save for the story to this point, a way that shapes the story still to follow."[128] Here, McClendon is working with narrative themes developed throughout his systematic theology. Much more will be said about this in the final chapter, but for the moment it is sufficient to note that for McClendon the notion of narrative with respect to Christ is in no sense merely illustrative, as if narratively-conceived presence is less than real presence. In fact, McClendon argues that a fruitful way of articulating the reality of Jesus's humanity and divinity is to speak of Jesus's humanity and divinity in the terms of the narrative in which he is revealed. That is, the storied identity of Jesus as

---

[123] Ibid.

[124] Ibid., 376.

[125] Ibid., 377

[126] Ibid., 376

[127] McClendon, *Doctrine*, 379.

[128] Ibid., 378

revealed in the gospel is indeed real identity with (for lack of a better word) ontological weight or significance.[129] Though McClendon does not explicitly draw the link, it is clear that the logic of the ethical strand of the Lord's Supper (a community forming practice) is spelled out in terms of Christ's presence with his disciples.

But, if worship itself is a 'medium' (a word McClendon does not use here) of God's presence, what is there to add doctrinally by way of the Lord's Supper? Here, McClendon draws some useful distinctions between the various signs of God, and in doing so articulates what he takes to be God's "language" of worship. First, there are the historic signs, those "crucial events in the history of redemption."[130] These are distinctive signs (often called miracles), "God's distinctive, self-disclosing signs, acts that make God's presence and power evident for redemptive purposes."[131] McClendon lists several (for example creation, the Exodus, birth of the Messiah). Then there are the remembering signs (McClendon identifies baptism, the Lord's Supper and preaching as three "classic" remembering signs), associated with the great historic signs "as their (repeatable) *monuments*."[132] But, these are no mere remembering signs, no mere symbols of something gone and past. Rather, "God acts to make these *remembering signs* effectual, just as God originally acted in the great historic signs themselves."[133] Finally there are providential signs, which are "instances of the distinctive guidance God gives to individual lives for designated kingdom tasks."[134] With respect to worship, then, "the centrality of Christ is witnessed by the place of the great signs of which his resurrection from the dead is chief; the remembering signs realize these divine sign-acts in our common worship; directed by these, the providential signs find in the baptist vision their checkpoint and norm."[135] That is, Christ is really present in Christian worship because he has promised to be, and the effective witnesses to this presence are the remembering signs—effective both because

---

129 See Ibid., 263-279. See also my exposition and appropriation in chapter 6 below.

130 Ibid., 381.

131 Ibid.

132 Ibid., 382.

133 McClendon, *Doctrine*, 382. McClendon uses John L. Austin's account of speech act to show how signs are rarely, if ever, *merely* symbolic; symbols perform work. See further, 388-389, and McClendon and James M. Smith, *Convictions: Diffusing Religious Relativism*, rev. ed. (Valley Forge, PA: Trinity Press, 1994; originally published as *Understanding Religious Convictions* [Notre Dame: Notre Dame University Press, 1975]), chapter 3 for an account of speech-act theory and its application to religious language.

134 McClendon, *Doctrine*, 382.

135 Ibid., 385.

they make real to the worshiping community the great historic signs (or, might it be better to say they make real to the great historic signs the gathered worshiping community?), and because they discipline and link providential signs to the reality of the historic signs.

The logic of the Lord's Supper in particular is linked most directly to the person of Jesus, and as such its "power . . . lies especially in its nearness to the person of Christ: Our beliefs about him theologically shape the meal that we call by his name."[136] The Supper is linked to Christ narratively insofar as in the celebration, the meal narrates the gathered community into the culmination of the story of Israel, that is, into Christ. There is, then, a "plurality of narratives" present in the celebration of the Lord's Supper, and this plurality may be spelled out (as McClendon does) in terms of several themes.[137]

The first narrative theme is solidarity, and this theme has already been explicated in McClendon's ethics (see above). The risen Christ is present in the celebration "to give us bread that is his, and so (by rights) his own body."[138] In so giving us his body, we are united with him and as a consequence "we are re-membered one to another as his members."[139]

The second narrative theme is forgiveness. McClendon argues that given that the meal is a community forming practice, and given that it is explicitly linked with Christ's self-sacrifice, the meal is a practice of community renewal. Such renewal occurs not merely as promises we make to one another, but promises we make to one another while sharing a meal with our God. Here, McClendon argues that the Roman Catholic Church is actually right to speak of the Lord's Supper as a sacrifice "if by sacrifice we mean a ritual meal that is shared between deity and worshippers" and not speak of the Lord's Supper as itself a means of forgiveness in some sort of functional competition with the once for all sacrifice of Christ.[140] Along with a meal of forgiveness, it is a meal of thanksgiving. The memorial identity of the meal is no mere recalling to mind, but a repeatable act of memorializing, a repeatable thanksgiving monument to God's act in Christ. Finally, a perhaps neglected theme of the Lord's Supper is its eschatological direction. McClendon notes that in the gospels the account of the Last Supper is linked with Jesus's teaching on last things.[141] So, the Supper not only looks back to Jesus's sacrifice, it looks

---

136 Ibid., 400.

137 Ibid., 401.

138 Ibid., 402.

139 Ibid.

140 McClendon, *Doctrine*, 402-403. McClendon notes approvingly that contemporary Roman Catholic theologians have corrected the abuses of the mass that were a central component of occasioning the reformation.

141 Ibid., 405. McClendon cites as an example Mark 13, where the "little apocalypse" is immediately followed by Mark's account of the last supper.

forward such that "God's future is immediately, presently relevant to this community."[142] But importantly, it is a looking forward not merely to some future heavenly bliss but, given that in the gospels the Supper is the last thing before crucifixion, a looking forward to judgment, to crisis for the followers of Jesus. Of course, given the overall eschatological thrust of the Bible, such crisis is not the last word. The crisis thrust upon Jesus and promised to his disciples is the crisis that opens up into God's future blessing, and hence the eschatological looking forward of the Supper is ultimately a looking forward to the full realization of God's kingdom rule on earth.

McClendon's theology of the Lord's Supper is narratively defined in terms of Christ's historical body insofar as it is the practice most clearly linked with Jesus himself, and insofar as more broadly the person of Christ is the "objective driving force" of worship. Furthermore, McClendon affirms that in the Supper Christ gives us his own body, though one might detect some hesitation in affirming this because McClendon often speaks of a meeting with Christ without explicit reference to his body. For instance, McClendon says that Christ is present "in a way that matters." Nevertheless, in light of McClendon's narrative Christology and his affirmation that the doctrinal significance of the Supper be spelled out in terms of the narrative of Christ's life and death, it is not an unfair comparison to the traditional affirmation of Christ's sacramental body insofar as narrative identity is real identity for McClendon. Much more will be said about this in the final chapter. Finally, the goal of the Supper is clearly the re-membering of the church as Christ's ecclesial body, and in this McClendon joins the Baptists so far described in their clear affirmation of the church as the 'product' of God's work in the Supper.

John E. Colwell

Few if any contemporary Baptists, be they North American, British, or otherwise, have done as much careful theological reflection on the notion of sacrament, and the sacraments themselves, as John Colwell. If one presumes that Baptists are by nature non-sacramental, as most contemporary Baptists do, then Colwell's *Promise and Presence: An Exploration of Sacramental Theology* is surprising, perhaps even shocking.[143] This is because not only does Colwell offer a careful and thorough theology of sacrament, Colwell undertakes something of a Baptist rehabilitation of the seven traditional sacraments of the Roman Catholic Church. While this rehabilitation is fascinating and worthy of further attention it is beyond the scope of this book to

---

[142] Ibid., 405.

[143] John E. Colwell, *Promise and Presence: An Exploration of Sacramental Theology* (Milton Keynes: Paternoster, 2005).

evaluate the project as a whole. Rather, I want to focus on Colwell's explication of the Lord's Supper. In order to do justice to Colwell's account of the Lord's Supper I need to give a brief overview of the sacramental theology out of which his reflection on the Lord's Supper arises.

Colwell argues that sacramental theology should be approached not as a distinct theological topic, but as a component of a doctrine of God, and so Colwell explicitly and carefully roots his sacramental reflections in the doctrine of the Trinity. This is because for Colwell the doctrine of the Trinity is the very logic of the gospel, and as such holds central place in theological reflection on any issue. Specifically, the doctrine of the Trinity defines the relationship of God to creation and so the theological context for articulating the mediation of God's presence to creation. That God's presence is mediated to creation is not merely a consequence of the fundamental distinction between God and creation, it is a consequence of God's own identity. The Spirit mediates the Father to the Son and the Son to the Father, and he does this as the personal mediator of the mutual love of Father and Son.[144] Colwell argues that the mediation of the Spirit is not a deduction from the oneness of God; rather, it is an inference drawn from the gospel story itself. And likewise, that God is constituted by loving relations of Father, Son, and Spirit is an inference from God's self-revelation. This is important for it shows that God's love is indeed free love. It is not necessitated by a 'nature' of God (although neither does God's revealed character leave it indeterminate); it is rather to name the free love of God within Godself. The Spirit's free, loving mediation of Father and Son, then, is constitutive of the free love of God, and hence constitutive of an account of grace in the sacraments.

That the gospel story reveals the Spirit to be the personal mediator of Father and Son is instructive for an account of the mediation of God's presence to creation. This is centrally important for Colwell because it shows that we must affirm God's self-mediation as a "mediated immediate" rather than "unmediated immediate."[145] This awkward locution signifies that the mediation of the Spirit is not in the manner of the mediation of, say the digital telephone network's mediation of my wife and me on a phone conversation. This would be a *merely* mediated relationship, one of two distant parties being virtually, not really, brought near; it is a mediation that presumes separation and distance. The Spirit's mediation is not a medium placed in between the Father and Son, such that the Father and Son are in some way separate from one another. Rather, it is the gospel way of articulating the immediate relation of Father to

---

144 Colwell carefully roots these relations in the Gospel story. See, for example, Ibid., 20.

145 Colwell, 40. Colwell credits Colin Gunton with claiming that Barth's theology produces such an unmediated immediate. The phrase "mediated immediate" comes from John Ballie *Our Knowledge of God* (London: Oxford University Press, 1939), 181.

Son—it is immediate (not screened, or blocked, or distant); but it is immediate *by means of* the person of the Spirit.

That God's love is free, though not arbitrary, and that God's love is mediated, though immediate love, is defining of the notion of sacrament. God's gracious presence to creation is mediated through the Spirit by means of tangible signs. Colwell notes that Scripture shows God's predilection for tangible signs. What constitutes some tangible signs as sacrament (for example, Lord's Supper) and other tangible signs as sacramental, but not properly a sacrament (for example, the burning bush) ultimately rests on God's promised presence in the signs to the church. That is, God in the burning bush, while certainly a sign and a means of grace, is not properly a sacrament because God has made no promise to mediate himself subsequently through burning bushes.[146] Furthermore, since God is doing the promising and the mediating, faith is not required for constituting the sacramental sign: "But it is a promise, rather than the faith, that constitutes the sacramental sign. Faith is not constitutive. Faith simply is a trustful resting on a given promise. . . . A sacrament is the promise of presence and action *whether that presence and action are discerned or not.*"[147] According to Colwell, the problem that occasions the reformation is not a Catholic theology of the sacraments in itself, but the way in which the sacraments came to be practiced as ways of manipulating or controlling God.[148]

Because the sacrament is ultimately a result of the promise of God, and because it is a consequence of God's triune identity, mediation of God's presence through sacramental signs is not a limitation on God's presence, as though the sacramental sign stands in between God and his people. Rather, as the Spirit mediates the immediate relationship of Father and Son through his person, so God mediates his immediate presence to believers by the Spirit's use of material signs. Hence, God's presence in the sacraments is always, in a way specific to the sacrament, a *real* presence; that is, sacraments are never *merely* signs, symbols of something (or, in this case someone) absent. Rather, they are signs that make effective, wholly by the work of the Spirit, that of which they are signs.

Colwell's account of the Lord's Supper affirms the real presence of Christ in the Lord's Supper in terms of his previous account of the sacraments. Colwell firsts notes that, like the Passover meal, this meal is no mere memorial but a participation in that which is commemorated; that is, the sacrificial meal, like the Passover, is a means of participating in the events themselves.[149] As a

---

146 Ibid., 57.

147 Ibid., 58. Italics in the original.

148 Ibid., 60.

149 Colwell, 157. Colwell is aware of some of the questions surrounding the link between the Passover meal and the Last Supper.

participation in the sacrifice of Christ, Colwell affirms by way of reflection on the book of Hebrews, that the Lord's Supper may indeed be termed a sacrifice. It is not a re-sacrifice, not a repetition of Christ's sacrifice. Rather, it is a re-presentation of the truly unique sacrifice of Christ, and re-presented not so much as an extension of the sacrifice, but rather as to make us present to it.[150] Colwell's hesitation with the usual Catholic way of articulating the presence of Christ is not with respect to it is as a sacrifice. He readily concedes that no "key" Catholic text speaks of the offering of the church as a mere repetition of Christ's sacrifice.[151] His hesitation is that he thinks the Catholic texts do not sufficiently state clearly and carefully that it is the *Spirit*, mediated through the instrumental means of priest and church, that does the work of re-presentation. So, he resists the claim that it is the Church or the priest that does the offering, even bloodlessly, and rather appeals to the notion of mediation: "But that Christ is truly offered again here (or better, that Christ's offering is re-presented here) is no mere human act: it is a divine act mediated through a human act by the Spirit; if it is a divine act in response to human prayer it is more fundamentally a human prayer in response to a divine promise." Colwell's affirmation of the notion of sacrifice, then, is an affirmation of a *real* sacrifice, and this because the Spirit, in response to prayer (which itself is a response to God's promises) ushers us into participation with the once-for-all sacrifice of Christ. In so doing, that which we participate in is indeed the true body and blood of Christ: "the participation in the body and blood of Christ attested by Paul in 1 Corinthians 10 and by Christ himself in the Synoptic Gospels and in John 6 is actual and real, it is no empty sign and no ineffective sign; we are truly changed here because we truly participate in Christ here."[152]

Colwell contends that this is what "the overwhelming majority of the Church, for the overwhelming majority of its history, and from its earliest extant confessions, has unequivocally affirmed: the risen Christ is made present here in a unique manner and to a unique degree."[153] And yet, rather than the visible sign of unity, the Lord's Supper is one of the more visible signs of *dis*unity in the church. Colwell claims (granting that it is an oversimplification) that the controversies tend to occur when the Church "has sought to define this 'mystery' more closely."[154] Here Colwell engages several attempts to more closely define the mystery. For my purposes, I want to attend briefly to three of these engagements: Aquinas, Luther, and Calvin.

In short, Colwell finds the most to commend about Calvin. Colwell's reservations about Aquinas are really issues of clarity and emphasis rather than

---

150 Ibid.,159-161.

151 Ibid., 161.

152 Colwell, 162.

153 Ibid., 162-163.

154 Ibid., 163.

substance; in fact, in substance, Colwell notes a striking similarity between Calvin and Aquinas. It is Luther who provides the real contrast to Calvin and Aquinas. In Luther, Colwell finds a troubling *lack* of unique mediation. Luther's use of the *communicatio idiomatum* is intended to show how it is that Christ can be bodily present in the Eucharist, while still in heaven, and to show how this could be the case without appeal to transubstantiation. But, Colwell argues that claiming Christ's body is present because it shares in all the attributes of divinity and hence can be bodily present under bread and wine, tends too closely to a physical account of the presence. If it is the case that both bread and body are substantially present, then why would it not follow that both are "accidentally" present, and as such one indeed chews the flesh of Christ?[155] Furthermore, "if Christ's presence at the Eucharist is simply an instance of a general ubiquity there is nothing distinctive, less still unique, about his presence at the Eucharist."[156] In light of his subsequent reflections on Calvin and Thomas, one might say that the problem here is that Luther really has no way to speak of the Spirit's work in response to God's promises since ultimately it is a point about divine and human nature that does the work of articulating this presence.

In contrast to Luther's suspiciously physicalist account, Colwell argues that Calvin and Aquinas both work hard to affirm a real presence, but one that is unique according to the mediation of the Spirit (though Aquinas is less clear here), and as such real without being crassly physical. In contrast to Luther, we cannot affirm the presence using the same terms as the incarnation. Aquinas affirms the uniqueness of this presence by claiming that the presence of Christ is not like any other presence. That is, Christ is not spatially located in the celebration of the Eucharist. He is rather there sacramentally, and "sacramentally" is, as Colwell observes, "to say something entirely distinctive, something entirely other than any general spatial presence: Christ's presence here is unique; he is present here in a manner in which he is present nowhere else; he is present here 'sacramentally.'"[157] Like Aquinas, Calvin affirms the uniqueness of the presence, and likewise affirms that what is present is Christ's true body and blood, although of course doing so in ways different from the creative use of Aristotle's categories of Aquinas's proposal. But, despite questions about the appropriateness of Aristotelian categories for contemporary accounts of the Lord's Supper, or even whether such a use in their historical context is really clarifying, Colwell's real hesitation with Aquinas, and concomitantly what is to be commended in Calvin, has to do with the presence and work of the Spirit in the making present of Christ's body. Thomas lacks

---

155 Ibid., 166.

156 Ibid., 167.

157 Colwell, 168.

Calvin's "explicit affirmation of the Spirit's mediating role" in the Eucharist.[158] Thomas certainly affirms that Christ is present by grace, and that God is the first cause of the presence acting through the authority of the priest, but he does so in a way that tends towards obscuring the personal activity of the Spirit. Colwell notes that where Calvin most often speaks of the personal presence and action of the Spirit, Thomas most frequently speaks of an impersonal grace (following the tradition of Augustine). Colwell thinks that, even if Aquinas himself is not guilty, this trajectory tends towards objectifying grace in a way that turns it into some sort of automatic deposit separate from the mediating work of the Spirit; and this is a problem because it obscures the way in which the sacrament is a work of God in response to his promises mediated through the material elements (priest, church, bread, wine) of the celebration.[159]

The point of the Lord's Supper is ultimately to conform the church to Christ by participation in the sacrifice of Christ: "The ultimate goal of the Supper, after all, is not the transformation of the elements but rather the transformation of the participants through their partaking of those transformed elements."[160] According to Colwell, both Aquinas and Calvin affirm this: participation in Christ through the mediation of the Spirit results in our transformation. This transformation is a result of God's promise and his consequent presence: God answers our prayers because he has promised to, not because we (or a priest) are able to manipulate the means God has provided. That the goal is transformation, and that the transformation occurs by participation in the real body and blood of Christ through the Spirit in response to God's free, loving promises, brings us back around to the problem of the church's disunity so evident in the practice of the Lord's Supper.

Colwell contends that, because the sacrament is what it is as a result of God's promises—Christ is present in the celebration because of the activity of the Spirit not because of the activity of the church—the Lord's Supper is properly understood to be a means of unity, not an expression of unity. Paul says, "Because there is one loaf, we, who are many, are one body, for we all partake of the one loaf" (1 Cor. 10:17, TNIV). That is, within the bounds of Christian orthodoxy

> it is not that we share communion as an expression of our unity (a unity defined and discovered in some other place or manner); it is rather that we are united by virtue of sharing communion. . . . [W]e do not share

---

158 Ibid., 171.

159 Ibid. Colwell follows Macquarrie's suggestion that it is really the Council of Constance (1414-1418) that moves the focus to the power of the priest to consecrate, rather than the priest as the one *through whom* the Spirit does the consecrating. See John Macquarrie, *A Guide To the Sacraments* (London: SCM Press, 1997), 129.

160 Ibid., 175.

> communion as an expression of our unity; we share communion as the means of our unity; to seek unity through agreeing forms of words is to seek an inadequate form of unity and to seek it by inadequate means.[161]

Hence, Colwell argues that confessional differences are a "wholly inadequate basis for continuing such disunity."[162] Though it is certainly true that the sacrament of the Lord's Supper calls for a response of faith on the part of the church, the sacrament depends upon the mediating power of the Spirit not on the dispositions of the participants; likewise, the unity of the church is ultimately a work of God in the Spirit and as such within the bounds of defined orthodoxy it is the Eucharist that makes the church, not the agreed upon formulations of doctrine among believers that makes the church. For Colwell, this is only fitting given that God is faithful to God's promises.

Of the Baptists surveyed here, Colwell has done the most thorough evaluation of the sacraments, and the most explicit engagement with the broader catholic tradition on the sacrament of the Lord's Supper. As such, the threefold articulation of Christ's body, especially Christ's sacramental body, is the most developed in Colwell. Colwell affirms that Christ himself is sacramentally re-presented as a result of God's promise. Furthermore, the point of this re-presentation is the unity of the church. Colwell clearly affirms that whatever is said about Christ's real presence in the Supper must include the real presence of Christ in the church.

Conclusion: Taking Stock

This extended survey of catholic Baptist reflection on the Lord's Supper has shown that there is a lively stream of contemporary Baptist theology articulating the identity of the Lord's Supper in terms of the body of Christ. Furthermore, this stream has freely and constructively appropriated the traditional threefold articulation of Christ's body, yet in distinctively Baptist ways. These Baptists affirm the thrust of the Supper as God's drawing the church into participation with Christ's body. Christ's sacramental body, his body in bread and wine is the medium of nourishment of the church as Christ's body.

Though articulating it in different ways, all the Baptists have implicitly affirmed the *unity* of this threefold articulation without collapsing that unity into indiscernibility. In other words, the same Jesus Christ, and hence the same body, is crucified on the cross, given in the Supper, and actualized in the church. Yet, that same body, the body on the cross, given in the bread, and actualized in the church must be distinguished in these three ways. That is, the

---

[161] Colwell, 176-177.

[162] Ibid., 177.

body of Christ crucified, shared in bread, and in the church is the same body, but not in the same manner of being the body of Christ. Such discernibility is necessary theologically to prevent problematic claims such as the church was crucified for the sins of the world, or Jesus is chewed by the teeth of the faithful, or Jesus has already returned from his ascension to heaven. Of course, this unity in diversity is constitutive of the broad catholic tradition of Eucharistic reflection, and so these Baptists are catholic insofar as they have drawn from that broad reservoir, and intend to contribute to it.

The purpose of my project here is to pursue this identity in diversity displayed in these Baptist theologians. Attention to analogous uses of language, and the constitutive role those uses play in identity claims, will allow me to trace the conceptual contours of this identity in diversity, of the 'fluidity' available in language to speak of the one body of Christ on the cross, in the bread, and in the church without confusion of each. Furthermore, attention to analogous uses of language will draw our attention to the baptist vision itself. The baptist vision, as I will show in the final chapter, is constituted by an identity claim, 'this is that,' which is real identity without collapsing 'this' into 'that.' As such, the baptist vision itself has an intrinsic interest in Eucharistic identity. Finally, this investigation will contribute to the catholic Baptist project by facilitating the sorts of claims about the Lord's Supper made by these Baptists. To be clear, in line with eschewing theory, attention to analogous uses of language will not *justify* what these Baptists say; those sorts of arguments will be exegetical and theological (outside the immediate scope of my claim). Yet, attention to analogous uses of language, and in particular the light shed by analogous uses of language on the baptist vision itself, will *clarify* what a Baptist is doing in identifying the bread and the church as Christ's body, and that such a theological identification is fittingly generated from the baptist vision itself.

CHAPTER 3

Analogous Uses of Language and Identity

Introduction

Having set the context of the book and outlined a method, I now turn to the programmatic issue: analogous uses of language. As indicated above, I will claim that attention to analogous uses of language can shed light on the intrinsic relationship between the baptist vision and Eucharistic identity claims. This chapter, then, aims to clarify analogous uses of language.

The chapter will proceed in two main parts. Each part will follow the lead of a central philosophical and theological guide. First, I set up the substantive issues attendant to an account of analogous uses of language. Using Garth Hallett as the guide of the first part, I will show why attention to language use is important, why it is so often overlooked, and how attention to actual uses of language displays the in-use boundaries, or grammar, of analogous uses of language. Furthermore, attention to actual use will display how pervasive (if often overlooked) analogous uses of language are. In the second part, I will turn to the work of David Burrell as the primary guide for characterizing the uses identified in the first part. Burrell's work on analogy has repeatedly, though not exclusively, centered on Thomas Aquinas, and so Aquinas will serve as something of a perspicuous example that will ultimately shed light on analogous uses of language in Eucharistic reflection.

Hallett on Analogous Uses of Language

Why, in a book pursuing the question of Christ's body in the Eucharist, should issues of language use be at the fore? After all, one might think that the primary issue is Christ's body itself, its presence or absence. What we say about Christ's body is a consequence of what we take to be real. Hence, the fundamental reality (and the epistemological issues attendant to our access to it) is the issue. What we say about that reality, the relevant words and sentences we use to talk about that reality, depends upon prior judgments we make about the reality. After all, is it not *just* language?

The above objection clearly embodies a dualism between language and reality, as though reality were 'real' and language not, at least not in the same sense that the world is real. Certainly we use language, but language, the objector might hold, is little more than a complex system of name tags we put on the stuff of the world, and so one might think that attending to language is attending to the wrong thing, or at least to a secondary thing. The heart of the matter is the reality; language is merely a consequence of what we say or write about the reality.

Any response will ultimately challenge the dualism of the question: the dualism that language and reality are two essentially or fundamentally different things; that language and reality are in competition with one another over that which is most important or most 'real.' And of course, one schooled by Wittgenstein cannot help but note the obvious conceptual confusion attendant to such a dualism. It appears that 'real' and 'reality' have started to lose their grip on the rough ground. Furthermore, I suspect that one voicing such an objection would remain unconvinced by an *argument* for the priority of language. What motivates the objection is likely not reliance upon a bad argument, as though someone convinced the objector by a series of claims in support of a thesis about the priority of 'reality' over language. Rather, I suspect that what motivates the objection is something like a lack of vision, a failure to see clearly.

That lack of vision, I submit, is fundamentally inattention to the role and complexity of language, particularly the variety of uses of language termed 'analogous.' The oversight may be motivated by the dualism, but the dualism is occasioned by a simple lack of awareness. Hallett warns that

> those who lack linguistic awareness . . . recognize that on most occasions there is little danger of bewitchment by language, hence little need to remove one's linguistic spectacles and examine them. What they do not recognize is that those who fail to reflect on language are thereby prevented from recognizing when and why such reflection does become necessary—why, for instance, speculative discourse requires constant vigilance whereas non-speculative discourse does not.[1]

In other words, language is largely invisible to language users, with the consequence that we are usually unaware of when our uses of language are themselves misleading us.

But, *bewitchment*? In what sense does language bewitch, mislead, or confuse? And how does the invisibility of language relate to such bewitchment? That is, if the realities are the issue, and language a secondary issue (i.e., something we *say about* realities), then is not the bewitchment on the level of our thoughts or perceptions of reality, not on the level of language? Or, put another way, is it not the case that any misleading or confusing language is a consequence or symptom of misleading or confusing thoughts? Get our thoughts and beliefs, our 'mental content,' right and language will

---

[1] Garth L. Hallett, *Essentialism: A Wittgensteinian Critique* (Albany: State University of New York Press, 1991), 131.

follow without difficulty. Language is not the issue; our beliefs and judgments about reality are the issue. Again, however, such an objection simply misses the role and complexity of language.

This complexity can more easily be shown by example than definition, and so an example from Hallett is worth quoting at length, for it gets at the often overlooked complexity of language use. (In the quote below, Hallett is presuming a prior stipulation he has made, that 'concept' will be used for "the meaning of a general term," and that the meaning of a term is "its use in the language to which it belongs"[2]):

> A useful illustration is the familiar concept "true." Out on the fringe of the concept, so to speak, lie true friends, true north, true blue, and the like. More central to the concept are true ideas, surmises, beliefs, opinions, and so forth, which are true in a different sense. Also true propositions, premises, conclusions, hypotheses, theories, creeds, principles, and so on, which are true for much the same reason, namely their being statable in true utterances. Utterances are true in still another sense: if their use of words conforms with the words' established uses, the utterances are true; if, not, they are false. The individual words however are neither true nor false, nor are constitutive phrases. Nor are commands, requests, recommendations, promises, invitations, questions, cheers, vows, and various other speech acts. Although they too employ their terms in accordance with rules laid down in practice or by stipulation, they lack that certain something which would make them statements, assertions, claims, declarations, or the like, and therefore true or false. Just what that special something is, philosophers of language are far from agreeing. And as for indubitable statements indubitably true, their "correspondence with fact" may mean various things, according as they are mathematical, logical, theoretical, or empirical, with the correspondence sometimes tighter or sometimes looser, as context, topic, or choice of phrase determines ("a hundred miles from Denver," say, being judged by less rigorous standards than "a hundred and five, and thirty-three thousandths"). The English concept "true," all by itself, is a linguistic labyrinth, which no one . . . has managed to map.[3]

On the one hand, 'true' is a word that we (English speakers) use regularly, and regularly use well. On the other hand, we use it in all sorts of ways. Inattention to all these sorts of ways is a cause of so much confusion: how do we theorize about a word used of such a range of things as friends and sentences? Of course, one might want to say, "but these are *words*, and we are interested in

---

2 Garth L. Hallett., *Logic For the Labyrinth: A Guide To Critical Thinking* (Lanham, MD: University Press of America, 1984), 2.

3 Ibid., 11.

truth itself," or some such. Yet, this is indeed worth noting: that we *sign* (talk, write, etc.) 'true.' That is, there is no reflection on truth without various uses of 'true' and 'truth.'[4] Of course, there are real differences in the way 'true' is used of a friend and of a sentence, and overlooking those differences may well cause confusion. But the felicitous approach is not to say that one is more truly 'true' than another, but simply to assemble enough reminders to help us go on. After all, English speakers just do use 'true' in all these different ways.

Still, if language is so important, why is it so often overlooked? It is not news to English speakers that 'true' is used of friends as often as it is used of sentences. Hallett suggests a response to why language is so often overlooked. Words are tools of communication. And yet, the tools themselves are of course not the point. The communication is the point. So, for the tools to do their job they must, in a sense, be invisible.[5] To communicate well in a natural language like English, I must be *fluent*. That is, I must be so familiar with the uses of the language that I use it without explicit reflection on it. For our lives to be occupied with things like eating, working, playing, etc. we must be fluent enough to speak the language with ease, to speak the language without being occupied with the language use itself.

Examples of this necessity are easy to come by, and most often found in the gaps between fluent speakers of a language and non-fluent speakers. For example, I spent six weeks one summer in Western China, and I recall taking long periods of time to order at restaurants where no one spoke English, because the waiter, my Chinese friends, and I were preoccupied with the language itself, and this preoccupation got in the way of efficient ordering and eating food. Or, consider a common conversation at the dinner table between my 18 month old daughter, learning the language still, and my wife and I: My daughter says, "Mo chuzz." My wife and I respond, "Huh?" "Mo chuzz!" "I'm sorry dear, I don't understand you." "Mo chueeeeeeeeze!" "Oh, more cheese." Until she is fluent, we will have constant stumbles over the language. Of course, these examples portray non-fluency, and as such display an important indicator of fluency: one is fluent in a language, we might say, when one has ceased to be occupied by the language. This ability to 'forget' *how* to speak, and just speak, is in some sense necessary for complex human ways of living. In other words, language is 'invisible' because it must be to facilitate complex human activities. As Hallett says, "We need to have such command of language that we are free to attend to the things we say, without figuring out how to say them."[6] (Compare with non-linguistic tools: The roofer never gets the roof completed because she constantly has to refer to the directions for her

---

4 For Garth Hallett's argument on the priority of linguistic truth to mental truth see *Language and Truth* (New Haven: Yale University Press, 1988), 47-50.

5 See Hallett, *Essentialism*, 134; and *Language For the Labyrinth*, 188.

6 Hallett, *Language For the Labyrinth*, 9.

pneumatic nail gun; or the carpenter never completes the house because he is constantly fiddling with his hammer and electric drill).

Still, what of the issue of bewitchment? It is one thing to say that language is invisible in this sense. But bewitching? The invisibility of language is rarely a problem in ordinary uses. We do get married, eat dinners, play games, go to work, celebrate birthdays and the like without ever attending explicitly to the uses to which we put language in those activities; and this 'overlooking' is not a problem. In fact, if Hallett is right, it is *required* in order to get married, eat dinners, play games, go to work, and celebrate birthdays without language itself getting in the way. But in philosophy, at least according to Wittgenstein, language itself frequently does get in the way. A primary cause of language getting in the way is misleading analogies. That is, in many cases, words "are of utterly different kinds, but look exactly alike."[7] Hallett identifies four "clusters" of misleading analogies (clusters because, as Wittgenstein himself notes, "the idea of an analogy being misleading is nothing sharply defined"[8]). Though all four are helpful for gaining a working sense of the misleading analogies, I want to focus on only two, both for sake of space, and because they are the sorts of misleading analogies that I suspect are a root of the original objection above about language and reality.

First is what Hallett labels the Reference Fallacy: "A substantive makes us look for a thing that corresponds to it."[9] When playing hide and seek with my toddler, I ask, "Where did Maddie hide?" Then I point to her ('hiding' in plain sight but with her hands over her eyes) and say, "there she is!" So, we are tempted when asking about knowing, hoping, believing, understanding and the like to try to point to a mental process, comparing, for example, understanding to a process "such as translation from one language to another; it suggests a similar conception of thinking, knowing, believing, wishing, intending, and so on."[10] Wittgenstein aimed to show, however, that even if such a mental or psychological process could be identified, it plays no role in our use of the terms. That is, when my students say in class, "we understand what you're trying to say about the Nicene Creed" they are not 'pointing,' so to speak, to a mental or psychological process; that is, if it is true that they understand, we

---

7 Ludwig Wittgenstein, *The Blue and Brown Books* (New York: Harper & Row, 1958), 56; cited in Garth L. Hallett, *A Companion to Wittgenstein's "Philosophical Investigations"* (Ithaca: Cornell University Press, 1977), 27.

8 Wittgenstein, *Blue Book,* 28; cited in Hallett, *Companion*, 27. The fallacies are the sense fallacy, descriptive fallacy, reference fallacy, and essence fallacy. See Hallett, *Companion*, 27-35.

9 Wittgenstein, *Blue Book*, 1; cited in Hallett, *Companion*, 31.

10 Ludwig Wittgenstein, *Philosophical Grammar,* edited by Rush Rhees, translated by Anthony Kenny (Berkeley: University of California Press, 1978), 74; cited in Hallett, *Companion,* 31.

need not find out anything about their mind or brain. The 'proof' would be in their ability to go on speaking in terms of Christological orthodoxy. The use of 'understand' simply need not link with a referent like a mental process, even if it turned out to be the case such a mental process could be identified.

Furthermore, 'understand' is used in different, though related ways. To understand the Nicene Creed, a mathematical formula, how a model train works, or what a French speaker is saying are not the same things. That is, there is no one experience that characterizes each. As Hallett notes, "were some single act or experience constantly, prominently present in all cases of meaning or willing or expecting or grieving (and so on), then talk of such a 'reference' would not be so misleading; but Wittgenstein argued that in these cases neither introspective reflection nor scientific research reveals a common core."[11] This suggests a close relationship between the Reference Fallacy and what Hallett calls the Essence Fallacy.

In the Essence Fallacy, a term like 'knowledge' or 'understanding' is taken to refer to one thing and one thing only:

> Essences in the traditional sense are core properties or clusters of properties present, necessarily, in all and only those things which bear the common name. Knowledge is one thing; language is one thing; beauty, meaning, humanity, life, law, justice—each is a single, invariant reality, present in the most varied instances, or in a separate realm of forms.[12]

Wittgenstein chalks this error up to the simple fact that we use the same word in varied contexts; and if we are using the same word, then the temptation is to assume one invariant, unchanging referent. The philosopher asks, "But why would we use the *same word* if there weren't something in common?"[13] In contrast, Wittgenstein said, "I cannot characterize the point better than by saying that it is opposed to that which Socrates represents in the Platonic dialogues. For if asked what knowledge is I would list examples of knowledge, and add the words 'and the like'. No common element is to be found in them all."[14]

Wittgenstein gave numerous examples in the *Investigations*, of which 'game' is perhaps the most well-known. We use the term 'game' of all sorts of things, and yet when asked to isolate its essence, we are at a loss. Or, to return to 'understand,' my students do in fact know how to use the word 'understand' in all its varied, but related ways: They understand the lesson for the day, and how to order food from the cafeteria, and why they are in trouble with their resident director for playing music too loud and so on. Philosophers, however,

---

11 Hallett, *Companion*, 32.

12 Ibid., *Essentialism*, 2.

13 Wittgenstein, *Philosophical Grammar*, 75. Cited in Hallett, *Companion,* 33.

14 Wittgenstein, Manuscript 302, 14. Cited in Hallett, *Companion*, 33-34.

get into trouble by supposing that there is one thing, understanding, and then trying to isolate that one thing from everything else. They operate as though there were a mental referent for understanding, and as though 'understanding' were essentially one thing, and one thing only.

Given these fallacies and the temptations and motivations that give rise to them, an immediate concern is whether or not we are left with any intelligible means of speaking. That is, if 'knowledge' is used in all sorts of different ways, then in what sense can we have knowledge? If we cannot say what 'understanding' is then how can we be sure that my students do in fact understand the lesson, how to order food, or why they are in trouble? But of course, this objection entirely misses the point. The claim is not that, since there are various ways of using 'understand' and 'knowledge' we are unable to know what understanding and knowledge are. Rather, the claim is that what understanding and knowledge are is fundamentally linked with how we use 'understanding' and 'knowledge.' That is, denying an essence in the sense above outlined is not denying sense to 'understanding' or 'knowledge.' It is simply calling attention to the fact that 'understanding' and 'knowledge' are used in related, though different ways. So, what is called for is attention to how the terms are used. To speak intelligibly of 'understanding' and 'knowledge' requires nothing more than fluency in use.

Still, the objection seems to be motivated by an uncomfortableness with the fuzziness, or fluidity, or variety of the uses of our terms. So, for this book, perhaps the most important feature of language to call attention to is the pervasiveness of analogous uses of language, that is, to the various, though related, ways in which terms are used. It is this to which I now turn.

Analogous Uses of Language Introduced

That 'knowledge,' 'understanding' and so many other of our words are used variously, though relatedly, is, again, a reminder of how pervasive analogous uses of language are. We have seen this in language use broadly through Wittgenstein and Hallett. Now, I want to turn to theological uses, specifically theological identity statements. Identity statements are important for reflection on the Lord's Supper ('This is my body') and important for McClendon's baptist vision ('This is that').

Hallett's reflections in his book *Identity and Mystery in Themes of Christian Faith* center on the way identity claims function in Christian discourse, and how sustained attention to the character of those claims aids us in locating and clarifying (which, he argues, is different than *explaining* or *solving*) mysteries of the faith. In Christian discourse, identity statements are a prime location to note mystery—'Jesus is God,' 'God is Trinity,' 'The church is the body of Christ,' 'This is my body', and so on. For example, Christian doctrine affirms whole-heartedly that Jesus is God—but of course that identity statement has led to much reflection on *how* Jesus is God, especially in light of another Christian identity claim, 'Jesus is human.'

The first thing to which Hallett calls our attention is a simple, yet perhaps frequently overlooked feature of identity statements, namely, that not all identity statements are identical. Consider the differences between these identity statements (Hallett's examples): "'Cicero is Tuly,' 'This is my wife' (gesturing to the person at my side), 'This is my brother' (pointing to a picture), 'Olivier is Hamlet' (in the movie), 'Klaus is the man on the left,' 'the evening star is the morning star,' 'ignorance is bliss,' 'war is war,' or 'life is a bowl of cherries.'"[15] It is not just ordinary usage that displays this variety. Consider these New Testament examples (again Hallett's): "'the varied responses to Jesus's question, 'Who do people say that the son of man is? . . . New Testament Eucharistic variants; Paul's living is Christ and dying is gain, you are the body of Christ, the gospel is the power of God for salvation."[16] All of these identity statements, and more, with even passing attention display a variety of kinds of identifications.

Hallett appeals to the essence fallacy as a reason for why this variety is overlooked. Recall that by essentialism, Hallett means the tendency to reduce things to essences—"core properties or clusters of properties present, necessarily, in all and only those things which bear the common name. Knowledge is one thing; language is one thing; beauty, meaning, humanity, life, law, justice—each is a single, invariant reality, present in the most varied instances, in a separate realm of forms."[17] Identity is usually thought of as one as well, and at least in the modern period, the prevalent account has been one of strict identity, or indiscernibility; that is, if two things are indeed identical, then they are indiscernible.[18] Philosophers, of course, granted that in ordinary speech such a strict standard was not always, perhaps even not usually, followed. But that was why philosophers needed to be extra careful and precise with their identity statements.[19] Furthermore, philosophers were ready to grant distinctions between, for instance, real identity and conceptual identity, or personal identity and physical identity. Yet, Hallett argues,

> the multiplicity, many would insist, does not entail that there is no single, absolute relation of identity or that the expression "the same" is equivocal, assuming different senses in different contexts. No, whatever *a* and *b* may be, if they really are identical, their identity is that of a thing with itself,

---

[15] Garth L. Hallett, *Identity and Mystery in Themes of Christian Faith: Late-Wittgensteinian Perspectives* (Aldershot: Ashgate, 2005), 7.

[16] Ibid., 7-8.

[17] Ibid., 2.

[18] Ibid., 3.

[19] Ibid., 2-3.

> and whatever is truly predicable of one must be truly predicable of the other. Identity entails indiscernibility.[20]

Hallett thinks that this sort of essentialism—that identity is *one* thing only, and that it is strict identity or no identity at all—has been an overlooked, yet influential factor in Christian identity claims. Hallett further argues that better attention to "the doctrine of analogy" can disabuse us of the tendency to essentialism. Of course, as Hallett notes, it is not that Christian theology has ignored analogy. Rather, Hallett thinks that what theology has not done well is attend to language *use*, and here, specifically with respect to what Hallett calls "competing claims of alternative expressions." [21]

By "competing claims of alternative expression" Hallett means to call our attention to the varying ranges and clusters of terms as they are used in natural languages. That is, if we were to map terms in relation to one another according to their uses, we would find some terms clustered more closely together, others spread farther apart. For instance, consider one of Hallett's examples, color terms. Crimson and scarlet are both reds, and both very similar reds at that. What keeps us from calling the color scarlet by the name 'crimson'? Hallett contends that it is the simple fact of the competing claim of the rival term 'scarlet.' In other words, while in many contexts it may be the case that 'crimson' could be easily stretched to include the color we call 'scarlet' without confusion—and it would not be much of a stretch in this case—those contexts are simply not *our* contexts (as English speakers). Our context includes the settled use of the term 'scarlet,' and this settled use is enough to prevent us from using 'crimson' for 'scarlet.'[22] The various terms denoting the family of red colors cluster closely together, and this close cluster means that they have fairly narrow ranges of use—'scarlet' is limited in use by the competing term 'crimson,' and the like.

Examples like this could be multiplied. Consider the relationship between 'tree,' 'shrub,' or 'bush.'[23] Bushes, especially big ones, are tree-like in many respects, yet we have the rival term 'tree' which limits the use of 'bush.' (My

---

20 Hallett, *Identity and Mystery*, 3.

21 Ibid., 4. Even Aquinas, on Hallett's read, so emphasizes similarity that he overlooks these competing expressions. For instance, Hallett cites Aquinas on wisdom: we say 'God is wise' because as the source of our wisdom we "imitate" God's wisdom (from *Summa Contra Gentiles* 1.31). In my judgment, David Burrell, who will be the primary guide in the second half of this chapter, could have helped Hallett here (Burrell is nowhere mentioned or referenced). Nevertheless, I do think Hallett's reflections here on analogy are helpful for identifying, in a rudimentary way, some boundaries for analogous uses, that is, its ubiquity as well as its limiters.

22 Ibid., 4.

23 Hallett's examples. See Hallett, *Identity and Mystery*, 4-5.

toddler regularly calls any plant bigger than she is 'tree,' and while this is cute and we know what she means, most of what we she calls 'trees' are in fact 'bushes'). Or consider the relation between 'ocean,' 'sea,' 'gulf,' and the like.[24] Hallett's point, again, is that in our actual uses of language, there are clusters of terms that limit the range of uses. 'Tree' regularly bumps into uses of 'bush,' 'gulf' to 'sea,' 'scarlet' to 'crimson.'

On the other hand, sometimes our uses range widely. Recall the earlier example of 'true' and its range of uses: said of friends, sentences, blue, and so on. The uses of 'true' here, while related, display a much wider range than 'scarlet,' for example. Why? Hallett's contention is the lack of a rival term of the kind mentioned above. That is, if we were looking at the map of language use, the location of 'scarlet' would be crowded with other terms, while the location of 'true' would be much less densely populated. Here, again, examples could be multiplied: 'good' said of boys, exams, and God; 'love' said of ice cream preferences, husband and wife relationships, and God; 'body' said of flesh, groups (e.g., 'student body'), and units (e.g., 'body of knowledge'). These terms, and so many others, occupy relatively open spaces on the map of language use, and it is just these open spaces that occasion us the liberty to use the terms more broadly.

We should note that there is nothing necessary about our current uses of terms. Nor is there any reason to argue that it will always be this way—for instance the cluster of 'crimson,' 'scarlet' and other reds; or the relative open spaces of words like 'true' or 'body.' As Wittgenstein observed, languages are like rivers and over time the river bed can shift. Hallett's point is only that for us, the river bed is in this place. In 100 or 1000 years if it has shifted and 'scarlet' is no longer used as it is used now, or at all, then 'crimson' will have lost its rival. But, Hallett would not want us to overlook the fact that there will almost certainly still be other rivals for other shades of red. That is, our use of a term does in fact seem to be limited by our other settled uses, even if any one particular use shifts over time.

Second, and significantly, there is no way to state *the* standard of similarity that would constitute a rivalry between terms. This is because different clusters of competing terms will have different degrees and even kinds of similarity and difference. For example, the difference and similarity between 'scarlet' and 'crimson' is of a different kind, not merely degree, than the similarity and difference between uses of 'good' (e.g., 'good' said of God and of anything else). In the latter cases, as Hallett says, "similarity may be looser."[25]

---

[24] Hallett relates the story of his two year-old niece calling the Gulf of Mexico a "big bathtub." Ibid., 5.

[25] Hallett, *Identity and Mystery*, 4.

Hallett thinks that these observations uncover something about analogous uses: in the creative task of analogous use, given that there are no absolute standards or criteria for dissimilarity and similarity, "a statements' use of terms should resemble more nearly the established uses of terms than would the substitution of any rival, incompatible expression."[26] That is, we do not use 'scarlet' for 'crimson' precisely because 'crimson' is one of our established uses. We do, however use 'true' in a wider range of uses, that is, we use it analogously, because there are fewer rival terms. Hallett's "criterion of relative similarity" (the name he gives the rule of thumb above; hereafter CRS for short) need not, however, be understood as a normative standard by which we *must* judge our ambiguous uses.[27] In fact, it is more helpful to see it as something like a descriptive claim, a grammatical remark on the ways in which we just do stretch our uses of terms. To see what I mean by calling it descriptive, consider again Hallett's color example. It is not that we do not use 'scarlet' for 'crimson' because there is a rule (say, CRS for example) that prevents us from doing so. Rather, we just do not use 'scarlet' for 'crimson.' We do not use 'scarlet' for crimson because we use 'crimson' for crimson. CRS calls our attention to the relative similarities and dissimilarities of terms clustered in ranges, and their consequent fluidity within boundaries marked out by established uses.

However, CRS also calls our attention to the fact that we do regularly use terms analogously. Consider 'good' said of a train robbery and 'good' said of a citizen.[28] When we add also 'good' said of God, we see the tremendous range over which 'good' stretches—indeed to the point that the concern for equivocation naturally arises. Yet, CRS reminds us that in the open spaces on the linguistic landscape we do so regularly speak; and the wide range of 'good' bears a family resemblance to the narrower range of color, for instance. After all, the criterion for what counts as sufficiently similar is not absolute, but indexed to the various clusters of uses. CRS does not explain why we use 'good' of a train robbery and 'good' of God. It only reminds us that, even given the wide range of use, there is nothing in our established usages that prevents

26 Ibid., 5.

27 The name 'criterion of relative similarity' is what Hallett calls the notion in *Identity and Mystery*, 7; In several of his other works, a similar principle is called 'principle of relative similarity (PRS),' for example in *Language and Truth*, 91. There are some revisions of the principle throughout his work, though the substance stays the same. The difference in appellations seems to have to do with the work he intends the principle to do. In most of his other works PRS is used to name a criterion of truth; whereas in *Identity and Mystery* Hallett is content for the sake of argument to let CRS name "a test of descriptive aptness and not necessarily of truth" (5).

28 These are Burrell's examples of uses of good. See Burrell, *Analogy and Philosophical Language* (New Haven: Yale University Press, 1973), 10.

us from doing so. Or, another way to put the same point, it suggests that the *limits* of analogous use are neither absolute, nor unchanging, and cannot be set ahead of our actual analogous uses. CRS is a license to proceed with creative uses, although of course there may be other reasons to refrain in certain circumstances.

What is the point of attending to CRS? On Hallett's account, CRS helps us target our questions on the analogous character of identity statements. Reflect again on the list of the various kinds of identity statements we make, both in ordinary language and in theological reflection. Owing to the influence of essentialism, so Hallett would argue, our tendency is to try to reduce all of those uses to one essential use—and because identity is essentially of one kind, then if they are statements of identity, the task is to investigate in what ways the terms being compared are identical. Consider theological affirmations. Hallett argues that Christian reflection on, for instance, the identification of Jesus as both God and human, tends to center on what it means to be the man Jesus, and what it means to be divine. Does divinity preclude the possibility of being human? Or does being human with all of the limitations it entails preclude affirming that a man is fully divine? Hallett argues, however, that Christian theology has by and large neglected the question raised by the relation itself.[29] CRS helps us see the variety of *kinds* of identity statements that are possible, which helps us see that perhaps the confusion, or in this case the mystery, is not precisely about what it means to be human or what it means to be divine (mysterious and relevant as they may be), but about the relation itself.

To continue with the example of the incarnation, on the essentialist read of identity, the underlying and unstated presumption is that the identity claim 'Jesus is God' states a strict identity, an identity of indiscernibility, what Hallett calls the Strict Identity Supposition (SIS). If the claim states a strict identity, then the two terms are indiscernible. If this is granted, then the task is to show how Jesus can be identical with God. As Hallett notes, if it is a statement of strict identity, then the identification must be reversible—God is Jesus. But, of course Christian reflection has not gone this route (after all, God the Father did not die on the cross). Hallett argues that neither the New Testament nor Chalcedon requires us to interpret the identity statement 'Jesus is God' in terms of strict identity. For instance, the prologue to John's gospel says that the Word was God, but also was *with* God. SIS would not allow one to be both identical to itself, and *with* itself, since *with* entails a differentiation. Furthermore, John says that the word *becomes* flesh. In both instances, the identity is never analyzed—"did the Word 'become flesh' in the way a person becomes an artist or a doctor, or rather in the way an actor becomes a character in a play, or perhaps in the way a mental word 'takes flesh' and becomes a spoken word . . .

---

[29] Hallett, *Identity and Mystery,* 18-22.

?"[30] Hallett's point is that the mystery of the faith is located *in the relation*—that is, if this is an identity statement but not one requiring strict identity, then the question becomes, what sort of identity? The purpose of articulating the question is not to answer it (Hallett argues that the mystery is located most fully, though not merely, *here)*, nor by any means to deny that Jesus really is God. Rather, the point is to clarify just what the question is. The upshot, on Hallett's read, is that we are better able to take account of the history of Christian reflection on these identity statements without presuming that the identity statements entail a strict identity.

For my purposes, these examples display that 'is' is used analogously in identity statements, and CRS suggests that this should not be surprising. 'Jesus is God', 'Jesus is Elijah,' 'the Church is the body of Christ,' and others—these statements are indeed claims of identity, but we need not presume that they are using 'is' univocally. But neither, of course, need we presume they are equivocal uses. They are indeed claims of identity. CRS helps us note that there is no better term than 'is' to name the relation—Jesus does not (merely) symbolize God—Jesus *is* God. No other affirmation will do. Yet, Hallett has sensitized us to the fact that though it is a real identity, it need not be the same kind of identity as, 'Cicero is Tuly,' 'the church is Christ's body,' or even 'this is my body.' In short, identity statements are constituted by analogous uses of language.

Criterion of Relative Similarity and Eucharistic Identity

Hallett thinks that we can clearly see SIS at work in Christian reflection on Christ's Eucharistic body. While the main point of this chapter of the book is gaining sensitivity to analogous uses of language, the identity of Christ's Eucharistic body is a helpful test case of sorts, and so useful to attend to in a preliminary way here. Furthermore, some of the issues raised here will be relevant throughout the book as I engage Aquinas, Hubmaier, and McClendon on the Lord's Supper, and hence for articulating the link between the baptist vision and Christ's Eucharistic body.

Hallett begins by observing that in several other identity claims, Christians have no problem accepting the reality of both poles of the identity. For instance, Paul's claim in 1 Corinthians 12:27 that "you are the body of Christ and individually members of it;" or Ephesians 1:23 which says that the church "is his body." Christians have consistently identified the church with the body of Christ without needing to deny either the reality of the church (as an institution, or as a gathering of believers) or the reality of Christ's body. Or, note the patristic theme of divinization, in which we are "transformed into

---

30 Hallett, *Identity and Mystery*, 28.

God" without being eradicated by or absorbed into God.[31] Or Vatican II's account of Christ's presence in the Eucharist in a four-fold manner: not only under the Eucharistic species, but also in the Eucharistic minister, in His word, and in the Church.[32]

These observations lead Hallett to ask the question, if Christians have repeatedly made these sorts of identity claims without feeling the need to argue that such an identification entails the absence of the other pole, then why is this not true of Christ's presence in bread and wine? Hallett's contention is that it is a result of the unexamined influence of SIS.[33] Recall that SIS holds that if some object contains all the properties, and only those properties, of another object which contains the same properties and no others, then they are the same object—i.e., there is only one object. With respect to Jesus's body, then, on SIS if there is a strict identity between bread and body, then there is in fact only one object, body. If, on the other hand, the identity is not strict, then there is really no identity at all and the relation can only be merely metaphorical. Hence, on SIS, either Christ's body replaces or eliminates bread, or Christ's body is not really present at all. One or the other pole of the relation must give way to the other. Of course, SIS need not be understood as having been explicitly formulated in Eucharistic debates. Nevertheless, Hallett's argument is that SIS is implicit throughout (at least from the 11th century on), and operates as a kind of unarticulated default position.

Of course, an obvious question is, why would this strict either-or option be applied here in the Eucharist, and not to the church as Christ's body or to Jesus as God? Hallett's answer is that SIS is a kind of default position that is overridden in those other cases because something strikes us as flat wrong about not recognizing the reality of the gathered community or the humanity of Jesus. In the identification of church as body we cannot simply eradicate the human element from the equation and so we let stand both poles of the identity while affirming that the identity is indeed a real one. Bread and wine, on the other hand, are not as significant and so put up less resistance to SIS.[34]

On Hallett's read, SIS does not begin to operate as a kind of implicit principle in Eucharistic theology until the 11th century. In fact, Hallett claims that the wedge that ultimately divides Catholics and Protestants is driven in the 11th century, not later. Hallett observes that prior to this, there was a comfortable fit between the presence of Christ in the Eucharist, and the presence of bread and wine. Paul, Ignatius, Justin and Augustine, to name just a few, all refer to the Eucharist as "bread" while identifying the bread with the

---

31 Hallett, *Identity and Mystery,* 90; citing Origen.

32 Ibid., 91; referencing Vatican Council II, "Constitution on the Sacred Liturgy."

33 Hallett, *Identity and Mystery*, 92. SIS is introduced first in chapter 2, 20-25.

34 Ibid.

body.[35] On Hallett's read, the shift begins in the 9th century with Paschasius Radbertus and Ratramnus of Corbie, though their debate was on the relation of the heavenly and Eucharistic presence rather than on the cessation of elements themselves. Nevertheless, the conclusion of the debate (as Hallett reads it through Schillebeeckx's summary) is that "a reality cannot at the same time be two realities," and hence there could be no "*reality* bread" where there was real Eucharistic presence.[36] Hallett affirms Edward Kilmartin's thesis that behind the shift is a transition from a Hellenic to Germanic mindset—namely, what before was comfortably mysterious yet real, teetered, and then split on the sharp edge of "thingly realism [contrasted] radically with the symbolic."[37] The question then becomes (again from Kilmartin), "how can one express the symbolism and realism of the Eucharist, when contemporary thought no longer understands the implications of the ancient image theology?"[38]

The answer which finally won the day in the 11th century was that to a degree one could not—if Christ's body was *really* present, then bread and wine could not be; and conversely, if bread and wine were really present, then Christ's body could not be. This trajectory comes to a head with Berengar and Lanfranc, for it was here that the question of whether or not bread and wine remained finally came to the fore. Berengar argued that the Eucharist was a sign insofar as it was a sacrament. Hence, though Christ was really present, the bread and wine must remain, else it is not a sign. Lanfranc took Berengar's position to require, then, that insofar as bread and wine remain, there can only remain a "symbolic presence (Germanically diluted)" of Christ.[39] Lanfranc then claimed that the Fathers had just this view in mind, for "who would believe that one thing is changed into another yet does not therewith cease to be what it is?"[40] But of course Hallett's contention is that only one who was operating implicitly on SIS would have such a hard time so believing. So, according to Hallett, it is SIS that makes such a wedge necessary—either Christ's body is present and the bread is not, or the bread is present and Christ's body is not. There is no middle or third alternative for Christ's real presence. For the Protestants, it is the other side of the wedge on which they fall—since the bread

---

35 Hallett, *Identity and Mystery*, 96. Recall also the list of quotes in chapter 1.

36 Ibid., 97. Citing Edward Schillebeeckx, *The Eucharist*, translated by N. D. Smith (New York: Sheed and Ward, 1968), 74.

37 Hallett, *Identity and Mystery*, 98. Quoting Edward Kilmartin, *The Eucharist in the West: History and Theology,* edited by Robert J. Daley (Collegeville: Liturgical Press, 1998), 79.

38 Hallett, *Identity and Mystery*, 79, again quoting Kilmartin, 143-144.

39 Hallett, *Identity and Mystery*, 100.

40 Lanfranc, *De corpore et sanguine Domine*, 419D, in Hallett, *Identity and Mystery,* 100.

and wine are obviously still present, Christ's body cannot be except symbolically.[41]

The purpose of this early excursion into Eucharistic reflection is to raise the issue developed later in the book: if identity statements are analogous, then what follows for Eucharistic reflection and the baptist vision if we reject the presumption that identity entails strict identity? That is, given the fact of analogous uses of language in theological identity statements, uses that open up identity statements beyond strict identity, are there ways of being true to the broad tradition of affirming Christ's body in the Eucharist and taking into account much of what Baptists have objected to? Attention to analogous uses of language helpfully directs attention to often overlooked features of the linguistic landscape, features useful for articulating the reality of Christ's body in the Eucharist. These are insights to be developed later, but for now I turn to further reflection on analogous uses of language.

Burrell, Aquinas, and Analogous Uses of Language

Hallett's reflections, particularly about CRS, are helpful reminders of the license to proceed with creative uses of language. The landscape of language use is such that there are places of open space where language can be used in ways unforeseen. I now want to say more about the nature of analogous uses of language, particularly with respect to Aquinas. Aquinas provides a classic focal point on the doctrine of analogy, as it is often called. As such a focal point, he has occasioned much discussion and disagreement. So, many of the relevant (for my purposes) issues attendant to analogous use are here. Also, I will contend in the next chapter that Aquinas's reflections on Christ's Eucharistic

---

41 Hallett goes on to cite some contemporary approaches to the Eucharist as possibilities for the middle way between two sides of the wedge. See Ibid., 114-117. Those who argue, for instance, that the substance of a thing, its essence, is constituted by its purpose or its intended use, have room to recognize the remainder of bread along with Christ's bodily presence. For instance, Franz Leenhardt argues that insofar as the reality of bread in the Eucharist is not dependent upon Jesus's intention for its reality, its substance, the bread is really Christ's body without ceasing to be bread. The consecrated host is indeed Christ—it is no less than real presence, at least so the various versions hold. But neither is the bread now thoroughly eradicated, for it does continue a kind of empirical presence. This is not the place to sort out whether or not the versions of transignification or the like are plausible, but only to note that at least on Hallett's read, they do provide a way out of the wedge, a way to recognize the reality of Christ's presence without denying the remaining presence of bread—in short, the sort of identity that Christians continue to comfortably make of the church as Christ's body. Of course, though providing a way out of the wedge, it is a different question whether or not they are theologically appropriate, much less consistent with transubstantiation.

presence depend on just such analogous uses of language. As such, attending to Aquinas on analogy will be useful preparation for the following chapters.

Here, I will proceed in three main sections. First, I will follow David Burrell's philosophical and theological leads in interpreting Aquinas on analogous uses. We shall see that a key insight of Burrell (who argues that it is a key insight of Aquinas) is that 'analogy' is itself an analogous term. That is, fruitful attention to analogous uses takes the form not of theorizing (where general definitions are given, and used univocally to make claims about what is essentially the case) but of assembling enough reminders, or objects of comparison, to be able to go on successfully.[42] That is, what I will seek from Burrell is neither an explanation of analogous use, nor a justification for it. Rather, I will attend to the fact that analogous uses are simply givens. Given this, what can we say to clarify how and why analogous uses are what they are? After attention to analogous use itself, I will attend to two examples, again following Burrell, one from Aquinas and one from Aristotle. From Aquinas, we will follow Burrell in noting how language used of God is inherently analogous. Aquinas's 'proofs' for God's existence and his account of God's 'attributes' in the first Questions of the *Summa Theologica* are a prime place to see analogous uses in practice. Aquinas on God's knowledge and will flesh out the simplicity of God, and hence the degree to which God-talk is analogous. Then, I will turn to Burrell's account of 'substance' in Aristotle. The purpose of attention to 'substance' is both to offer an example outside of God-talk, and to begin to set up issues of analogous use in Aquinas's reflections on the Eucharist.

Burrell on Analogous Uses of Language

Burrell notes that, contrary to much of the literature, Aquinas simply does not have a theory of analogy. Cajetan, others have argued, is largely responsible for this mistaken impression insofar as Cajetan holds up a:b::c:d as the schematic formula for all analogous use.[43] The formula, as traditionally conceived, suggests a kind of algorithmic application of analogous terms. The schema works for numbers (2:4::3:6), and it is this model or picture that is applied to the relationship between, for instance, 'good citizen' and 'good train robbery.'

---

42 For an account of the use of general terms in theory, see Hallett, *Logic For the Labyrinth,* 39-40.

43 Ralph McInerny in particular has done extensive work in the area of analogy, and of challenging received accounts of Aquinas on analogy. More than once Burrell expresses his indebtedness to McInerny. See, for instance, McInerny *The Logic of Analogy; An Interpretation of St. Thomas* (The Hague: Nijhoff, 1961), McInerny, *Studies in Analogy* (The Hague: Mijhoff), 1968, and McInerny, *Aquinas* (Cambridge: Polity Press, 2004).

On the traditional reading, what the schema shows is that the analogy is reducible to a common property or feature. This is what renders the analogy intelligible. We can use 'good' of a train robbery and 'good' of a citizen without equivocating because there is something common that belongs to both.[44]

However, Burrell wants us to notice how the schema obscures the oddness of using 'good' of a train robbery and 'good' of a citizen. For anyone trained in rudimentary math the relation between the numerical sets is obvious. The analogy 2:4::3:6 holds because both relations are reducible to 1:2. Yet, though there is some kind of relation between good citizen and good train robbery (we do not take ourselves to be equivocating), that relation is ambiguous in a way the proportionality scheme is not.

Aquinas's favorite example of analogous speech is 'health,' and here too we can see how a:b::c:d simply does not capture the ambiguity of analogous predication. As Burrell notes, 'healthy' is a term most properly applied to organisms.[45] We can see this by paying attention to how the other uses of 'health' depend on this use. Were we to specify what it means to say an organism is healthy, we would point to the growth of the organism, its flourishing in its environment, its vigor, etc. When we specify what it means to say medicine is healthy, we do so as it is indexed to the health of the organism: medicine contributes to the health of an organism. We speak of urine as healthy because urine is a sign of the health of the organism. But note, then, that the way in which an organism is healthy is unlike the way in which medicine, or urine is healthy. Urine is not healthy because it is flourishing, but only insofar as it is a *sign* of the flourishing of the organism. Yet, we say that urine and medicine are healthy, and when we do so we are not equivocating. This is because there is a connection, but, it is a connection *we make* by judgment—we judge that though there is no common, identifiable essence between medicine and organism, we can use 'healthy' of both without equivocating.[46] In the case of medicine and health we can of course say something about what the connection is. But, as there is no common essence, it is the connection as we judge it. That is, the way in which medicine contributes to health is a judgment we make, and there is nothing necessary about that connection.[47]

---

44 Burrell, *Analogy and Philosophical Language*, 9-12.

45 Burrell, "From Analogy of 'Being' to Analogy of Being," in *Recovering Nature: essays in Natural Philosophy, Ethics, and Metaphysics in Honor of Ralph McInerny*, edited by Thomas Hibbs and John O'Callaghan (Notre Dame: University of Notre Dame Press, 1999), 257.

46 Judgment will turn out to be a key to Burrell's take on analogy, and I will say more about it below.

47 Burrell, "From Analogy of 'Being' to Analogy of Being," 259-261.

The problem with the schema, then, is that what holds for numbers simply will not hold for 'good' said of citizens and train robberies, or 'healthy' said of organisms, urine and medicine. There simply is no underlying, specifiable, *unambiguous* proportion of those uses of 'good' and 'healthy' respectively. As Burrell notes, this "systematic ambiguity" is precisely what names the relation as analogous and not mathematical in the first place. Hence, a:b::c:d simply will not do the work of an unambiguous formal account of analogy.[48]

The failure of the formula a:b::c:d to work as a systematic account displays that it is itself *analogous*.[49] Hence, it cannot function as a theory of analogy. Insofar as it purports to, it reduces the analogical relation to a mathematical one, which simply does not account for the ambiguity in analogical use Even so, as we saw Wittgenstein reject crystalline purity for its own sake, only to note its usefulness in some cases as an object of comparison, so too with the formula a:b::c:d for Burrell. It may well display something helpful, even important about analogous use, but it does not do so systematically, or in the mode of a philosophical thesis that would justify analogous speech. At the very least what the schema displays is that there is indeed *some* relation between the several uses of 'good.'

Here, we can see one way that Wittgenstein has influenced Burrell. The received account of analogous use functions as a *model for purposes of comparison*, rather than a systematic, formalizable account of analogous predication. Furthermore, that the formula functions in this way is displayed by assembling reminders, perspicuous examples that surface the relevant features. Burrell has noted how the formula a:b::c:d simply will not do the work that the theoretician (or logician) wants it to do. The supposed advantage of a theory is precisely that it is stable. It can be employed in various contexts as an isolatable, 'plug and play' sort of logical device. However, for a theory to be stable it must be justified, for justification is the process by which its innards are laid logically bare for scrutiny. And of course, a bare minimum of justification is that the theory not be circular. Yet, argues Burrell, this is precisely what we find in the received formula for analogous predication. We cannot use it to specify analogous relations because it itself is analogous.

Aquinas, contrary to the way Cajetan reads him, has no such theory of analogy. In fact, as Burrell notes, Aquinas favorite phrase is "analogously speaking."[50] Rather than a theory, Aquinas makes observations along the way about how we use language analogously. To the extent that he lacks a theory, Aquinas also lacks any formal justification for analogous use. Burrell notes that in an important sense Aquinas's lack of justification for analogy anticipates

---

48 Burrell, *Analogy and Philosophical Language*, 9-10.

49 Ibid., 10.

50 Ibid., 121, 125.

some of the insights of Wittgenstein.[51] Wittgenstein noted that lots of ways we use language would not stand up to analysis. But this is not a mark against our using language the way we do. Wittgenstein reminded us that *we* use language for *our* purposes.

That analogous uses of language are fruitfully used, even though lacking a systematic justification can be observed in the use of what Burrell calls "transcategorical terms."[52] These terms are distinguished from other terms in that they are "equally at home in every category and mode of discourse."[53] The transcendentals (e.g., good, true, beautiful) are the most obvious examples. The price for their transcendence, however, is the loss of "any definite meaning."[54] The meaning of the terms depends upon their context, the inquiry in which they occur. They are proper within each framework, but have no "'carry-over' meaning of their own."[55] These terms are particularly useful for talking about God because they do not depend upon any particular category, and God does not fit into any category because, as we will see below, God is not a categorizable thing.

If the terms themselves have no carry over meaning of their own, how are we not just equivocating when we use them? Burrell argues that for Aquinas, what carries the meaning, so to speak, is not any transcendental meaning, but *judgment*: "We *do* recognize the possibility of extending the proper meaning to form a common notion, but we simply affirm that what we know in a way that is proper to us is most perfectly *verified* in God as in its source."[56] This does not assume a common or transcendental meaning. Rather, what carries the meaning is "the drive native to the intellect to seek the relevant, a demand of rational consciousness to recognize the fact that there must be an explanation, even when equally aware of its incapacity to grasp what that explanation might be."[57] Of the transcategorical terms, then, "this inherent need [to use such terms] may well be the only meaning proper to them, as the instance of 'being' suggests."[58] The context of inquiry includes the inquirer, and thus the judgment of the inquirer.

What is it about the inquirer that makes analogy meaningful? Human creatures, owing to the kind of creatures they are cannot help but presume that

---

51 Burrell, *Analogy and Philosophical Language*, 176-177.

52 Ibid., 222-226.

53 Ibid., 222.

54 Ibid., 223.

55 Ibid., 223-24.

56 Burrell, "Religious Language and the Logic of Analogy: Apropos of McInerny's Book and Ross's Review," *International Philosophical Quarterly* 2 (December 1962): 654.

57 Ibid., 656.

58 Burrell, *Analogy and Philosophical Language*, 223.

existence is intelligible. The intellect naturally seeks "order and intelligibility as its perfection."[59] Take *being* as an example. Says Burrell, "'being' (x is a . . .) reflects no answer in particular, but simply notes that the *question*: 'what is (the nature of) *x*?' is a question that will not down [sic]."[60] Being is not a thing, or a feature that can be investigated. Yet, we cannot help but ask questions about it. Intellect seeks intelligibility.

Burrell seems to be after something like this: In the world we come to learn to use a term like 'good.' Through practice and correction we learn to use the word well in various contexts. We learn to talk of a 'good train robbery,' 'good car,' a 'good pet', and even a 'good person.' Through use, the intellect, in the drive for intelligibility, begins to recognize a pattern, or a range of situations in which 'good' is correctly, if unevenly, applied. The unevenness of application suggests that the term can be 'stretched.' This stretching is discerned in tendency or direction of usage. In the sequence from a 'good car' to a 'good pet' and on to a 'good person' there is a tendency discernable. The uses of 'good' are related. And yet the relation is not in a common meaning carried through the various contexts. For talking of a 'good person' is quite different from talking about a 'good car.'

It is important to recall here that the 'stretch' between the uses of 'good' need not presume any underlying, unchanging commonality between uses, as though there were a conceptual univocal substratum that extended to include all uses. Rather, the commonality may be, to borrow two examples of Wittgenstein, of a family resemblance, or a twisting of fibers. On family resemblances, Wittgenstein wrote, "For various resemblances between members of a family: build, features, colour of eyes, gait, temperament, etc. etc. overlap and criss-cross in the same way."[61] Or, consider the variety of sorts of numbers. What is the link between cardinal numbers and quaternions or transfinite numbers? Is there a common core of properties? Wittgenstein suggests, "We extend our concept of number as in spinning a thread we twist fibre on fibre."[62] As Hallett observes, "By the time we reach quaternions or transfinite numbers there may be nothing in common between the two ends of the series."[63] Of course, the 'stretch' observed in uses of 'good' may be of neither of these kinds, but the point is that the commonality between uses, the similarity that warrants the appellation 'analogous use' need not be of the kind of a set of core properties remaining unchanging throughout uses. That is, the

---

59 Burrell, *Analogy and Philosophical Language*, 142.

60 Ibid., 223.

61 Ludwig Wittgenstein, *Philosophical Investigations*, translated by G.E.M. Anscombe (New York: Macmillan, 1958), § 67.

62 Ibid. Hallett uses this analogy to make the same point in *Logic For the Labyrinth*, 30.

63 Hallett, *Logic For the Labyrinth*, 30.

'stretch' identified in the 'tendency' presumes no common, unchanging, core between uses.

What is crucial for Burrell with respect to this 'tendency' is the way it is linked inextricably with the activity of human inquiry. We would misunderstand Burrell if we took him to be offering something like Duns Scotus, a substratum in which the related senses cohere. If we call it a 'tendency' we can only mean a tendency as we are led on by our practices of questioning. There is nothing outside of the practice of inquiry itself that anchors the meaning of the terms. Hence, that 'stretchability' from a 'good car' to a 'good pet' to a 'good person' says more about human inquirers than it does about the language itself. Appeal to a tendency or stretchability is not an attempted justification for why the uses are not equivocal. It is rather something of a grammatical remark about the stubbornness of human inquiry, and the need for such terms in the practice of inquiry.

So, when we say God is good, *we* the language users make a judgment that 'good' applies most fully to God, even though we cannot say *how* it is that it applies to God.[64] We have already noted Hallett's contention that the open spaces in the landscape of language use license creative uses of language. But Burrell points further, arguing that we make the judgment that God is good not on the basis of some common notion of God and humans, or between 'good' as applied to God, and 'good' as applied to humans. Rather, we make the judgment because we *must*.[65] The intellect seeks intelligibility, and thus takes advantage of the open spaces on the linguistic landscape. We judge that God is good, and what keeps us from equivocating is not a common meaning, or tendency abstractable from human inquirers, but that drive for intelligibility, that recognition of a pattern, and the judgment that shows the limits of the pattern. The relation is important—but it is the relation as judged by the language user. Judgment is the very activity where "the twin requirements of intelligibility—order and fulfillment—make themselves manifest."[66] Judgment is the way we use terms to make claims about a properly unknowable God. It is the expression of this drive for intelligibility.[67]

If Burrell is right on analogy, "nothing appears to be able to provide canons for the correct use of *these* expressions."[68] The context is indeed central. But, this fluidity is not a problem because "the context is shaped *to fill the purposes we have in mind.*"[69] Recall, yet again, Hallett's claim that the

---

64 Burrell, *Aquinas: God and Action*, 2nd ed. (Scranton: University of Scranton, 2008), 58-67.

65 Burrell, "Religious Language and the Logic of Analogy," 651.

66 Burrell, *Analogy and Philosophical Language*, 153.

67 Ibid., 164.

68 Ibid, 168.

69 Ibid. Emphasis added.

differences and similarity in uses of terms are of different *kinds* not merely degrees. It does not follow, then, that because we cannot nail down the relation *before* we speak analogically that we are then speaking equivocally, because though the context is indeed a universe of discourse, it is a universe of discourse as used by discours*ers*. That is, the inquirer is included inextricably in the description of how these transcategorical terms get their meaning.

Cajetan, as we have noted, made just this mistake—working as though there were something intrinsically common to both. Hence, his emphasis on proportionality as necessary for any analogical predication. However, we can see here the limits of the proportional scheme. Analogous predication, on Burrell's read, depends upon the skill of the language user. Hence, the scheme a:b::c:d cannot do the work of justifying analogous speech; for analogous speech is a skill. The schema may be helpful in certain cases, but in the end it is the language user who judges it to be so.

This insight about analogous use is what allows Aquinas to remind us that we can in fact speak about God, and do so without equivocating, even though God is properly unknowable to us. There need not be any common thing between us and God in order for us to speak of God, just as there need be no common thing between medicine and an organism to be able to call both 'healthy,' and to do so without equivocating. Of course, we can specify something of a connection between medicine and an organism, even if the connection depends on judgment and is not reducible to something common to both. Can we do so of God and creatures? Aquinas says yes, but it is because of a theological account of creation. God is creator, and as such creation participates in the perfections which are properly of God. We do not *know* this; rather we *judge* this to be so on the basis of revelation. The biblical story, then, furnishes us the narrative necessary for the connection. But again, this does not provide us with a 'nugget' of knowledge that we can claim about God. In fact, it precisely affirms that there can be no 'nugget'—for the creator is not one of his own creations and hence is not susceptible to the same sorts of knowledge-claiming sentences that we make of created things. To call God creator is not a philosophical presupposition for an argument, but a statement of faith that turns out to be philosophically illuminating insofar as it helps us elucidate how we can say anything at all about God, even though we cannot properly know any bit of data about God.

What Burrell takes Aquinas to be doing, then, early in the *Summa Theologica* is displaying to us the ways in which our language in its very structure embodies this distinction between us and God. To anticipate what will be seen below, we say God is 'simple,' but this cannot be a bit of information about God. It rather displays to us the way in which God is precisely the sort of 'thing' about which we can have no bits of data, because God is not a thing in the first place. Such a reminder about our language, as we stated above, does not amount to saying that we can know nothing of God, that we are just gassing when we say God is good. Rather, it reminds us that just as there is no common essence between 'healthy' said of medicine and 'healthy' said of an organism—yet, neither are we equivocating when we so speak—so there is no common essence between 'good' said of God and 'good' said of Socrates—and likewise, neither are we then equivocating. And as we have seen, that we are not equivocating is not an argument having to do with any necessary 'ontological' similarity between us and God, but a claim about the ways in which we use language for the purposes of inquiry.

To put it differently, that we affirm God to be creator need not be a *justification* for saying what we say about God, but rather faith throwing the necessary light on our language to remind us that though we cannot properly know God we can make true affirmations about God. In other words, to say that we cannot specify the way in which God is good, even though 'good' is a term that most properly belongs to God, is to say that there is no philosophical ladder sufficient for carrying our understanding up to God, that whatever we know of God we know improperly, and only because God graciously reveals himself as creator and redeemer. As Burrell suggests, God as creator is precisely the reminder we need to illuminate why the *proportional* model of analogous use is both unnecessary and philosophically dangerous—unnecessary because we just do speak of God analogously even though, owing to the radical distinction between creator and created, we can specify no common thing between them; and dangerous because insofar as the proportionality model requires just such a common thing, it threatens to erase that all important distinction, all the while throwing mounds of confusion on the ways in which we do in fact speak analogously.

Aquinas's Five Ways

A central place to see Aquinas's use of analogy at work, and how attention to analogous uses of language displays the grammar of the Christian claim that God is wholly distinct from creation, is Aquinas's account of how we speak of God in the *Summa*. As Burrell reads Aquinas, Aquinas's 'proofs' of God's existence, and Aquinas's accounts of the 'attributes' of God display the degree to which language is stretched in order to speak of God. Burrell argues that Aquinas's 'proofs' of God's existence are in fact not proofs in the traditional sense, but rather explorations of the role 'God' plays in inquiry. Similarly, Aquinas's discussions of the 'attributes' of God are not intended to identify bits of data about God, but rather display the ways in which anything we say about God is said 'improperly.' In both cases, the stretch that is required of language occasions analogous uses of language.

First, consider Aquinas's 'proofs' for the existence of God. Burrell returns repeatedly to Aquinas here to make the point.[70] On the prevalent

---

[70] Burrell, *Analogy and Philosophical Language*, 115-118; see also Burrell, "Aquinas on Naming God" *Theological Studies* 24 (June 1963): 187-89.

'introduction to philosophy' view, we have in the five ways the perfect example of what Burrell calls a philosophy of religion of certitude, philosophy of religion whereby we justify the otherwise suspicious enterprise of theology, in this case by proving God's existence. On this traditional view, Aquinas is laying the groundwork for a philosophy of religion. In order to first speak of God, we must be certain that God in fact exists, else, whatever we say will be suspect insofar as the object of our speaking remains undetermined. Hence, Aquinas offers five 'proofs' of God's existence, and after having done so can then move on to say more specific things about this God. On this view, whatever we say must be justified according to the canons of some universal reason, "the pattern of rationality itself."[71] Hence, to speak of God, we would have to show God's existence according to this supposed pattern in order to be justified in speaking of God theologically; for the way to achieve certainty on anything just is to justify it according to this solid pattern of rationality.

Burrell, on the contrary, argues this completely misses the point of Aquinas's text, bewitched as we are by the modern preoccupation with certainty by justification. It is in contrast to this prevalent view of philosophy of religion that we can see the way in which Aquinas is teasing out the contours of analogous speech about God.

On the surface, it might look like Aquinas is up to something like this intro to philosophy account. He notes that everyone has some vague notion of God apart from revelation: "To know that God exists in a general and confused way is implanted in us by nature, inasmuch as God is man's beatitude" (I.2.1, Reply 1).[72] But, argues Burrell, this "general and confused way" of knowing that God exists amounts to little more than the fact that even an agnostic can form a meaningful sentence using the term 'God.'[73] The proofs are something like demonstrations clarifying the meaning of the term 'God,' and hence were never intended by Aquinas to do preparatory work of justifying speech about God.

Burrell notes that in Article 3 of Question 2, Aquinas does not use the word best translated as 'proof' (*demonstrare*). Rather, Aquinas uses the term

---

71 Burrell, "Philosophy and Religion: Attention to Language and the Role of Reason," in *God, Reason and Religions: New Essays in the Philosophy of Religion*, edited by Eugene Thomas Long (Dordrecth: Kluwer Academic Publishers, 1995), 116.

72 When citing Aquinas's *Summa* I will adopt the convention of listing the Parts in Roman numerals, followed by questions, followed by articles and replies. So, the citation above is from the First part, Question 2, Article 1, the first reply. Unless otherwise noted, all quotes are from the translation of the Fathers of the English Dominican Province, originally published in the United States by Benzinger Brothers, now available from numerous publishers.

73 Burrell, "Aquinas on Naming God," 187-89.

probare, 'test,' or as Burrell prefers, "proving ground."[74] "The existence of God can be proved [*probari*] in five ways"—not that we can go hunting for God through the five ways, rather we can take 'God' for a test spin, so to speak. It is the difference, for example, between proving that a stealth bomber exists, and proving it on the battle field, putting it through its paces. The difference is important, for it is the difference between certitude and elucidation. On Burrell's read, what Aquinas is elucidating is the meaning of the term 'God.'

Burrell does not note this, but *demonstrare* does appear in Question 2 more than once in the passive infinitive form (the same form *probare* occurs in Article 3), for instance in Aquinas's reply to Article 1 of Question 2: The proposition "God exists" is not self-evident and so must be demonstrated (*demonstrari*). In his third reply to Article 2 of Question 2, Aquinas uses it to signify that we can demonstrate (*demonstrari)* God's existence from God's effects. Significantly, however, Aquinas only uses *demonstrare* in response to the way the question or objection is posed. For instance, in Article 1 Aquinas's claim that the proposition "God exists" must be demonstrated (*demonstrari)* seems to be in reply to the second objection, which cites "the Philosopher" and his rules for demonstration (*demonstrationis*). Likewise, the question asked in Article 2 is whether or not it can be demonstrated that God exists, and hence Aquinas uses *demonstrari* in his response. Aquinas picks up the way his interlocutors pose the questions and objections, and then carefully leads them through the thicket, not by meeting the objection, but by challenging the picture by which the objection operates. The whole line of questioning is posed in terms of *demonstrare*, proof. But rather than *proving* God's existence, Aquinas leads us out of the puzzle in another direction, by seeing how far 'God' can go, by 'testing' its usefulness, even necessity, with respect to ultimate questions. This is consistent with Aquinas's general method of approaching God, as Burrell reads it, a method of "taking-by-the-hand-and-leading-along" (*manuductio*).[75]

Aquinas seems to be saying something like this: "if you are asking whether or not God can be demonstrated, I recognize the philosophical tools (demonstration) with which you are working. But this whole line of approaching God's existence misses the point. What we need is not a demonstration, proof, but attention to the work that 'God' does with respect to situating ourselves in the universe. Hence, what we need is to *probare* 'God,' not *demonstrare* God." In effect, Aquinas uses the very terms of the objections to press them to their limits, and then offers us a clarification, an elucidation, by redirecting what it is that we are after when asking about God's existence. Hence, as Burrell argues, for Aquinas it is *probare* that does the important

---

74 Burrell, "Philosophy and Religion," 117.

75 Burrell, *Aquinas: God and Action*, 15.

philosophical work, and consequently displays the limitations of any supposed proof (*demonstrare*) of God's existence.

By testing 'God' what we are in effect testing is the adequacy of any all-encompassing explanation: "The best strategy would be to take schemes purporting to explain all-that-is, and show that none of them could possibly be completed, so the gap left would only be filled by this One from whom all has come forth freely."[76] Of course, this gap is not an *empirical* one that can be filled with more observation (God of the gaps). Rather, it is a *logical* gap that displays the limits of our discourse. Given the structure of discourse we are simply unable to circumscribe fully the limits of our own discoursing, and hence fail to be able to give a completely adequate explanation of our world insofar as we can only do so *in* language. This is not to say that we cannot gesture at the limits, nor take good account of them. But we cannot get outside language to have a God's-eye view of it, which would be necessary for a full account of our own existence. The five ways, then, elucidate this limit; they in effect "test the explanatory waters, as it were, by indicating how diverse schemes proposed to explain the universe fail to do so unless supplemented by this very One to *whom* such schemes inadequately point."[77] Yet, this is not a 'proof' (in the 'certainty' sense) of that One, for that would make that One superfluous—our demonstration would itself be the god.

Consequently, the five ways display that what is "general and confused" about the term 'God' is that we do not normally recognize the way in which we have to break the ordinary rules of language to be able to speak of God. This will be worked out further in Questions 3-11, the often-called 'attributes' of God. The five ways, or five elucidations we might say, display to us in a preliminary way how whatever 'God' is, it is not the sort of thing of which we can say it is moved, or it is caused, etc; and in so noting this we note something about the limits of our explanatory schemes that would leave 'God' out. Put differently, 'God' is not the sort of thing our explanatory schemes can take account of. The five ways, then are neither *descriptions* of God (that thing which is not caused), nor *justifications* for our speech about God (we talk about God because we can prove God exists). They rather specify the way 'God' works in our language.

Taking the five ways as elucidations helps clarify also the relation of Aquinas's reflections here to what he says about faith. That God exists is indeed a preamble to faith. But this cannot mean that faith is built upon natural knowledge (note the way certainty functions here as a specific picture—one builds knowledge on a solid, certain foundation), in the sense that one starts at natural knowledge and ends up at faith on the pattern of 'universal reason.' Rather, faith is articulated using the term 'God,' a term which even pagans

---

76 Burrell, "Philosophy and Religion," 115.

77 Ibid., 117.

know how to use. Aquinas ends each of these five ways with some variation of "and this everyone calls God." Though in the articulation of faith 'God' gets importantly re-described, nonetheless a well-informed atheist could formulate a sentence using 'God' to which a devout believer might assent, even though of course the atheist would then not. Natural reason and knowledge as preambles of faith are not bits of knowledge on which faith is built, but the human capacity to form meaningful statements using the word 'God.'

Hence, for Burrell, to name God's existence a preamble of faith is not to name the *foundation* of faith, but to engage in what Wittgenstein called therapy, elucidating the ways language works when speaking of God.[78] Revelation can be *spoken* in natural languages (English, for example), and to that degree presupposes nature. However, it does no work of *justifying* our talk of God. It rather displays to us the intelligibility of our talk of God. It does not render such talk intelligible, but it does cast light on the fact that when we do so speak, we are not babbling unintelligibly. Furthermore, the five elucidations clue us into the ways our language must stretch in order to be able to so speak. The elucidations are expanded in the next part of the *Summa*, the so-called attributes of God.

Aquinas on God-Talk

In the first questions of the *Summa* about God, Burrell argues that we patently misread Aquinas if we think he is offering a description of God.[79] It may well be true that scholastic commentators and theologians took Aquinas to be doing something like this. Such a trajectory cannot help but lead eventually to the divorce of the so called God of the philosophers from the God of the Bible. In fact, while Burrell thinks Process Theology itself displays a fundamental misreading of Aquinas, the challenge of Process Theology also displays that taking these as *attributes* renders a God insufficiently relatable to creation.[80]

---

78 Burrell, "Philosophy and Religion," 116.

79 For Burrell's extended treatment of the 'attributes' of God, see Burrell, *Aquinas: God and Action*, 12-41. I follow Burrell closely throughout.

80 Burrell has engaged Process Theology several times throughout his career. See, for instance, *Aquinas: God and Action*, 78-89, and "Does Process Theology Rest on a Mistake?" *Theological Studies* 43 no. 1 (1982), 125-135. For my purposes, I do not need to track Burrell's engagement with Process Theology, but only to note the challenge he sees from Process Theology and how philosophy as therapy helps to meet that challenge. For instance, Burrell notes an irony in that Process Theology's account of God works largely on models taken from the natural processes, which emphasizes abstract concepts. And yet, one of the driving motivations behind Process Theology is a way of talking about the real relatability of God to creation. Burrell simply notes that the "classical" account of God had as its model that of agent or person, which would appear to be a better model of relatability than natural processes.

Yet, if Burrell is right, such a divorce is more a product of misunderstandings about language use than it is about competing accounts or understandings of God. Indeed, for Aquinas, any description of God is simply impossible for human discourse, which is itself a claim gesturing to the created limits of humans.

Aquinas tells us upfront that "we cannot know what God is, but only what he is not" (I.3.intro). Some immediate questions: if that is the case, then what are we doing when we say that God is good, for instance? What are we to make of Aquinas's statement that God is "the beginning and end of all things and of reasoning creatures especially" (I.2 intro)? And furthermore, when Aquinas goes on to tell us that God is simple, unchangeable, and the like, do we not now have data about God? Yet, Burrell would have us take Aquinas's claim about our inability to know what God is seriously—all of this, then, is still by way of displaying to us what God is *not* rather than descriptions of what God *is*.[81]

First, note what the locution "the beginning and end of all things and of reasoning creatures especially" tells us. On Burrell's read, what it tells us is something about the limit of our own speech about God, for whatever "the beginning and end of all things and of reasoning creatures especially" is, it cannot be a piece of the furniture of the universe. Yet, all of our discoursing is precisely about things in the universe.[82] For Plato and Aristotle, language was an indication of the way the world is. There was an isomorphism between the form of our language and the form of our world. Something as basic as the subject predicate marriage displays to us something important about our world—namely, that it is composed of things. That the sentence "the chair is red" has any sense at all is important, for attention to the form of the sentence suggests to us that whatever we make of any particular chair, chairs are the sorts of things that are describable, that are composed. Such an acknowledgement need not amount to anything 'metaphysical,' in the sense that it begs arguments about whether properties (e.g., red) are as real as the chair. The point is simply to note that constitutive of the very use of the word 'chair' is a marriage of subject and predicate. Indeed, constitutive of any sensible discourse of our world includes just such a basic grammar. This need not deny that we can do all sorts of interesting and puzzling things with language. (Consider 'the chair *is*'—does it have sense? Perhaps in the right context). Again, the point is merely to note that our usual ways of speaking fit hand in glove with what we take the world to be.

The point, then, is a formal one, and "although a formal feature cannot be used to identify an object or be part of its description, it is everywhere displayed—provided we are as sensitive to what our language shows as we are

81 Burrell, *Aquinas: God and Action*, 13.

82 Ibid.

to what it *says.*"[83] What language shows is that we discourse of a world of composed things. To say that Aquinas is making a formal point is to say that what Aquinas is doing is giving us something like a metalinguistic post-it note reminding us of the 'logical neighborhood' in which speech about God resides. This is a pre-theological enterprise, and hence to claim that we can never describe God is not to claim that locutions like 'God is wise' are meaningless or somehow linguistically prohibited. It is rather a way of showing that verifying whether or not God is wise is a much different enterprise than verifying whether the chair in the corner is in fact red. Evaluating the truth and serviceability of statements like 'God is wise' is the domain of theology. But philosophy can clue us into the sorts of linguistic moves involved in making such claims at all, and display to us both the limits and possibilities of such language. This is not a theological claim that we ought not bother confessing God as wise because we cannot know God to begin with. Rather, we are being reminded that when we say God is wise we are using language in a way improper to its own structure. It is a formal point about the language used, rather than a substantive point about the veracity of such language. In fact, Burrell argues that Aquinas "is engaged in the metalinguistic project of mapping out the grammar appropriate *in divinis.*"[84] Aquinas is pointing out to us the logical neighborhood of speech about God. Such a project in its own right tells us nothing about God, but rather clues us into the ways in which our speech about God outstrips itself.

We ought to pause here and note the ways Burrell has appropriated the philosophical method of Wittgenstein, and the degree to which Burrell thinks modern philosophy has blinded us to analogous methods of Aquinas. As Burrell reads Aquinas, what we have are grammatical remarks that elucidate the way our God-talk works. What Burrell here calls formal features Wittgenstein might have termed grammatical remarks. The import for both is that they *clarify* rather than *justify*. As with 'proof,' what Burrell, following Aquinas, is after is not a justification of our God-talk, but clarity about what we are doing when we so speak.

So return to the puzzling phrase, "the beginning and end of all things and of reasoning creatures especially." Whatever else it may or may not tell us about God, what it certainly says is that God is not one of things in the universe of which we normally speak, for "beginning and end of all things" serves to put us on notice that what we are speaking of is not of the same kind as the objects of the universe, the things of which we normally speak. In other words, the locution does not furnish us with facts or data *about* God, but rather serves as a reminder that whatever we say about God will be improper insofar as whatever we say is in manner properly said of things in the universe. Aquinas, then, is

---

83 Burrell, *Aquinas: God and Action*, 16.

84 Ibid., 17.

cluing us into what to expect next: namely a display of the limits of the sorts of things we are able to say about God, something far from a doctrine or description of God.

So in Question 3 Aquinas begins by claiming that God is simple. On the classical doctrinal read, this is taken as the first attribute of God. However, on Burrell's read such a claim does not provide any data about God, as though Aquinas were picking out one feature among others as a starting point of a description of God. Rather, Aquinas is providing us a formal feature of God (elucidating the grammar of 'God'), which might just as well be described as a formal feature of our use of language, working out the claim of "beginning and end" in such a way that what we are confronted with is not a description of God, but a display of the limits of the way our language can take account of God. As Burrell says, "God escapes our grasp because every bit of knowledge we possess is knowledge *about* something."[85] And consequently, all our ways of talking are about things as they are in the world. But to call God simple is to remind us that God is not a thing (things are composed), which of course itself is but a tortured way of gesturing to the limits of our understanding of God.

Aquinas organizes Question 3 on simplicity into eight articles, dealing with such issues as whether or not God has a body, or whether God is composed of form and matter, and so on. But again, on Burrell's read Aquinas is not listing the ingredients that make God up: "we are not asking whether God is composed of sugar and spice, but whether he is composed at all;"[86] and as Burrell goes on to note, the sense of "composed" here has shifted, from an empirical claim about the constitutive ingredients of a thing, to a logical point about the conceptual limitations of speech about God (an anticipation of how speech about God is always analogous). What Aquinas is doing, then, from the very start is showing us why *no* formula can ever hope to give a definitive description of God, to tabulate all the information about God, so to speak. If God is simple, then God is strictly beyond our grasp. That God is beyond our grasp is again not a claim *about* God, so much as an acknowledgment of our own limitations with respect to God. On Burrell's read, then, what else Aquinas has to say about God ought to be read in this light: Aquinas is not offering us here a doctrine of God, but a sort of map of the logical space in which our speech about God resides.

This is the same sort of approach we should look for as we think more carefully about analogous use. In fact, for Aquinas, analogous use is the key to getting a grasp on what we are doing when we talk about God. This is so because what we are after is not a description of God, but the logical neighborhood in which such speech is most at home. 'God is wise' is certainly true, but the ascription 'true' is an ascription that belongs to the theological

---

85 Burrell, *Aquinas: God and Action*, 18.

86 Ibid., 17.

project of speaking well of God. Hence, what Aquinas needs to do in his philosophical (that is clarificatory) mode is not justify speech about God, or lay out criteria for verifying which ascriptions of God can and cannot be true. Rather, he simply needs to nudge us into paying attention to the features of the language we use. Noting that speech about God is analogous is neither a theory of how we can speak intelligibly about God, nor a justification for such speech, but a marker along the way reminding us that any speech of God is not quite of the same kind as speech about trees. This serves the larger theological purpose for it clarifies for us the difference between idol-making and faithful confession.

God, then, is simple, by which we mean only that God is not composed like anything in existence. For Aquinas, a clarifying way of saying this is to identify God's essence with God's existence. Simpleness[87] is in effect an expansion of Aquinas's claim that God's essence is God's existence, which is another display of what it means to say that God is the beginning and end of all things. On Burrell's read, as we have noted, Aquinas does not offer simpleness as an attribute, but a grammatical reminder of the limits—as well as the usefulness—of our God-talk; for what could we say of one for whom the distinction between essence and existence does not hold?

Furthermore, insofar as God is not composed, this means God is not subject to change; for to change presupposes that existence and essence are separate. Of course, to say that God is immovable is not to say that God is bolted to the ground. It is rather to say that God does not admit of the ascriptions we apply to changing things. This is because God's nature is nothing other than God's own existence. The point is that insofar as God does not admit of change, God does not properly admit of tensed verbs. The result is the classical 'attribute' of eternity, a God who is timeless. However, mere 'timelessness' for Burrell misses what is essential about God. Here Burrell cites Boetheius' definition of eternity: "the possession all-at-once (*tota simul*) of unending *life*."[88] Burrell continues, "Whatever is eternal, in the full-blooded sense in which that is intended when claimed as a formal feature of divinity, must be alive—existing or actual, if you will—and not merely the sort of thing to which temporal becoming is irrelevant, as it is to mathematics."[89]

What Burrell wants us to note is that this way of securing God's simpleness and eternity (God's essence is God's existence) "seems tailored to a

---

87 Burrell says he prefers 'simpleness' to 'simplicity,' though without any real explanation. Burrell, *Aquinas: God and Action*, 18.

88 Burrell, "Distinguishing God from the World," in *Language, Meaning and God: Essays in Honor of Herbert McCabe*, edited by Brian Davies (Longdon: Geoffrey Chapman, 1987), 80.

89 Burrell, "Distinguishing God from the World," 80.

characterization of God as creator: the One who bestows existence."[90] This is important for the challenge from Process Theology (and other approaches raising a similar worry) because a central component of the challenge is that the classical doctrine cannot adequately relate God to creation. And yet, on Aquinas's read, simpleness, eternity, and the like is just the sort of logical space that the creator must inhabit if it is to render creation intelligible at all, for the creator cannot be another object in the creation subject to change in order to be creator; and taking note of this again elucidates why statements such as 'God is wise' are neither gibberish, nor idol-making—for they are not straightforward descriptions of the same kind as the 'tree is tall.'

But before continuing, let us get our bearings. We have followed Burrell in claiming that Aquinas's reflections on God in the *Summa* are not so much a list of characteristics describing God, as they are clarifying remarks about how language must stretch to speak of one who is not a piece of the universe. Because God does not admit of description, we speak analogously. That is, to speak 'improperly' of God, we take advantage of the open spaces on the linguistic map and we use language creatively, or improperly, to speak of what properly belongs to God. Failure to attend to this stretch leads to conceptual confusions.

God's Knowledge

The fact that failure to attend to analogous uses of language with respect to talk of God leads to conceptual confusions can be further illustrated by attending to another example of this, what Aquinas says about God's knowledge and will in relation to God's simpleness. We will see that 'knowledge' 'will,' and 'existence' are all (unsurprisingly by now) used analogously of God. Burrell argues that catching the significance of the identification of essence with existence is illuminated by noting what is at stake with existence. This can be approached by looking at what Aquinas says about God's knowledge and will.

On Burrell's read, the problem of relating God's knowledge to God's will is a problem rooted in unclarity about existence, and it is a problem that leads directly to the claim that the classical account of God renders a God unrelateable to the world. If existence is taken merely as a given, an equivocal term used indifferently of God and anything else, then simpleness remains a mystery. How could divine knowledge and will be in one God who is formally simple, without thereby confusing knowledge and will? Beginning with properties without attending to existence-as-given is precisely what creates the confusion.[91]

---

90 Ibid., 79.

91 Burrell, "Distinguishing God from the World," 85.

So let us first get clear on existence. Of course, getting clear on existence is not to say that we can give a full account of it. Existence, like language, is something we cannot get out of, so to speak, and hence cannot give a full account of. Nevertheless, we can take note of it. Burrell argues that taking note of it is itself clarifying. On Aquinas's account, existing "is to be conceived as a constituent feature of whatever is, as toads are constituted toads by the constituent structure called toadness."[92] Toadness is merely formal. We can attend to toadness without attending to any existing toads. That is, a student could learn the defining characteristics of toads without ever experiencing an actual toad (for instance, learning about toads from textbooks without ever getting into the field and catching toads). If we are talking about any particular toad existing, then this is not merely formal, but actual: we cannot attend to any actually existing toad without attending to that actually existing toad. A definition of 'toad' in a dictionary may be instructive about toads, but attending to the definition is not attending to an actual toad. That is, existence is constitutive of any particular existing toad, and not merely a logical given or presupposition. Existence on the model of act helps clarify this: "existence as *act* (not *an* act) perfecting the essence as form does matter, by realizing the nature in an existing individual."[93] Existing, then, becomes the source for what an individual can do: "In other words, certain ranges of actions are typical of certain types of things, but only the existing individuals of the species can *do* them."[94] This point is not to be missed. It may be that constitutive of toadness is the power to cause warts, but only *actually existing* toads cause warts in Timmy.[95]

The payoff for Burrell is that we are reminded that while formal features are defining of what a thing is, existence is not one of those formal features. 'Existence' is a way of linguistically gesturing to actually existing things, not only their definitions. In other words, existence is never merely a given, and failure to attend to this creates confusion. Of course, existing is again not something we can get out of, so to speak, in order to analyze completely. But, though it cannot be analyzed, it can be displayed. And displaying it in terms of act helps clarify not only Aquinas's account, but divine simplicity. We can begin to see what Aquinas could mean when he says that though knowledge and will in God signify one thing, they are not simplistically identifiable. (In terms of Hallett, they need not be understood in terms of strict identity). This is because we will speak of them in terms of "distinct powers in a subject capable

---

92 Ibid., 84.

93 Ibid., 85.

94 Ibid.

95 I realize that toads do not cause warts. But I passed up many an opportunity as a kid to poke a toad because of this fear (better for the toads).

of acting."[96] Of course, in the case of God we will want to be careful to remember that "the distinct acts (knowing and willing) need not be rooted in separate powers."[97] After all, God is simple. This of course does not *explain* how knowledge and will remain unconfused in God. Furthermore, as we ought to expect by now, this is not a description of God's knowledge and will, but a grammatical remark displaying the limits of our God-talk. Such grammatical remarks about what Burrell has called formal features of God help clarify the claim of divine approval of creation in Genesis: "'and God saw that it was good', in which a single knowing act, carried to its term, reaches its fruition in the enjoyment of what is—insofar as it is—then the knowing and willing which are distinct acts for us will be but the articulations of a single act of knowing in God."[98]

Consider the perplexing puzzle for Christians (and Jews and Muslims) of how to speak of distinct created agents: "that in knowing God's own to-be, God knows and takes pleasure in bringing forth individuals 'according to their kinds.'"[99] The problem here is that we are tempted to think of God's creating as God choosing one option among many possible options. On this picture, it is difficult to see how we could articulate creation in terms other than distinct acts of knowing and willing (God knows all the options and wills or chooses one in particular).

The picture that bewitches us bewitched Moses Maimonides too on Burrell's read—namely the picture of the act of creation on the model of speculative knowledge rather than practical knowledge. For Maimonides this was rooted in an account of knowledge that held that speculative reason was superior to practical reason. Maimonides says that "'*the* function of the intellect is to discriminate between the true and the false,' not good and evil."[100] For Maimonides, Adam knew completely that which was true, but could not make the sort of discriminations Aristotle would have classified under practical knowledge. It was only after the fall, when Adam gained the knowledge of good and evil that he was able to make these practical judgments. This grows out of Maimonides' read of Genesis 3:7, from which he judges that Adam and Eve gained a new faculty, where now they knew right and wrong, not merely true and false. Burrell notes that this account may sound strange to ears schooled in Aristotle, where there was one intellectual faculty with distinct

---

96 Burrell, "Distinguishing God from the World," 85.

97 Ibid.

98 Ibid.

99 Ibid., 86.

100 Cited in Burrell, "Why Not Pursue the Metaphor of Artisan and View God's Knowledge as Practice?" in *Neplatonism and Jewish Thought*, ed. By Lenn E. Goodman, vol. 7 *Studies in Neoplatonism: Ancient and Modern*, ed. R. Bain Harris (Albany: State Univeristy of New York Press, 1992), 207-216, 208.

functions or objects—speculative and practical. Burrell attributes this view to Maimonides following Ibn Sina, who had a "single-minded devotion to speculative reason as *the* paradigm for knowing, and, correspondingly, for the relation between the universe and its source."[101] Hence, for Maimonides, it is speculative reason that exhausts what it means, properly speaking, for humans to know anything. Practical knowledge is a knowledge that, while necessary in our current state, is a result of the fall, and hence is somehow 'improper.'

The problem with talking about God's knowledge on the model of speculative reason is that it would render knowing and willing as distinct powers. If knowing is on the model of a demonstration where conclusions follow directly from premises, then willing must be a separate act of *choosing*.[102] Maimonides solved the problem by simply denying that we can say anything at all about God's knowledge. Even analogical discourse was cut off as a way of speaking of a God whom we could not know. Hence, for Maimonides, equivocation goes all the way down, so to speak, when we try to speak of God's knowledge.

Burrell, however, wants to press Maimonides on this picture of knowledge as speculative reason. Note how it determines his account—for even though he denies it describes God's knowledge, it so traps him that any other account of knowledge, say the knowledge of the artisan, is likewise unable to play any functional, analogical role. Burrell suggests that it is here that Aquinas is helpful, for though he did not pursue it far, he seemed to recognize that what causes the confusion is precisely this speculative model of knowledge coupled with the negative claims about God's divinity.[103] For Aquinas, no one, including God, can know anything that has not happened yet, just because there is not yet anything to know—a grammatical remark about 'know' rather than a descriptive claim about God's knowledge. But, if we operate on the picture of an artisan, we can speak of what has not yet happened as present in intention—the potter who has not yet made the pot but knows what she is making. Hence, the model of the knowledge of an artisan releases the mental cramp caused by operating on the model of knowledge of speculative reason. It provides us a way to 'go on' in the Wittgensteininan sense. Of course as we have just noted, for Aquinas this does not amount to a description of God's knowledge, but a grammatical remark about our uses of 'knowledge.'

Returning to the puzzle of how to think of God's act of creation in terms of simplicity—how can we articulate it without speaking of two distinct powers, knowing and willing? If we operate on the picture of the knowledge of the artisan "then no distinct act of choosing will be needed, since the object made is the term of artistic knowing . . . . Choices are entailed, certainly, in

---

101 Burrell, "Why Not Pursue the Metaphor of Artisan . . . ?", 209

102 Ibid., 212-213.

103 Ibid., 213-214.

human execution, but they subserve the intention coming to realization in the object."[104] Or, to repeat a quote given earlier, "a single knowing act, carried to its term, reaches fruition in the enjoyment of what is—insofar as it is—[so that] the knowing and willing which are distinct acts for us will be but the articulations of a single act of knowing in God."[105] Here also we can make some sense out of God's creating *freely* which keeps us from making the neoplatonic mistake of creation as a necessary emanation from God. The problem is our penchant for conceiving of freedom as primarily freedom of choice. But if we conceive of freedom as the freedom to move where good draws us "so that following the bent of one's nature can be at once natural and free, why cannot creation be similarly understood?"[106]

The payoff: "These considerations are meant to persuade us of the plausibility of a simple divine nature whose unitary act of loving knowing of itself issues in a making (creating) universe."[107] Hence, we have here a way of recognizing the challenge of the worry that God is not intimately related to creation without losing the all important distinction between God and creation. For on Burrell's read of Aquinas, there is no *real* 'gap' between God and creation, but we still recognize God as creator to the degree we acknowledge the *logical* distinction: God as the beginning and end of all things is not one of the things in the universe. In fact, it is precisely the distinction that allows us to elucidate God's loving, intimate, personal relation with creation, for that relation is one of loving and sustaining creator.

Such an elucidation helps us also make sense of the personal involvement of God with creation, as well as the real personal involvement and participation of creation in the life of God "in the measure that the animating spark of one's own being can be said to be a participation in the very to-be of the One from whom all existence flows . . . ."[108] Hence, the disciplines of spiritual practice are elucidated by God's simpleness and eternity, for it is in simpleness and eternity that we can begin to name what it means for God to be present, and for us, then to be present to God.

Up to this point we have seen pictures that bewitch us. The modern view of philosophy as a preparatory, justificatory enterprise blinds us to the way Aquinas pitches his five ways and his account of God, which further breeds confusion about how such a God could be related to creation. By working on the model of philosophy as therapy, we have seen how Burrell has dissolved the problem. Aquinas's 'proofs' say nothing about how God relates to creation—that would be a theological confession—but simply displays the

---

104 Burrell, "Distinguishing God from the World," 86.

105 Ibid., 85.

106 Ibid., 86.

107 Ibid.

108 Ibid., 88.

linguistic structure of such a theological claim. Existence on the model of act clears up attendant confusions of God's knowledge and will, and along with the knowledge of the artisan shows those to be grammatical reminders that God neither knows nor 'chooses' as humans do. Of course these alternative pictures are not theories of our God-talk. Rather, they serve as objects of comparison that throw light on the confusion that arises from our bewitchment.

What they elucidate is, as we have said, the grammar of our God-talk, the logical neighborhood of speech about God. To say that talk about God is not of the same kind as talk about chairs is simply to elucidate the structure of discourse. Aquinas himself, if Burrell's read is plausible, is doing something similar. As we have alluded to already, one inescapable feature of our God-talk is its analogical character. All that we say about God is said by analogous uses of language—'existence,' 'simpleness,' 'eternity,' 'knowledge,' 'will,' and so on. We just do speak about the One who is properly unspeakable, and we do so by creative uses of the open spaces on the landscape of language use.

Burrell on Aristotle's 'Substance'

Of course, if one follows Aquinas it is not at all surprising that we would need to speak analogously of God owing to the utter distinction between God and creation. It is useful, then, to recall the pervasiveness of analogous uses of language beyond theology and philosophy. Wittgenstein points out the fluidity present even in our ordinary, general use of terms, as we have seen. One of his most celebrated examples is that of 'game.' Wittgenstein notes that all of the various ways we use the term are not really susceptible to any one, all-encompassing definition. Yet, this does not suggest that our use is confused or vague or equivocal. In fact, through practice we become quite skilled at discerning between a game and something else, even if we are then unable to formulate a precise definition of what a game is. Wittgenstein multiplies examples, showing the fluidity of terms like 'knowledge,' 'understand,' 'read,' etc. And again, his point is not to suggest that we are confused, or that the meaning of these terms is up for grabs. Rather, he simply means to point out the variety of ways we use these terms. We do use them, and for the most part we are able to go on. Language users use language, and we do so quite successfully for the most part even though we cannot iron out the imprecision, or even though in many cases we are unable to say *why* we use language the way we do. Hallett, following Wittgenstein has made much the same point.

This is important to note for it ought to suggest to us that we would be wise to keep our logical ears attuned to places where analogous use is operative, but perhaps unnoticed. Burrell's take on Aristotle and substance is just such a place, and will be useful when we return later to Aquinas's account of the Eucharist. But one immediate benefit is to introduce another instance of analogous use pervading our discourse, perhaps without our noticing.[109]

Burrell begins his analysis of 'substance' by asking us to note how we are generally skilled at negotiating the shifting senses of 'unit,' 'one,' 'component,' 'element,' and the like.[110] We know what it means to say, for instance, that iron is a component of steel, and steel in turn a component of an automobile. So can we then say that iron is a component of an automobile? Of course—but note that to do so presumes already a context of inquiry. Iron is not an 'element' of a car in the same sense as a steering wheel if the context of inquiry is the interior design of the cabin where the basic elements of the car are the steering wheel, dashboard, seats, etc.

Even so, the car example illuminates the way in which we almost compulsively search for what is *most* basic. There is something that nags at us in the example of the interior designer. Perhaps we want to object, "sure, the *relevant* components are seats and steering wheels, but iron is still a more basic component." Note, however, that 'relevant' here takes on something more robust than 'merely interesting,' as the objection seems to mean by 'relevant.' Were the interior designer unable to focus attention on the *relevant* components of the car, then the object of the designer's work suffers; or, put differently, 'relevant' in this case clues us into what is constitutive about the activity of interior designing, which itself elucidates how what is most basic is never so apart from a context of inquiry.

But perhaps we again want to object—"the seats and steering wheels are themselves made up of more basic components. Just because those more basic components may not have any direct bearing on interior design, on what grounds do we privilege 'large' things like steering wheels as basic?" But why stop here? Iron is itself made up of atoms, which are made up of neutrons, protons, electrons, which are themselves made up of . . . and so on. Note how there is inextricably a certain amount of 'privilege' involved in discerning what is most basic. Perhaps it seems arbitrary to consider steering wheels as basic—but on what grounds? Just because there are *smaller* parts than a steering wheel? Atoms may be measurably smaller than a steering wheel. But on what grounds do we privilege *physical size* as most basic? Furthermore, note that we

---

[109] Most of what follows is taken from Burrell's essay, "Substance: A Performatory Account," in *Substances and Things: Aristotle's Doctrine of Physical Substance in Recent Essays*, edited by M.L. O'Hara, 226-249. However, Burrell follows this general line of reasoning elsewhere, most especially in the argumentative thread about inquiry and analogous use that runs throughout *Analogy and Philosophical Language*.

[110] Burrell, "Substance: A Performatory Account," 226-227. The point I make is Burrell's, though I have expanded on the point that specifying 'unit' is context dependent, and the degree to which this displays the analogical character of the uses.

just do draw lines about what is relevant. Atoms are smaller than iron, but we are happy to call iron a basic component of a car. The point of course is a logical one, not an empirical one. Where we draw the line between relevant and not relevant is as much a logical question, about the scope of inquiry and the purposes we have in mind, than it is an empirical one about measurable, material components.

Here we start to see more clearly the way in which 'component,' 'unit,' 'basic,' and the like are used analogously. In the case of the interior designer the steering wheel is the relevant unit. No matter that the chemist or physicist would contend that it is a unit only insofar as it is made of smaller components—which itself suggests the way in which modern science so pervasively grips our pictures of the world that we fail to see the *logical* point Burrell wishes to make. It makes no difference whether neutrinos are finally the smallest object we can measure. That would give them no better claim to absolutely *most* basic than steering wheels because what is 'most basic' is fluid depending on context. The logical point, then, is that any statement about what a thing is is to some degree irreducibly analogous insofar as it presumes a 'basicness.'

How does this bear on substance? In sum, for Aristotle, substance names the basic unit of intelligibility.[111] Aristotle is often taken as proposing something like this: whatever substance is, it is best identified with the subject of a sentence. That is, whatever we put in the subject category of grammar, we call that substance. So, for instance, a horse is a primary substance, because in a sentence we would put 'horse' where the subject (or nominative case) is, and then we say things of that primary substance using predicates—'The horse is white' but not 'white is a horse' (unless 'White' is the name of a horse and not the name of a color).

What this analysis misses, on Burrell's read, is the way that Aristotle was taken not so much with what could be said of a substance, but precisely that though we say things *of* a substance, we *know* substances.[112] In other words, versions of the usual interpretation fail to see that when we say 'the horse is white' we do not mean to say that we have in mind a bare substance to which we add color. We simply mean to say that *that* horse *is* white. Rather than identifying substance with 'horse,' it better fits our use of language to say that substance is identified with 'the-horse-is-white.' The subject predicate marriage, not the grammatical subject alone identifies substance.

For Aristotle, then, the "statement-making sentence is primary" rather than the components of such a sentence.[113] Of course, sentences contain elements (names, predicates, etc.), but as attention above to the shifting senses of

111 Burrell, "Substance: A Performatory Account," 230.

112 Ibid., 231.

113 Burrell, "Substance: A Performatory Account," 228.

elements suggests, that sentences are *composed* is itself no automatic argument for why sentences are not the most basic units of this use of language, which is suggestive of why it is "more proper to speak of matter/form and name/verb as principles rather than elements."[114]

Burrell's analysis hinges on the emphasis Aristotle gives to statement-making sentences. There are of course lots of ways we use sentences—asking, marrying, acting, etc. So why privilege one use of a sentence—statement-making—as the best location for elucidating substance? On Burrell's read, Aristotle focuses on statement making sentences not because there is anything necessarily or in principle privileged about them over other ways of speaking. Rather, Aristotle's focus is *inquiry*, and in the context of inquiry, statement-making sentences in fact play an important part. Their role can be seen from what Burrell calls the basic question form: what is *that*? As Burrell says,

> coming to know what anything is involves learning a number of things *about* it, and these items are held fast in statements which purpose to assert or deny something of the thing in question . . . . Although Aristotle did not use this language, what is known about the object in question is just that: a knowing-about it, or a fact. And what states the fact is a statement-making sentence, asserting something about the object or state of affairs in which we are interested.[115]

So again we are back to the role language users play in the use of language. Substances are things most at home in inquiry, the way we identify the formal feature of the object of our inquiry. Though Aristotle emphasizes prime substances (like horses) we need not limit it to such things. Substance formally considered is simply that which is the object of inquiry—which could be an animal, a tree, a state of affairs, and so on. In Burrell's words, "Substance, or *what-is*, becomes a shorthand way of referring to any object of inquiry—in the inescapable fashion that (a) everything which we ask about becomes in that capacity an object and hence a kind of substance, and (b) we feel an inquiry resolved when it returns to explicate some facts about the world of this's and that's."[116]

This analysis of substance of course emphasizes language. But the above quote also ought to clue us into how such a linguistic analysis need not deny something like metaphysics, except that we will want to note how the activity of metaphysical inquiry is just that—*inquiry* and hence inextricably a linguistic activity. For Aristotle, then, substance in metaphysics is primary being, and 'primary being' means something that is one and is a 'this-something.' That is, what in metaphysical inquiry we call substance is just that which both confronts

114 Ibid.

115 Ibid., 230.

116 Ibid., 242.

us as a 'some-thing,' and which further has an intelligible unity to it. If substance properly belongs to the realm of inquiry, then substance is precisely that which terminates our inquiry, or the object of inquiry.

This account of substance and statement-making sentences can be illuminated by Wittgenstein's reflections on pointing. Consider my pointing three feet to the left and asking "what is that?" You are likely to answer "dog." But let us suppose that I am a veterinary student and we are in a lab dissecting a dog. We have been learning about a particular organ, the name of which I have forgotten, and I am pointing to that particular organ. Of course, the general direction of pointing will be the same, but what distinguishes pointing-to-the-dog and pointing-to-the-dog's-appendix is nothing about the gesture itself, but the context of the inquiry. So with substance. What distinguishes one substance from another is as much the context of inquiry as anything else. This itself points to the ways in which we not only seek unity in intelligibility, but again the terms we use to articulate unity in intelligibility are used analogously.

I passed over rather quickly the prevailing take on Aristotle—that substance is identified with subject. In the *Categories*, Aristotle does give an analysis that on the surface looks as though names or terms in a sentence are most basic; and furthermore that substances are identified with the subject of the sentence. Yet, Burrell notes that if we take Aristotle here not as offering a definition of substance, but observations of how we speak, then it makes perfect sense to note that in statement-making sentences, "whatever *functions* as subject [is] in the domain of substance."[117] Nevertheless, insofar as we talk in *sentences* when we speak of substances ("the tree in my yard has no leaves"), then it misses the import of what we say and how we say it to limit substance to the subject of the sentence, as though subjects simply refer to substances. We say *of* the tree that it has no leaves, but what I know as a result of saying is the-tree-with-no-leaves, not a bare subject. This, then, is why names or terms are not more basic in terms of substances than the sentence itself, and why we ought not misunderstand what Aristotle is doing here. Parts of a sentence may signify ('tree' alone signifies), but what those terms cannot do apart from the sentences is assert anything about the tree. Furthermore, even then they only signify separately if their ambiguity is settled. Burrell's example is to consider a question like 'where was Paul today?' The one word answer 'walking' signifies plainly, unless of course you happen to be near a town named Walking. Then, the answer would be followed by further questions, for instance, '*out* walking or *in* Walking?' Signification is always linked with the context and purposes to which we put it.[118]

Aristotle's analyses, then, are elucidations that bring to the fore the twin formal components of anything of which we speak—its thereness, and its

---

[117] Burrell, "Substance: A Performatory Account," 237.

[118] Burrell, "Substance: A Performatory Account," 235.

whatness, its existence and essence.[119] That I say anything at all about the tree out my window presumes a logical neighborhood, a neighborhood made up of intelligible units of discourse. On Burrell's read, Aristotle does not offer us a theory of substances, or intelligence, or knowledge, or even sentences and signification for that matter, but clarifying remarks about what we are doing when we speak of anything at all. That I can form any sentences at all about the tree—'the tree is ugly,' 'it is in my way,' 'it is a maple,' 'is there a tree there or is there something in my eye?'—bears a certain formal feature in the very speaking of them. Substance, then, is a mark on the map of the logical neighborhood—it is here, when these sentences function in these ways that we find ourselves. In an important sense, it is this unity that *makes* substance primary insofar as it functions as intelligible object.

For Aristotle, then, it is statement-making sentences that disclose substances to us in their very form. As Burrell notes, among statement-making sentences, definition serves an important role.[120] The import of a definition is the role it plays in inquiry; namely, definition serves a unifying function. The ideal definition would be the one from which we could deduce any other fact about an object. Though Aristotle suggests that it would need to be one sentence, Burrell notes there is no reason why we could not take it to be a conjunction of several. The important thing, however, is that it would serve to unify the object of inquiry insofar as anything else could be derived from the definition. To this degree, it serves as something like a hypothesis in modern scientific inquiry (though Burrell notes that Aristotle either was not aware, or at the very least made no use of the important distinction between affirming and entertaining an assertion). Of course, that we can fruitfully specify 'definition' in this way does not guarantee that in our inquiries we will always or perhaps even ever come up with such an ultimately ordering description. Again, the import is to note the logical shape of the domain of substance—its logical neighborhood is inquiry, and how we specify substances are by descriptive sentences, and definitions are a privileged route to so specifying insofar as they gather up the inquiry into an ordered unity. Our inquiry has met its object when we can specify some sort of a definition, even if never an ultimate or all-encompassing one.

What we have here, then, is something like the ideal of definition serving the purpose of helping us elucidate what we in fact do when we inquire, and the role substance plays in that inquiry. It is worth noting, then, how the ideal works here for Burrell similarly as it worked for Wittgenstein. The claim is not that we do not have a definition until we can formulate one matching the ideal. The ideal here is not normative, but *illuminating*. By making note of this picture of definition we can throw fruitful light on inquiry, and specifically the

---

119 Ibid., 243-245.

120 Ibid., 239-242.

way inquiry provides the necessary context for substance. The ideal itself does not stand in judgment over definitions we might offer. Rather, it displays to us the logical neighborhood of such definitions and what they have to do with specifying substances. For my purposes, it notes the link between substances and sentences, and the role language users, in this case inquirers, play in the approach to substances. The ideal has no ultimate significance, as though what we are after in our inquiry is "crystalline purity," to recall Wittgenstein's phrase. Rather, its significance lies precisely in what we make of it, namely a helpful picture that serves as an object of comparison for the purposes of illuminating and clarifying—and again, clarifying not in the sense of delineating the *goal* which we seek, but clarifying insofar as it throws light on what we in fact do when we inquire, whether or not our inquiries ever gain such 'purity' themselves.

In summary, then, Burrell has offered a read of substance in Aristotle which achieves at least three helpful results. First, here we have another instance of analogous use. One of the conclusions we cannot help but reach is that 'substance' itself is an analogous term. That is, we can outline some helpful markers that aid us in negotiating 'substance,' but we cannot specify in advance exactly what 'substance' means apart from its actual use in specific inquiry. This recalls again the ways in which analogous use pervades our speech, something we will want to note when looking at Aquinas on Eucharistic identity.

Second, we noted here, as we did in the section on analogous use, that it is language *users* who put language to various uses, and consequently, the context of inquiry is centrally important in elucidating what is going on. This feature of language ought continually to be before us; for a natural temptation will be to try to solidify what we have gathered up into a theory or system. Yet, if our speaking, thinking, reflecting, etc. are all linked with our purposes, then no system can adequately capture what is going on precisely because a *system* must be at some remove from us and our purposes. What we need is not a theory, but clarity.

Finally, though we will need to wait until we tackle Aquinas, it is worth noting here how helpful such an account of substance will be when dealing with Aquinas on substance and the Body of Christ. For instance, as we have noted, what is most basic, or what is a unified whole depends upon the context. This reminder will serve us well when we turn to Aquinas's account of real presence, for we will see that the presence of Christ's body does not strictly map to the geography of the bits of material stuff we call bread and wine. By keeping in mind Burrell's elucidation, we can help ourselves navigate the philosophical puzzles such claims about presence entail if we continually recall that even in our ordinary modes of discourse and action, what we take to be most basic is inextricably linked to the purposes with which we operate.

Conclusion

In this chapter I have accomplished two things. First, I have used Hallett to note the pervasiveness of analogous uses of language, and to show how those uses can be seen as creative uses of the open space on the landscape of language use. Second, I have used Burrell's engagement with Aquinas to set the context of language use in terms of human inquiry broadly speaking, and within theological inquiry more specifically. Examples from Aquinas on God-talk show analogous uses of language at work; 'substance' in Aristotle provides a further example, one that will provide helpful conceptual clarification looking forward to Eucharistic reflection in Thomas.

I have intentionally avoided offering a theory of language or of identity or of analogous uses of language, and have rather sought the wisdom of Hallett and Burrell to help us 'go on' in pursuit of clarity on Eucharistic identity and the baptist vision. This chapter is programmatic for the book, if not 'foundational,' insofar as we have traced the conceptual contours that we will set against the varied uses of language employed in Eucharistic theology and the baptist vision to illuminate both.

CHAPTER 4

Analogous Uses of Language and Transubstantiation

Introduction

The doctrine of transubstantiation teaches that in the Eucharist the bread and wine become Christ's body and blood in such a way that there is no longer the substance of bread and wine, but only Christ's body and blood. This is Thomas's claim. Not only is Christ's body truly in the Sacrament (*Summa Theologica* III.75.1), but it is there by a conversion of the bread and wine into body and blood such that bread and wine no longer remain (III.75.2, 4). The import of such a claim is that for 'this' to be body it *cannot* be bread.

We saw in the previous chapter Hallett's contention that the dichotomy in the claim that for 'this' to be the body of Christ entails that 'this' *cannot* be bread, is a dichotomy that in form "has no parallel in comparable Christians beliefs."[1] Other sorts of theological identity statements retain both terms of the identity, for example 'Jesus is God,' or 'the church is the body of Christ.' In fact, Hallett's contention is that in Eucharistic theology there really is *no* identity established between both poles of the relation. On transubstantiation, it is not the case that bread is body, for there is no bread *to be* body.[2] Bread is converted into body, and as a complete conversion there is no bread remaining. Hence, in transubstantiation, the identity of bread is bread, and the identity of body is body. Transubstantiation names how bread identified as bread *becomes* body identified as body. We saw Hallett's contention that the reason the two poles of the identity are not allowed to remain was the unexamined influence of SIS in conjunction with the fact that bread and wine were not 'substantial' enough to resist elimination in the identification.

We saw in chapter 1 the number of theologians prior to the ninth century who were comfortable affirming that 'this' bread is Christ's body, and that the presence of bread *and* body apparently did not trouble them. As noted in the previous chapter, Hallett thinks this mode of engaging the Eucharist remains broadly unchanged until the ninth century. From then into the eleventh century SIS begins to dominate, such that *either* the bread is converted into Christ's

---

1 Hallett, *Identity and Mystery*, 89.

2 Ibid.

body with no remainder of bread, *or* there is no conversion at all, and hence Christ is only symbolically identified with the bread.[3]

In this chapter I am not interested in the historical circumstances that give rise to this view, nor other factors at work in making implicit judgments about the relative significance or insignificance of bread. However, I do want to pursue this question: is it possible to affirm within the context of Thomas's account of transubstantiation the reality of Christ's body and still affirm the reality of bread? That is, must we conclude with Thomas that "this opinion cannot stand" (III.75.2), namely the opinion that the substance of bread might in fact remain in the sacrament after consecration? [4] Aside from historical and doctrinal interest in this question, asking this question will bring to the fore the role of analogous uses of language in Thomas's account of transubstantiation. On the basis of this observation, I will argue that attention to analogous uses of language requires us to attend to the way in which this 'is' and 'is not' bread, and the way in which this 'is' and 'is not' body. In fact, I will argue that Thomas's account of transubstantiation may be read not as an affirmation of body *in place of* bread, but rather bread *as* body. I recognize, of course, that this is against Thomas's explicit claim about the fate of the substance of bread. But even so, I will argue that the direction of Thomas's account leads us to affirming what Thomas himself did not. Thomas failed to see where his words were leading him. This argument is of more than historical and even doctrinal interest, for whether or not one accepts my claim, we are led necessarily into the dense but fruitful landscape of analogous uses of language, a landscape that we will find ourselves traversing in the following chapters.

This chapter will proceed in four parts. First, I will consider P.J. Fitzpatrick's objection to transubstantiation, namely that Aquinas's account is neither right nor wrong, but simply nonsense. Fitzpatrick's objection is useful because it suggests the necessity of carefully attending to analogous uses of language in an account of transubstantiation. In fact, this is just the line that Herbert McCabe takes in defense of Aquinas. Second, after considering Fitzpatrick's objection and the suggestion to attend to analogous uses of language, I will consider the role of metaphysical conceptual tools in Thomas's theology, highlighting again the way in which metaphysical terms' susceptibility to analogous uses of language make them useful tools for a theological articulation of Christ's body in the Eucharist. Third, I will consider a second objection to transubstantiation from the Orthodox theologian Alexander Schmemann. Schmemann contends that transubstantiation is an attempt to *explain* the mystery of Christ's presence in terms inappropriate to the presence itself, and that in so doing transubstantiation misses what is central

---

3 Hallett, *Identity and Mystery*, 97-101.

4 The translations of Thomas are from *Summa Theologica,* trans. by Fathers of the English Dominican Province (New York: Benziger Bros, 1948).

about Christ's presence in the Eucharist, namely the Eucharist as the actualization of the Church as Christ's body. Finally, with Schmemann's objection in mind, I gather up what has been gained from the previous sections on analogous uses of language and argue that Aquinas's account, despite his express conclusion, leads in the direction of an affirmation at home in patristic theology: the bread is Christ's body. I will show how this read of Aquinas's account addresses part of Schmemann's criticism, while also suggesting that what remains unaddressed opens the way for a consideration of Hubmaier's theology of the Lord's Supper in the following chapter.

Fitzpatrick's Objection

According to P.J. Fitzpatrick, in order to see the problem of intelligibility in Aquinas's account of transubstantiation it is important to be clear on the use of the terms within their Aristotelian context.[5] Following Aristotle, Aquinas affirms two basic sorts of changes: accidental change and substantial change. Consider a lump of play-dough. My 18 month old daughter says to me, "play-dough ball?" So I take a small lump of play-dough and roll it lightly between my fingers until I have a play-dough ball, a rough spheroid made out of play-dough. I put the play-dough ball on the table and she squeals "squash it!" and smashes it with her hand. Now, instead of a play-dough ball we have a play-dough pancake. Something has changed, but what has changed is not what the thing is, the *substance* (play-dough), but an *accident* of the thing (its shape). Of course, we could change not only the shape of the play-dough, but the play-dough itself. We could burn the play-dough and what we would have is no longer play-dough, but residue or ash (or whatever would happen if we burned up play-dough). This is a substantial change.

Any sort of change, be it accidental or substantial, presumes a more basic distinction between potentiality and actuality. Any play-dough ball is potentially a play-dough pancake; and any lump of play-dough is potentially a lump of ash. But the way in which the play-dough ball is potentially a play-dough pancake and the way in which the play-dough is potentially ash is importantly different. There is a subject in common to the play-dough ball and

---

5 See P.J. Fitzpatrick, *In Breaking of Bread: The Eucharist and Ritual* (Cambridge: Cambridge University Press, 2006). For a briefer account of the same basic argument see the exchange between Herbert McCabe and Fitzpatrick (writing under the pseudonym G. Egner) reprinted in Herbert McCabe, *God Matters* (London: Continuum, 1987); Fitzpatrick [G. Egner], "Some Thoughts On the Eucharistic Presence," in *God Matters*, 130-145; Fitzpatrick [G. Egner], "More Thoughts on the Eucharistic Presence," in *God Matters*, 155-164. Fitzpatrick follows Aquinas's commentary on Aristotle's *Metaphysics*. I follow the main points of Fitzpatrick's explication, using my own examples and order of presentation.

the play-dough pancake, namely the lump of play-dough. The beginning point of the change (play-dough ball) and the end point of the change (play-dough pancake) are the same lump of play-dough. But what of the change of play-dough to ash? Here, the change is a change in the sort of thing it is, not merely a particular quality of the thing. We cannot speak of *play-dough* as the subject in the same way as before since *play-dough* is only present at the beginning of the change. The continuing subject is not the substance, since the change is precisely a change from one substance to another.

Here, Aristotle and Aquinas appeal to prime matter, something that is pure potentiality. As pure potentiality, prime matter is capable of receiving different forms, in this case different substantial forms, in this case play-dough and ash. Prime matter, pure potentiality, serves as the subject of a substantial change. As Fitzpatrick points out, Aristotle and Aquinas generally want to guard against a possible danger here, a danger evident in speaking of prime matter as a 'something,' as I do above.[6] The danger is a reification of substance, accident, form and the like. Like Aristotle, Aquinas emphasizes that what changes is not some thingy form or formless matter, but the composite object, in the above example the play-dough ball.[7] As Fitzpatrick succinctly notes, "forms do not change or come into being, but . . . it is the composite, the individual, which comes to be of such a form."[8] There is no sense in which we can properly speak of a form changing, or a form coming to be. Rather, we speak of play-dough balls becoming play-dough pancakes, or lumps of play-dough becoming lumps of ash. The reason that we cannot reify form and matter is because to do so would involve us in an infinite regress:

> The distinction between matter and form is drawn as part of construing all change in terms of matter that is first of all one form and then of another form; so if I now make the *form* change as well, I must make the same distinction there, and have a matter and form of the form itself; and so shall be involved in an infinite regress.[9]

Hence, reification creates conceptual, not just practical problems. So, the terms are used by Aristotle and Aquinas to make conceptual distinctions that aid in describing change, not to identify constituent 'things' or dissectible 'parts' that make up play-dough balls and the like. Whatever one thinks of Aristotle's system, to this point Aquinas's account of change follows it in broad outline.

---

6 Fitzpatrick, "Some Thoughts," 132-133.

7 Fitzpatrick, *In Breaking of Bread*, 13.

8 Ibid., 7.

9 Ibid., 6.

Transubstantiation and the Problem of Intelligibility

Transubstantiation is, according to Aquinas, a unique sort of change, sharing some similarities but some important differences with substantial changes. There is of course an ordinary and regularly recurring occasion when bread is changed into a body, the occasion of a person eating bread. [10] What is bread goes into a person's body and through the usual processes of digestion is changed into one's body. On the terms of Aristotle's system, there is a sense in which a person's body is 'made out of' bread (or food in general). However, this cannot be a good parallel for the change of the Eucharistic bread into Christ's body, for Christ's body in the Eucharist is in no way 'made out of' the elements themselves. And so, Aquinas says, the change of bread to Christ's body is importantly *not* like usual substantial changes. It is a substantial change in the sense that bread is now body, but it is a unique sort of substantial change (III.75.4). What is unique about it is that in this change (from bread to Christ's body) there is no common material subject between the two ends of the change. When in the usual course of events bread is changed into a body, the substantial change is 'carried along' by the prime matter; that is, prime matter accounts for the continuity that is conceptually required for a change. For example, to say that the play-dough ball is changed into ash presumes some sort of continuity between this lump of play-dough and the ash.

It is of course possible for there to be a kind of change in which there is no material continuity and one substance is simply replaced by another. Suppose when my daughter turns away I sneak a pile of ash from a pot underneath the table and put it where the lump of play-dough was. But of course, this is not really a substantial change, but a change of place. Aquinas explicitly denies that this is the case with respect to the change from bread to body, that Christ's body *replaces* bread. Aquinas is clear that Christ's body does not merely replace bread, as though God through a slight of hand removes the bread and puts Christ's body in its place. This is so, according to Aquinas, because then Christ's body would have to be present by a local motion, a change of place. But this cannot be right since Christ's body remains in heaven, on account of the ascension (III.75.2). So it is in fact the case that bread is converted into Christ's body; there is a substantial change that takes place, but a unique change such that there is no common material subject between the two ends of the change.

This is precisely the problem that Fitzpatrick sees with Aquinas's account. Fitzpatrick argues that Aquinas simply renders 'change' incoherent in Aristotle's system. That is, the terms in which change is described are terms that are marshaled to accounting for the continuity between the ends of the change (the play-dough as the subject of the change from round to flat; and the

---

10 McCabe, *God Matters*, 133-34.

matter as the subject of the change from play-dough to ash). Remove the subject, the common element, that which accounts for continuity, and you have simply removed any sense of substantial *change* Aristotelianly described.[11]

This is why Fitzpatrick thinks it does not help Aquinas to appeal to God's power, as Aquinas does. In Objection 1 of III.75.4 Aquinas raises basically the objection above: how can there be a change without a subject? Aquinas in his main argument repeats that it is a supernatural change, unlike any other, and is brought about by God's power. In response to the particular objection, Aquinas says that the objection only holds for formal changes; but this is not one of those changes. Yet, Fitzpatrick claims that this only begs the question: if not a formal change, then what? A conversion of one substance to another substance just is a formal change, a change of substantial forms. Hence, Aquinas's response leaves standing the question of *intelligibility*. The objection is not whether or not God is powerful enough to pull this off, but whether or not the 'it' in question has any intelligible content at all. To say that God cannot make a square circle is not to put a limitation on God, but to put a limitation on the intelligibility of 'square-circle.' This, thinks Fitzpatrick, is the principle problem of Aquinas's account of transubstantiation.

But of course Aquinas does not think transubstantiation is unintelligible. Why not? Fitzpatrick thinks it is because of a creeping reification of the terms themselves. Recall that in their original context, form, substance, accident, and the like serve as something like conceptual tools for making conceptual distinctions necessary to describe change. The only 'thing' in question is the composite thing—play-dough balls, ash heaps, and loafs of bread. The terms do not indicate constituent *things* that make up play-dough balls and ash heaps for Aristotle and Aquinas, at least when Aquinas is not talking about transubstantiation. And yet, argues Fitzpatrick, this is precisely what happens with transubstantiation—substance, accident, form, and matter become not mere conceptual distinctions, but "dissections," thingy, constituent components of the things in question.[12] They become "hypostatised," and this is how

---

[11] Germain Grisez has a similar concern (though to a different end). Grisez argues, "If it is meaningful to talk about converting A into B without anything of A contributing to the reality of B, God no doubt can do it. But the very idea of converting A into B seems to me to imply that something of A contributes to the reality of B. So, it seems to me that Aquinas's account of transubstantiation is unintelligible. And since the unintelligible is impossible, not even God can do it." Grisez, "An Alternative Theology Of Jesus' Substantial Presence In the Eucharist," *Irish Theological Quarterly* 65 (Summer 2000): 119. For a response to Grisez, see Roch Kereszty, "On the Eucharistic Presence: Response To Germain Grisez," *Irish Theological Quarterly* 65 (Winter 2000): 347-352.

[12] Fitzpatrick, *In Breaking of Bread*, 14.

Aquinas gets around the problem of intelligibility.[13] In this case transubstantiation "now becomes the replacing of one substance by another (each in turn composed of matter and form) under the unaltered veil or surface of the accidents."[14]

Fitzpatrick thinks Aquinas's reification can be seen clearly in his discussion of the *manner* of Christ's presence. Fitzpatrick focuses on III.76.1 where Thomas says that Christ's dimensions are present only by way of substance, not by way of quantity. As Fitzpatrick notes, Aquinas does not fully spell out what all this would entail, except to say that the "proper totality of substance is contained indifferently in a small or large quantity; as the whole nature of air in a great or small amount of air, and the whole nature of a man in a big or small individual" (III.76.1, Reply 3). Fitzpatrick argues that the vocabulary that Aquinas uses "goes against the grain of what he is trying to suggest."[15] Fitzpatrick continues:

> The 'specific totality' of a substance, he writes, *is contained* just as much in a small as in a large quantity . . . [sic] and so the whole substance of Christ *is contained* in the sacrament after the consecration, just as the substance of the bread *was contained* there before the consecration (*ST* 3.76. 1 ad 3). Argument goes one way, the associations of 'is contained' (*continetur*) go another. Which is what happens again when he contrasts 'presence by way of dimensions' with 'presence by way of substance': in the former, the dimensive quantity of something is *under* the dimensive quantity of a place; in the latter we have presence in the way that substance is *under* its dimensions (*ST* 3.76.3). One and the same preposition (the Latin *sub*) holds together what Aquinas is trying to keep apart.[16]

Here Fitzpatrick's immediate point is again one about intelligibility: The very terms Aquinas uses to make one point (that Christ is not dimensively located) in fact make the opposite point, despite his intentions. Aquinas changed the use

---

13 Fitzpatrick, "More Thoughts," 157.

14 Fitzpatrick, "Some Thoughts," 134. See also *In Breaking Of Bread,* 13-14.

15 Fitzpatrick, *In Breaking Of Bread,* 114.

16 Ibid., 114-115. Grisez has similar, though not identical reservations about 'under' and 'contained.' Grisez concludes, "When Aquinas says Christ's body is present in the Eucharist 'in a certain special way that is proper to this sacrament,' he either does or does not intend to exclude all the sameness of meaning between *what is contained* said of Jesus and of the bread. If he does intend to exclude all sameness of meaning, his answer to the question about the meaning of *this* in the formula of consecration is incoherent. But if there is some one sense in which both the unconsecrated elements and Jesus can truly be said 'to be contained' under the accidents, what can that unambiguous sense of *contained* be?" Grisez, 117.

of the terms without changing their conceptual context, and this leads to two problems. Already mentioned is the problem of infinite regress, but furthermore treating 'substance' as a dissection rather than a distinction would have us affirm a contradiction: 'substance' is not a *thing*; and yet substance is being treated as a *thing*. Both of these issues, according to Fitzpatrick, go to intelligibility.

Analogous Uses of Language and Transubstantiation

Early on, well before Fitzpatrick published *In Breaking of Bread*, he (under the pseudonym G. Egner) and Herbert McCabe engaged in a critical, but friendly exchange on Fitzpatrick's claims.[17] Much of the substance of the critique of Thomas's account of transubstantiation found its way into Fitzpatrick's book. I want to turn to that exchange because it clearly introduces the issue of analogous uses of language. McCabe's response is that in sum theological language, especially when making use of metaphysical terms, is unavoidably constituted by analogous uses of language.

McCabe argues that Fitzpatrick is right on at least one point: Thomas is not a good Aristotelian. McCabe concedes that Aristotle himself would have found an account like transubstantiation to be nonsense.[18] And yet, contends McCabe, this should not surprise us at all since "theology is not done within a philosophical system but at its margin."[19] Though Thomas uses the conceptual tools provided by Aristotle, transubstantiation is "not a notion that can be accommodated *within* the concepts of Aristotelian philosophy, it represents the breakdown of these concepts in the face of a mystery."[20]

---

17 In McCabe, *God Matters*, 116-179.

18 Ibid. Robert Jenson says that it is a mistake to think that Thomas "adopted" Aristotle. Says Jenson, "that is exactly what he did not do. He *conversed* with Aristotle, and in the conversation was stimulated and helped to his own metaphysical positions, the key items of which could hardly be less Aristotelian." Jenson, *Systematic Theology*, vol. 1 (Oxford: Oxford University Press, 1997), 21. Jenson shows how Thomas must "upset" Aristotle in order to be able to speak of God (212-214). Along similar lines, John M. Rist says, "Certainly much Thomistic interpretation of Aristotle goes beyond Aristotle. By that I do not mean that if Aristotle had lived in the thirteenth century, he would necessarily have repudiated the thought of Aquinas; what I mean is that if he had been willing to accept the thought of Aquinas, he would have had to abandon some of the ideas he himself proposed in the fourth century B.C., as well as allow that Aquinas had raised new, strictly metaphysical questions which he himself had not considered." John M. Rist, "Augustine, Aristotelianism, and Aquinas," in *Aquinas the Augustinian*, ed. Michael Dauphinais, Barry David, and Matthew Levering (Washington, D.C.: Catholic University of America Press, 2007), 82.

19 McCabe, *God Matters*, 146.

20 Ibid.

McCabe follows Thomas and appeals to the doctrine of creation as an illuminative, comparable case. Thomas says in III.75.8 that there is something similar about creation and transubstantiation, namely that in both cases there is no subject common to the terms of the change.[21] In creation, God makes out of nothing, which of course is not to say that nothing is the stuff out of which the universe is made, but rather that "God did not make the world out of anything."[22] This is a sort of making that does not fit within an Aristotelian system. Like change, ordinary sorts of making are an actualization of a potential. To say that I make a play-dough ball just means that I actualize the potential of the lump of play-dough; or, to use a substantial change as an example, to say that I make ash out of play-dough (by burning it, for example) is to say that I actualize the potential for this matter to actualize the substantial form of ash. So, Thomas is using 'make' here analogically. God makes the world, but the way in which God makes the world is not like other makings, and so, in some respect when we say that God makes the world "we do not, strictly speaking, know what we are talking about."[23] We have already seen that this sort of language use pertains to our speech about God. To say that God is good is true, but we do not know the way in which God is good since "we do not know what it is for God to be God."[24]

McCabe presses this comparison to transubstantiation: to say that bread is converted into body is to say that strictly speaking we do not know what we are talking about. Transubstantiation, in this respect like creation, "takes place neither at the level of accident nor at the level of substance but at the level of existence itself. When the host is consecrated it means a different thing for it to be a substance, a different thing for it to exist."[25] McCabe continues,

> For [an] Aristotelian, to say that when the host is consecrated it means a different thing for it to exist, would simply mean that a substantial change had taken place, the host had become a different kind of thing . . . . [But] The notion of transubstantiation depends upon the idea that there can be a

---

21 Of course, transubstantiation is also different from creation, and so has something similar to natural changes, namely that in transubstantiation, like natural change, "one of the extremes passes into the other, as bread into Christ's body, and air into fire; whereas nonbeing is converted into being . . . [and] that on both sides something remains the same . . . for the same matter or subject remains in natural transmutation; whereas in this sacrament the same accidents remain" (III.75.8).

22 McCabe, *God Matters*, 148.

23 Ibid., 149.

24 Ibid.

25 Ibid.

> kind of transformation in what it *means* to exist which is not simply a change in *what it is* that exists.[26]

Later in this chapter I want to pick up McCabe's distinction, especially with respect to substance, but for now I only want to press McCabe's point: 'change' here is used analogously. Thomas has used both creation and natural change as something like objects of comparison to illuminate the relevant differences between the use of 'change' with respect to ordinary change and transubstantiation.

Analogous uses of language continue with respect to the identity of the bread. McCabe argues that Fitzpatrick has too "mechanistic" a view of language.[27] Fitzpatrick claims that after the consecration bread is bread, on account of the fact that 'bread' has clear criteria for use in the English language, and that after the consecration those criteria are all met. McCabe says that if one makes the claim that 'this is *not* bread' one could be claiming a number of things:

> We *might* be saying that it is zinc or that it is miraculously disguised human flesh or whatever, but we *might* also be saying that here the ordinary criteria for deciding whether this is bread or zinc or any other stuff just are not relevant . . . . What happens at the consecration is not that the proper description of the host shifts within our language (from 'bread' to 'Body of Christ') but that it no longer becomes possible to give an account of it *within* our language at all.[28]

An indication of this is Thomas's account of the manner of the presence of Christ's body. Christ's body is truly present, but not in a manner at all expected of bodies. For instance, according to Thomas Christ's body is located in heaven, and is present on the altar not according to local motion or dimensive quantities (III.76.5). Says McCabe, "certainly when we speak of Christ's body we are using the word 'body' analogically . . . . "[29] We rightly say that 'this is

---

26 McCabe, *God Matters*, 150.

27 Ibid.

28 Ibid., 152.

29 Ibid. McCabe asks, then why not think that 'bread' is used analogously? If bread were used analogously, then we might have an easier time at least consenting to Fitzpatrick's claim that 'this is bread,' if not the route by which Fitzpatrick gets there. However, McCabe explicitly rejects this possibility, claiming that the English word 'bread' is too "attached to the particularities of its ordinary context to be free to be used analogically" (153). I concur with McCabe that in this context, as it is currently used, 'bread' has too settled a use for it to have the 'flex' of other analogous uses. I emphasize *in this context* because, as Wittgenstein reminds us, the riverbed of language can and does shift over time. However, I will suggest another way to reach the same conclusion

Christ's body,' but do so in a way that acknowledges that we do not, strictly speaking, know the way in which it is body. So McCabe's response to Fitzpatrick is to say that contrary to being problematic, transubstantiation is of a piece with all of Christian theology insofar as it uses language in analogical ways.

In his reply, Fitzpatrick grants that theologians often make use of analogous uses of language, but insists that in the case of transubstantiation, this appeal fails. This is because in the case of transubstantiation "the Aristotelian vocabulary of change is too context-bound for its Eucharistic employment."[30] Continuing the debate further on the particularities of these uses would take us too far afield.[31] However, we can suggest a related avenue of response by attending to how Aquinas conceives of the practice of theology. Matthew Levering has perceptively suggested that the source of the trouble Fitzpatrick finds with transubstantiation is not so much a difference of view on how particular terms are used, but rather a broader understanding of what it is that the theologian does. Levering claims that Fitzpatrick "tends not to grasp Aquinas's perspective, in part due to the differences between his analytic

---

Fitzpatrick does, that 'this' is bread, though by route of McCabe's reminder about analogous uses of language.

30 McCabe, *God Matters*, 156.

31 Though, if we were to continue the pursuit of a response, along with McCabe, Joseph Bobik might be helpful. In reflecting on Thomas's comparison of the change to creation and to physical changes, Bobik says, "And so, it is not difficult to see how this conversion is both like, and unlike, physical change, and thereby to see that it is something intelligible, or understandable, to us humans." Joseph Bobik, *Veritas Divina: Aquinas on Divine Truth: Some Philosophy of Religion* (South Bend: St. Augustine's Press, 2001), 170. Following Bobik's claim, we might say that what makes transubstantiation intelligible is precisely the ability to articulate how the change is "both like, and unlike, physical change." That is, intelligibility does not hang on precisely the 'settled' meaning of the terms, but on the ability to specify how the meanings (or, more precisely, the uses) of terms are similar and dissimilar to one another. We might pursue this line of reasoning to suggest that contrary to Fitzpatrick, the intelligibility of transubstantiation is not parasitic on the intelligibility of physical changes even though it uses terms we (or, at least, Aristotelians) use in describing physical change. Rather, the related, though not simply identical uses of the important terms ('subject,' 'accident,' 'substance,') and the like are explicated by way of comparison and contrast. The contours of the analogous uses of the terms are traced along careful observations of the ways in which the uses are like and unlike one another. All that is required for intelligibility is the acknowledgement of analogous uses of language by means of a leading step by step from one use of a term to another; and this Thomas provides.

framework and Aquinas's metaphysical theology."[32] I think we can get at what Levering means by considering now what Thomas conceives theology to be, and in particular the relationship between theology and metaphysical language. Attending to this will help set up what I will claim about analogous uses of language in transubstantiation.

Aquinas and Mystical Theology

As we have seen, a central objection for Fitzpatrick is that Thomas's account of transubstantiation is held captive by Aristotelian philosophical categories. The result is that Thomas's articulation of the conversion of bread and wine is for Fitzpatrick unintelligible. This objection, however, fails to adequately account for the fact that while Thomas certainly makes use of Aristotelian terms, Thomas is in the final analysis not merely an Aristotelian.[33] He is, fundamentally, a theologian who makes use as is fitting of conceptual tools provided him by philosophy. Yet, as will be argued, in so using those categories he does not leave them as they are. The conceptual tools do not serve as simple, self-contained building blocks. Rather, as part of his whole theological project, the 'blocks' themselves take on new shape. Such, we will see, is the importance of recalling the flexibility of language, for *especially* in 'metaphysical' sorts of questions, analogous uses of language are central. In fact, W. Norris Clarke has suggested that "the great metaphysical concepts and linguistic terms" that are so useful to the metaphysician are useful precisely because they are analogous in nature.[34] It is their susceptibility to analogous usages that allows Thomas to so creatively employ and 'stretch' them for his theological purposes. We shall see that for Aquinas it is just this 'flex' that makes possible an account like transubstantiation.

Flexibility is only an asset if it is a disciplined flexibility. Careless use is always in danger of becoming *equivocal* use. Thomas is not without discipline as evidenced by his careful approach to metaphysics, an approach well versed in Aristotle. And yet, to say that Thomas was an Aristotelian is to neglect the degree to which he was a practitioner of, in A.N. Williams's terms, "mystical theology."[35] Williams notes that as it is currently practiced, theology is separate from spirituality to the extent that spirituality is often culturally associated with

---

32 Matthew Levering, *Sacrifice and Community: Jewish Offering and the Christian Eucharist*. (Malden: Blackwell, 2005), 115, footnote 1.

33 Recall from above Jenson, *Systematic Theology*, 21.

34 W. Norris Clarke, *The One and the Many: A Contemporary Thomistic Metaphysic* (Notre Dame: University of Notre Dame Press, 2001), 57. See further 42-58.

35 A.N. Williams, "Mystical Theology Redux: The Pattern of Aquinas' *Summa Theologiae," Modern Theology* 13 no. 1 (January 1997): 53.

"any number of forms of religiosity undifferentiated with respect to their doctrinal foundations."[36] This is not the case with the church fathers, who "knew no distinction between the various branches of theology, nor even between theology and spiritual discipline."[37] Williams notes that while the "first cracks" of the split may be present in the Middle Ages, it is really the product of a "modern mentality."[38]

In contrast to contemporary means of doing theology apart from spirituality, Williams endorses doing theology integrated with spirituality. She defines mystical theology as "theology concerned with the conditions of the possibility of union with God."[39] Thomas is the example that Williams offers. Though frequently understood as a philosopher, Williams notes that in his *Summa* Thomas's treatment of God "relentlessly portrays God intent upon union with humanity."[40] Williams notes that Thomas begins the *Summa* by claiming that God "has destined us for a goal that lies beyond the grasp of reason" and that the teaching required to pursue this goal is "based on premises known by the light of a higher science, God's own knowledge of himself, shared with the blessed in heaven."[41] This goal beyond reason, and the pursuit of that goal which depends foundationally on God's revelation are the goal and source of theology, and as such propel theology to spirituality insofar as God himself is the end.

This end pervades Thomas's theology. In fact, Thomas claims that the unity of theology as a science comes from the fact that everything is related to God, theology's principle object. And yet, precisely because God knows everything, there is no principled distinction between theoretical and practical knowledge. The result is that "even in its most practical moments, the *Summa* is to be read as an act of contemplation whereby we are united to the mind of God."[42]

If Williams is right, then all the conceptual tools of Thomas's theological enterprise are used for purposes that in the end outstrip the tools themselves. That is, if God is the subject of theology, and God is properly unknowable by creatures, as Thomas affirms, then for the philosophical tools available to him to do the work he wants, they must be carefully worked to this purpose. Williams argues that this can be seen when reading Thomas's discussion of divine attributes in light of what Thomas says about prayer in the second part of part two of the *Summa*. There, Thomas unites love and knowledge, the will

---

36 Williams, 53.

37 Ibid., 55.

38 Ibid.

39 Ibid., 56.

40 Ibid., 57.

41 Ibid., 58.

42 Ibid., 59.

and the intellect, so that prayer becomes the purpose of contemplation, and contemplation provides the motivation to prayer.[43] The result is that "the careful, often technical, discussion of divine simplicity, goodness, perfection and all the rest, may now be viewed as a form of meditation which is meant to incite the love that leads to union."[44] In fact, Williams makes clear that for Thomas, contemplation as an act pursuing unity is thoroughly theocentric: "grace is given that we might be made deiform. Our transformation is not into better or happier human beings, but into partakers of God's own life."[45] So, for Thomas, all theology and philosophy ultimately serve the purpose of humanity's loving union with God.

Matthew Levering follows Williams's trajectory and claims that Thomas's theology can be read as an exercise in metaphysical *ascesis*. Levering articulates this in the context of Thomas's Trinitarian theology, a theology that engages both "scriptural and metaphysical modes of reflection," a way of doing theology that has contemplation as its end.[46] If contemplation is the end of theology, then theology "belongs to the interior spiritual conversion by which self-centered human beings become *God-centered*."[47] This de-centering of the human, in order to re-center on God constitutes metaphysical *ascesis*. Following Giles Hibbert, Levering argues that metaphysical reflection is required because God-talk, including that found in Scripture, is always human language. God's revelation of himself in Scripture is by means of creaturely language. Creaturely language is "inevitably metaphysical in content."[48] By 'metaphysics' Levering means, again following Hibbert, that way of reflecting on divine revelation which "belongs to the personal encounter by which human words truly express *divine* revelation."[49] But why call this 'metaphysics?' Burrell has noted that the question, 'what is metaphysics,' is itself a metaphysical question. This is because 'metaphysics' "has come to refer to the paradigmatic activity proper to philosophy: one which enquires into the nature of things, indeed of anything at all."[50] But, one might object, "now that God

---

43 Williams, 63. See *Summa Theologica* II.II.82-83.

44 Ibid., 64.

45 Ibid., 69.

46 Matthew Levering, *Scripture and Metaphysics: Aquinas and the Renewal of Trinitarian Theology* (Malden: Blackwell, 2004), 2. In fact, Levering asserts that scriptural and metaphysical modes of reasoning "came unglued . . . when theologians no longer recognized contemplation as the rightful 'end' of Trinitarian theology."

47 Ibid., 3.

48 Ibid., 5.

49 Ibid.

50 David Burrell's review of *Rethinking Metaphysics* edited by L. Gregory Jones and Stephen E. Fowl, in *Modern Theology* 12 no. 1 (January 1996), 109. Cited in Levering, *Scripture and Metaphysics,* 7.

has revealed himself in Scripture, why would Christian theologians still rely on the insights of Greek metaphysics?"[51] Far from attempting to explain God in terms of Greek metaphysics, Levering argues that as a discipline tending toward contemplation, "the practice of metaphysical questioning constitutes a spiritual exercise that purifies from idolatry those who would contemplate the self-revealing God."[52] In this mode, metaphysical reflection seeks to de-center humanity in the theological quest. In this sense, metaphysical reflection is about human transformation, and so what is required is "grasping how human transformation occurs within the movement whereby we rise from idolatry and, instead of primarily contemplating creatures (ourselves), contemplate God for his own sake rather than for the sake of creatures."[53] Metaphysical reflection is required, then, in order to train us to use our creaturely language to speak not of ourselves, but of God.

Williams and Levering, up to this point, have focused on our language about God himself. However, metaphysical *ascesis* is also required to understand Thomas's account of transubstantiation, as Levering makes clear.[54] According to Levering, metaphysical *ascesis* comes into play because of the necessity that we "purify our minds of attachment to our imagistic understanding of 'bodily.'"[55] This is required because the claim at issue is 'this is my body.' The Church affirms that Christ's body is present in the sacrament, and Thomas has offered us a scriptural argument for why the presence of body is necessary.[56] But the Church, following Thomas, affirms that Christ's body is not present 'bodily,' at least not in the ordinary way in which bodies are present. Rather, it is present sacramentally. Thomas affirms the reality of Christ's body, but it is not present locally, as bodies usually are. Thomas says that Christ's body remains locally in heaven. Also, Christ's body is present at all celebrations of the Eucharist, and so not limited to one time and place. Furthermore, Christ's body is not present 'empirically' insofar as touching and chewing the species is not simply touching or chewing flesh. To say that Christ's body is present sacramentally is to that his body is really present, but not in the same way bodies are usually present. To say that Christ's body is present sacramentally is perhaps a clue that analogous uses of language are at work.

Of course, Thomas articulates an account of Christ's body in terms of substance and accident. Levering argues that what Thomas is doing with the

---

51 Levering, *Scripture and Metaphysics*, 8.

52 Ibid., 9-10.

53 Ibid., 17.

54 Levering, *Sacrifice and Community*, 150-154.

55 Ibid., 150.

56 Ibid., 135-140.

language of substance and accident is metaphysical *ascesis*.[57] However, rather than continuing Levering's account, I want now to pause and consider another criticism of Thomas's account of transubstantiation. This is because my purpose for going this route has been to raise two issues, namely analogous uses of language in Eucharistic theology, and the manner in which those analogous uses are disciplined by metaphysical *ascesis*. Below, I will continue reflecting on 'substance' and 'accident,' paying particular attention to the way in which Thomas's account uses 'substance' and 'accident' analogously in order to subvert the usual ways in which we conceive of substance and accidents in the world of empirical causes and effects. That is, I intend to spell out below my own account of the way in which transubstantiation is an exercise in metaphysical *ascesis*.

But in order to do this, it is helpful to introduce now another objection to Thomas's account of transubstantiation, that from the Eastern Orthodox theologian Alexander Schmemann. As I will argue below, Schmemann's criticism of western Eucharistic theology helpfully reframes the inquiry from Fitzpatrick's concern with intelligibility, to a concern about theological appropriateness. Schmemann accuses transubstantiation of something of a category mistake. On his read, transubstantiation is an attempt to talk about the change and consequent presence of Christ in terms of "this world," when this world is simply incapable of accounting for what it is that God accomplishes in the Eucharist. I will suggest below that Thomas's account can answer these objections, but only if one attends to analogous uses of language, and how such analogous uses of language constitute an exercise in metaphysical *ascesis*. I will give a more extended explication of Schmemann's criticism than I did with Fitzpatrick because some of what Schmemann addresses will be useful when it comes time, in the next chapter, to consider Hubmaier's theology of the Lord's Supper.

Schmemann's Objection

Schmemann's criticism of transubstantiation is part of a broader criticism of the development of both the Eastern and Western Churches' liturgical tradition, and occurs in the context of his liturgical theology.[58] However, for my purposes, I want to focus on two central claims that Schmemann makes with respect to transubstantiation, as these claims get to the question of identity and analogous uses of language. First, Schmemann argues that Western (and "by imitation" Eastern) "school theology" illegitimately reduces Eucharistic

---

57 Levering, *Sacrifice and Community*, 154.

58 For an account of Schmemann's understanding of liturgical theology see Alexander Schmemann, *Introduction To Liturgical Theology*, trans. Asheleigh E. Moorehouse (Crestwood, NT: St. Vladimir's Seminary Press, 1966), 16-27.

theological reflection to two basic questions: when does the conversion of bread and wine happen, and how does it happen.[59] This reduction misses the central theological meaning of the Eucharist, namely that the whole liturgy actualizes the Church as the Body of Christ. Second, because this approach misses the centrality of the Church to the Eucharist, and in its place puts questions about the mechanisms of the conversion, school theology ends up articulating the body and blood of Christ in terms of "this world" mechanisms and processes, terms which "reduce the heavenly and otherworldly to the earthly, to their own 'human, only human,' impoverished and feeble 'categories.'"[60] This reduction of the heavenly to the earthly then reinforces the first problem insofar as it turns Eucharistic theology away from the church to the mechanisms of the conversion. Hence, the fundamental problem is that theological reflection on the Eucharist misses the Eucharist's purpose as the realization of the *Church* as Christ's body.

The Relation of the Eucharist and the Church

Schmemann claims that one of the great achievements of liturgical theology is its "discovery of worship as the life of the Church, the public act which eternally actualizes the nature of the Church as the body of Christ," an achievement that has reestablished the essential link between the Eucharist and the Church.[61] The poverty of school theology with respect to the Eucharist, in Schmemann's judgment, is that insofar as it neglected the liturgy of the Church as the source of Eucharistic theological reflection, it also neglected the Church itself. In so doing, a diminishing of the Eucharist to the moment of consecration is likewise a diminishing of the Church as the gathered assembly, that is, the assembly 'gathered into' the body of Christ.

Schmemann argues that from an analysis of the liturgy it is clear that rather than one among many dispensers of grace, the Eucharist is instead "*the* sacrament of the Church, i.e., her eternal actualization as the Body of Christ,

---

[59] By "school theology," Schmemann means to identify a broad theological trajectory in which the liturgy ceases to play a central role in the theological task itself. Schmemann says that school theology "arose after the break with the patristic tradition, and chiefly from a western understanding of both the method and the very nature of theology." Schmemann, *The Eucharist: Sacrament Of the Kingdom*, trans. Paul Kachur (Crestwood, NY: St. Vladimir's Seminary Press, 1987), 12-13. It names, simply, that mode of theological reflection that proceeds from other sources than the liturgy. Schmemann identifies transubstantiation as a doctrine resulting from this trajectory. Schmemann, *The Eucharist*, 160.

[60] Schmemann, *The Eucharist*, 163.

[61] Schmemann, *Introduction To Liturgical Theology*, 14.

united to Christ by the Holy Spirit."[62] Conceiving of the Eucharist as an instrument for dispensing grace misses the fact that the Eucharist is

> the very manifestation and *fulfillment* of the Church in all her power, sanctity and fullness. Only by taking part in it can we increase in holiness and fulfill all that we have been commanded to be and do. The Church, gathered in the Eucharist, even when limited to "two or three," is the image and realization of the body of Christ, and only those who are gathered will be able to *partake*, i.e., be communicants of the body and blood of Christ, because they manifest him by their very assembly.[63]

Of course, the conversion of bread and wine is indeed important for Schmemann because it gets to the central question: "*what is accomplished in the eucharist*?"[64] This, says Schmemann, is the most important question to be asked of the Eucharist, and he distinguishes it from questions asked by school theology about *how* and *when* the transformation occurs. Schmemann presses this distinction repeatedly: theology has been concerned about mechanisms and has missed the essence of the Eucharist. This leads us to the second objection of Schmemann. Excessive interest in the conversion itself rather than the way in which the conversion facilitates the participation of the Church in Christ's body, results in an explanation of the conversion in 'this world' terms, terms which fundamentally misunderstand what the conversion, and consequently what the Eucharist, is.

'This World' Explanations

Because school theology, in Schmemann's judgment, fails to attend to the liturgy as a primary source of theological reflection, it is left to articulate a theology of the Eucharist in terms foreign to the Eucharist itself. Of course, theology has always made use of philosophical concepts to articulate theological truths.[65] But in this case, rather than making appropriate use of philosophical concepts for the purposes of theology, Schmemann thinks that philosophical categories have in the end determined a foreign articulation of the Eucharist.[66]

---

62 Schmemann, *Introduction To Liturgical Theology*, 24.

63 Schmemann, *The Eucharist,* 24.

64 Ibid., 163.

65 The Russian Orthodox theologian Sergius Bulgakov makes much the same claim: while theology has made regular use of philosophy, in this case philosophy has trumped theology. See Bulgakov, *The Holy Grail and the Eucharist*, trans. Boris Jakim (Hudson, NY: Lindisfarne Books, 1997), 74-77.

66 Similarly, Bulgakov thinks that Aquinas's account of transubstantiation (an account that he says "has a determining significance" for Western Eucharistic reflection)

As already said, the problem with theology's alienation of Eucharistic theology from the liturgy of the Church is that theology has substituted the wrong questions. Rather than pursuing the question of what is accomplished in the Eucharist, school theology focuses on "answering the questions of *how*, i.e., on account of what 'causality,' and *when*, i.e., at what moment did the change occur."[67] Yet, those questions are by nature asking about processes in terms of this world. They are questions "rooted not in the experience of the Church, but in the 'seekings of this age'—categories of thought, one can almost say in the curiosity of fallen reason, which has not been reborn and enlightened by faith."[68] While Schmemann is in no way satisfied with a simplistic 'just believe it' response, he nevertheless contends that the articulation of such a complex, mysterious teaching must be in terms which affirm the fundamental mystery, and as such must reject any attempts at explanation. Precisely because the conversion is a mystery, it

> is a mystery that cannot be revealed and explained in categories of "this world"—time, essence, causality, etc. It is revealed only to faith: "I believe also that this is truly Thine own most pure Body, and that this is truly Thine own precious Blood." Nothing is explained, nothing is defined, nothing has changed in "this world."[69]

Nothing is explained: this appears to be a central point of resistance for Schmemann. Of course the mystery must be articulated carefully and precisely. But such articulation of a mystery is different than an *explanation* of the mystery.

This is why Schmemann objects to an articulation of the change in terms of substance and accident. Schmemann asks,

> what in fact does the distinction of *essence* and *accidents*, which goes back to Aristotle and which the scholastics made use of to answer the question of how the transubstantiation of the bread and wine into the body and blood of Christ is accomplished, mean—not philosophically, not abstractly, but really—for our faith, our communion in the divine, our spiritual life, our salvation? Does transubstantiation consist, according to this experience, in the change of the "substance" (essence) of the bread

owes too much to Aristotelian categories of substance and accident. Of course, theology has regularly borrowed concepts from philosophy, but in this case, the church has been held captive by them, and the result is an account of the presence of Christ that is too physical, that makes Christ's glorified body subject to the physical, material change of this world. Bulgakov, 68-69.

67 Schmemann, *The Eucharist,* 27-28.

68 Ibid., 162.

69 Ibid., 226.

> into the essence of the body of Christ, while the "accidents" of the body remain the accidents of the bread? To faith, which confesses every Sunday, in the fear of God and with love, that "this is truly Thine own most pure Body . . . this is truly Thine own precious Blood," this explanation is unnecessary, and for the mind itself it remains an equally incomprehensible violence to those very "laws" on whose foundations the explanation is supposedly constructed.[70]

On the one hand, an explanation in terms of Aristotelian categories is simply unhelpful in 'this world' anyway (here, Schmemann articulates a concern similar to Fitzpatrick). But this concern is secondary for in the end, even if an account of transubstantiation is intelligible, it adds nothing to faith. The primary concern of the Eucharist is not the conversion itself, but the Church, and as such an account in terms of substance and accident, even if it holds together conceptually, simply misses the point. "Nothing is explained, nothing is defined, *nothing has changed in 'this world.'*"[71] The bread on the altar still has all the 'this worldly' quality of bread. Nothing has changed with respect to this, and so the change, though certainly a *real* change, is simply not a change about material components and causes.

To spell out *why* the change cannot be articulated in terms of 'this world' we now need to return to the link between Eucharist and Church, with a view to spelling out what it means to say that the Eucharist 'actualizes' the Church as Christ's body. This will allow us to see why Schmemann thinks that transubstantiation is an explanation in terms of 'this world,' and why Schmemann thinks his alternative account is more in line with patristic theology.

The Church as Christ's Body and Time

To say that the Eucharist "actualizes" the Church as Christ's body requires an articulation of the nature of that actualization, both in terms of the identity of the Church as the Body of Christ in relation to the unrepeatable, singular event of Christ's life, death and resurrection, and in terms of the Church's anticipation of the bodily return of Christ, the final ushering in of the fullness of God's kingdom. Both of these issues are directly related to time—how it is that one singular event of the past can be actualized in the Church, and how the actualization in the Church relates to a future, to the anticipation of an as yet unrealized completion of God's plan. The link between 'this world' and God's kingdom is indeed a timeful link, one made through the celebration of the Eucharist: "The liturgy is served on earth, and this means in the time and space

---

70 Schmemann, *The Eucharist*, 162.

71 Ibid., 226. Emphasis added.

of 'this world.' But if it is served on earth, *it is accomplished in heaven, in the new time of the new creation*, in the time of the Holy Spirit."[72]

Time is here a central concept, and it is worth articulating the relationship of the time of 'this world' to God's time. Schmemann does so by contrasting two problematic views of the relationship between time and Christian expectation of God's future. In spiritualism, there is a "rejection of time," an attempt to leave time because it is thought to be evil. But for Christians, time is part of God's "good" creation. Of course, it is true that as part of God's fallen creation, time 'in this world' is likewise fallen, and this is what Schmemann says that the "activists" forget: "They do not sense that it not only reflects the fall of the world but is itself the 'reality' of this fall, the triumph of 'death and time,' which reign on earth."[73]

Time is created good by God, and yet is fallen with all creation, and so it is into time that Christ comes: "In it he proclaimed that the kingdom of God which is to come, salvation from sin and death, 'the beginning of another life, new and eternal,' had drawn near."[74] Christ accomplished this through his life, death and resurrection, and this new life appeared at Pentecost through the pouring out of the Holy Spirit, through whom the "new time [descended] onto the Church." Schmemann continues,

> The old time did not disappear, and outside in the world nothing changed. But to the Church of Christ, which lives in the Spirit and by the Spirit, the commandment and the power to convert it into the *new time* was given. "Behold, I make all things new" (Rev. 21:5). This is not the *replacement* of the old with the new, not an exit into some "other" world. It is the same world, created through the love of God, which in the Holy Spirit we see and receive as God created it: heaven and earth, full of the glory of God.[75]

The relationship of the old time and of the new time is now a relationship of faith and sight. From the perspective of 'this world,' nothing has changed. Time continues to dominate towards death and destruction. And yet, from the perspective of the 'new world,' a world only visible by faith, a world made manifest in the liturgy, the time of 'this world' is transformed through the very timeful, sequential progression of the liturgy, into the 'new time,' in which time becomes the medium of created creature's worship and participation in the life of God rather than the medium of death and destruction. Hence, until the second coming of Christ, both times are 'present,' though their manner of presence is different: one by sight according to the 'natural' progressions and

---

72 Schmemann, *The Eucharist*, 218.

73 Ibid., 219.

74 Ibid.

75 Ibid.

processes of 'this world'; one by faith according to the already accomplished work of Christ.

It is in light of this 'new time' that the Church as the sacrament of unity, the actualization of the body of Christ can be articulated. That the Eucharist is accomplished in heaven and "served on earth" means that what is

> most important is the fact that what is accomplished in heaven is already accomplished, already *is*, already *has been accomplished*, already *given*. Christ has become man, died on the cross, descended into hades, arisen from the dead, ascended into heaven, sent down the Holy Spirit. In the liturgy, which we have been commanded to celebrate "until he comes," we do not *repeat* and we do not *represent*—we *ascend* into the mystery of salvation and new life, which has been accomplished once, but is granted to us "always, now and forever and unto ages of ages." And in this heavenly, eternal and otherworldly eucharist Christ does not come down to us, rather we ascend to him.[76]

The descent of the Spirit is theologically central, for "the Liturgy is accomplished in the new time through the Holy Spirit."[77] That what the Spirit transfigures becomes manifestation is central for reintegrating sign and reality *eschatologically*:

> [In] its outward appearance, in the time of "this world," the liturgy is a *symbol* and is expressed in *symbols*—but "symbol" [understood as] a reality that cannot be expressed or manifested in the categories of "this world," i.e., to the senses, empirically, visibly. It is the reality that we termed the *sacramentality* inherent in everything created by God, but which man has ceased to sense and recognize in "this" fallen world.[78]

This is why Schmemann thinks it is a mistake to try to articulate the conversion of bread and wine in terms drawn from this world, for the conversion "is accomplished invisibly. Nothing perceptive *happens*—the bread remains bread, and the wine remains wine."[79] That is, in 'this world' all that makes bread what it is—its chemical structure, its material attributes, its relation to physical causes and effects—remain the same. And so, according to Schmemann,

> any attempt to *explain* the conversion, to locate it in formulas and causes, is not only unnecessary but truly harmful . . . . [For] in "this world" no knowledge, other than that disclosed in faith, and no "science" can explain what is accomplished in the new time, in the coming of the Holy Spirit, in

---

76 Schmemann, *The Eucharist*, 221.

77 Ibid.

78 Ibid., 222.

79 Ibid.

> the conversion of life into the new life of the kingdom of God, which is "in our midst."[80]

So, Schmemann thinks that transubstantiation is an attempt to explain something heavenly, something of the 'new time' in terms which are proper to 'this world,' the old time.

Inattention to the distinction between old time and new, this world and heaven, results in confusion about the role and identity of the bread in the Eucharist. Bread and wine serve as apt signs of the body precisely because of their role as food in human life. As Schmemann says, food was part of God's creation, food being one of the creaturely requirements of life. And yet, in creation, "the meaning, essence and joy of life is not in food, but in God, in communion with him."[81] In the fall, humanity fell away from this food, such that "food came to reign in him, but this reign is not unto life, but unto death, disintegration and separation."[82] That which God gave to communicate life, and in so doing to facilitate creaturely participation in communion with God, became instead a sign of death, for without material food, God's creatures now die. So Schmemann says, "that is why Christ, when he had come into the world, called himself 'the bread of God . . . which comes down from heaven, and gives life to the world (Jn 6:33).'"[83]

In so doing, Christ destroys the supposed "self-sufficiency" of bread, of all of creation. Such self-sufficiency "constitutes the essence of sin and [makes] bread only bread—the mortal food of mortal man, a partaking of sin and death."[84] But as the bread of God, the food that genuinely gives life, "in Christ our earthly good, which is converted into our flesh and blood, into our very selves and our lives, becomes that for which it was created—participation in the divine life, through which the mortal is clothed in immortality and death is swallowed up in victory."[85] Bread becomes what bread *truly* is. The bread of 'this world' is not genuine food; the bread of 'the world to come' is genuine bread for it becomes the food of immortality.

In this sense, then, the bread of the Eucharist becomes not only a sign of Christ's body, but a sign of the future of the world. Schmemann says,

> Christian sanctification consists in the restoration to everything in the world of its symbolic nature, its "sacramentality," in referring everything to the ultimate aim of being. All our worship services therefore are an ascent to the altar and a return to "this world" for witness to "What no eye

---

80 Schmemann, *The Eucharist*, 222-223.

81 Ibid., 225.

82 Ibid.

83 Ibid., 225.

84 Ibid. 110.

85 Ibid.

has seen, nor ear heard, nor the heart of man conceived, what God has prepared for those who love him" (1 Co 2:9).[86]

This is why it is inappropriate to isolate the conversion of bread and wine from the whole liturgy, for *"what is accomplished in the eucharist* [is] the transformation of the bread and wine, with us, with the Church, with the world, with *all through all.*"[87] The transformation of the bread is a realization of what will happen to all creation. This is fundamentally why the change cannot be described in the terms of this world. To ask about what happens to the bread in the Eucharist is to ask about the nature of all food in God's 'new time,' not to ask about physical or natural mechanisms of change. The terms of this world can only describe the world in terms of its fallenness, its capture by death and decay. But the change of bread and wine is something 'other-worldly' in the sense of transforming this world to something other than it is now, and yet to something that it is created to be.

In this sense, then, the bread becomes the sacramental sign of the ascent of the Church. Schmemann says that in Western theology, the liturgy is perceived

> not in the key of *ascent* but of *descent*. The entire western eucharistic mystique is thoroughly imbued with the image of Christ *descending* onto our alters. Meanwhile the original eucharistic experience, to which the very order of the eucharist witnesses, speaks of our *ascent* to that place where Christ ascended, of the heavenly nature of the eucharistic celebration.[88]

This, of course, links with why it is that the Eucharist cannot be described in 'this worldly' events, for at its core it is not an event of this world, but of heaven. It is not that Christ is 'brought down' from heaven to dwell with the Church, but that in the liturgy the Church is 'brought up' to heaven to dwell with Christ: "The divine liturgy—the continual ascent, the lifting up of the church to *heaven*, to the throne of glory, to the unfading light and joy of the kingdom of God," such is the consequence of the descent of the Spirit. Of course, the ascent of the church while realized in the Eucharist is not the final, full realization of the kingdom. The church is still in 'this world,' subject to the time of 'this world.' Rather, "for 'this world' [the kingdom] is as yet in the future, but in Christ it is already revealed and in the Church it is already 'anticipated,' and the eucharist raises and elevates us to this heavenly kingdom of God from on high, and in it the eucharist is accomplished."[89]

---

86 Schmemann, *The Eucharist*, 61.

87 Ibid., 166.

88 Ibid., 60.

89 Schmemann, *The Eucharist*, 68-9.

The anticipation of the Church, an anticipation by means of a sacramental realization affirms again why the Eucharist cannot be described in terms of 'this world':

> For Christ has ascended to heaven, and his altar is "sacred and spiritual." In "this world" there *is not and cannot be* an altar, for the kingdom of God is "not of this world." And that is why it is so important to understand that we regard the altar with reverence—we kiss it, we bow before it, etc.—not because it is "sanctified" and has become, so to speak, a "sacred object," but because its very sanctification consists in its *referral* to the reality of the kingdom, in its conversion into a symbol of the kingdom. Our reverence, our veneration is never related to "matter," but always to that which it reveals, of which it is an *epiphany*, i.e. a manifestation and presence.[90]

This is a central claim for Schmemann for it displays the logic of the relationship of the church and the material elements of the Eucharist to the world. The material of bread and wine is important not in itself, but as it participates in the anticipation-by-way-of-realization of the liturgy. The material elements of the creation 'make plain,' at least to faith, the reality of the future of all of creation. In so doing, the ascent of the Church makes known to the world its eschatological end.

Transubstantiation as Metaphysical *Ascesis*

Having in mind Schmemann's insight that the Eucharist is a liturgical act whereby the Church ascends to God's throne in worship, as well as the exhortation to attend to analogous uses of language, I will argue that transubstantiation, rather than a 'this-worldly' explanation of Christ's presence is instead an instance of mystical theology by way of an exercise in metaphysical *ascesis* whereby human language is made available to speak of things outside the ordinary course of the world—an exercise in disestablishing conceptual idols in order to speak well of God and what God does. This argument will then allow me to make the claim I suggested at the beginning of the chapter, namely that despite his express conclusion, Thomas's account of transubstantiation leads in the direction of an affirmation of the reality of the bread *as* the reality of Christ's body, an identification of bread as body. This can be seen by attending to analogous uses of language in Thomas's account of transubstantiation. In fact, metaphysical *ascesis* here is constituted by analogous uses of language, uses which display that our very notions of substance and accidents—that is, what it means to be anything at all in this fallen world—are themselves 'transubstantiated' into the language of faith, an

---

90 Ibid., 60-61.

affirmation of the presence of Christ's body and blood in bread and wine. Similar to the claim that language about God signifies truly, but in a way improper to language itself, so too an affirmation of Christ's body in the bread and wine signifies truly and meaningfully, but improper to the usual uses of language.

The comparison with language about God is a legitimate one, even though talking about (relatively) ordinary things like bread and body, for two reasons. First, as Thomas's account makes clear, while bread and body are ordinary notions, the way in which bread and body are present in the Eucharist is mysterious, a mystery that requires us to use language in ways out of the ordinary. It is just these uses that occasion Fitzpatrick's objection. Of course, Thomas takes transubstantiation to be an account of a conversion in which bread is changed without remainder into Christ's body. But, I will suggest that it rather results in a claim about the manner in which the bread is present, a manner that, like body, is mysterious and 'out of the ordinary.' Second, the unique manner of presence of the body (and, as I shall claim, bread) in the Eucharist hinges ultimately, Thomas says, on the mystery of God as first cause. Consequently, transubstantiation is an identification of a mystery in terms of God's own action and being, which of course requires us to speak analogically.

Analogous Uses of Substance

It will be helpful to return up front to McCabe's suggestion, in response to Fitzpatrick, that transubstantiation is a change on the level of existence itself, that when the host is consecrated "it means a different thing for it to be a substance, a different thing for it to exist."[91] I want to pursue the claim that 'substance' is one of those words that McCabe identifies as being susceptible to creative uses, and that its use in Thomas's account of transubstantiation can be understood as creative linguistic rule-breaking.

To say that 'substance' is used analogously is not in itself a novel claim. In fact, Aristotle and Thomas both use it so. For Aristotle, and Thomas following him, 'substance' is used both of an individual existing thing (e.g., Socrates), and for the species and genera that the thing is (e.g., human, and animal, in the case of Socrates). Thomas accepts these usages, and in fact at one point indicates such uses of substance as analogous. Thomas says that the distinction between substance in the first sense (Socrates) and in the second sense (human) is not a division according to genus. That is, Socrates is not a species of the genus human. Rather, Socrates is an *instance* of a human, and so the division "is analogous rather than specific."[92] Furthermore, 'substance'

---

91 McCabe, *God Matters*, 149.

92 *De Potentia,* q. 9. A. 2. Reply to the 6th objection: "The division of substance into 'first' and 'second' is not a division into genus and species, since 'second'

when used of 'human' (in 'Socrates is a human') is to be distinguished from 'substance' as used of 'humanity.' We say that Socrates is a human, but we do not say that Socrates is humanity. So, 'substance' used secondarily is not to be conflated with 'substance' said of a nature or quiddity.[93] In short, 'substance' is a term susceptible to analogous use.[94]

W. Norris Clarke argues that for Aristotle, substance names the "principle of self-identity . . . , that which stands under all its changing phases as their principle of continuity and self-identity."[95] 'Accident' names those "changing phases," that which "happens to the substance but [does] not constitute or change its essential self-identity."[96] As Clarke says well, the contrast between accident and substance is not between that which changes and that which does not change. Rather, the contrast is between the *way in which* a thing changes. In an accidental change "the substance itself changes, but not substantially or essentially, only accidentally."[97] In a substantial change, the thing ceases to be what it was and becomes something else. The distinction between substance and accidents helps to articulate the different ways in which a thing changes. Insofar as self-identity is at issue, we can say that for Thomas, substance is "a thing whose quiddity it belongs to exist not in something else."[98] In contrast, accident is "a thing to which it belongs to be in something else."[99]

---

substance covers nothing that is not covered by 'first' substance: but it is a division of a genus according to different modes of existence. Thus 'second' substance denotes the generic nature in itself absolutely, while 'first' substance signifies that nature as individually subsistent: wherefore the division is analogous rather than specific." Of this passage, John F. Wippel says, "Hence, Thomas adds, this is more a division of something analogous than of a genus. By this I take him to mean that this is really a division by reason of diversity in modes of being rather than the division of a genus into its species by specific differences." See John F. Wippel, *The Metaphysical Thought of Thomas Aquinas: From Finite Being to Uncreated Being* (Washington, D.C.: Catholic University of America Press), 207.

93 Wippel, 207.

94 Wippel rightly connects the analogous use of substance with analogous use of 'being.' That is, 'beings' exist in different ways and substance names one of those ways of existing. Furthermore, the way in which a thing exists as a substance can be spoken of in different ways. See Wippel, 199-202.

95 Clarke, 128.

96 Ibid.

97 Ibid.

98 Wippel, 234. Wippel calls this a quasi-definition, suggesting implicitly that 'substance' resists rigid formulation.

99 Ibid. It is worth noting here that Wippel contends that it was Thomas's Eucharistic concerns that led him to state the quasi-definition of accident in this way, for

However, for Thomas substance is not inert, static, 'stuff,' but rather dynamic presence in the world. As Clarke says,

> Substance for Thomas interpreted in the light of his fundamental conception of real being as dynamic act of presence ordered naturally to flow over into self-expressive, self-communicative action, is itself a highly dynamic notion. The substance of any being, as a nature (= "a center of acting and being acted upon"), is intrinsically oriented toward expressing and fulfilling itself through its operations and relations of giving-receiving with others.[100]

That is, 'substance,' used of what a thing is, is not signifying the 'inner constitution' of the thing separable from its relation to everything else, as though 'what it is' is simply and only a self-contained unit irrespective of anything else. Rather, substance is used of what a thing is in itself, and yet by the nature of being as act, what a thing is in itself is the thing dynamically acting in the universe of things. We might even say that its own self-identity is dynamic. In fact, Clarke, in reflection on human life says that substance is "the necessary metaphysical underpinning of every human life as a *story* with a point to it. No perduring substantial self = no story; no abiding center of natural potentialities = no growth toward fulfillment, *no meaningful story*!"[101] Of course, non-human objects do not have the same sort of narrative or point that humans do. And yet, narrative is helpful for identifying substance. Consider Leo Elder's claim that insofar as being and act are linked, things have a "kind of action which consists in making themselves known, i.e., a process by means of which they radiate forth and communicate their likeness to the sense faculties of man and animals."[102] All of this gets at the way in which substance is not a static, inert thing, and the substance-accident distinction is not the distinction between the thing and the 'covering' of the thing. Rather the distinction is in the various ways in which a thing exists and changes; and, by the lights of Thomas, things exist in activity, in the constant flow of giving and receiving.

The contrast with Descartes on substance, and for that matter John Locke and David Hume is instructive. For Descartes, substance indicates an "isolated self-enclosed" thing that exists "by itself."[103] For Locke, substance names the

---

in transubstantiation the remaining accidents are not *in* the substance of bread, but held in place by God's power. Wippel, 237.

100 Clarke, 129.

101 Ibid., 130. Emphases and exclamation are Clarke's.

102 Leo J. Elders, *The Metaphysics of Being of St. Thomas Aquinas In a Historical Perspective,* trans. John Dudley, Studien Und Texte Zur Geistesgeschichte Des Mittelalters (Leiden: E.J.Brill, 1993), 259, referencing *De Potentia*, q.5, a.8.

103 Clarke, 133.

"inert, static, unknowable . . . underlying substratum needed to support the properties and accidents of a thing, which are all we can know."[104] And for Hume, substance is in an important sense at best abstraction, if not simply an absurdity. This is because if substance were really distinct from attributes, it would have to be able to exist separable from them. And yet, the only observable things are bundles of attributes.[105]

In contrast to Descartes, for Thomas and Aristotle substances are not isolated things that exist *by* themselves; rather substance is "that which exists *in* itself."[106] As Clarke notes, the change in preposition is central. Substance for the ancients was "naturally oriented toward action, hence toward *relations* of giving-receiving to all around it."[107] In contrast to Locke, rather than a static, unknowable substrate, substance was "oriented toward self-expressive action."[108] And in contrast to Hume, substance was a "metaphysical co-principle," not a separably existent *thing*.[109] All of which is simply to repeat the point above: substance names the self-identity of a thing, and more fundamentally, the way in which self-identity is constituted by the distinctive and dynamic way in which the thing gives of itself and receives from all to which it is related.

Laurence Paul Hemming considers substance as it appears in transubstantiation. Hemming notes that in transubstantiation, Thomas makes clear that the truth of Christ's body is knowable only by faith (III.76.7). This of course indicates that there is no empirical test to detect Christ's body in the bread (it cannot be seen by a bodily eye); but neither can it be seen by unaided intellect. As Hemming nicely puts it, "if it can be demonstrated (*probare*) through the scientific reflection on faith that is theology, it cannot be proven (*demonstrare*) by any means that we would understand as conforming to the modern definition of scientific method."[110] As Thomas says, substance is known by the intellect. And yet this particular substance can only be known by faith. We might say that though Christ's body for Thomas in no way depends upon an individual human's faith for its existence, nevertheless its *manner* of communicative existence (to recall Elder's point above) is as an object known by faith rather than by empirical observation.

Hemming argues that Thomas's use of "eye" and "seeing" here is crucial. In response to the question of whether or not Christ's body can be seen in its

---

104 Ibid.

105 Ibid.

106 Ibid.

107 Ibid.

108 Ibid.

109 Ibid.

110 Laurence Paul Hemming, "Transubstantiating Ourselves," *Heythrop Journal* 44 (October 2003): 421.

sacramental mode by a glorified eye, Thomas answers negatively. He notes that "the eye is of two kinds, namely, the bodily eye properly so-called, and the intellectual eye, so-called by similitude" (III.76.7). Thomas goes on to note that substance in itself is never visible to a bodily eye. Substances are known by way of their accidents, even though what is known by the intellect is the substance. In fact, the object of the intellect is substance, which is "*what a thing is*" (III.76.7).[111] Hemming's understanding of what Thomas means to say is worth quoting at length:

> Already it is clear from what Aquinas says here that substance has something to do with the manner of *our* presence to what it is that we are present to. This is quite separate from the question of the manner of the presence of Christ in the sacrament—which is a matter known only in faith. The question of substance has nothing, therefore, to do with the question of Christ's presence in the sacrament, which is there by divine power, and so there, and always there, insofar as and as long as God chooses it to be such. I repeat, substance has no bearing on this at all, despite what textbook after textbook has attempted to say over the years. The question, I repeat again, is our manner of being present to what it is we are present to, on which basis we may know what in fact we do know in faith. Let us, for a moment, reverse the point: if there were no intellect present to this thing, then no substance would be present at all. For Aquinas, the only reason that there is always substance present is because, irrespective of our presence, the divine intellect is always present, and so for this reason and no other, the substance always remains. Indeed, at this point the question becomes tautologous, because if there were no God, there would be no presence of Christ.[112]

This, we might say, is yet another way of affirming how Thomas's faith adopts and transforms philosophical concepts. For, in short, what Hemming is suggesting is another way of affirming God as creator, and as the creator who knows and sustains his creation. That anything exists as itself at all is dependent upon God's loving knowledge of it. And hence, insofar as we, and for that matter, all of creation participate in God's life in ways appropriate to the sorts of creatures we are, to speak of substance is to speak of co-presence. We need not understand Hemming to be saying that an individual's faith is effective for the presence of Christ's body, but rather he is speaking of the way in which Christ's body is gift—not as a self-contained, isolated 'thing,' but present dynamically as substance, as self-identity always giving to be known, but known by faith in this case, not by empirical detection.

---

112 Hemming, 431.

At this point, it is worth recalling what Burrell said about substance in Aristotle. Recall that Burrell claims that for Aristotle, substance identifies the basic unit of intelligibility.[113] The need for a notion like substance is at least partly occasioned by the analogous use of words like 'unit,' 'one,' 'component,' and so on. For Aristotle, as Burrell says, statement making sentences are primary. What we know is substances, that the horse is white or that the bread is stale. Recall that on Burrell's read, the reason to privilege statement making sentences as elucidating substance is because they are the fitting conclusions to *inquiry*. Substance, in this sense, is simply the object of inquiry. To say that substance is the object of inquiry is to note that it is naming a kind of co-presence. The thing about which we are inquiring of course does not depend upon human intellect for its being. But for it to exist as *substance*, as a knowable, communicative, dynamic substance does of course depend upon God. Human inquiry is a practice that participates in the being of a thing in a way appropriate to knowing creatures.

The purpose of this survey of substance has been two-fold. First, to suggest that 'substance' is a term susceptible to analogous uses. Second, this susceptibility to analogous uses is indicated by the way in which 'substance' is used not for the identity of a thing in relation only to itself, but rather a thing's self-identity as it dynamically exists in relation to others. That a thing's self-identity is not insulated from its relation to the world in which it belongs will play an important role in my account of the substance of bread and the substance of body in transubstantiation. But for now I turn to Aquinas's account of the accidents of bread, as what he says there provides the clearest clue to the identity of the bread in the Eucharist, and the necessity of being attentive to analogous uses of language.

Analogous Uses of Accident

The accidents of bread and wine do much work in Thomas's account of transubstantiation. In fact, Thomas's articulation of the surviving accidents occupies an entire question. In Question 77, Article 1, Thomas argues that the accidents that remain are there because of God's power as first cause. As the first objection says, in "the order which God established in nature," accidents are accidents of a subject, and as accidents of a subject they are the signs of the nature or substance of the subject (III.77.1, Obj. 1). That is, accidents participate in the being of a thing dependently as the signs of what the thing is. So, says the first objection, it is simply impossible for an accident to remain without a subject, and besides such a remaining accident would be deceptive

---

113 Burrell, "Substance: A Performatory Account," in *Substances and Things: Aristotle's Doctrine of Physical Substance in Recent Essays*, edited by M.L. O'Hara, 230.

since it would be a sign that misled as there would be no substance of which it was a sign.

Thomas in reply says that in fact the accidents do remain without a subject, because God's power sustains their existence (III.77.1, Reply 1). God can do this because God is the first cause of all things, and effects depend to a greater degree on the first cause than on a secondary cause. The subject is a secondary cause as it itself depends upon the first cause, God's power. So, Thomas says that God "by His unlimited power [can] preserve an accident in existence when the substance is withdrawn whereby it was preserved in existence as by its proper cause" (III.77.1). While the accidents received their individual existence first from the bread and wine as accidents of individual bits of bread and wine, now their individual existence is preserved by God, and so, Thomas says in reply to the third objection "they are individual and sensible" (III.77.1, Reply 3). Finally, in response to the fourth objection, Thomas says that as accidents of bread and wine the accidents had no existence of themselves since they existed in the bread and the wine. However, after the consecration "the accidents which remain have being; hence they are compounded of existence and essence [similar to angels]; and besides they have composition of quantitative parts" (III.77.1, Reply 4). And again, this is a consequence of God's power.

These remaining accidents account for the continued material interactions of the consecrated host on their surroundings. Under natural conditions, says the first objection to Article 3 of Question 77, accidents act on the world by means of their material habitation: "forms which are in matter are produced by forms that are in matter, but not from forms which are without matter, because like makes like" (III.77.3, Obj. 1). Because the sacramental accidents are without a subject, they are without matter. Thomas has previously identified being and act, and reminds us here that "everything stands in the same relation to action as it does to being" (III.77.3). And so, because God's power has preserved the being of the accidents without a subject, they are able to continue their action. In reply to the objection, Thomas says that this is why even though they exist without matter they are still able to act: "The sacramental species, although they are forms existing without matter, still retain the same being which they had before in matter, and therefore as to their being they are like forms which are in matter" (III.77.3, Reply 1).

That the accidental forms retain the same being they had before the consecration is what Thomas will appeal to frequently throughout the rest of the question. For example, in Article 4 the issue is whether or not the sacramental species are corruptible. The first objection claims that they are not because corruption comes from the separation of form from matter. But, the matter of bread and wine do not remain, so there cannot be corruption. Second, forms are only corrupted accidentally when the subject is corrupted. But again, after the conversion there is no subject in which these accidents inhere. Thomas responds that corruption is "movement from being into non-being" (III.77.4).

Yet, as already shown, the accidents retain the being they had when the bread and wine were present, and so they can be corrupted according to their continued being. So, to the first objection Thomas says that though the accidental forms are not in matter, their being is "like such being as is in matter," and so subject to corruption (III.77.4, Reply 1). The reply is similar to the second objection: "Although the sacramental species are forms not in matter, yet they have the being which they had in matter" (III.77.4, Reply 2). So, again, that they are preserved in the being they had when they were the accidents of bread and wine accounts for their corruptibility.

That the accidents are corruptible accounts also for their generative effects on the world. When something is corrupted, something else is generated. When play-dough balls are corrupted with respect to being play-dough, ash is produced; when play-dough balls are corrupted according to shape, play-dough squares are produced. Interestingly, Thomas devotes a longer response to this question, surveying the various proposals for how to account for the corruption and generation that is evident to the senses. He concedes that though "the senses are witness that something is generated . . . . Nevertheless, it is difficult to see how anything can be generated from them" (III.77.5). This is because we cannot say that generation happens as a result of Christ's body. Christ's body is glorified and so incorruptible. If the matter of bread and wine remained, that might account for corruption and generation, but this is not the case. "Others" have suggested that generation occurs not from the sacramental species "but from the surrounding atmosphere" (III.77.5). Thomas dismisses this for a number of reasons which need not concern us here.

Another option suggested by "others," one that is important for my purposes, is that the substance of bread and wine returns on the occasion of corruption and generation, so that the worms and ashes that are generated from the corruption come from the returning substance (III.77.5). Thomas says that it is impossible for the substance of bread and wine to return and gives several reasons, again not immediately relevant here. For my purposes, however, I want to note what Thomas leaves unchallenged by the suggestion: that if we could appeal to substance we would be able to explain the effect of the species on the world. I will return to this. Thomas's solution is that "it seems better to say that in the actual consecration it is miraculously bestowed on the dimensive quantity of bread and wine to be the subject of subsequent forms. Now this is proper to matter; and therefore as a consequence everything which goes with the matter is bestowed on dimensive quantity," and consequently what would be generated or corrupted from the matter of bread and wine can be generated or corrupted by the remaining accidents of bread and wine (III.77.5). In the reply to objection 2, Thomas states tersely, "those sacramental species are indeed accidents, yet they have the act and power of substance, as stated above" (III.77.5, Reply 2). Note what Thomas is saying: the power of substance to act is bestowed on the accidents by their continued being by God's power, and their continued being is rooted in the dimensive quantity, something proper to matter. That is, by God's power, the remaining accidents are able to account for *everything* that matter, substance, and accident account for with respect to the relation of bread and wine to the sensible world. Having established this, Thomas says that it "presents no difficulty" to see that the sacramental species nourish, the subject of Article 6 (III.77.6).

To repeat, the consequence of this line of argumentation is that the accidents fulfill all of what Schmemann might identify as the 'this-worldly' requirements of substance and matter as well accident. Anything that bread and wine can do, the remaining accidents can do; the active power of bread and wine is retained in the divinely sustained being and act of the accidents.

Now, it is precisely this sort of argumentation that Fitzpatrick objects to. 'Accidents' that act just like substances are simply not Aristotelian accidents; and for Fitzpatrick, the only reason that there is even an appearance of sense is because of the tendency to treat accident and substance as dissections, as constituent parts, something that Aristotle, and Thomas in other places, expressively forbids. However, I think we should take seriously what we noted above: Thomas is not, strictly speaking, an Aristotelian. There is no doubt that his theology has been influenced by Aristotle. But he does not simply 'translate' Christian theology into an Aristotelian system. He rather makes use of Aristotle as Aristotle is helpful to articulate truths that ultimately rest on divine revelation and authority. Furthermore, in using those tools they are reshaped to his theological purposes.

This Bread is Christ's Body

The reshaping of these tools, that is their susceptibility to analogous use, can be seen by considering further Thomas's appeal to the distinction between first and second causes. Recall that in the order of secondary causes, that is, the world with respect to the natural order of causes and effects, substance and accident are used to articulate the kind of change in question. Substance is used for "a thing whose quiddity it belongs to exist not in something else," and accident for "a thing to which it belongs to be in something else."[114] As we noted, these uses of substance and accident are helpful in keeping track of the different ways a thing might change: with respect to what it is (play-dough to ash), or with respect to some other characteristic of the thing (from play-dough ball to play-dough pancake).

But now, considering the world with respect to its first cause, God, these uses of substance and accident shift. This is because *everything*, even that which is 'substance' in the order of natural causes is "a thing to which it belongs to be in something else" insofar as in the order of first cause, everything exists *in God* as creator. Of course, the way in which something

[114] Wippel, 234.

exists in God is not univocal to the way in which shape, for instance, exists in a substance. But neither is it equivocal, for in both instances there is a real causal link.[115] What I am suggesting, then, is that Thomas's appeal to first and second cause function here to indicate that 'substance' and 'accident' are being used analogically. To be clear, I do not mean to claim that Thomas himself had this in mind. However, I do mean to claim that in fact his usage indicates this move: insofar as with respect to first cause everything is in God, uses of substance in transubstantiation are closer on the map of language use to ordinary uses of accident than to ordinary uses of substance. But furthermore, Thomas's insistence that the remaining accidents of bread and wine are sufficient to account for everything that substance ordinarily accounts for, suggests that accidents in transubstantiation is used in a way closer to ordinary uses of substance on the map of language use.

Substance used ordinarily with respect to the order of secondary causes generally accounts for the sorts of interactions a thing has in the world. Play-dough can be squished from a ball to a pancake because it is play-dough and not a rock; bread can nourish because it is bread and not arsenic. Yet, for Thomas, it is the remaining accidents that account for the same thing: the species nourish as ordinary bread nourishes even though (Thomas contends) it is no longer bread. To be clear, I am not claiming that substance said of consecrated bread is used exactly the same as accident said of the qualities of unconsecrated bread; but I am claiming that accident and substance are used analogously of consecrated and unconsecrated.

These analogous uses of substance and accident, uses indexed to the order of first cause and the order of second causes, are uses that make possible differentiating *the way in which* the consecrated host is bread, and the way in which the consecrated host is not bread but body. Prior to the consecration, what is on the altar is bread and wine and not body. This is because prior to the consecration, God as first cause operates mediately by second causes, and so identity claims about what is on the altar are articulated by ordinary uses of language within the order of second causes. God is *always* first cause, and so bread is always 'in' God. But ordinarily, the way in which bread is in God is mediately by second causes—bread comes to be from the baking of the baker, and the stuff the baker bakes comes to be from the growth of plants, and so on. Likewise, in the order of second causes, the accidents of bread are in a substance. Of course accidents, like substance, are always in God as first cause, but in the order of second causes their manner of being in God is mediately through their participation in the being of the substance. After the consecration, after the change which is brought about "by a power which is infinite" (III.75.

[115] Of course, 'cause' is itself used analogously. See Burrell, *Aquinas: God and Action* (Scranton: University of Scranton Press, 2008; originally published Notre Dame: University of Notre Dame Press, 1979), 150-154.

7) we must speak analogously of substance and accidents and their various manners of being. We must so speak analogously precisely because God has acted immediately as first cause, outside the ordinary order of second causes. The consequence is a manner of being accident that depends upon God's immediate power as its cause. Recall, Thomas explicitly affirms this (III.77.1). As long as the accidents remain, God's power acts immediately to sustain them without a subject, without their being in a substance.

Now, as I have suggested, this recognition that when speaking of consecrated bread we are speaking of the immediate effects of God as first cause outside the ordinary order of causes, is an indication that we must be attentive to the shifting contexts of language use. That is, language used ordinarily, properly within the order of second causes is now used improperly of effects sustained by God as first cause. Hence, to speak of substance and accident after the consecration is to use substance and accident analogically. The consequence of attending to these analogous uses of language is, I contend, the possibility of affirming that 'this *bread* is Christ's body.' And, as Hallett has suggested, one advantage of this recognition is perhaps the ability to stick with more natural understandings of many of the church fathers' sayings about bread and body.

Because of the analogous use of accident identified in this account, a use that is closer to the ordinary uses of substance, and a use that takes into account the fact that the remaining accidents do everything substance does with respect to substance's participation in the order of secondary causes, it can be truly said that, even after the consecration 'this *is* bread.' Of course, it is not bread in just the same way it was bread before the consecration, but with respect to the order of second causes it is still now everything bread was prior to the consecration. The analogous uses of substance and accident are linguistic clues to the various ways in which bread *is*. However, it is also the case that there is no contradiction in affirming that after the consecration 'this *is not* bread, but body.' There is no contradiction because the analogous uses of substance and accident indicate the analogous uses of 'is.' There is no contradiction because 'is' is not used univocally in both claims. It is bread *with respect to* its relation to the order of secondary causes, a way of being mediately in God. It is not bread but body with respect to its participation immediately in God's power as first cause. *Both* can be true, because the identity claims are indexed to different orders of causes and effects, different ways of participating in being. Of course, these orders of cause and effect are not simply different or unrelated. To speak of 'different' orders of causes and effects is not to posit some ultimate distinction between them. But it is to recognize a *relative* distinction between them. The order of second causes always participates in God as first cause; however, it also has its own, gifted integrity, a kind of relative autonomy such that it is possible to give true (if incomplete) descriptions of it without explicit reference to God as first cause. It is this relative distinction that makes possible both claims—'this is bread,' and 'this is not bread', because the 'is-ing' of each is not said univocally.

Thomas's affirmation of the presence of Christ's body likewise hints at this relative distinction. Christ's body is in substance under the accidents. But for Thomas's own account, the effects of Christ's body are not within the order of second causes. All the ordinary effects of eating (or of corruption) are indexed to the remaining accidents. The effects of the substance of Christ's body are unrelated to the ordinary effects of food. Rather, Christ's body "works in man the effect which Christ's passion wrought the world" (III.79.1). Thomas says, "the sacrament does for the spiritual life all that material food does for the bodily life, namely by sustaining, giving increase, restoring, and giving delight" (III.79.1). Thomas concludes, "and since Christ and his passion are the cause of grace; and since spiritual refreshment and charity cannot be without grace, it is clear from all that has been set forth that this sacrament bestows grace" (III.79. 1). So, I suggest, there is no competition between the substance of Christ's body and the substance of bread, because 'substance' is used analogously, and this analogous use is indicated by appeal to the relatively distinct orders of cause and effect.

To be clear, I am not suggesting an account of consubstantiation, where 'substance' is used univocally, and said of both bread and body. Nevertheless, contrary to Thomas, I do claim that we can truly say the substance of bread is present as well as the substance of Christ's body because substance is used analogically. Furthermore, I claim that, despite his express conclusion, Aquinas's account leads us in this direction. What it means to be the substance bread prior to consecration is not simply the same as what it means to be the substance bread after consecration. This is because, as McCabe has suggested, it now "means a different thing for it to be a substance, a different thing for it to exist."[116]

From Explanation to Identity

Attention to analogous uses of 'substance,' 'accident,' 'is,' and others, accomplishes at least some of what Schmemann takes to be missing in transubstantiation. First, recall that Schmemann thinks that transubstantiation fails insofar as it is an attempt to explain the presence of Christ's body in terms of 'this world.'[117] But, analogous uses of substance, accident, and the like, rather than explaining the mystery, instead indicate where our language runs up against the boundaries of what is sayable. We can, because of our ability to bend language use to various purposes, say without contradiction 'this bread is Christ's body.' Furthermore, we can indicate by use *why* there is no

---

116 McCabe, *God Matters*, 149.

117 Schmemann, *The Eucharist*, 222-223, 216.

contradiction: because the terms in which we articulate this identity (substance, accident, is) are used analogously. We can use language to speak of God's power as first cause because we can speak analogously of God in the first place. But we do run into our limits. We can say truly that 'God is good;' but as McCabe succinctly put it of creation, "we do not, strictly speaking, know what we are talking about."[118] Likewise, we can speak of Christ's body in the bread, but we cannot properly know the way in which it is in the bread because the way in which it is bread is according to God as first cause. So, I claim that attention to analogous uses of language in an account of transubstantiation is precisely what is required to speak *truly*, without thereby *explaining* what is fundamentally mystery, namely, that this bread is Christ's body.

Second, my account addresses Schmemann's claim that "Nothing perceptible *happens*—the bread remaining bread, and wine remaining wine."[119] Within the order of second causes, this is true. As Thomas himself would acknowledge, the baker and the scientist would have the exact same cause and effect relationship *as baker and scientist* to the bread before and after the consecration. "Nothing perceptible happens." Yet, as Schmemann would affirm, this is not to say that *nothing at all* happens. Bread truly has become, by God's power, Christ's body. But this is only knowable by faith, which is to say that from every possible angle of inquiry apart from faith—that is, from every possible angle of inquiry within the order of second causes—nothing has happened. Of course, every possible angle of inquiry within the order of second causes is still an angle of inquiry that can give only an incomplete account of what has happened. For the God who as first cause creates and sustains all of creation has acted in the sacrament to bring about something not knowable or explainable by the lights of 'this world.'

But still, one might ask, which is it *really*? Attention to analogous uses of language suggests that this question is not precise enough. This is because we can inquire of the bread, even after consecration, as to its being with respect to the order of second causes. In this sense it is still *really* bread insofar as it fulfills all the requirements of bread within the created integrity of the order of second causes. Yet, to be clear, this context of inquiry has been decisively relativized by God's act of converting bread to body. It is *really* Christ's body because of God's action. Yet again, God's action has not obliterated the order of second causes. One could still inquire of the bread in the order of second causes, and one would give the same answer both before and after the consecration. But this answer is decisively incomplete apart from faith. From faith, one sees that it is really bread in a relativized sense, for by God's action the order of first cause became the primary, proper context of inquiry. All of this, in the end, is a way of suggesting that 'really' is likewise used

---

118 McCabe, *God Matters*, 149.

119 Schmemann, *The Eucharist*, 222.

analogously. What it means for it to be 'really' bread is not univocal to what it means for it to be 'really' body.

To be clear, I am not suggesting that a context of inquiry *makes* it to be the case. This business about contexts of inquiry does nothing to make bread what it is (or is not). God has decisively acted, both in creation and in the conversion of bread and wine. Even so, appeal to contexts of inquiry is a way of appealing to the care required in our speech about that which is on the altar after the consecration. "Is this still bread?" to which we can say, Yes, but it is bread in the limited sense of its relation to the order of second causes and insofar as there is creational integrity to second causes. "Is this body?" to which we can say, Yes, but understand that when we so signify we acknowledge that the way in which it is body is not the same as the way in which it is bread. "So, is it no longer bread because it is now body?" Within the order of second causes it is bread; but with respect to what God has done as first cause, it really is Christ's body. Of course, this is but the long-handed way of saying that 'is,' etc. are used analogously. Furthermore, it displays the way in which theological reflection is metaphysical *ascesis*. In order to affirm that this is body and this is bread, we must work our language to its limits in order to disestablish our conceptual idols of what it means to *be* anything at all.

Transubstantiation and the Church

Recall that a central point of Schmemann's objection to transubstantiation was that transubstantiation functionally overshadowed the ultimate point of the Eucharist, namely the actualization of the Church. My proposal above likewise ignores the link between the Church and the Eucharist. Perhaps this is evidence, in an oblique way, of the validity of Schmemann's concern. My 'repair' of Thomas requires no account of the intrinsic relation of the Church to the Eucharist, which of course for Schmemann would suggest that at best my account can be a severely limited repair, one that misses the main point. So, is Schmemann's objection fair to Thomas, and presumably by extension to my suggestion?

There is no doubt that for Thomas, as for the early Church, the Eucharist is indeed the sacrament of the unity of the Church. Aquinas says this explicitly more than once. For example, in the opening question on the Eucharist in part 3 of the *Summa*, Question 73, Article 3, Thomas says in response to the question of whether the Eucharist is necessary for salvation, "the reality of the sacrament is the unity of the mystical body, without which there can be no salvation . . ."(III.73.3).[120] Furthermore, explicit identifications of the sacrament of the

---

[120] Gregory Dix calls this a "medieval summary" of the early Church's unmistakable link between the Eucharist and the unity of the Church. Dix, *The Shape of*

Eucharist as the sacrament of the Church as Christ's body occasionally appear in passing in the context of other sacramental issues. For example, on the relationship between the priestly office and baptism, Thomas says that the "sacrament of Christ's Body . . . is the sacrament of ecclesial unity" (III.67.2). The point is to show that priests are consecrated primarily for the purposes of celebrating the Eucharist, and insofar as baptism is the entrance to celebrating the Eucharist, it likewise belongs to the office of the priest to baptize. Consequently, it would be obviously inaccurate to say that Thomas completely neglects the link between the Eucharist and the unity of the Church.[121]

However, despite these affirmations, Schmemann's objection has a ring of truth to it. The bulk of Thomas's Eucharistic theology in the *Summa* is given over to issues that de-emphasize, if not outright ignore the intrinsic relation of the Eucharist to the Church. The evidence that I marshaled to defend Thomas in the above paragraph is evidence drawn exclusively from in-passing comments. Furthermore, Thomas's treatment of Christ's body in the sacrament is suggestive of the trajectory that de Lubac and Dix identify, namely the overshadowing of Christ's ecclesial body by his sacramental body.[122] To the degree this is true, Thomas serves as an apt representation of what Schmemann judges to be the West's fixation on the when and how of the consecration and the nature of Christ's presence rather than on what the Eucharist accomplishes, namely the actualization of the Church.

This can be seen in the articles specifically on Christ's true body (Questions 75-77) where there is no intrinsic link articulated between Christ's sacramental ("true") body and Christ's ecclesial ("mystical") body. Of course, the point of the questions is to articulate *the way in which* Christ's true body and blood are present, so to note that Christ's ecclesial body is almost entirely absent from Thomas's theological reflections may be nothing more than to

---

the Liturgy, with additional notes by Paul V. Marshall (New York: Seabury Press, 1982), 248.

[121] David N. Power makes this point clearly: "Aquinas also related the entire sacramental economy to the Eucharist, and specifically to the communion in the body and blood of Christ whereby he joins the faithful to himself in the communion of the Church and thus brings them into his communion with the Father. For him, this central act of worship is one in which Christ acts directly, without the mediation of a minister, creating a spiritual communion in which the Church is 'as though one person' with himself." Power, *Sacrament: The Language Of God's Giving* (New York: Crossroad Publishers, 1999), 53.

[122] Dix, 598-597; Henri De Lubac, *Corpus Mysticum: The Eucharist and the Church In the Middle Ages*, translated by Gemma Simmonds with Richard Price and Christopher Stephens, ed. by Laurence Paul Hemming and Susan Frank Parsons (London: SCM Press, 2006), 95-96. For both, Thomas himself is not an instance of the full-blown development of the trajectory, but is identifiably on the path.

recognize the obvious: the questions are about Christ's sacramental body, not his ecclesial body, and so the absence of a link is only because of the particular subject matter, not a result of any necessary entailments of the logic. Though this is certainly true, the almost complete absence of even passing references to the link between Christ's sacramental body and his ecclesial body is, in light of Schmemann's comments, significant. Even if Thomas himself assumes such a link, evidenced by his explicit affirmation of such a link elsewhere, such that he sees no need to articulate it at length here, the effect of such an absence is to call into question that link; for Thomas's logic, if not necessarily entailing a disjunction between sacramental body and mystical body, strongly suggests it insofar as Christ's true body is intelligible at all apart from its continuity with the Church.

Perhaps this suggestion can be seen in Question 79, where Thomas is discussing the effects of the sacrament of the Eucharist. One might reasonably expect something to be said about the Church as an effect, especially since, in Question 73, Thomas has explicitly (though briefly) affirmed the link between the sacrament and unity. However, in Question 79, Thomas says surprisingly little about the corporate unity of the Church, emphasizing instead the consequences of grace for the individual communicants' sins and eternal destiny. That is, the effect which pre-occupies Thomas is the effect on the individual destiny of the communicant.

The Eucharist as the sacrament of unity does make a brief appearance in Question 79. In Article 1 on whether the sacrament bestows grace on participants, Thomas says that the effect of the sacrament can be considered in several ways (III.79.1). The effect to be considered "first of all and principally" is the presence of Christ, a presence that through spiritual nourishment unites communicants with himself. Second, the sacrament effects the benefits of Christ's passion, namely the remission of sins. Third, the sacrament is contained in food and drink and so "this sacrament does for the spiritual life all that material food does for the bodily life, namely, by sustaining, giving, increasing, restoring, and giving delight." Fourth, the effect of the sacrament "is considered from the species under which it is given." Here Thomas cites Augustine who says that just as out of many grains and grapes unity flows, so too in the sacrament: "O sacrament of piety, O sign of unity, O bond of charity!" This fourth consideration is the sole extended reference to the sacrament as the sacrament of unity in Question 79.[123] Again, Thomas himself explicitly affirms the connection elsewhere, but it plays at best an ancillary role in this question. One could of course argue that Thomas's account of the effects of grace *assume* that, as he says elsewhere explicitly, there is no salvation

123 In the following article Thomas makes a passing reference to the "unity denoted by the species of bread and wine" though the context is explicitly about whether or not one receives from the sacrament the attainment of glory (III.79.2).

outside the Church. And so the absence of the Church is because it is assumed in *any* discussion of grace and salvation. That may well be correct, but again the effect is nevertheless to suggest what Schmemann worries about, namely the detaching of the Church from any intrinsic account of the sacrament. As noted above, my 'repair' of Thomas leaves this objection standing.

Conclusion

I have claimed that Aquinas's account of transubstantiation, rather than an explanation of the Eucharistic mystery, is an exercise in metaphysical *ascesis*, of running our language up to its own boundaries in order to disestablish what Schmemann would call 'this world' explanations. Doing so allowed me to argue that Thomas's own account of transubstantiation leads us to an identification of bread and body. Using Schmemann as the orienting criticism allowed me, in light of an account of mystical theology, to redirect Fitzpatrick's criticism of transubstantiation. Fitzpatrick is right to raise the issue of language, but fails to grasp the radical *ascesis* required to speak well of Christ's body. And yet, it will be part of the task of the next chapter to show why the move to attend to metaphysical *ascesis* proves useful, both for articulating the identity of Christ's body in bread and in the Church, and for assembling more reminders along the way to showing the intrinsic link between Eucharistic identity and the baptist vision.

For my purposes, as I do not intend Thomas as a rung on any theoretical ladder, though Schmemann's concern about transubstantiation's relationship to the identity of the Church stands, we can leave it as it is. This is because my purpose has been to suggest how attention to analogous uses of language allows us to trace the contours of the sort of identity at issue with respect to bread and body, and to suggest a way to read Thomas that does not require the collapse of bread into body. There may be a way to more thoroughly repair Thomas, so that analogous uses of language that identify bread and body can be shown to have an intrinsic relationship to the identity of the Church. However, *that* the account would have so decisively shifted to attention to analogous uses of language in order to articulate the identity of body, bread and Church would be sufficient for my immediate purposes. Furthermore, without attending any further to Schmemann in particular, the identity of the Church turns out to be central to the account of the Lord's Supper found in the 16th century Anabaptist Balthasar Hubmaier. That is what I will turn to in the next chapter.

CHAPTER 5

Analogous Uses of Language and the Suffering Church

Introduction

If transubstantiation is the doctrine that bread is converted into Christ's body so that there is only Christ's body and no longer bread, one might think that Balthasar Hubmaier, a 16th century Anabaptist, stands as an apt and radical contrast. Hubmaier says of the Lord's Supper, "Here it is obvious that the bread is not the body of Christ but only a reminder thereof."[1] On the account of transubstantiation, what is on the altar is not bread, but body. For Hubmaier, what is on the communion table is not body, but bread. Of course, the apparent contrast is in the content of the claims only. In form, they share the common conclusion that there really is no identity claim to be made between bread and body; bread *is not* body for Hubmaier; and for transubstantiation, at least as Thomas expressly concludes and Catholic theology has largely followed, Christ's body *is not* bread, as there is no remaining bread *to be* body.

In the last chapter I argued that Thomas's account of transubstantiation helps us to attend to the identity claim made of bread and body, of the linguistic nimbleness required to attend to the ways in which this 'is' and 'is not' bread and body. I suggested that attention to analogous uses of language sheds light on Aquinas's account, with the conclusion that Aquinas's words lead to an affirmation of the identity claim made between bread and body, despite the fact that his own express conclusion is that the bread is converted into body such that bread no longer remains. Thomas's account of transubstantiation was an

---

1 Balthasar Hubmaier, "Summa of the Entire Christian Life," in *Balthasar Hubmaier: Theologian of Anabaptism*, trans and ed. H. Wane Pipken and John H. Yoder (Scottdale, PA: Herald Press, 1989), 87. All citations of Hubmaier's work will be taken from Pipken's and Yoder's authoritative translation. In their text they include the corresponding page numbers in the German collection of Hubmaier's writings, *Balthasar Hubmaier: Schriften*, ed. Gunnar Westin and Torsten Bergsten (Heidelberg: Gutersloher Verlagshaus Gerd Mohn, 1962). In the instances that I include the original German in brackets, the German can be found in Westin and Bergsten on the page corresponding to the page listed in Pipken and Yoder.

exercise in metaphysical *ascesis*, the purpose of which was to assemble enough linguistic reminders to help the theologian go on talking about the conversion and identity claim in terms of an Aristotelian idiom. This exercise in metaphysical *ascesis* was part of Thomas's contemplative theology, theology bent toward prayer and contemplation.

Hubmaier clearly rejects transubstantiation (as well as a host of other ways of attempting to articulate the presence of Christ's body in bread and wine).[2] Yet, in so doing, he does not simply reject the identity of Christ's body with the bread in the Lord's Supper. Hubmaier's theology of the Lord's Supper does not constitute a simple claim about the *absence* of Christ's body, but rather, as I will argue, constitutes reflection on the *modes* of presence of Christ's body. I will suggest that Hubmaier, like Thomas, skillfully makes use of analogous uses of language, though he appears to be thematically less reflective than Thomas is about *how* he makes the claims he does. What we will see is that Hubmaier affirms the identity of Christ's body in the Supper, but preeminently in the mode of the suffering church. If Thomas undertakes metaphysical *ascesis* in order to bend human language toward prayer and contemplation, for Hubmaier, language must be reworked, bent towards the habits of speech fitting of a church of martyrs, and these habits of speech must include ways of articulating the identity of Christ's body in the church. For Hubmaier, then, the Lord's Supper provides the conceptual 'vocabulary' by which the church articulates its identity as a *suffering* church on the way to martyrdom. As I will suggest, this conceptual vocabulary makes prolific, if unreflective use of analogous terms.

In order to make this case, the chapter will proceed as follows. First, I will argue that Hubmaier's Eucharistic theology must be understood in light of his desire to restore a church of faithful disciples. I will review the work of Kenneth Davis in particular, who has done much work in connecting Anabaptism with an ascetic tradition, and that such a connection helps bring into clear relief the obsession of the Anabaptists with the life of holiness and purity. Next, I will turn specifically to Hubmaier's Eucharistic theology. After describing a number of clusters of identity claims, I will briefly engage three

---

[2] In his "A Simple Instruction," Hubmaier lists 15 various ways of understanding the presence of Christ in the Lord's Supper from the Roman Catholic tradition (319-320). Elsewhere, he explicitly mentions Thomas's account of the change (326). Just before the reference to Thomas, he cites the confession that was forced upon Berangar (325). This is the infamous confession in which it is affirmed that "the bread and wine which are placed on the altar after the consecration are not only signs, but also the true body and blood of our Lord Jesus Christ, and that sensually . . . they are handled and broken by the hands of the priest and crushed by the teeth of the faithful . . . ." Cited in Gary Macy, *Treasures from the Storeroom: Medieval Religion and the Eucharist* (Collegeville, MN: The Liturgical Press, 1999), 21.

contemporary interpretations of Hubmaier, interpretations which turn out to radically diverge from one another. I will then suggest how attention to analogous uses of language can move past these divergent interpretations while providing yet another illustrative example of the importance of analogous uses of language to Eucharistic identity claims.

Hubmaier's Context

Hubmaier's theology as a whole might be best characterized as the articulation of what it means to be a church of martyrs, a holy church in an unholy world. Kenneth Davis's work showing the roots of Anabaptism in the ascetic tradition is helpful here.[3] Davis builds on the initial suggestion of Albrecht Ritschl who argued that Anabaptism is linked in its origins to "a late medieval, Catholic, ascetic reform tradition."[4] While he judges Ritschl's claim to be "overstated," he notes that a number of scholars of Anabaptism have traced at least some possible links between Anabaptist origins and medieval asceticism.[5] Davis's

---

3 Kenneth Ronald Davis, *Anabaptism and Asceticism: A Study in Intellectual Origins* (Scottdale: Herald Press, 1974). C. Arnold Snyder affirms a connection between asceticism and the Radical Reformation as well: "But on this score [how faith alone related to practice] the 'radical' reformers turned out to be more conservative than Luther, and retained the ascetic, late medieval piety that saw humankind as capable of regeneration and a new life in the here and now; that saw grace as efficacious; that expected 'true' faith to lead to moral reform; and that assumed that external behavior was a good sign of the presence or absence of faith." Snyder, *Anabaptist History and Theology: An Introduction* (Kitchener, Ontario: Pandora Press, 1995), 48-49. While I find Davis's link with asceticism plausible and helpful for my purposes, Hans-Jurgen Goertz's opening sentence of his study of Anabaptism is important to keep in mind: "Much has been written on the origin, development and nature of Anabaptism, yet there is still no unanimous judgment—indeed quite the opposite." Goertz, *The Anabaptists*, trans. Trevor Johnson (London: Routledge, 1996), 1. Likewise, William R. Estep says of accounts of the roots of Anabaptism, "Almost everything that could be said has, at one time or another, been said—and by competent scholars at that." William R. Estep, *The Anabaptist Story: An Introduction to Sixteenth-Century Anabaptism,* 3d ed. (Grand Rapids: Eerdmans, 1996), 24. Though no consensus is to be found, Goertz notes the general trend of moving away from a single source or movement to many sources and many movements (4). In any case, Davis' study is fruitful as, at minimum, one important, and for my purposes illuminating, contribution to the study of Anabaptist origins. For a general overview of the Radical Reformation, including Hubmaier's part see George Huntston Williams, *The Radical Reformation*, 3d rev. ed. (Kirksville, MO: Sixteenth Century Journal Publishers, 1992).

4 Davis, *Anabaptism and Asceticism,* 29.

5 See Davis's list, *Anabaptism and Asceticism*, 30.

central claim is that the major issue for Evangelical Anabaptism was the concern for holiness in life, and that this concern "parallels in a general way traditional ascetic ideals and practices."[6] As suggested by a number of theologians, this concern for holiness was rooted in the Anabaptist notion of the church as a church of martyrs.[7]

The concern for the holy life is evident in Hubmaier. As Davis notes, for Hubmaier the true Christian is one who is saved *and* who grows in holiness.[8] The theology of Anabaptism almost universally emphasized not only regeneration, but the holy life that follows from sanctification. There is, in the words of Davis, a "qualitative conception of eternal life which must begin in this life."[9] Davis notes that Anabaptists most frequently spoke of being "made" saved or holy, rather than the more Lutheran terminology of "reckoned."[10] Consequently, what it meant to be a Christian was to be made new in God's grace. Davis summarizes,

> Therefore holiness, as conceptualized and defined by the Anabaptists, follows the traditional pattern of ascetic expression and includes: *internally*, the supremacy of love for God and one's fellows, and a kind of relativistic, creaturely 'divinization' which involves regeneration and a new citizenship; *externally*, the development of Christlike [sic] virtues, and the renunciation of vices according to an ascetic code of conduct in a social and corporate context; and a radical sense of separation related to cosmic, dualistic tension.[11]

---

6 Ibid., 34.

7 Tripp York offers a read of Balthasar Hubmaier's Eucharistic theology in light of the Anabaptist understanding of martyrdom. See his "Martyrdom and Eating Jesus: Two Neglected Practices?" in *Conrad Grebel Review* 22 (Winter 2004): 71-86. For a more in depth account of an Anabaptist understanding of martyrdom (from which York draws), see Ethelbert Stauffer, "The Anabaptist Theology of Martyrdom," *Mennonite Quarterly Review* 19 (July 1945): 179-214. See also Cornelius J. Dyck, "The Suffering Church in Anabaptism," *Mennonite Quarterly Review* 59 (January 1985): 5-23; and Brad S. Gregory, *Salvation at Stake: Christian Martyrdom in Early Modern Europe* (Cambridge, MA: Harvard University Press, 1999), 197-249. For a brief overview of the history and traditions of the various ways Anabaptists have celebrated the Lord's Supper, see John D. Rempel, "The Lord's Supper in Mennonite Tradition," *Vision: A Journal Of Church and Theology* 2 no. 1: 4-15.

8 Davis, *Anabaptism and Asceticism,* 135; see Hubmaier, "On Fraternal Admonition," 373.

9 Ibid.

10 Ibid., 136.

11 Ibid., 142-143.

Davis argues that this can be clearly seen in Hubmaier's account of a three stage development of holiness, an account that serves as a useful pattern for Anabaptism as a whole:

> 1) an initial transformation of man's nature, relating to the spirit and soul, sufficient to permit an effective willing to do good and live holily, which [Hubmaier] calls the inner baptism; 2) a placing of oneself into the care and discipline and fellowship of a brotherhood by the pledge of baptism, which is the outer or believers baptism; 3) a baptism of blood, or suffering and persecution, which, as a mortification of the flesh, works a developing purification in the yielded Christian and which terminates only with death.[12]

Hence, Hubmaier's theology, in line with the broad trajectory of Anabaptism is always theology aimed at instructing a church on the way to holiness, and a church on the way to holiness will be a church of martyrs, suffering like Jesus at the hands of a hostile world.

Hubmaier's account of the sacraments is fruitfully seen in this context. More will be said about the Lord's Supper below, but Hubmaier's understanding of baptism and of Christian admonition (which was not properly a sacrament, but for Hubmaier was related to baptism and the Lord's Supper as the means of disciplining the Christian from her initial initiation in baptism, to her maturity enacted in the pledge of love of the Lord's Supper) is helpful here. Davis argues that while Anabaptist baptism is a response of a person's faith in the forgiveness of their sins, it was from the beginning inseparably linked with the corporate realization of the church.[13] The concern for the holy life was not primarily an individual achievement, but rather was the necessary condition for a holy church.[14] Davis says that the corporate aspect of baptism "was derived

---

12 Davis, *Anabaptism and Asceticism*, 143. The concise summary of Hubmaier's thinking to which Davis refers is Hubmaier, "A Brief Apologia," 301.

13 Davis, "No Discipline, No Church: An Anabaptist Contribution To the Reformed Tradition," *The Sixteenth Century Journal* 13 (Winter, 1982): 43-44. Davis relies on the work of Jean Runzo for the specific claim that the restoration of church discipline occurred early on across a broad spectrum of Anabaptist reformers. See Jean Runzo "Communal Discipline in the Early Anabaptist Communities of Switzerland, South and Central Germany, Austria and Moravia, 1525-1550, (PhD diss., University of Michigan, 1978), 218-222, cited in Davis, 45.

14 As Waltner says about the Anabaptists, "Their practical concern was the actualization of a visible and true body of Christ on earth, which would be in accord with the New Testament pattern." Erland Waltner, "The Anabaptist Conception of the Church," *Mennonite Quarterly Review* 25 (January 1951): 8. Robert Friedmen likewise says that in contrast to the notion that the invisible church is the "ideal—of which the established state churches were but weak images," for the Anabaptists "*Theirs was*

from [Anabaptists'] understanding of the goal of salvation as not just forensic pardon or personal forgiveness but as the restoration of both the holy life and the holy community."[15] This corporate aspect meant that baptism was indeed a visible sign of a personal, inner reality. However, it was necessarily expressed in corporate as well as individual outward behavior, behavior that contrasts with the world to the degree that "the believing person will come to experience suffering and persecution."[16] The visibility of the holy church was the medicine for all Christians, since all Christians needed discipline in order to faithfully follow the teachings of Jesus. The link between the ban (the form of admonition by exclusion) and the corporate life of the church was such that "the ban was essential to the 'being of the church'," and thus, as Hubmaier argues, without it there is no true church, no true reform.[17]

For Hubmaier in particular, the ban was important because it was a response to what he perceived to be a general moral laxity on the part not only of the Roman Catholic Church of his day, but also throughout regions influenced by the Magisterial Reformers. This is perhaps a central reason why Hubmaier so strongly linked the reality of the church with the ban.[18] Hubmaier explicitly said that as necessary as reforms of baptismal and Eucharistic theology and practice were, in themselves they were not sufficient to reform the life of the church since discipline was required for true reform.[19] Their necessity, as Davis makes clear, is constituted by their purpose. They were

---

always a visible church, the living brotherhood-congregation which they regarded, at least in part, as the nucleus of God's kingdom on earth or its attempted realization." Robert Friedmann, *The Theology of Anabaptism: An Interpretation* (Scottdale, PA: Herald Press, 1973), 117.

15 Davis, "No Discipline," 43.

16 Christof Windhorst, "Balthasar Hubmaier: Professor, Preacher, Politician," in *Profiles of Radical Reformers: Biographical Sketches From Thomas Muntzer to Paracelsus*, ed. Hans-Jurgen Geortz, English edition ed. Walter Klaasen (Kitchener, Ontario: Herald Press, 1982), 151.

17 Davis, "No Discipline," 45.

18 Ibid., 47.

19 See for example, Hubmaier, "On Fraternal Admonition," 375: "Unless fraternal admonition is again restored, accepted, and used according to the earnest behest of Christ, it is not possible that things might proceed aright and stand well among Christians on earth. Even if we should all shout, write, and hear the gospel until we are hoarse and tired, still all our shouting, effort, and industry is in vain and useless. Yes, even water baptism and the breaking of bread are vain, pointless and fruitless, if fraternal admonition and the Christian ban do not accompany them, admonition belonging to baptism as the ban belongs to communion and fellowship." This is also one of the texts cited by Davis though from the German. Davis, "No Discipline," 47.

"only tools to the greater goal" which was the restoration of a holy church whose members faithfully followed the teachings of Christ.[20]

Clusters

With these observations in mind, that Hubmaier and Anabaptism were concerned for the establishment of a holy church set apart from the world, and that his theology has as its ultimate aim the instruction of such a church, I now turn to Hubmaier's Eucharistic theology. In what follows, I will first describe several important clusters of theological claims that Hubmaier makes with respect to the Lord's Supper. I say clusters, because in my judgment Hubmaier's theology of the Lord's Supper cannot be successfully 'systematized' in the sense that a clear, 'geometric' ordering can be discerned.[21] That the clusters cannot be so 'systematized' will occasion some

---

20 Davis, "No Discipline," 48.

21 The appellation 'geometric' is from Kevin Vanhoozer, who in turn is following Colin Gunton. In an essay on systematic theology, Vanhoozer says that "'strong' theological systems resemble geometrics and exposit Scripture with a comprehensive set of categories and a definite logic . . . . Typically, this means interpreting the meaning and truth of Scripture in terms of some comprehensive conceptual scheme." Thomas Aquinas is the given example. Vanhoozer, "Systematic Theology," in *Dictionary for Theological Interpretation Of the Bible*, 776; citing Gunton, "A Rose by Any Other Name? From 'Christian Doctrine' to 'Systematic Theology,'" *International Journal of Systematic Theology* 1 (March 1999): 4-23. A 'soft' systematic theology "requires only that one take responsibility for the overall consistency of one's beliefs." Vanhoozer, 776. Such an account presumes no necessary understanding of what constitutes coherence. In this broader sense there is a "systematicity" (Vanhoozer's word) to Hubmaier's theology insofar as there is a coherence, though as I will suggest the coherence is found in his analogous performance of language, rather than in principles extrinsic to those performances.

Another way to attempt to organize Hubmaier's theology in a 'systematic' fashion is to understand it primarily in terms of its development over time. For example, as I will outline below, Rempel thinks that Hubmaier's early Eucharistic theology follows roughly the traditional paradigm of associating bread with Christ's body in some way, but that Hubmaier makes a more or less clean break with this tradition in his later theology (see in particular John D. Rempel, *The Lord's Supper In Anabaptism: A Study in the Christology Of Balthasar Hubmaier, Pilgram Marpeck, and Dirk Philips* (Waterloo, Ontario: Herald Press, 1993), 49-57. Rempel thinks that the few remaining references to this paradigm in Hubmaier's later theology are a result of Hubmaier's lack of time before his martyrdom to critically reflect on his theology, with the result that some vestigial ways of speaking remain, but at odds with his overall theology. As I will suggest, another way of reading the same evidence is to suggest that rather than a more

overlap in my description of the clusters. For some inductive evidence of the inability to systematize Hubmaier's theology of the Lord's Supper, after describing these clusters of identity statements I turn to three prominent interpreters of Hubmaier on the Lord's Supper, each of whom attempt to interpret Hubmaier's Lord's Supper theology in just such a 'geometric' fashion. Yet, their interpretations are so divergent that one hardly recognizes them as interpretations of the very same theologian. I will then suggest that the mistake made is an inattention to analogous uses of language, and that attention to analogous uses of language allows us to order the conceptual clusters in an intelligible, if not linearly systematic way. The fruit of this investigation will be two-fold. First, it will help resolve a clear and deep lack of clarity in how to understand Hubmaier's theology of the Lord's Supper. Second, as before with Thomas, it will show the necessity of attending to analogous uses of language in Eucharistic identity statements.

The Mass is Not a Sacrifice

Early on and throughout his brief career as an evangelical reformer, Hubmaier rejects the Roman Catholic claim that the mass is a sacrifice. In one of his first public statements on the matter, his participation in the Second Zurich Disputation of 1523, Hubmaier says, "Concerning abuses in the mass—which I would rather call a testament of Christ or a memorial of his bitter suffering—without doubt this is the main point of the abuse, that we interpret the mass as a sacrifice."[22] If not a sacrifice, then as a testimony to Christ's suffering it is a "proclamation of the covenant of Christ," proclamation by means of a remembrance of the one "who offered himself once for all on the cross, and never more will again be offered."[23] If the mass is not a sacrifice, then Hubmaier says that the role of the priest is simply to preach nothing other than "the pure, true, clear word of God."[24] Hence, preaching and testimony replace sacrifice as the action of the Lord's Supper.

With one exception, the explicit rejection of the Lord's Supper as a sacrifice disappears after Hubmaier's earlier writings, but it is clear that this is because it was a point he deemed obvious enough to assume.[25] However, the

---

or less linear development, Hubmaier is continually testing and retesting in a kind of looping pattern the various ways (both 'traditional' and 'constructive') of speaking about Christ in the Supper.

22 Hubmaier, "Statements at the Second Zurich Disputation," 27.

23 Ibid.

24 Ibid.

25 The exception is in Hubmaier's "A Simple Instruction," 333. Hubmaier there rehearses the claim that since the Supper is a remembrance of Christ's suffering, it cannot be a sacrifice. His assertion that it is not a sacrifice is relevant there because in

Lord's Supper as testimony and proclamation continue. As a commemoration of Christ, the Supper proclaims Christ, and an implication is that it should be held in common languages.[26] The proclamation that occurs is not only when the preacher proclaims Christ, but the Supper itself is a proclamation. Proclamation occurs parallel with the notion of commemoration of Christ's suffering.[27] It also occurs with the notion of the obligation to serve one another.[28] The implication of both appears to be that the commemoration of Christ's suffering in the Supper is itself a proclamation; and that the living service of members of the church is a proclamation of Christ's serving us in his death and resurrection. Even so, as indicated above the preacher must proclaim the Lord's death. In his instructions for how to celebrate the Lord's Supper, Hubmaier gives suggestions for appropriate passages of Scripture to be used for instruction, and says "there must be diligence so that the death of the Lord is earnestly proclaimed" and by this proclamation the church will be instructed and prepared for Christian discipleship.[29]

The Lord's Supper is a Memorial Meal

The rejection of the mass as sacrifice, and also his articulation of it as testimony and proclamation, was linked by Hubmaier, as indicated in the citation from the Second Zurich Disputation above, with the notion of memorial. Rather than a sacrifice, which in Hubmaier's view would repeat all over again what was a unique, past event, the Supper was a "memorial of his bitter death."[30] That it is Christ's suffering that is memorialized is noted frequently by Hubmaier.[31] For Hubmaier, Christ's words, "Do this in remembrance of me" (Luke 22:19; 1 Cor. 11:24) are decisive—in the sharing of bread in the meal Christ's body, in particular its suffering, is remembered. That the Supper is a memorial provides the context for Hubmaier's claims that the bread and wine are memorial signs. Says Hubmaier, "Here everybody can see that bread is bread and wine is wine, like other bread and wine. But it is instituted by Christ as a reminder and memorial."[32] More will be said about bread and body below, but here the purpose is to note their role in this

---

this document he deals explicitly with the way in which Christ's body is related to the bread in the celebration.

26 Hubmaier, "Eighteen Theses Concerning the Christian Life," 33.

27 Ibid., "Several Theses Concerning the Mass," 74.

28 Ibid., 76.

29 Ibid., "A Form for Christ's Supper," 395.

30 Ibid., "Second Zurich," 27.

31 For example, see his "Several Theses" (1525), 74; "Summa" (1525); "A Christian Catechism" (1526), 355; and "Apologia from Prison" (1528), 557.

32 Ibid., "Summa," 87.

memorial meal. Whatever else is (or is not) claimed for the bread and wine, fundamentally they are memorials of Christ's suffering body.

The Lord's Supper is a Meal of Commitment to Sacrificial Service

A pervasive and consistent theme in Hubmaier's theology of the Lord's Supper is the commitment entailed by the Supper to serve, at times to the point of death, one's brothers and sisters in Christ. Hubmaier's earliest claims about the Lord's Supper emphasize that it is not a sacrifice, but a memorial of Christ's sacrifice; and yet, sacrifice nevertheless quickly becomes one of the central themes of his understanding of the Lord's Supper. The difference is that rather than Christ's sacrifice on the cross as the referent, it becomes the sacrifice of believers for one another. For Hubmaier, the commitment to sacrifice is a bond made in the Supper, and this bond is similar to the commitment one makes at baptism.

Hubmaier placed the bond made with God at the center of his baptismal theology, and as early as his "Letter to Oecolampad" (1525) he links the bond of baptism to the bond of the Lord's Supper: "In baptism there is made a bond with God . . . and a renunciation of Satan and all his pretentiousness . . . . The bond made in the Lord's Supper is like it, whereby I commit myself to lay down my body and blood for his sake, as Christ did for me."[33] The antecedent of "his sake" is ambiguous. The most immediate grammatical candidate is God himself. However, in the next sentence Hubmaier says, "And so we have the laws and the prophets."[34] This is presumably an allusion to Matthew 7:12: "So in everything, do to others what you would have them do to you, for this sums up the Law and the Prophets" (NIV). If this is so, then it appears Hubmaier means to say that the believer lays down her life for the sake of her neighbor. This suggestion is confirmed by a similar turn of phrase in his 1526 "Christian Catechism," again drawing a parallel between baptism and the Lord's Supper: "Indeed to state it bluntly, the Lord's Supper is a sign of the obligation to brotherly love just as water baptism is a symbol of the vow of faith. The water concerns God, the supper our neighbor; therein lie all the Law and Prophets."[35] So for Hubmaier, just as Christ laid down his life for my sake, so I should also lay down my life for the sake of my neighbor; and as Hubmaier will make clear, a commitment to lay down my life for God entails the commitment to lay down my life for fellow believers.

That such a commitment to God entails commitment to others is found in Hubmaier's 1525 document, "Several Theses On the Mass." There, Hubmaier

---

33 Hubmaier, "Letter to Oecolampad," 70.

34 Ibid., 70.

35 Ibid., "A Christian Catechism," 355.

links the theme of remembrance with the commitment of service to fellow believers by way of the symbol or sign of bread and wine:

> The Supper of Christ is a commemoration of his suffering and a proclamation of his death until he comes to us again. The breaking of his bread and the drinking of the wine in the Christ meal is an outward sign or symbol instituted by Christ before his death, which signifies to us how he offered his body for us and shed his blood *so that we also do the same for the sake of our neighbor.*[36]

Hubmaier clearly affirms that the sacrifice of Christ is a unique sacrifice which is for taking away the sins of believers.[37] At the same time, it is a sacrifice to be emulated by believers in that it shows the pattern of faithful discipleship—service to others even to the point of death. Consequently, the Lord's Supper as the memorial of Christ's suffering serves as the occasion of renewing the commitment to serve one another just as Christ served us.

Hubmaier repeats in various ways the claim that the Supper is a meal of obligation to serve fellow believers. One particularly striking articulation, to be considered further below, occurs at the end of his "Several Theses:"

> We conclude that the bread and wine of the Christ meal are outward word symbols of an inward Christian nature [*wesens*] here on earth, in which a Christian obligates himself to another in Christian love with regard to body and blood. Thus as the body and blood of Christ became my body and blood on the cross, so likewise shall my body and blood become the body and blood of my neighbor, and in time of need theirs become my body and blood, or we cannot boast at all to be Christians.[38]

That the commitment to service includes my very body and blood is repeated in his "Summa of the Christian Life" (also 1525):

> The person who practices the Supper of Christ in that way [as a memorial meal] and contemplates the suffering of Christ in a firm faith will also give thanks to God for this grace and goodness. He will surrender himself to the will of Christ, which then is that we also should do to our neighbor as he has done to us and give our body, life, property and blood for his sake.[39]

In 1526, Hubmaier makes clear that this obligation to service is a public obligation, that in the celebration of the Supper the commitment to service is made corporately and visibly before the congregation:

---

36 Hubmaier, "Several Theses," 74. Emphasis added.

37 Ibid., "Summa," 87.

38 Ibid., "Several Theses," 76.

39 Ibid., "Summa," 88.

> Likewise, in love, in which he obligates himself now, and with this breaking of the bread and drinking of the cup publicly before the church commits himself and promises that for the sake of his neighbor he is also willing to let his flesh and blood be broken and sacrificed, with which he has now become one bread and one drink.[40]

Of course, the commitment is *always* to be public in the sense that Hubmaier presses for a church of disciples; there is no such thing as a merely 'inward' or 'spiritual' Christian. Here, however, the emphasis is on the commitment itself that makes possible such a faithful life. Hubmaier's point seems to be that the making and renewing of the commitment itself is likewise never merely 'spiritual' and 'inward' (though it is inward in the sense of a personal commitment to such service), but is corporate and visible.

In Hubmaier's instructions for how to celebrate the Lord's Supper (1527), the obligation to serve fellow believers is prominent. Early in the service, roughly at the point where the traditional mass would have the public confession of sin, Hubmaier has a time of "examination" in which the believer affirms belief in Christ's sacrifice for sin. On the basis of Christ's sacrifice, the believer likewise affirms that "he be of an attitude and ready will to do for Christ his God and Lord in turn as he had done for him."[41] But, says Hubmaier, Christ does not need anything we can give since "heaven and earth are his and all that is in them," and consequently "he points us toward our neighbor, first of all to the members of the household of faith . . . that we might fulfill the works of this our gratitude toward them physically [*leiblich*] and spiritually, feeding the hungry, giving drink to the thirsty, clothing the naked, consoling the prisoner, sheltering the needy."[42] He emphasizes again the public nature of the commitment:

> So that the church might also be fully aware of a person's attitude and will, one holds fellowship with her in the breaking of bread, thereby saying, testifying, and publically assuring her, yea making to her a sacrament or sworn pledge, and giving one's hand on the commitment that one is willing henceforth to offer one's body and to shed one's blood thus for one's fellow believers.[43]

In the order of service, just before the "bishop" blesses and distributes the bread, the congregation corporately vows to fulfill the obligation to serve one another that each believer is making in the celebration of the Supper.

---

[40] Hubmaier, "A Simple instruction," 333-334.

[41] Ibid., "Form," 397.

[42] Ibid. Hubmaier is referencing Matthew 25 (in-line in Yoder's and Pipken's translation; in the margin in the German text).

[43] Ibid., 397-398.

The theme of obligation is repeated yet again in Hubmaier's "Apologia from Prison" at the end of his life. Hubmaier wrote his Apologia while in prison under the authority of King Ferdinand. In articulating to his Catholic opponents his views, Hubmaier summarizes his views on the Lord's Supper: "I have taught that it is a testimony of brotherly love, that as Christ loved us unto death so we should also love one another and each perform toward one another the works of mercy, concerning which Christ will demand an account on the judgment day, Matt. 25:40."[44] Throughout the document, while never recanting or misleading his opponents about his views, he nevertheless emphasizes the elements of his theology that would be more in line with Catholic theology.[45] So it is not surprising that Hubmaier leaves out his rejection of the Lord's Supper as sacrifice, and his emphasis on the bread and wine as memorial symbols. Still, that he condenses his teaching on the Lord's Supper to essentially an obligation to brotherly love is indicative of the centrality of the concept to his theology of the Lord's Supper.

Communion with Christ and Others.

There is a natural link between the obligation to serve one another and the fellowship or communion that both accompanies the life of service to one another, and is one of its preconditions. Hubmaier more than once links communion or fellowship with the service that the Lord's Supper demands of believers. Early on in particular, the communion that we share with one another is explicitly a result of the communion of Christ with us. Hubmaier says that the Spirit that "makes us alive" accompanies the Word and brings assurance.[46] Though the thought process is unclear, this Spirit-brought assurance is linked with the bread and wine as symbols of Christ's body and blood

---

44 Hubmaier, "Apologia From Prison," 557.

45 Pipken and Yoder in their editorial introduction to "Apologia" cite Sachsee's work of carefully documenting everything said in "Apologia" with Hubmaier's previous work, so that "everything he says here echoes earlier writings." Pipken and Yoder, 535; see Carl Sachsse, *D. Balthasar Hubmaier Als Theologe* (Berlin: Trowitzsch & Sohn, 1914), 231-271. In his authoritative biography of Hubmaier, Torsten Bergsten agrees with this assessment. Torsten Bergsten, *Balthasar Hubmaier: Anabaptist Theologian and Martyr*, trans. Irwin J. Barnes and William R. Estep, ed. William R. Estep (Valley Forge: Judson Press, 1978), 379-380. Earlier in his career, while imprisoned in Zurich under the authority of the city council with the clear blessing of Zwingli, Hubmaier did recant his views under torture, though when released he left the city and continued his reformation. He later regretted his weakness in recanting. See Bergsten, 300-311 for an account.

46 Hubmaier, "Several Theses," 75.

> by which we remember how he, Christ, was our Christ, and how we also are always to be Christ to one another. We all are one bread and one body—we all, who have fellowship in one bread and in one drink. As one little kernel does not keep its own flour, but shares it with the others, and a single grape does not keep its juice for itself, but shares it with the others, so should we Christians also act—or we eat and drink unworthily from the table of Christ.[47]

Consequently, "As we now have communion with one another in this bread and drink of the Christ meal, so also should the body and blood of all of us be shared with each other, just as the body and blood of Christ is shared with us all."[48] Hence, the sacrifice of Christ serves as the basis of our communion with Christ; our communion with Christ is the basis for our communion with one another; and our communion with one another is the occasion of the bond of mutual service to one another. The Lord's Supper is the sign of this service-fellowship as well as an occasion for it.

In Hubmaier's later theology, explicit references to communion with Christ disappear almost entirely from his theology of the Lord's Supper and are replaced by the fellowship of believers with one another. In his 1527 document, "On the Christian Ban," Hubmaier makes a passing reference to the presence of Christ in the context of the bread and wine of the Supper. However, here Christ's presence is intended as a rebuke of the claim that Christ is somehow 'specially' present in the Lord's Supper: "For he is with [the church] by his grace until the end of the world . . . although bodily [*leiblich*] he has ascended into heaven where he sits at the right hand of his heavenly father."[49] Here, grace is clearly intended as an alternative to body: Christ is bodily in heaven, and hence there is no communion in the Lord's Supper with him other than the communion we have with Christ generally based on his finished work on the cross. Of course, this is no 'mere' communion any more than the work of the cross is 'mere' work. It is nevertheless the case that there is no 'special' communion with Christ in the Lord's Supper.

Having said that, Hubmaier retains the notion of communion with Christ. However, it is communion with Christ in and through communion with one another. That is, our participation in and communion with one another *is* communion with Christ.[50] This notion is already implicitly present in the

---

47 Hubmaier, "Several Theses," 75.

48 Ibid., 75.

49 Ibid., "On the Christian Ban," 413-414.

50 The language of participation is suggested by Dyck with respect to an Anabaptist understanding of suffering, service to one another, and the suffering of Jesus. He says, "Although [in the martyr literature suffering] is often referred to as *imitation*, there is also present a deeper strand which might best be called *participation*, for the

"Several Theses" (1525), in a section cited above. Hubmaier says that the bread and wine remind us "how he, Christ, was our Christ, and how we also are always to be Christ to one another. We all are one bread and one body—we all who have fellowship in one bread and in one drink."[51] We have fellowship with one another; and we are to be Christ to one another. Hubmaier goes on to confirm this understanding when he says that "the bread which we break means and commemorates the communion of the body of Christ with us." In his "Form for the Lord's Supper," in a passage already cited, Hubmaier says that what we owe to Christ we are to do to one another since Christ in heaven does not need anything. The result is that "it is certain and sure that all the good that we do to the very least of his, that we do to Christ himself."[52] Hence, fellowship with one another is fellowship with Christ.

Elsewhere Hubmaier affirms that the church is the body of Christ. He says in his "Form for the Lord's Supper" that "all have become one loaf and one body [*leib*], and our Head is Christ;"[53] and again, "the church is the body [*leib*] of Christ. Christ is the head and we are the members of the body of Christ, 1 Cor. 12; Eph 2; 4; Col. 1; 3."[54] In both cases, Hubmaier draws no conclusions with respect to communion with Christ in the Lord's Supper, and yet in conjunction with the above affirmations, these claims about the church are significant. It appears that Hubmaier means to say that if Christ's physical body is absent from the Lord's Supper, nevertheless his body is present in the church, and hence fellowship with and in the church is fellowship with Christ. Recalling that Hubmaier has previously linked service to one another with fellowship with one another, there again is the implication that in serving one

---

mood is not one of legalistic obedience but of an eager entering into the very suffering of Christ himself." Dyck, 14. J. Denny Weaver connects this with Hubmaier's account of the Lord's Supper, such that "Hubmaier thus envisions the Lord's Supper as an enactment of each believing individual's participation in the body of Christ." J. Denny Weaver, "Discipleship Redefined: Four Sixteenth Century Anabaptists," *Mennonite Quarterly Review* 54 (October 1980): 273.

51 Hubmaier, "Several Theses," 74.

52 Ibid., "Form," 397.

53 Ibid., 405.

54 Ibid., "Apologia From Prison," 546. Hubmaier's language here is of course drawn from Scripture. Erland Waltner notes that for the Anabaptists, the notion of the church as the body of Christ was no 'mere' metaphor, rather "the church in its vertical relationship is the body of Christ of which He is the real and living Head." Waltner, 8. Waltner quotes Menno Simons (Dutch Anabaptist leader, whose conversion to the evangelical Reformation occurred shortly after Hubmaier's death). Menno Simons's articulation, drawn from the analogy of marriage, is overtly 'physical': "For all who are in Christ are new creatures, flesh of his flesh, bone of his bone, and member of his body." Waltner, 8, citing from the 1871 edition of Simons' Complete Works, 1:161-162.

another we are serving Christ, and hence in fellowship with Christ. So, it appears that at least one reason that explicit references to communion with Christ drop out of his theology of the Lord's Supper is that for Hubmaier communion with the church *is* communion with Christ.

Bread is and is not Christ's Body

There is much to be said here about bread and body, so much so that at this point I want only to introduce two important themes related to the identity of the bread and wine, themes that will then be further explicated in the following sections. These themes have been introduced already in the above sections, though they are worth making explicit here in order to help orient the following discussion. In his 1525 "Several Theses on the Mass," Hubmaier succinctly articulates the themes together. Though expressed with variation over the course of the next two to three years before his death, this early statement captures well the pervasive themes: given that the Supper is a memorial, Hubmaier says that the "breaking of his bread and the drinking of the wine in the Christ meal is an outward sign or symbol instituted by Christ before his death, *which signifies to us how he offered his body for us and shed his blood so that we also do the same for the sake of our neighbor*."[55] That is, the bread in the Lord's Supper has here a double referent: 1) Christ's broken body; and 2) our bodies in service to fellow believers.

At times in his theology of the Lord's Supper Hubmaier will emphasize one side or the other, but the two are never entirely separated. Earlier in his career, in attempting to articulate an account of the bread and body in opposition to the popular Roman Catholic view, Hubmaier emphasizes that the way in which the bread symbolizes Christ's body is as memorial emblem, that the bread is *not* Christ's body but a reminder of it. Later, when articulating the identity of the bread outside of the immediate issue of received Roman Catholic theology, Hubmaier will emphasize how the bread is the sign of the church, those who continue the pattern found in Christ of sacrificial service.

However, those two claims—that bread symbolizes Christ's body and that bread symbolizes the church—are never sundered from one another. Later in his career he articulates them together. In his "Form for the Celebration of the Lord's Supper" in 1527, he says,

> How much someone cares about the flesh and blood, that is about the suffering and death of Christ Jesus, about the shedding of his crimson blood, about the forgiveness of sins, about brotherly love and communion in God the Father, Son, and the Holy Ghost, yea the communion of the whole heavenly host and the universal Christian church outside of which there is no salvation, just this much he should care about the bread and

---

55 Hubmaier, "Several Theses," 74.

> wine of God's table. Not that here bread and wine are anything other than bread and wine; but according to the memorial and the significant mysteries for the sake of which Christ thus instituted it.[56]

Bread, in other words, bears not only the sign of Christ's body, but the sign of the whole church. In his Apologia of 1528, he makes a similar point. Referencing what he has taught about the commitment to service made in the Lord's Supper, he says "This witness of love occurs through the breaking of the bread, which is eaten in memory of Christ's suffering which he endured for us out of love, for the remission of our sins."[57] Again, the bread bears both the identity of Christ's body and the obligation of love. Here, Hubmaier succinctly states a conceptual link between the two that appears elsewhere, though not always explicitly: The way in which the bread refers both to Christ's body and the church is in the way in which the breaking of the bread as a reminder of Christ serves as the occasion of the church's commitment of love. In other words, the bread in memory is something like the 'idiom' in which one makes the commitment to serve fellow believers.

As indicated above, there is an especially dense cluster of identity claims contained in Hubmaier's articulation of the bread and wine, and so to that I now turn. Noting the conceptual clusters, rather than attempting to synthesize all that Hubmaier says, it would be better to attend to Hubmaier's most sustained defense of his views, that found in his "A Simple Instruction" of 1526. So, first I offer an explication of that. "A Simple Instruction" is not Hubmaier's final word on the matter, but it is his most sustained attention to the identity of bread, wine, body and blood. Then, I will gather up some of the other relevant claims about bread and body from Hubmaier's other writings, particularly those addressing the central issues of "A Simple Instruction," in order to assemble the central identity claims. Following that, I will offer three contemporary accounts of how best to understand Hubmaier's theology of the Lord's Supper, and the identities of bread, body, and church.

A Simple Instruction (1526).

"A Simple Instruction" is one of three works Hubmaier wrote devoted to the Lord's Supper. The other two are "Several Theses on the Mass" (1525), and his "Form for the Lord's Supper" (1527). Both of these will be further consulted in the next section. However, while important in their own right neither contains anywhere near the density of identity claims found in "A Simple Instruction," and so for clarity it will be better to note the relevant identity claims below rather than devote attention to each individually.

---

56 Hubmaier, "Form," 399.

57 Ibid., "Apologia From Prison," 557.

As Pipkin and Yoder note, Hubmaier's "Simple Instruction" appeared at a time of heightened interest in the Lord's Supper for the Reformers. Hubmaier's work appeared in two editions, which Yoder and Pipkin surmise suggests it received relatively widespread attention, at least in Moravia. Hubmaier at this point was "at the height of his influence as an Anabaptist."[58] Hubmaier begins by listing fifteen various ways of understanding the Lord's Supper, all drawn from the Roman Catholic theological tradition. Hubmaier's reason for listing them is explicitly to note that in "ancient times there has always been great disunity on the sacrament (as they call it) of the altar."[59] So, the unstated implication is that it should not be surprising that there is disunity in Hubmaier's day, which is an occasion for renewed debate and study rather than anger or offense.[60] Hubmaier's "Simple Instruction" is intended as a study and argument for how to understand Christ's words, "this is my body."

Early in his writings, Hubmaier articulated a view that was essentially the same as Karlstadt's.[61] Karlstadt held that when Jesus uttered those words, Jesus was basically pointing to himself rather than bread. Likewise, Hubmaier wrote: "When Christ commands, 'Take, eat, this is my body given for you,' he means his mortal body, for he himself suffered for us, and not the bread on the table which he gave them to eat."[62] However, in the "Simple Instruction" Hubmaier abandons this approach, and instead he focuses on how to understand the use of 'is.' He rejects Zwingli's view that *est* should be understood as *significat*, on the grounds that not only does it simply not stand exegetically, but "if this is the practice then no one would be certain as to where *est*/is/ stands in the Scripture for *significat*/signifies or for itself."[63] In contrast, Hubmaier argues that 'is' ought to be "taken [as] in the Old Testament for *is*, Genesis 1:3: 'God said let there be light and there was light.' Likewise in the New Testament: 'And the word became flesh [John 1:14]."[64] In light of Paul and Luke's longer account of Jesus words, 'is' must be understood in light of the memorial aspect of the Supper, that Jesus is by those words instituting a memorial meal. So, if the Supper is a memorial, and 'is' is to be taken in its straightforward sense, Hubmaier argues:

> From all these words follows the final conclusion that the bread offered, broken, taken, and eaten is the body of Christ in remembrance. Thus also the cup taken, distributed, and drunk is the blood of Christ in

58 Pipken and Yoder, 314.

59 Hubmaier, "A Simple Instruction," 319.

60 Ibid., 320-321.

61 Bergsten, 193-194.

62 Hubmaier, "Several Theses," 75.

63 Ibid., "A Simple Instruction," 321.

64 Ibid., 322.

> remembrance . . . . In the power of this saying everyone must confess and say that this baked bread is the body of Christ who was crucified for us. Now, however, bread in itself is not the body, for this bread was not crucified and did not die for us, so the bread must be the body of Christ in remembrance, so that all the words of Christ can remain in their plain and simple sense . . . . For these words, "in my memory" testify in the entire previous saying that the breaking, distribution, and eating of the bread is not a breaking, distribution, and eating of the body of Christ, who is sitting at the right hand of God the Father in the heavens, but all that is a remembrance of his being broken and distributed in suffering.[65]

This formulation, "the body of Christ in remembrance" serves as the catch phrase for the entire work; and, in fact, the rest of the document is basically working out the limits of the notion, as well as its implications.

In particular, Hubmaier more than once explicitly notes that the remembrance that governs the identity of bread as body is dynamic and is a character of the celebration itself. For example, he says "what is more understandable than to say, 'The bread is the body of Christ in active, practiced, or held memory,' so that justice is done to the little word *facite* or 'do';"[66] and later, "'This is my body.' Understand, it is not in itself that the bread-eating is the body of Christ really [*wesenlich*], but only in the celebrated remembrance;"[67] and finally, a few sentences later, "As the bread is the body of Christ in enacted remembrance, so also is the drink the blood of Christ in the enacted remembrance."[68] These various ways of articulating the identity of bread as body show that the remembrance is a character of the celebration of the meal itself, rather than a 'mental' activity of the individual recipients.

If the bread is Christ's body in remembrance, than for Hubmaier several things follow, things which, on Hubmaier's view, happily cohere with the rest of Scripture. One implication is that "nothing is taken into the hands, broken, distributed, and eaten except the bread. If now the bread is the body of Christ, then Christ must be touched with the hands, grasped, broken, divided, and eaten with the teeth."[69] If the bread is chewed and not Christ, then the inverse holds: it was Christ who was crucified for us and not the bread.[70] Furthermore, Hubmaier thinks that understanding the bread as Christ's body in remembrance makes the right sense of the ascension and future return of Christ: "Now follow the Scriptures, according to which Christ does not bodily come to us until the

---

65 Hubmaier, "A Simple Instruction," 324.

66 Ibid., 325.

67 Ibid., 330.

68 Ibid.

69 Ibid., 325.

70 Hubmaier, "A Simple Instruction," 331.

hour of the last judgment, and then we will see him as he ascended;"[71] and similarly, "'Until he comes': it follows that he is not present;"[72] and finally, that he is not present is the reason for the meal as memorial, "for where a person is essentially [*wesenlich*] and bodily [*leiblich*] present, there a remembrance is not necessary."[73] So, Hubmaier summarizes, "All of these [texts of Scripture] together and thoroughly testify that Christ Jesus ascended into heaven, sits at the right hand of God his heavenly Father, and also will not come from there until the time of the last day when he will come to judge the living and the dead."[74]

Hubmaier was a trained scholar (one of the very few in the early Anabaptist movement) and explicitly references Thomas's account of transubstantiation.[75] Consequently, he would have known that, at least as Thomas understood it, transubstantiation can likewise account for Christ's *bodily* ascension. Yet, it was more than Reformation polemics that led him to such statements. He cites just before Thomas the confession that Berengar was forced to sign:

> You say: "Yes, Christ is not broken and eaten and also not the bread, but the form [*gestalten*] of the bread under which the body of Christ is hidden." Answer: Pope Nicholas forced Berengarius to speak otherwise. *De Consec.* di. II c. *Ego* . . . . However, I leave such a speech to be an Anaxagorean but not a theological issue.[76]

It would appear, then, that Hubmaier is reflecting something of the popular German Roman Catholic piety of his day through the lens of medieval Eucharistic battles over the 'physicalism' of Christ's body. In any case,

---

71 Ibid., 329.

72 Ibid., 333.

73 Ibid.

74 Ibid., 336.

75 Ibid., 326-327: "Therewith the word and meaning of Christ is ripped apart and violated, since he says of the bread 'This is my body,' and does not say, 'Under the form [*gestalt*] of the bread is my body,' as the dream and Thomistic addition of these miserable people states. . . . For according to such expositions created out of their own brain, the little word *hoc*, 'this' does not point to the bread which has already gone away and has disappeared according to their speech, but only to the form of the bread." In an editorial footnote on the same page, Pipken and Yoder say, "Hubmaier is referring to the view of Thomas Aquinas, whereby the substance of the bread has been transformed (transubstantiated) into the body of Christ, but the form (accidents) of the bread remain as bread."

76 Hubmaier, "A Simple Instruction," 325. Yoder and Pipkin note that Anaxagoras "was a favorite name used by Reformers to refer to Scholastics," 112, footnote 20.

Hubmaier clearly thought that his view was better able to handle the real *physical* absence of Christ from the world.

Of course, up to this point nothing has been made of a theme that I claimed earlier was prevalent in Hubmaier's understanding of the Supper, namely the bond or commitment believers made to one another in the Supper. While "A Simple Instruction" is devoted to understanding the relationship of the bread to Christ's body, Hubmaier does turn to the commitment when dealing with 1 Cor. 11:23. There, he says that when Paul warns against eating of the Supper unworthily, Paul is instructing the believer to have "a real internal and intensive hunger and thirst for this bread and drink," as it is the sign of Christ's sacrifice for him; and as the sign of his sacrifice for him, it follows that "in love, in which he [the believer] obligates himself now, and with this breaking of the bread and drinking of the cup publicly before the church commits himself and promises that for the sake of his neighbor he is also willing to let his flesh [*fleisch*] and blood be broken and sacrificed, with which he has now become one bread and one drink."[77] So, while the identification of the Supper as a meal of obligation is minimized in "A Simple Instruction," it is present. This, I will suggest later, is important to keep in mind for it suggests that for Hubmaier there is no intrinsic competition between Christ's body and the commitment of the congregation.

Further Articulations of Bread and Body

As noted, "A Simple Instruction" is not the last word on the identity of the bread. However, what Hubmaier says there, while said differently and with different emphases, is nevertheless representative of the general trajectory of his articulation of the identity. So, in light of what he says in "A Simple Instruction," we can gather up some of his other scattered claims and their implications.

First, Hubmaier says a number of times that bread is bread, not body. In his 1525 "Summa of the Christian Life," in reflection on Luke's and Paul's "Do this is in remembrance of me," Hubmaier says: "Here everybody can see that bread is bread and wine is wine, like other bread and wine. But it is instituted by Christ as a reminder and memorial."[78] In breaking and distributing the bread, the church remembers "his body broken for us on the cross and distributed to all those who eat and enjoy it in faith."[79] In his "Christian Catechism" (1526), Hubmaier repeats a common assertion, that "the bread and wine are nothing but memorial symbols of Christ's suffering and death for the

---

77 Hubmaier, "A Simple Instruction," 334.

78 Hubmaier, " Summa," 87.

79 Ibid.

forgiveness of our sins."[80] In his "Form for the Lord's Supper" (1527), in an explanation of the meal as memorial and occasion for obligation, Hubmaier says, "Not that here bread and wine are anything other than bread and wine; but according to the memorial and the significant mysteries for the sake of which Christ thus instituted it;"[81] and later, Hubmaier instructs the "priest [to] point out clearly and expressly that the bread is bread and the wine wine and not flesh and blood, as has long been believed."[82] In Hubmaier's *On the Sword*, a treatise dedicated to the issue of coercion in government and religion, Hubmaier uses the Lord's Supper to illustrate how to interpret Scripture. He says:

> When Christ says, "This is my body," that is a half-truth . . . . However, if he says, "This is my body which is given for you, do this in my memory," that is now a whole truth. Whoever now judges on the basis of the half-truth says that the bread is the body of Christ, and errs. However, whoever judges on the basis of the whole truth says that the bread is the body of Christ given for you. He is not bodily [*leiblich*] or essentially [*wesenlich*] in it himself, but is in the held memory in the power of the institution of Christ which took place at the Last Supper.[83]

Hubmaier's point is clear enough: the identity of bread as body is an identity in terms of memory. In light of "A Simple Instruction," the bread *is* the body of Christ, but it is the body of Christ *in memory*, and for Hubmaier this means that bread is bread essentially [*wesenlich*], and body in memory.

Like "A Simple Instruction," several things follow from the fact that bread is Christ's body in memory rather than in essence. For example, if Christ is not essentially in bread and wine, then Christ is not subject to various bodily forces on earth. Christ is not, despite what the "mass priests" might say, sacrificed on the altar since Christ is not there bodily, but rather in memory.[84] Christ is not subject to the teeth of the faithful or the hands of the priest: "Yea, Christ, as far as [the mass priests] are concerned they raise you in the air, they make three pieces out of you, they drown you in wine, and finally crunch you with their teeth."[85] But of course, none of this actually happens to Christ since, as even the priests know, "you are not there, but sit at the right hand of your heavenly father."[86] Hubmaier's logic is clear: if Christ's body is not physically or essentially in bread and wine, then none of what happened to Christ's body

---

80 Ibid., "Catechism," 354-355.

81 Ibid., "Form," 399

82 Ibid., "Form," 403.

83 Ibid., "On the Sword," 514.

84 Ibid., "A Brief Apologia," 303.

85 Hubmaier, "A Brief Apologia," 303.

86 Ibid.

happens to the bread, and none of what happens to the bread happens to Christ's body.

As the last citation indicates, for Hubmaier a reason for denying the presence of Christ's body in the bread is the fact that Christ has ascended and is no longer bodily on earth. Hubmaier says in commenting on 1 Cor. 11, "Notice he [Paul] says 'until he comes.' From this we hear that he is not present but will come only at the hour of the last judgment, in his great majesty and glory and shining visibly to everybody as the lightning from east to west."[87] Because of the ascension, Hubmaier says in prayer form, "It is therefore needless, my meek Christ, to worship thee either here or there, yea neither in bread nor in wine, for thou art to be found sitting at the right hand of thy heavenly Father, just as also the holy Stephen saw and worshiped thee."[88] If not worshiped in the bread, then "I worship Christ seated at the right hand of his heavenly father . . . . Then we shall see him descended as he ascended; for this we wait and will not seek him in bread or wine."[89] Because of the ascension the eating is not a physical eating: "For the same ascended into heaven and is sitting at the right hand of God his Father . . . . Thus Christ cannot be eaten or drunk by us otherwise than spiritually and in faith."[90] For Hubmaier, the ascension serves an important purpose. It indicates that any reference to Christ's body in the Supper must be Christ's body in memory. If Christ were bodily present, then no remembrance would be necessary. But since the Supper has been given in memory, he must be bodily absent, and the ascension is a confirmation of this.

If Christ is absent, then it is the church that carries on the work of Christ. The power of the keys (the power of inclusion in, and exclusion from the church) is exercised by the church in the absence of Jesus.[91] So, for example, Hubmaier says that the authority that we exercise was exercised by Christ "as he walked among us bodily."[92] But, because of the ascension, he "no longer [remains] bodily with us on earth," and has as a result of his bodily absence given the church the power of the keys.[93] Consequently, "Whoever now says that Christ is bodily present in the bread and wine . . . is not saying the whole

---

87 Ibid., "Summa," 88.

88 Ibid., "The Twelve Articles in Prayer Form," 237.

89 Ibid., "Catechism," 355.

90 Ibid., "Form," 407.

91 For an overview of Hubmaier's understanding of the keys, and his exegesis of key biblical texts, see Carl M. Leth, "Balthasar Hubmaier's 'Catholic' Exegesis: Matthew 16:18-19 and the Power of the Keys," in *Biblical Interpretation In the Era of the Reformation: Essays Presented to David C. Steinmetz In Honor of His Sixtieth Birthday*, ed. Richard A. Muller and John L. Thompson (Grand Rapids: Eerdmans, 1996): 103-117.

92 Hubmaier, "Ban," 411.

93 Ibid.

truth."[94] This matters, because on Hubmaier's account the claim that Christ is bodily present in the bread and wine "unbuckles the keys from the side of the Christian church, which Christ with serious words attached to her side and gave her and commended to her until he come again [citing 1 Cor. 11]."[95] Since the church exercises these powers, as commanded by the New Testament, Christ cannot be bodily in the bread and wine; and, as before, this is confirmed by the ascension of Jesus to heaven.

The church exercises the power of the keys on Christ's behalf. That the church does so is indicative of how Christ remains present to the world during his bodily absence. In a treatise on baptism, Hubmaier argues that the charge for the disciples to preach and to baptize is a clue not only to the nature of discipleship, but also the present bodily absence of Jesus. Hubmaier says, "In the same way now after the resurrection they have themselves received the same office: namely, to announce the pardon of sins through Christ, who now was present no longer bodily, but henceforth in his Word and through his disciples, in which way he wants to remain among us until the end of the world."[96] The Father sent the Son to preach repentance, and Jesus instructed his disciples to do the same: "Likewise his disciples should now represent him henceforth during the time of his bodily absence and guarantee to all believers a sure and certain remission of their sin through him."[97] Hence, the disciples have been given by Jesus authority to preach and to discipline the church, and in so representing him continue the 'bodily' consequences of Jesus's life, even though bodily Jesus has ascended.

We saw above that for Hubmaier the Lord's Supper has a twin focus, namely a remembrance of Jesus's suffering and the commitment of his followers to serve one another. So, it is not surprising to find Hubmaier linking the church to Christ's body, as Paul of course does. Hubmaier says that in the meal when the church eats and drinks the bread and wine in the memory of Christ, Christians have fellowship with one another, and hence "have become one loaf and one body, and our Head is Christ."[98] Elsewhere, he says, "We all are one bread and one body—we all, who have fellowship in one bread and in one drink."[99] I noted above a particularly striking version of Hubmaier's identity claim for the disciples, and it is worth reconsidering here: "We conclude that the bread and wine of the Christ meal are outward word symbols of an inward Christian nature [*wesens*] here on earth . . . . Thus as the body and blood of Christ became my very body and blood on the cross, so likewise shall

---

94 Ibid., 413.

95 Ibid.

96 Ibid., "On the Christian Baptism of Believers," 104.

97 Ibid., 116.

98 Hubmaier, "Form," 405.

99 Ibid., "Several Theses," 75.

my body and blood become the body and blood of my neighbor, and in time of need theirs become my body and blood, or we cannot boast at all to be Christians."[100] Here, it appears that Hubmaier intends nature [*wesens*] to clearly limit the presence of Christ's body: the nature that is present is an "inward Christian" one indicative of the disciples. Even so, it occasions identity between Jesus's body and my body in his sacrifice, and consequently my body and my neighbor's body. Hence, we must consider below not only Jesus's historical body, but again the church as Christ's body.

Ways of Understanding Hubmaier

Now, I will consider three contemporary interpreters of Hubmaier's understanding of the Lord's Supper. Two things will quickly become evident. First, all three interpreters wrestle with what to make of Hubmaier's identity claims relative to the bread and body. Bread is bread not body; but bread is the body of Christ in remembrance; Christ is our body on the cross; we are the body of Christ; we become one another's bodies. Second, they come to strikingly different conclusions about just what these identity statements mean. This lack of consensus runs the gamut from more or less subjective remembering experience to an ontological physicalism. Why the striking variation? No doubt it is largely due to Hubmaier's own writing style. As noted, he was frequently writing in and to hostile contexts. Though he never reversed himself on a substantive issue, neither did he straightforwardly and linearly develop his thinking. His mind was constantly searching and testing, and this led, if not to contradiction, at least tension and a lack of 'geometric' consistency. Furthermore, his creative mind was pushing past even the creative insights of his contemporary Reformers.

All three interpreters agree with Bergsten, who said that "to the observance of the Lord's Supper, Hubmaier gave a distinctive shape according to his own particular insights."[101] However, as I will suggest below, the various

---

[100] Ibid., 76.

[101] Bergsten, 241. Mabry says Hubmaier "produced a doctrine of the Lord's Supper which was neither medieval nor typically sixteenth century, but was essentially his own." Eddie Mabry, *Balthasar Hubmaier's Doctrine of the Church* (Lanham: University Press of America, 1994), 177. In this, the three interpreters consulted here agree. MacGregor claims that Hubmaier produced "a radically new conception of the Eucharist." Kirk R. MacGregor, *A Central European Synthesis Of Radical and Magisterial Reform: The Sacramental Theology of Balthasar Hubmaier* (Lanham: University Press of America, 2006), 217; and Rempel says that Hubmaier "completely broke with the conventional eucharistic scheme as it had been formulated since the time of Augustine." Rempel, *Lord's Supper*, 52. According to Rempel, the way in which

interpretations are a result of a failure to attend to analogous uses of language in Hubmaier's theology of the Lord's Supper. For my purposes these three interpreters are helpful, then, because their various ways of reading Hubmaier will aid teasing out the contours of Hubmaier's analogous uses of terms, and his general failure to explicitly reflect on those analogous uses. Noting this failure will suggest once again why attention to analogous uses of language is important for a theology of the Lord's Supper.

Eddie Mabry

Eddie Mabry's understanding of Hubmaier's theology of the Lord's Supper emphasizes the remembering done by the community in the celebration. As Hubmaier himself makes clear, if the Supper is a memorial occasioned by Christ's ascension, then Christ's "actual body" cannot be present.[102] Hence, Hubmaier's remarks about the identity of the bread and wine are fundamentally arguments against transubstantiation.[103] As a memorial, the action of the Supper was focused almost exclusively on the act of remembering by the congregation. Says Mabry,

> the Supper stood in memory of the suffering and death of Christ on the cross, and, through the observance of the Supper, the participant recalled from memory the passion of Christ. The faithful were to go back in remembrance and participate with Christ on Calvary in His suffering. Through memory, one vividly experienced the suffering of Christ, and was reminded of the obligation to live a saintly life, and of the covenant that he or she had with God and with each other.[104]

Note that both prominent themes identified above in Hubmaier's theology—bread and wine as signs of Christ's suffering, and bread and wine as signs of the commitment of the community to mutual sacrificial service—are understood by Mabry to be 'mediated' by memory. That is, the Supper signifies just to the degree that the believers remember. Christ is in no way present; rather, he is remembered in his bodily absence. In the Supper no actual commitment is made or renewed; rather, the commitment made at baptism is remembered.

Mabry contends that for Hubmaier, this notion of memory nevertheless includes a "real presence."[105] Mabry says that "For Hubmaier, as for the

---

Hubmaier broke from the conventional scheme was that for Hubmaier, "the role of a sacrament as a bridge between the human and the divine has been rejected," 56.

102 Mabry, *Doctrine*, 169.

103 Ibid.

104 Ibid., 166-167.

105 Mabry, *Doctrine*, 172.

Anabaptists, the Supper was not a matter of Christ's presence with the believer at the celebration of the Supper, either by being bodily eaten or symbolically there; but rather, the believer went back in memory to be with Christ in His suffering on Calvary."[106] Elsewhere, Mabry contends that for Hubmaier

> memorial means more than just recalling by memory the passion of Christ. In Hubmaier's theology of memorial the person who receives the Lord's Supper also goes back in memory and participates with Christ in His suffering on Calvary. The participant in the Supper is actually there, suffering with Christ, instead of Christ coming to be present with the recipient at the Supper. In this way one not only vividly experiences the suffering of Christ, but he or she is also reminded of the covenant that was made with Christ and with the members of the community.[107]

So for Mabry, real presence is the presence of the disciple through the medium of memory to Christ's suffering.

The cluster of identity claims in Hubmaier are organized by Mabry in terms of the notion of memorial. Apart from memory, there simply is no identity to be found—bread is not body; we are not one another's bodies. However, in the active remembering of the congregation, the identities are found. In remembering Christ, the bread is (in the memory of the believer) Christ's body, and we are one another's insofar as believers remember the covenants made. In effect, Mabry's read of Hubmaier turns the Eucharistic identities into subjective memorial experiences. Mabry's articulation of the notion of real presence is limited by memory, such that real presence can only entail an *experience* by way of memory.

John D. Rempel

For Mabry, the identity claims that entail real presence hold only in the memory of believers. If Mabry emphasizes the notion of memorial, such that the relevant identities hold only in the remembering mind of the believers, Rempel argues that Hubmaier's theology retains a notion of a real presence not

---

[106] Ibid.

[107] Eddie Mabry, *Balthasar Hubmaier's Understanding of Faith* (Lanham: University Press of America, 1998), 7. For Alvin J. Beachy, even Mabry's understanding of a kind of commemorative participation goes too far. Beachy contends that Hubmaier's understanding of the memorial aspect of the meal forbids any account of participation: "Hubmaier stresses the *memorial* aspect of the Supper. The breaking, distribution, and eating of the bread is not a participation in the body of Christ. . . . The bread and wine are the body and blood of Christ in memorial only, and not otherwise." Beachy, *The Concept of Grace In the Radical Reformation* (Nieuwkoop: B. De Graaf, 1977), 105-106.

reducible to subjective experience. However, the novelty of Hubmaier's theology is that the real presence is not the bodily presence of Jesus in the bread and wine, but rather the real presence of Jesus in the life and action of the church. In effect, "the church is the real presence of Christ's humanity on earth."[108]

With respect to Hubmaier's theology of the Lord's Supper, there are two key moves that Rempel identifies. First, Hubmaier's articulation of the memorial aspect of the meal serves to remove Christ's physical body from the Lord's Supper. For Hubmaier, that Christ is remembered entails that Christ is not corporeally present. Hence, memorial becomes a "limiting characteristic" in the sense that it says all that can be said about Jesus's body, namely, that it is remembered in the celebration of the Supper.[109] The way Hubmaier understands the ascension of Jesus "removes him from the plain of history."[110] Rempel notes that Hubmaier strives to stick with biblical language, eschewing much of the traditional language about the Lord's Supper. Emphasizing the memorial aspect of the Supper, relying in particular on Luke and 1 Corinthians, allows Hubmaier to rule out other views, especially transubstantiation.

If Hubmaier first emphasizes memorial in order to displace the traditional link between the real presence of Christ in the Supper, the second key move is to 'realize' the church in the pledge that is made in the Lord's Supper. Recall that for Hubmaier, the bread serves not only as the sign of Christ's body remembered, but as a sign of the pledge of the church. In breaking bread, believers not only recall Christ's suffering, but pledge to suffer for one another. Hubmaier, as we saw, emphasizes that the pledge made in the breaking of the bread occasions the identity of the church as the body of Christ insofar as all share in the one loaf, in the one body. Rempel suggests that "in this emphasis on the church becoming the body of Christ, there is a resonance with Augustine's notion of the mystical body."[111] However, for Hubmaier "the transformation . . . is not sacramental, that is, a divine pledge in which the word is added to the 'element.' This transformation is an ethical one, brought about by the sanctified human pledge."[112] In Rempel's understanding of Hubmaier, the Supper has ceased to be a divine act, and is instead an act of the church, and hence the transformation of the church is occasioned by the pledge. The consequence is that "Hubmaier overturned the traditional *res* and *signum* of the sacrament. He held that the thing signified by the bread was the church."[113]

---

108 Rempel, *Lord's Supper*, 83.

109 Ibid., 62.

110 Ibid.

111 Ibid., 63.

112 Rempel, *Lord's Supper*, 63.

113 Ibid., 64.

If the bread is a sign of the church, then it is no longer the case that Christ is "in some fashion . . . the present reference point for the communion elements. [Hubmaier] fashioned a Eucharist which had, instead, only a historical and an imitative relationship to Christ."[114] Consequently, in the pledge of service to one another the believers themselves became Christ's body, and in so doing "they made him present to the world. To put the matter into traditional sacramental language, the 'real presence' in the Lord's Supper is that of the church."[115] Hence, for Rempel, "the church—instead of the Lord's Supper—perpetuates the power of the incarnate Christ through history."[116] The way in which the church perpetuates the incarnation is not corporeally; Christ's body is not *physically* identified with the church. Rather it perpetuates the incarnation ethically. The "ontological shift" occasioned by Hubmaier's theology is a real presence, but one analyzed in terms of the ethical identity of the church with Christ's body, rather than the physical identity of the church with Christ's body.[117] Rempel summarizes these two key moves:

> As a weapon in Hubmaier's hands, the memorial broke the Supper lose from its relationship to the presence of Christ. Once that was accomplished, it became possible to make the church, in its pledge of imitative love, the thing signified by the elements. What required ritual embodiment in the community was not Christ's sacrifice but obedience to its grace and willingness to act it out in the present.[118]

For Rempel, then, the real presence is not 'in' the Supper; rather the Supper is a sign of the real presence of the church in the world. The real presence is 'in' the church, and the Supper points to this presence in the church. For Rempel, this is the key to the cluster of identity statements in Hubmaier's theology: bread is identified as Christ's body in memory, which displaces Christ's physical body so that the church can be identified with the bread, and in being so identified with the bread the church is identified ethically, though not physically, with Christ's body on earth. In contrast to Mabry, Rempel affirms a real presence, but a real presence following from "an ontological shift" in which the church is the real presence.[119]

Though this ontological shift is articulated in ethical terms, Rempel argues that the way in which an ethical identification of church and the body of Christ achieves the presence of Christ is left unarticulated by Hubmaier. This is

---

114 Ibid.

115 Ibid., 65.

116 Ibid., 72.

117 Ibid., 53.

118 Ibid., 72.

119 Rempel, *Lord's Supper*, 53.

because Hubmaier is clear that Christ is "essentially and corporeally" absent from history, and yet, on Rempel's read, Hubmaier "never developed a profile of Christ's nonessential, noncorporeal presence in the world."[120] So, according to Rempel, the church is indeed the body of Christ ethically, but not corporeally or essentially. The church is the body of Christ in the sense that the church "perpetuates the power of the incarnation," but this perpetuation is not the same as if Christ himself had not ascended. *What* this perpetuation is, or how it is that the church's ethical identification with Christ's body is sufficient for an identification with the incarnation is left unanalyzed by Hubmaier, except for the negative claim that it cannot be essential and corporeal because Christ has ascended.

Kirk R. MacGregor

MacGregor's understanding of Hubmaier is close to Rempel's with one striking and important difference: MacGregor rejects Rempel's dissociation of ontological from physical, claiming that for Hubmaier the ethical, ontological shift entails that the church is "ontologically transformed into the physical body of Christ," and in this way is a "continuation of the incarnation."[121] The way in which the church perpetuates the power of the incarnation is, in contrast to Rempel, essentially and corporeally. Hubmaier did not reject the corporeal realism of the Eucharist taught by Roman Catholicism and by Luther.[122] Rather, he simply shifted that which bore the corporeal real presence of Christ—not the bread and wine, but the church. MacGregor claims that Hubmaier affirms a "literal consubstantiation (*i.e.*, the possession of two natures at once), in which each recipient is consubstantiated into the humanity of Christ."[123] Hence, the cluster of identity claims brings Christ's body to bear on the church, rather than the bread and wine, such that the church is identified with the *physical* body of Christ.

Like Rempel, MacGregor says that Hubmaier's emphasis on the memorial aspect of the Supper serves to sunder the relationship between bread and Christ's physical body. Bread serves as a sign of Christ's body in remembrance. This is because Christ has ascended. However, MacGregor argues that Hubmaier makes use of the Anselmian distinction between

---

120 Ibid., 66.

121 MacGregor, 180.

122 MacGregor says that Hubmaier "rejected the Catholic and Lutheran positions because he believed that both had misplaced that which bears the real presence of Christ and mistaken the vehicle of the real presence for the bearer of that presence." Ibid., 188.

123 MacGregor, 200. MacGregor cites Luther as the relevant understanding of consubstantiation as MacGregor means it, the only difference being that for Hubmaier it is not bread that is consubstantiated into Christ's body, but the church.

definitive presence and repletive presence, such that Christ's body is definitively present in heaven, but repletively present "at all points in the space-time universe without being limited by it."[124] Hence, the memorial aspect of the Lord's Supper serves to sunder Christ's physical body *definitively present* from the plane of history, and in particular from identification with the bread and wine, but in no way demands that Christ's physical body be simply absent.

In fact, MacGregor contends that Hubmaier's claims about the identification of the Supper as memorial is what allows Hubmaier to affirm the presence of Christ's physical body such that "through participation in the bread and wine, the recipients literally commune with the physical body and blood of Christ."[125] That is, Christ's body is present not in the bread and wine, but in the congregation who participates in the breaking of the bread and the drinking of the wine. That Christ is present in the celebration itself indicates that the bread can only be identified as body mediately through the action of the church. This affirmation is affirmed in two steps. First, Hubmaier claims that Christ's body is present "in active, practiced or held memory,"[126] and secondly he identifies the Supper as a "living commemoration [of Christ] in the breaking of bread."[127] These two affirmations allow Hubmaier to make the church itself the sign of the Supper. This is because the medium of the presence is the celebration of the church itself. The bread and wine are only signs insofar as they are actively broken or poured and consumed by the church in the celebration. In other words, communion with Christ happens in the celebration of the Supper itself, and in so communing the church becomes the body of Christ, such that bread and wine are signs of the *church* rather than Christ's body. MacGregor argues that Hubmaier's "language seems to imply that the transformation which takes place in [his] new order of the Supper is that of the congregation rather than of the elements."[128]

---

124 Ibid., 184-185, 189. Here, MacGregor argues that Hubmaier is working from an Alexandrian Christology, rather than an Antiochene Christology, which allows Hubmaier to exploit the notion of *communicatio idiomatum* so that Christ's humanity participates in the omnipotence of divinity. In this way, Christ is not simply absent from history. Rempel, without explicitly appealing to Alexandrian and Antiochene Christologies nevertheless argues that Hubmaier rejected the implications of such an Alexandrian Christology. For Hubmaier, the ascension was decisive and Christ could in no way be corporeally present. See Rempel, *Lord's Supper,* 29-37, and 66. For a brief overview of these two 'types' of Christology, see J.N.D. Kelly, *Early Christian Doctrines*, rev. ed. (New York: HarperCollins, 1978), 281.

125 MacGregor, 191.

126 Hubmaier, "A Simple Instruction," 326.

127 Hubmaier, "Form," 398.

128 MacGregor, 193.

MacGregor claims that further evidence of this read is Hubmaier's use of theological language (*wesen* and *wesenlich*, usually translated 'nature' or 'essence,' and 'essentially' or 'substantially'—see some of my citations from Hubmaier above). Hubmaier uses the language to indicate an "ontological shift" that happens in the Lord's Supper.[129] If Hubmaier denies that Christ's body is essentially (*wesenlich*) present in the bread, it is to affirm that the Christian becomes essentially (*wesenlich*) Christ's body. MacGregor understands Hubmaier's appeal to "an inward Christian nature [*wesens*]" not as a description of the 'inward,' personal, subjective aspect of faith, but rather as the transformation of the believer into the physical body of Christ.[130] MacGregor argues that Hubmaier defines this nature as "the state where Christ's person 'is essentially and bodily present'."[131] Consequently, "Hubmaier clearly affirms that the bread and wine are outer signs of the human essence of Christ present on earth."[132] The result is that the participants in the Supper are changed *in essence* such that they become the physical body of Christ on earth. For MacGregor, like Rempel, there are clear ethical implications of such an ontological change. However, unlike Rempel, strictly speaking the ethical identification of the church as the body of Christ is not itself the ontological identification; rather, the identification is physical with ethical implications.

Hubmaier, the Lord's Supper, and Analogous Uses of Language

Why these wildly divergent understandings of Hubmaier's theology of the Lord's Supper? These three scholars are all interpreting the same figure using the same texts, yet come to strikingly different conclusions about what Hubmaier was trying to say. Of course, it is possible that one reason for the variation is that perhaps Hubmaier himself was confused, and so his writings simply say lots of different things, some of which hold together coherently, some of which do not. It is also possible that one or more of these three scholars simply misunderstands Hubmaier.

However, I want to suggest that the variations are a result of an oversight by all three, namely inattention to analogous uses of language. I want to suggest that Hubmaier's theology of the Lord's Supper can fruitfully be understood as an exercise in teasing out the various ways in which Christ's body *is*, ways that admit of more evaluations than a binary 'physical or not physical,' 'ontological or remembered,' or even 'body in bread' or 'body in church,' and that these varied evaluations while not reducible to a 'geometric'

129 Ibid., 195.

130 Ibid. Citing Hubmaier, "Several Theses," 76.

131 MacGregor, 195, citing Hubmaier, "A Simple Instruction," 333.

132 MacGregor, 195.

systematic whole can nevertheless be ordered intelligibly by careful skill in language use.

Perhaps a return to the metaphor of the landscape of language use would help indicate what I mean to say about Hubmaier. I suggested above that Hubmaier is not a systematic theologian in the sense that his theology is linearly comprehensive. Rather, I want to suggest that Hubmaier is more like the intrepid explorer, setting out in a territory largely unexplored (or, if explored before neglected now for too long). The territory to be explored is the linguistic thickets of Eucharistic identity statements. Because unexplored or neglected, there are no comprehensive maps available, only the vestigial linguistic 'sensibility' (or, to anticipate the following chapter, 'vision') of the attentive traveler for feeling his way through the tangle. For orienting guides Hubmaier has the Scriptural identity claims, in particular 'this is my body' and 'the church is the body of Christ;' the overarching narrative of Scripture, particularly the narrative of Jesus and the church that provides the contextual home for those identity claims; and his pursuit (certainly Scriptural as well) of a holy church, a church of disciples faithful to the way of Jesus even, or especially, to the point of death.

So, what we find Hubmaier doing in his Eucharistic theology is exploring various linguistic trails, various ways of speaking about Christ's body. As it turns out, there are numerous interconnected trails that all seem to be leading the same general theological direction, but none taking the very same route. Furthermore, the more he explores the more he gets the sense that the direction the trails go are not leading to the top of a mountain, where one can survey and get a comprehensive map of the theological landscape. Rather, the further one goes down the trails the more one begins to realize that the trails lead right back to the cross, to the way of suffering in the world for the sake of Christ and for fellow believers. In this sense, there is no 'final account' of 'this is my body,' for there is always the need for training in habits of speech, and for that matter in habits of living, that are conducive to a suffering church. The fruit of the trails, then, is a character capable of suffering, that is, a character in conformity with the character of Christ. The trails' destination is faithfulness, rather than theological comprehensiveness or systematization. In the case of the Eucharistic identity statements, what a careful and attentive traveler discovers is that the way through the linguistic thickets is sensitivity to analogous uses of language, as it is by means of analogous uses of language that one can successfully affirm and deny what must be affirmed and denied in order to rightly teach how to be a martyr for Jesus.

Perhaps the metaphor is carried too far, but hopefully it illustrates the point. In any case, it ought to be noted up front that aside from his explicit remarks in opposition to Zwingli on the use of 'is,' Hubmaier gives little indication that he is consciously doing what I suggest he is doing. Even so, I think it can be shown that what Hubmaier is in fact doing in his theology of the Lord's Supper is tracing the contours of analogous uses of language in theological reflection on the Lord's Supper. I will suggest at the end that though lacking an explicit theological account of and reflection on analogous uses of language, it was precisely Hubmaier's repository of patristic theology gained through his Catholic education and subsequent study as a Reformer that supplied him with the linguistic nimbleness (or, what I called linguistic 'sensibility' above) to so explore analogous uses of language.[133] Furthermore, to be explored in the following chapter, it was Hubmaier's 'baptist' vision that operationalized that patristic repository in service to the shifting senses of the way in which bread, body, and church are Christ's body.

Analogous Uses: Limit Setting

An important clue to Hubmaier's analogous uses of language (even if he himself was not cognizant of what he was doing), is Hubmiaer's reply to Zwingli's substitution of 'signifies' for 'is.' After the negative claim that if Zwingli's proposal is accepted, then no one would know how 'is' is being used at any given time, Hubmaier offers constructively two biblical *examples* of uses of 'is.' His logic runs like this: Here are two other uses of 'is' in Scripture; the use of 'is' in the Lord's Supper is like those uses. His argument against Zwingli is followed immediately by a dismissal of the understanding of 'is' of "the papists" (though he does not tell us here what their objectionable understanding of 'is' is), and also of a "third group" which understands body as "a figurative body and the like," while still maintaining that "bread is bread and the wine, wine."[134] So, Hubmaier has explicitly rejected Zwingli, "the papists" and the third "figural" proposal and offered his own alternative, that 'is' should be understood in light of 'is' elsewhere in Scripture.

The two Scriptural examples Hubmaier cites are Genesis 1:3 ("God said let there be light and there was light") and John 1:14 ("And the word became flesh").[135] He clearly intends those uses to witness against the three uses he mentions. Though he does not spell out explicitly how they are witnesses

---

133 Hubmaier was a trained a theologian, and so "one of the most theologically learned of the early Anabaptist leaders." David C. Steinmetz, *Reformers in the Wings: From Geiler von Kaysersberg to Theodore Beza*, 2nd ed. (Oxford: Oxford University press, 2001), 139. James William McClendon, Jr. sees the key to understanding Hubmaier's theology and role in Anabaptism in his "Catholic origins, education and pastoral service prior to the radical turn of 1524-1525." See, James William McClendon, Jr., "Balthasar Hubmaier, Catholic Anabaptist," *Mennonite Quarterly Review* 65 (January 1991): 20-33.

134 Hubmaier, "A Simple Instruction," 322.

135 The Scriptural citations are as translated by Yoder and Pipken from Hubmaier's German.

against the three alternatives, his reasoning is fairly clear.[136] The objection to the first option ('signifies') is clearest. When God said let there be light, he meant that there should really be light; and the Word does not merely signify flesh, the word becomes flesh. The objection to the third option is also clear enough. God created light, not a figure of light; and the Word became real flesh, not a figure or symbol of flesh.

The objection to the second option is a bit less clear because Hubmaier does not tell us here what constitutes the "papist" 'is.' However, a reasonable guess can be made from other places where Hubmaier polemically attacks the Roman Catholic view (a few have been cited above). Hubmaier appears to take the Roman Catholic 'is' to mean that, for instance, when the priest raises the bread, the priest raises Christ; when the faithful chew the bread, the faithful chew Christ; if the bread is Christ's body then the bread would have had to have been crucified for us.

So, it would appear that Hubmaier means the two cited biblical examples to witness against this "papist" 'is.' How so? In the case of John, perhaps Hubmaier means to appeal to the distinction between Word and flesh in the union of the one person of Christ (something like Chalcedon's affirmation of a non-confusion of divinity and humanity), such that the Son truly suffers in the humanity of Jesus, but not in his divinity. The 'is' in 'the Word became flesh' does not confuse the two poles of the relation as the "papist" view does. The appeal to Genesis in this context is a bit less clear. Perhaps Hubmaier means to say that the relation of non-light to light is clearly not the relation of bread to body in the papist view. In other words, when God says (to the realm of non-light?), "let there be light," it does not follow that whatever is true of light is likewise true of non-light.

This way of approaching Hubmaier brings something sharply into focus, something that it appears Hubmaier himself may not have seen, though elsewhere he exploits it: namely, the use of 'is' in Genesis 1:3 is not strictly identical with the use of 'is' in John 1:14. When the Word became flesh, the Word did not cease to exist; however, when creation without light becomes creation with light, the original term does cease to exist. Once God calls for light, there is no longer creation without light (of course, there are regions of space-time where light does not penetrate; but that light may not be in any particular place or time is not equivalent to light not existing). So, Hubmaier's two chosen examples from Scripture turn out to be indicative of analogous uses of language, in this case of analogous uses of 'is.'

---

[136] R. Baine Harris's exposition of Hubmaier's understanding of 'is' is both bracing in its straightforwardness, and in its brevity suggesting of just how much care is required to be clear: "*is* means is (is identical with), and nothing else." R. Baine Harris, "The Anabaptist View of the Supper," *The Journal Of Religious Thought* 33 (Autumn/Winter 1976): 61.

Now, given that 'is' in Genesis 1:3 and John 1:14 is not used univocally, which use does Hubmaier mean to appeal to for his understanding of the Lord's Supper? Initially, Genesis 1:3 might seem to suggest something like transubstantiation or related accounts (i.e., in the Lord's Supper bread is converted, or changed into, or annihilated into body, and hence is no longer bread). But of course Hubmaier rejects these. On the other hand, John 1:14 *might* suggest something like consubstantiation. But Hubmaier's insistence that Jesus's physical [*leiblich*] body is in heaven and not on earth would seem to militate against that. However, while transubstantiation *may* follow from 'is' in Genesis, and while consubstantiation *may* follow from John 1, neither follow *necessarily*.

Though he shows no evidence of being explicitly aware of the uses of 'is' as analogous, his argument in "Simple Instruction" displays an implicit 'sensibility' for so reading. To see this 'sensibility' for reading the analogous uses of 'is' in these two passages in action, it may be more helpful to approach Hubmaier's identity statements not first with an eye to his view of *what the bread is*, but rather to his explorations of *what can and cannot be said about bread*. Of course, one of the things that can be said about bread is what it is, but I mean to suggest that we take the metaphor I offered earlier seriously: Hubmaier is an explorer in the landscape of *language use*, and so we should see which trails he explores, and where they lead him.

We might read Hubmaier as implicitly exploring the question, "if we want to affirm the Scriptural claim that 'this is my body' (and we should), what sorts of habits of speech are conducive to this affirmation?" Consider Hubmaier's negative claims, what it is that we *cannot* say about bread and body. According to Hubmaier we cannot say of the bread that it was crucified for us; nor can we say of the body of Christ that it is lifted in the air by the priest, broken, chewed, etc. We cannot say of the bread that we should worship it; we cannot say of the body of Christ that it is on the altar to be worshiped *there*. For Hubmaier, we cannot say these things because in his view, Scripture will not allow it. Christ's sacrifice was a unique event in the past, and so we cannot attribute the event to the bread; only God is worthy of worship and so we cannot worship the bread. Scripture affirms that Christ is ascended, and so we cannot say of Christ that he is lifted, broken, chewed etc., and we cannot say that we worship him on the altar because he is not *on* the altar to be worshiped.

These negations of what can be said constitute the content of Hubmaier's rejection of 'bodily' or 'physically' [*leiblich*], and of 'essentially' or 'by nature' [*wesenlich*] said of Christ's body in relation to the bread. That is, when Hubmaier says that Christ is not bodily or essentially in the bread, he does not mean to say that Christ is simply *absent*. Rather, he means to say that it is forbidden by Scripture for us to say of Christ's body all the things that we say of bread. This is how Hubmaier understands Scripture's identification of the Supper as memorial. Luke and Paul make clear what is only implicit in Matthew and Mark: We cannot say of the bread merely what we say about

Christ's body; and we cannot say about Christ's body merely what we say about bread; and that the Supper is a *memorial* meal is the reminder of these linguistic limits.

A comparison with Thomas is instructive because the sorts of limits that Hubmaier sets with respect to what can and cannot be said about the bread as Christ's body shows a family resemblance to Thomas's account of transubstantiation. On transubstantiation, to say that the bread is truly Christ's body is to follow similar habits of speech: bread is not crucified for us; bread is not worshiped; Christ's body is not lifted, torn, etc.; it is indeed the case that Christ's body is at the right hand of God. Both Thomas and Hubmaier up to this point could affirm with Herbert McCabe, that if we ask how Christ is present in the Lord's Supper, we must say that "he is present because the food and drink have become his body. If, however, you ask how his body is present, the answer is that it is present sacramentally."[137] In the previous chapter I suggested that Thomas's affirmation of Christ's body present sacramentally functioned more or less negatively. That is, what it means for Christ's body to be present sacramentally is for Christ's body to be really and truly present, but not in any of the ordinary ways bodies are present. While Hubmaier eschews language like 'sacramentally' with respect to the identification of bread as body, he does appear to use the notion of memorial in a roughly similar way. If you ask what it means for the bread to be Christ's body in remembrance, the answer you get is a series of negative judgments: it means that Christ is not torn, the bread is not sacrificed, etc.

If you press Thomas for a positive statement of 'sacramentally,' the best you will get is 'spiritually' and 'invisibly.' I take 'sacramental' here to be a shorthand way of saying that Christ's body is really and truly present by the power of God, but the manner of its presence is fundamentally beyond our grasp. If you press Hubmaier for a positive account of remembrance, you get a bit more. Contra Mabry, he is clear that it is not reducible to an individual's subjective memory. Hubmaier says that the bread is Christ's body in "active, practiced, or held memory;"[138] and that the bread is Christ's body "in the celebrated remembrance."[139] Still, if you press Hubmaier and ask what it means for bread to be body in the celebrated remembrance, what you will get is the same set of negative judgments. Hence, the notion of remembrance appears to be something of a linguistic limit setter rather than a positive account of the simple *absence* of Christ's body. That the bread is Christ's body in remembrance is to indicate that there a number of things that cannot be said about the bread and about the body.

---

137 Herbert McCabe, *God Matters*, 117.

138 Hubmaier, "A Simple Instruction," 327.

139 Ibid., 330.

What of Hubmaier's identification of the *church* as the body of Christ? Here, in striking contrast to what he says about the relation of bread to body, Hubmaier offers only constructive indications of what must be said. That is, unlike what can be said about Christ's body in the bread, explicit limits on what can be said about the church as Christ's body are missing. Consider yet again Hubmaier's most succinct statements on the matter: "Thus as the body and blood of Christ became my body and blood on the cross, so likewise shall my body and blood become the body and blood of my neighbor, and . . . theirs become my body and blood, or we cannot boast at all to be Christians;"[140] or "Christ was our Christ, and . . . we are to be Christ to one another;"[141] or, Christ is now present "in his Word and through his disciples, in which he wants to *remain among us* until the end of the world."[142] Hubmaier shows no reticence to speak of these identifications in 'physical' language: Christians must fulfill their obligations to their neighbor "physically [*leiblich*],"[143] and consequently, what we do "physically [*leiblich*] and spiritually" to our neighbor we "do to Christ himself."[144] Of course, because of the ascension Christ is physically in heaven; yet, what we physically do to neighbors we do to Christ. Compared to the reserve of what can be said about bread and body, there is a surprising boldness in what can be said about the church. There is a sort of physical participation in the body of Christ such that though Christ's body is physically in heaven, it is physically served in the mutual service of the church. These are bold implications. Yet, with the exception of advertence to the ascension, Hubmaier sees no need to work over such language with the same sorts of linguistic limits on the identification of church and the body of Christ that he does on the bread and the body of Christ.

The Church and Christ's Body

I suggested above that Hubmaier sees no need to work over language affirming the church as Christ's body in the way he does with respect to the bread and the body. Why not? If pressed, Hubmaier would surely want to articulate some of those limits. To say that I become Christ to my neighbor is obviously not to say that I become sinless, or that my genuine act of self-sacrifice on their behalf accomplishes just the same things that Christ's unique act of self-sacrifice accomplished; and furthermore, my physical doings would surely not entail that just as I lift my arm Christ's physical arm lifts, or that Christ is somehow no

140 Ibid., "Several Theses," 76.

141 Ibid., 74.

142 Ibid., "Christian Baptism," 104. Emphasis added.

143 Ibid., "Form," 397.

144 Ibid.

longer ascended to heaven but is instead walking around at the local grocery store.

Perhaps he refrains from explicit limit setting because those limits are obvious. However, it may also have something to do with how Hubmaier perceived the state of both the Roman Catholic Church, and the churches of the Protestant Reformers. Dix claims that the Christianity with which Hubmaier was familiar was shaped in some negative ways relevant to Hubmaier's later Medieval context by the official sanction of the church by the Roman Empire in the fourth century. As a result of this official sanction, there was an influx of barbarians into the church, who, while following their leaders into official Christianity nevertheless "did not make them responsible Christians."[145] The result is that "all through the dark and middle ages there is an immense drab mass of nominal Christianity in the background, looming behind the radiant figures of the saints and the outstanding actions of the great men and women . . . [which] was never fully absorbed by the church."[146] Aside from a relatively prevalent (at least from Hubmaier's perspective) moral laxity, this contributed to the general trend of infrequent lay communion with the result that, even allowing certain exceptions and a mild improvement around the twelfth and thirteenth centuries, "it remained true, broadly speaking, of even later mediaeval religion, that the priest as such was normally the only communicant."[147] This meant that lay Christians had no active part remaining in the liturgy. Consequently, the emphasis went to *seeing* over *doing* in the liturgy; the point was to observe the consecration of the elements. As Sarah Beckwith puts it, "the mass was becoming more and more of a spectacle and less and less of a communion. The emphasis was increasingly on watching Christ's body rather than being incorporated into it."[148]

For Hubmaier, infrequent lay communion and moral laxity would both have been problematic, and there is some passing evidence that he connected the 'spectacle' of the Medieval mass with such moral laxity.[149] When Hubmaier

---

[145] Dom Gregory Dix, *The Shape of the Liturgy*, 2nd ed. (London: A&C Black, 1945; reprint New York: Seabury Press, 1985), 595.

[146] Ibid., 596. Stauffer suggests in a related vein that the result of this influx and official sanction is that the "church of the Roman Empire as well as later on the church of the Papacy, were no longer churches of martyrs." Stauffer, 182.

[147] Dix, 598.

[148] Sarah Beckwith, *Christ's Body: Identity, Culture and Society In Late Medieval Writings* (London: Routledge, 1993), 36. Beckwith cites, along with Dix 599-600, Theodor Klauser, *A Short History of the Liturgy*, (Oxford: Oxford University Press, 1969), 97.

[149] To be clear, Hubmaier's concern about moral laxity was not limited to Roman Catholicism. He was clearly concerned that Luther's reform was still characterized by moral laxity (Estep, 97). Furthermore, Christof Windhorst suggests that several of

polemically attacks the medieval mass it is frequently in terms of its 'showiness' instead of its faithfulness. As one example, in his "18 Theses," early in his career, he begins by affirming the Reformation principle of justification by faith, and then immediately turns to the necessity of true Christians to "break forth in gratitude toward God and in all sorts of works of brother love toward others. This casts down all artifice such as candles, palm branches, and holy water."[150] He goes on to dismiss "fish and flesh, cowl and tonsure," and then to deny that the mass is a sacrifice.[151] What is clearly at issue for Hubmaier here is more than doctrinal: it is a church that (in his view) has substituted 'show' for faith. Hubmaier's desire is to constitute a holy church, a church of disciples, and he understands the Lord's Supper as one of the essential practices of the church: "a return to true Christianity will never be effected unless baptism and the Lord's Supper are brought back to their nature and genuine purity."[152] And so, his reasons for such explicit limit setting on what can be said about the bread and body may be because he thinks the 'spectacle' of a misplaced emphasis on Christ's body in the bread has obscured the church as the body of Christ. Consequently, he encourages a bold, perhaps even daring articulation of the identity of the church as Christ's body as a corrective. For Hubmaier, these of course were not idle theological speculations, for as I suggested above, what was at stake was how to teach and instruct a church of martyrs.

In this sense, Hubmaier shows continuity with the early church on the Eucharist. For the early church, *anamensis* was understood not as a recalling to the mind something absent, but as "a 're-calling' or 're-presenting' of a thing in such a way that it is not so much regarded as being 'absent,' as itself *presently operative* by its effects."[153] In so accomplishing this perpetuation of the one unique sacrifice, Christ accomplishes the unity of the church. Reflecting on Paul in light of pre-Nicene writers, Dix comments, "for the whole of catholic tradition the Eucharist is the *representative* act of the whole Christian life, that in which it finds its continuance and its supreme manifestation."[154] That is, in the perpetuation of this one unique sacrifice, the church is made a body which itself is prepared to suffer, to offer herself on behalf of Christ who has offered himself on behalf of her. In this sense, the *anamnesis* of the Eucharist is the

---

Hubmaier's later writings (in particular, "A Christian Catechism," "On Fraternal Admonition," and "On the Christian Ban") were written by Hubmaier to combat moral laxity within the reforms instituted by him in Nicolsburg. Windhorst, 152-153.

150 Hubmaier, "Eighteen Theses Concerning the Christian Life," 32.

151 Ibid.

152 Ibid., "Letter to Oecolampad," 70.

153 Dix, 245.

154 Ibid., 254; see also pp. 248-249.

realization of the church—the body of Christ prepared to suffer for Christ as an offering to Christ.

With this, Hubmaier would have much sympathy. Though early on Hubmaier rejects the notion of the Eucharist as a sacrifice, his brief comments make clear that what it is that he rejects is the crassly physical understanding of a re-sacrificed Christ. I further suggested that there is a sense (admittedly loose, perhaps) in which Hubmaier understands the Lord's Supper as a kind of sacrifice, insofar as in the Supper believers commit their lives to one another, even to death. In this sense, Hubmaier's practice and understanding of the Lord's Supper have a rough parallel to the early church, insofar as the Lord's Supper "is the *representative* act of the whole Christian life," to cite Dix's words above.

The early church fathers may also be a source of the vestigial 'sensibility' Hubmaier displays in his tracing the contours of the different ways words are used. I noted that Hubmaier shows little indication that he was consciously aware of the theological linguistic limit setting that I argue largely constitutes his Eucharistic theology. Yet, there is a source for the pattern of thought and speech that has implicitly habituated his mind, namely the patristic literature.[155] We know that Hubmaier was not only aware of the church fathers, but had studied many of them.[156] He even uses several in his defense of believers

---

[155] Here, recall Hallett on the variety of identity statements available in patristic theology. Hallett, *Identity and Mystery*, ch. 5.

[156] For an in depth and exhaustive study of the church fathers available to Hubmaier and used by him, see Andrew P. Klager, "Balthasar Hubmaier's Use of the Church Fathers: Availability, Access and Interaction," *Mennonite Quarterly Review,* 84 (January 2010): 5-65. Klager argues that "Hubmaier used the fathers for apologetic purposes as historical allies in his defense of credobaptism and free will. Clearly, he viewed the fathers favorably, not merely by giving cognitive assent to their teachings, but by accepting them as co-affiliates in the universal church as he understood it" (9). For a briefer survey of Hubmaier's use of the church fathers with respect to baptism, see Rollin Stely Armour, *Anabaptist Baptism: A Representative Study* (Scottdale, PA: Herald Press, 1966), 49-54. MacGregor takes a remark by Hubmaier to be indicative of Hubmaier's dating of the "downfall of the church" *after* the patristic period (Macgregor, 95; citing Hubmaier, "Christian Catechism," 349, where Hubmaier says that true baptism has been "lost for a thousand years"). MacGregor elsewhere notes that of the early church fathers, Augustine is the one most despised by Hubmaier because he thought Augustine most responsible for the spread of infant baptism (138-139). Hence, it was not all church theology that Hubmaier rejected, but (along with Augustine) theology after the patristic period. Todd E. Johnson would concur with the general point of MacGregor's claim, as he notes that "Hubmaier's doctrine of the Church [was] founded on scripture, early church writings, and Reformation sources." Todd E.

baptism. There is also good reason to think that Hubmaier's objections to Roman Catholic theology are self-consciously rejections of late Medieval Roman Catholic theology, not everything from the end of the New Testament on. Aside from Augustine (whom Hubmaier thought largely responsible for the popularization of infant baptism), the only theologians Hubmaier ever calls out by name for rebuke are theologians well after the patristic period. The reason cannot be because he did not know any other theologians—again, he makes extensive use of the church fathers in his baptismal theology. I want to suggest that it was the early church fathers' articulations of the various identity statements related to the Lord's Supper that vestigially shaped the linguistic patterns that made possible his use of analogous uses of language. It is true that, unlike his baptismal theology he never explicitly references the patristics in his Eucharistic theology. Yet, it would be unrealistic to think that, in his reading of the fathers, they had *no* impact on his Eucharistic theology. Hence, there is no reason to think that, even if unable to articulate *what* he was doing, he was nevertheless capable of doing it.

Conclusion

For Hubmaier, then, tracing the contours of analogous uses of language allows the body of Christ with respect to the Lord's Supper to flicker back and forth seamlessly between Jesus's 'historical' body on the cross, his 'remembered' body in the bread, and his 'ecclesial' body in the church. What governs this 'flickering' is not any theoretical principle, but skill in analogous uses of language.

This 'flickering' of the identification of Christ's body is what helps sort out the three interpretations described above. Mabry turns out to be the one most alien to Hubmaier's thought. No doubt the notion of remembrance was crucial to Hubmaier, but not in a way that says that Christ is present only to the degree that individual disciples call him to mind. Rather, remembrance served as a key linguistic marker of the limits of what could be said about *the way in which* the bread is Christ's body. Rempel is on the right track, though his insistence that Hubmaier *replaces* Christ's body in the bread with the church overstates the case. While it is true that the emphasis of identity claims goes to Christ in the church (for reasons perhaps related to his context), Hubmaier's tracing out of the contours of analogous uses of language in Eucharistic identity claims allows him to suggest the different ways in which Christ is present in bread and church, and the relationship of those identity claims. MacGregor, like Rempel overstates the displacement of body from bread, and in doing so misidentifies what Hubmaier is doing with language like 'physical' and

---

Johnson, "Initiation or Ordination? Balthasar Hubmaier's Rite of Baptism," *Studia Liturgica* 25 (1995): 68-85.

'essentially.' MacGregor fails to attend adequately to the 'ethical' thrust of such language, such that the appropriate parallel is not transubstantiation or consubstantiation (only the change directed to the church rather than the bread), but the active, self-sacrificial life of the church.

Earlier I suggested that the fruit of Hubmaier's explorations of the various linguistic trails in the landscape of theological identity statements related to the Lord's Supper is the production of a character capable of suffering. For Hubmaier, the Lord's Supper participates in the formation of such a character by training the disciples of Jesus to articulate the identity of bread-body-church in terms of the church's own suffering understood in terms of Christ's suffering. The bread is the body of Christ in remembrance, and what is being memorialized is the suffering of Jesus on behalf of the world. The memorial serves as more than a recollection of something in the past. It is rather the present participation of the disciples in that suffering body in their commitment to one another, a commitment made in the 'idiom' of the breaking of bread. This participation consists of mutual service and self-sacrifice. The participation is 'ethical,' 'ontological,' and 'physical.' Ethical: participation in the body of Christ is at least partly constituted by the active, self-sacrificial love of disciples on behalf of others. Ontological: the participation effects a real identification of church and body of Christ, one that cannot be reduced to 'mere' figure or to individualized, subjective recall. Physical: the real identification partly constituted by active, self-sacrificial love means that believers' physical, embodied selves *are* Christ's physical, embodied participation in the world.

Hence, Hubmaier's theology of the Lord's Supper contributes to a character capable of suffering by training the church in patterns of speech that bend identity claims about Christ's body toward a description of the suffering church. Furthermore, his theology provides the linguistic resources for bending language in this way without confusing the body of Christ in the church, the body of Christ in the bread, and the body of Christ on the cross. Language can be so bent without confusion because of attention to analogous uses of language, and hence the analogous nature of identity claims. Hubmaier's theology bears an implicit witness to Hallett's claim that strict identity neither exhausts the sorts of identity claims relevant to the Lord's Supper, nor is even the one most appropriate to it in light of the church as the body of Christ.

CHAPTER 6

Analogous Uses of Language and the 'baptist' Vision

Introduction

In chapter 3 I argued that attention to analogous uses of language allowed a reading of Thomas's account of transubstantiation facilitating a claim about the bread contrary to Thomas's own conclusion, namely that the conversion of bread to body is a conversion that constitutes a real identification of bread and body without the collapse of one pole of the identity into the other. What brought order to the analogous uses of language that made possible such a claim was advertence to God's power as first cause in bringing about the change. In the previous chapter, I argued that attention to analogous uses of language suggested a read of Hubmaier where his theology serves to trace out the contours of language about Christ's body in the Lord's Supper in which Eucharistic identity flickers seamlessly between Christ's body on the cross, Christ's body in the bread, and the church as Christ's body. There I suggested that what orders that flickering is not any one or even set of theological principles, but a vestigial sensibility for analogous uses of language.

While there are obviously important differences between Hubmaier and Thomas, I suggested that one thing they had in common was a reticence to speak positively about the *way in which* Christ's body is present in the bread. For Thomas, transubstantiation was not an explanation of the presence of Christ's body, but metaphysical *ascesis* teasing out the limits of what could be said about Christ's body. My constructive argument to repair Thomas was that analogous uses of language opened the way for us to affirm the identity of bread as Christ's body without the eradication of one pole. Even so, my argument affirmed Thomas's reticence insofar as it leaves unsaid just *how* bread is body, only that it is on account of God's action as first cause. Likewise, Hubmaier's insistence that Christ's physical body was in heaven and that the bread was Christ's body in remembrance was not a simple claim about the *absence* of Christ's body from the Lord's Supper, but about the limits that must be in place to speak well of Christ's body in the Supper.

One obvious point of difference is their treatment of the church. As I noted, it would certainly be unfair to Thomas to claim that the church had nothing to do with his Eucharistic theology. And yet, Schmemann's worry about transubstantiation appears founded insofar as for Thomas the church as the body of Christ has no substantive role in articulating the conversion of bread and wine. Again, taken as a whole Thomas's theology may suggest the links between the church and the conversion of bread and wine, but that he speaks of the conversion of bread and wine without a substantive account of the church as Christ's body in practice obscures the point of the conversion, namely (in Schmemann's words) "the actualization of the church." Hubmaier, in contrast to Thomas, makes the identity of the church as Christ's body central, so that the identity of the bread as Christ's body is explicitly directed to the church: in sharing the bread, which is Christ's body in remembrance, the church pledges and enacts the giving of oneself to others, so that the church is Christ's body.

In this final chapter, I want to suggest that our engagement of these two previous examples of tracing the contours of analogous uses of language provide useful parallels for engaging McClendon's baptist vision. Attention to Thomas and Hubmaier in light of analogous uses of language in Eucharistic identity claims illuminates a way of approaching the baptist vision in such a way as to show the intrinsic relationship between the baptist vision and Eucharistic identity, intrinsic insofar as the shape of the baptist vision itself is generative of just such an identity claim. In chapter three our linguistic ears were clued in by Hallett to identity claims that do not reduce to strict identity, and to the fact that, by way of Burrell, analogous uses of language are at the heart of such identity claims. In subsequent chapters, those insights were exercised in explorations of Thomas and Hubmaier.

Consequently, we will now be in a position to see that the identity claim that constitutes McClendon's baptist vision is real identity, yet not strict identity. In turn, the baptist vision will prove constructive for a conceptual investigation into Eucharistic identity insofar as the analogous uses of language that constitute the identity statement that is the baptist vision are shown to be uses that constitute real identity, though not strict identity. This will be shown by teasing out the contours of the analogous uses along the lines of baptists' (usually implicit) narrative reading strategy of Scripture. As will be shown below, for McClendon baptists read Scripture narratively. By reading Scripture narratively, I mean that for McClendon baptists read Scripture in light of an overarching biblical narrative in which they then render and make sense of their own stories. This convergence of identities in the narrative reading of Scripture constitutes the sensibility or fluency necessary to order the analogous uses of language that constitute real, but not strict, identity claims in baptist life. The use of narrative in this sense parallels the way in which Thomas and Hubmaier disciplined their uses of language, advertence to God as first cause for Thomas, and reliance upon a vestigial sensibility for Hubmaier (though, the conclusion of this chapter will suggest that a further source of Hubmaier's sensibility was the baptist vision itself).

Furthermore, bringing McClendon's baptist vision to bear on Eucharistic identity will bring to the fore the intrinsic relationship between the two. In other words, Eucharistic identity may be articulated in just the narrative logic that disciplines the analogous uses of language in the baptist vision itself. Hence, I will suggest that Eucharistic identity and the baptist vision ought not be foreign to one another. They are organically related to, and even generative of one another. This suggestion will provide a modest contribution to Baptist sacramentalism, as well as to catholic Eucharistic theology more broadly. Furthermore, the link between the baptist vision itself and Eucharistic identity will enable us to return to the issue of the relation of the church to Eucharistic identity.

In order to accomplish these goals, the chapter will proceed as follows. First, I will offer a description of McClendon's baptist vision, highlighting the centrality of narrative to the baptist vision. In this first section, the use McClendon makes of narrative will dominate in order to bring to the fore what will later be shown to be the primary way of disciplining the various analogous uses of language that constitute, and flow from, the baptist vision. Second, I will turn to three instances of the baptist vision at work to trace the contours of the sort of identity that constitutes the vision, with the goal of showing that the analogous uses of language that constitute the vision constitute a real, though not strict, identity claim. I will set up these three instances with McClendon's comparison of the baptist vision to Roman Catholic Eucharistic identity claims, suggesting that this latter comparison is problematic, and yet still illuminating. The fruit of this section will be to show that what disciplines analogous uses of language in McClendon's theology is the narrative reading strategy of baptists. Third, I will offer an account of McClendon's theology of the Lord's Supper, and draw out how the baptist vision provides the resources for ordering the various uses of language constituting the identities involved in the Lord's Supper: Christ crucified, Christ's body in the bread, and the church as Christ's body. As indicated, the primary means of so ordering the uses of language that constitute these identities is the narrative reading strategy of baptists. Then, in a final section serving as the conclusion to both the chapter and the book, I will make explicit how the baptist vision contributes not only to the loose project of Baptist sacramentalism, but also to broadly catholic Eucharistic reflection.

McClendon's 'baptist' Vision

In this section, I will first offer an overview of McClendon's baptist vision: 'this church is that church.' Then, I will show that for McClendon, the narrative reading strategy that embodies the vision itself provides the conceptual framework that shows the identity claim that constitutes the vision to be ordered along just those narrative lines. Third, I will show that, for McClendon, this narrative ordering that disciplines the uses of language that constitute the baptist vision generates the articulations of the identity of Jesus, his disciples, and the church, articulations that I will call, for sake of brevity, narrative identity. The exploration in this section, then, will emphasize the role of narrative in McClendon's theology. The emphasis here on narrative will bear its fruit when, later in the chapter, I will show how narrative in McClendon's theology proves illuminating of the analogous uses of language that constitute the identity statements at issue. What I intend to show later by the exploration of narrative here is that, though McClendon makes no explicit use of the concept of analogous use, analogous uses of language are at the heart of his theology and are disciplined by the narrative of Scripture as read in the baptist vision.

'This is That' and the 'baptist' Vision

Given the fact that 'baptist' names no one single group or denomination, but a variety of communions, marked by relatively differing confessions of faith, doctrine, and church practice, there is a special challenge for a theology that calls itself 'baptist.' McClendon contends that what the various groups share is a vision, and it is this vision rather than any one doctrine or church structure that stands "at the center of this way of life and belief."[1] If this is the case, then the articulation of that vision must serve as the entry point into a baptist theology.

Yet, the danger is that if there is indeed variety in baptist life, an articulation of a vision may hover over all, disconnected from any one as a remote theoretical abstraction. So, McClendon explains,

> By such a vision, I do not mean some end result of theoretical reflection, remote from the daily life of a rather plain people. Nor do I mean a detachable baptist Ideal—what baptists ought to be (but of course are not). Instead, by a vision I mean the guiding pattern by which a people (or as here, a combination of peoples) shape their thought and practice as that people or that combination; I mean by it the continually emerging theme and tonic structure of their common life.[2]

The articulation of the vision, if it is to accurately express what is at the heart of baptist life and thought, must not be a surprise to any of the various groups. Even if they have not so articulated it themselves, they must be able to recognize it as their own. If this is no detachable ideal, but the guiding pattern of life, then it is a vision that must be already operative in baptist communities. It ought not seem alien to baptists.

If the vision McClendon articulates meets this test, then it should "serve as the touchstone by which authentic baptist convictions are discovered, described, and transformed, and thus as the organizing principle around which

---

[1] James Wm. McClendon, Jr, *Ethics*, 2nd. ed., vol. 1 of *Systematic Theology* (Nasvhille: Abingdon Press, 2002), 27.

[2] Ibid.

an authentic baptist theology can take shape."[3] No doubt baptists have and will continue to differ over particular doctrines. But McClendon's claim is that, if he has rightly articulated the vision common to all, then they will recognize one another's articulations as growing organically out of the common vision, and hence have a common vision out of which to test one another's claims.

McClendon surveys five frequently suggested "marks" of baptist life and finds them all to be in some way rightly descriptive of baptists: biblicism, liberty, discipleship, community, and mission (evangelism). Yet, McClendon asks, why these? "What is the vision that unites, organizes, guides these assorted elements into one whole?"[4] Biblicism is perhaps the most likely candidate, and McClendon's baptist vision shares with this option an emphasis on the centrality of Scripture. But biblicism, argues McClendon, does not sufficiently account for the *way in which* baptists read Scripture. This, suggests McClendon, is where to find the vision: not Scripture itself, though Scripture is central, but the "hermeneutical principle" by which baptists read Scripture: "*shared awareness of the present Christian community as the primitive community and the eschatological community*. In a motto, **the church now is the primitive church and the church on judgment day**."[5] This motto, argues McClendon, adequately expresses the centrality of Scripture in the life of baptists by capturing the way in which baptists read Scripture as the governing paradigm for all of life. Scripture is in no way incidental or secondary to baptist life: "The whole Bible is for the church *the* book: we are people of that book."[6] Yet, as important as Scripture is there is always the danger (especially in baptist life) of bibliolatry. McClendon thinks that his articulation of the baptist vision both accurately and faithfully names how baptists read the Bible, as well as suggesting how to do so without making an idol of the Bible. By noting not just the Bible, but the hermeneutical principle by which baptists read it, "we avoid a dogmatic bibliolatry which could substitute attention to the book for

---

3 McClendon, *Ethics*, 27.

4 Ibid., 28.

5 Ibid., 30. Italics and bold are McClendon's. McClendon offers an earlier formulation of a similar claim in his *Biography as Theology: How Life Stories Can Remake Today's Theology* (Nashville: Abingdon Press, 1974). He says there, "Our doctrine, then, must be that men of biblical faith are those who find in Scripture what is centrally there—great dominant images, such as those of Kingdom of God, and Israel, and sacrifice, and Son of Man, *and who apply them as the makers of Scripture applied them*—to themselves" (95; emphasis is McClendon's).

6 McClendon, *Ethics*, 31.

participation in its life."[7] That is, the *point* of reading the Bible is to become faithful people.[8]

McClendon offers two "illustrative parallels" to the 'this is that' articulation of the baptist vision.[9] First, Roman Catholic theology about the Eucharist, where the bread is the body of Christ: "Not 'represents' or 'symbolizes,' but *is*. No lesser word will do."[10] The parallel McClendon intends to draw is explicitly about the non-falsifiability of the claims. On the Catholic claim, there is no evidence of the usual kind that can disprove it. After the consecration bread is still bread, at least as the scientist, the baker, and the hungry traveler would judge it. So too the baptist vision. That the historian would remind us that Jesus ministered some time chronologically distant from any particular baptist church is beside the point: "The church now *is* the primitive church; *we* are Jesus' followers; the commands are addressed directly to *us*. And no rejoinder about the date of Jesus' earthly ministry verses today's date can refute that claim."[11] McClendon distinguishes the identification of the present church with the primitive church from the way in which a Catholic might do so, by means of succession or development. In contrast, the 'is' in 'this is that' is "mystical and immediate; it might be better understood by the artist and poet than by the metaphysician and dogmatist."[12]

The second illustrative parallel is Acts 2. There, Peter makes an identification of Pentecost with the prophecy of Joel. McClendon cites the King James rendering of Acts 2:16: "*this is that* which was spoken by the prophet Joel."[13] As before, that Joel's prophecy occurs some centuries before and perhaps has some immediate reference to events of his time is no evidence against Peter's claim. McClendon appeals to B. Davie Napier:

> We have in the Old Testament no past which has not already been appropriated in the present, and so appropriated as to *be* the present, to *live* in the present. [For the prophets, the past] *was* past, but it now *is*. The event lives in faith. It has been culticized. . . . As such, it is . . . not so

---

7 McClendon, *Ethics*, 31.

8 Barry Harvey reflects McClendon's understanding of the relationship of Scripture reading to discipleship when he says that "the baptist vision names both a reading strategy for the church confronting the witness of Scripture and the way of Christian existence." Harvey, "Beginning in the Middle of Things: Following James McClendon's *Systematic Theology*," *Modern Theology* 18 (April 2002), 255.

9 McClendon, *Ethics*, 31-33.

10 Ibid., 31.

11 Ibid., 32.

12 Ibid.

13 Ibid. Italics are McClendon's.

> much (if at all) merely memorialized as reexperienced—created and lived again.[14]

Hence, McClendon's articulation of the vision is especially appropriate insofar as it captures, on McClendon's judgment, Scripture's own way of interpreting itself.

Typology is the model here. Typology, what McClendon calls the spiritual sense of the text, or the point of the text, consists in reading the plain sense as type or antitype. Similar to Peter at Pentecost, Hosea appropriates the pattern of the Exodus and proclaims that a new Exodus will be brought about by God (Hosea 2:15-23). For Hosea, the Exodus from Egypt is a type for grasping and appropriating the promised renewal by God.[15] The promised renewal *is* the Exodus of Israel from bondage. Paul's identification of Adam as a type of Christ in Romans 5:14 is another example. In this instance, Christ has fulfilled or completed the type, accomplishing what Adam was unable to accomplish.[16] McClendon says, "We are here in the presence of a regular motif in biblical literature in which language about one set of events and circumstances is applied under divine guidance to another set of events or circumstances."[17] That it is a regular motif, and that the motif is likewise found in baptist life, is fitting for the baptist vision.

In appealing to typology, McClendon is appealing to what he calls "the main course of Christian Bible reading over the centuries."[18] That is, though many interpretive strategies have been present, by and large Christians have read the Bible in terms of its "plain sense . . .—its stories were read as (in the main) real stories about real people; its history real history; its declarations about God and God's creatures as saying what they meant and meaning what they said. The Bible was not a code or cipher to be cracked; it was not a book of secrets; it was realistic; it spoke plain."[19] Yet, it was no *mere* history.

---

[14] B. Davie Napier, *Interpreter's Dictionary of the Bible*, vol. 3, ed. George A. Butterick, et al. (Nashville: Abingdon Press, 1962), 906; Quoted in McClendon, *Ethics*, 32-33. In citing Napier, McClendon notes that Napier is both "Biblical scholar and poet" (32).

[15] James Wm. McClendon, Jr., *Doctrine*, vol. 2 of *Systematic Theology* (Nashville: Abingdon Press, 1994), 37.

[16] Ibid.

[17] Ibid.

[18] Ibid. 36.

[19] Ibid. McClendon references Hans Frei, "The 'Literal reading' of Biblical Narrative in the Christian Tradition: Does it Stretch or Will It Break?" in *The Bible and the Narrative Tradition*, ed. Frank McConnell (New York: Oxford University Press, 1986): 36-77; and David Tracy, "On Reading the Scriptures Theologically," in *Theology and Dialogue: Essays in Conversation with George Lindbeck*, ed. Bruce D. Marshall

Christians read this plain sense as indicative of God's active work in the world, and in particular of God's continuing work in the life of the church. Hence, the plain sense was read not merely for information, but for instruction in how to participate in God's action. There was then a "spiritual sense" to Scripture, which did not replace the plain sense, but rather appropriated it "into the whole story of divine and human relations; [the spiritual sense] meant the way the plain words bore upon readers' lives in relation to all that God had done and would do in their regard."[20] The means of making the links between the plain sense and its point were various interpretive devices, chief among them typology.

So, the baptist vision is constituted by a particular way of reading Scripture, a way that McClendon thinks is, on the whole, consistent with the broad stream of Christian readings of Scripture. Furthermore, the particular way in which Scripture is read is as real stories about real people, real stories that open up into myriad appropriations in different contexts by means of a 'this is that' hermeneutic. The character of that 'this is that' identification, that is the conceptual approach to the 'this is that' hermeneutic at work in this way of reading Scripture is, as I will suggest below, fruitfully traced along the lines of narrative. As I will show, for McClendon, narrative is a central theological category, and for my purposes later in the chapter a central category for tracing the contours of baptist analogous uses of language. To this narrative character I now turn.

Narrative Links

This link between the church now and the church then, between the Jesus of the gospels and the Jesus Christians worship, the link effected by the various interpretive devices, typology being the most prominent, is a link ordered by the reading strategy of baptists, a strategy that is constituted by a series of what I will call narrative links between the church now and then, between the Jesus of the gospels and the Jesus of worship. Before turning specifically to Jesus and the church, I will describe the centrality of narrative to McClendon's systematic project.

(Notre Dame: University of Notre Dame Press, 1990): 35-68. For a brief overview of Frei's contribution to narrative, and also narrative identity, see Dan R. Stiver, *The Philosophy Of Religious Language: Sign, Symbol, and Story* (Cambridge: Blackwell Publishers, 1996), 140-145. For an interesting description of the debate between Frei and Tracey on narrative particularity and theology, see M. A. Higton, "Hans Frei and David Tracy on the Ordinary and the Extraordinary in Christianity," *The Journal of Religion* 79 (October 1999): 566-591.

[20] McClendon, *Doctrine*, 36.

McClendon articulates the centrality of narrative in the context of a defense of his narrative approach to ethics, and it continues to characterize his doctrinal approach as well.[21] To see this, first note that for McClendon the Bible is itself a grand, overarching narrative.[22] Of course, not all parts of the Bible are in narrative form, but a large portion of it is. Even so, more important is the fact that the narratives, along with other genres (poetry, personal letters, proverbs, etc.) together constitute the overarching narrative of God's relationship with the world, which, for baptists, is the narrative that orders and

---

[21] Narrative, of course, has played a huge part in contemporary theology, philosophy, and ethics. However, as Stanley Hauerwas and L. Gregory Jones say, "it is not readily obvious what, if anything, the varieties of appeals to narrative have in common. The category of narrative has been used, among other purposes, to explain human action, to articulate the structures of human consciousness, to depict the identity of agents (whether human or divine), to explain strategies of reading (whether specifically for biblical texts or as a more general hermeneutic), to justify a view of the importance of 'story-telling' (often in religious studies through the language of 'fables' and 'myths'), to account for the historical development of traditions, to provide an alternative to foundationalist and/or other scientific epistemologies, and to develop a means for imposing order on what is otherwise chaos." Hauerwas and Jones, "Introduction: Why Narrative?" in *Why Narrative? Readings in Narrative Theology*, ed. by Hauerwas and Jones (Grand Rapids: Eerdmans, 1989), 2.

Dan R. Stiver has provided a helpful overview of narrative theology, surveying three general trajectories: the Chicago School (represented by David Tracy, Langdon Gilkey, and Paul Ricoeur); the Yale School (represented by Hans Frei, George Lindbeck, and Ronald Thiemann); and what Stiver calls a California School (represented by McClendon, Michael Goldberg, and Terrence Tilley). See Stiver, *The Philosophy Of Religious Language*, 134-162. Stiver says that a central issue is "irreducibility," the fact that narrative is an "irreplaceable" category for theology. In investigating narrative, "we can distinguish between *the* story, the canonical Scripture; our story, the cultural narratives and myths that form the background framework of our lives; and my and your story, the personal autobiography and biographies that constitute a central part of our identity. Interestingly, each one of these emphases is represented by a different school, if this analogy is not pushed too far. The Yale School focuses on the biblical story. The Chicago School tends to center on the broader cultural, narrative framework. And we can identify perhaps a California School centered around the work of James McClendon . . . who focuses on biography and autobiography." Stiver, 135. Stiver notes that McClendon is working on a systematic theology, but clearly privileges his early work. Thus, McClendon's systematic theology as a whole is not helpfully considered by Stiver in terms of personal autobiographies and biographies, even though McClendon clearly remains committed to the importance of each (which is why several biographies appear in each of the three volumes).

[22] McClendon, *Ethics*, 329.

makes sense of *all* narratives. Furthermore, this grand narrative finds its narrative focus in the stories of Jesus Christ, which of course involves the narratives of the disciples. Thus, for McClendon, narrative is theologically important precisely because Scripture itself is narrative in form.

Second, and related to the first, is the "realistic" or "historylike" quality of the narrative content of Scripture.[23] McClendon argues that there are three essential features of any realistic narrative: "character, social setting, and circumstances or incident."[24] He argues that these three features map well onto his three stranded account of ethics, an account of ethics that is narrative in shape.[25] McClendon clarifies that it is not that ethics itself is a story, but rather the analysis of "a way of life, a morality, that is itself story-formed."[26] In this case, the subject of this analysis is "those who share in a certain ongoing real story—a story whose link with its primitive past is established by anamnesis or memory, and whose link with its final end is fixed by the anticipation or hope of the sharers of the Way."[27] Hence, the 'realistic' quality of the biblical narrative is of no mere antiquarian or literary interest. Rather, it turns out that the biblical narrative relates "a living Lord whose timely life confronts our stories with his own."[28] It is in this sense that the baptist vision is fundamentally narrative in nature—the link between the church now and the church past is a narrative link, the re-storying of the church as the story of the disciples.

---

[23] McClendon, *Ethics*, 328-329. Here, McClendon cites Robert Alter, *The Art of Biblical Narrative* (New York: Basic Books, 1981) and Hans Frei, *The Eclipse of Biblical Narrative: A Study in Eighteenth and Nineteenth Century Hermeneutics* (New Haven: Yale University Press, 2974), and *The Identity of Jesus Christ: The Hermeneutical Bases Of Dogmatic Theology* (Philadelphia: Fortress Press, 1975). McClendon says that Alter in literary studies and Frei in theology "choose not to engage in the modern critical debate about how well the Bible serves the interests of the critical historians. Rather they call attention to the style of the biblical books, found both in the individual narratives that constitute a great portion of both Testaments . . . also in the overall story implied by the lesser stories. (For Christians, that Great Story must include the whole account of Israel, of the kingdom Jesus proclaimed, and of the church that followed)." *Ethics*, 329.

[24] McClendon, *Ethics*, 329. The quotation is McClendon's summary, but he cites Frei, *The Identity of Jesus Christ*, 321.

[25] McClendon's three strands are embodied witness (part 1 of *Ethics*), a community of care (part 2), and the sphere of the anastatic (part 3).

[26] McClendon, *Ethics*, 330.

[27] Ibid.

[28] bid., 331.

Narrative Identity, Jesus, and Disciples

Having articulated the centrality of narrative to McClendon's theological project, I now turn to the role narrative plays in identity claims about Jesus and the church. Recall that the purpose up to this point is simply to bring to the fore the role that narrative plays in McClendon's theology, for the purpose of later showing how the narrative reading strategy of baptists serves as a kind of disciplining regimen for analogous uses of language.

Narrative is the way in which McClendon approaches the identity of Jesus. McClendon follows Hans Frei in claiming that the primary purpose of the Gospel narratives is to identify Jesus Christ. McClendon applies speech act theory. As in any speech-act, identifying has its own criteria for aptness. Titles and proper names are tools for identification, but often lack specificity. What is needed is a "definite description." McClendon's example: "'Mount Everest' is only a proper name, but the 'tallest mountain on earth above sea level' is a definite description, and to know that Everest is that mountain is to identify it unambiguously."[29] On this paradigm, the gospel of Mark, for instance, serves as a definite description of Jesus Christ: "it says, to be brief, that Jesus Christ . . . is the one who: was baptized by John, was tempted by Satan, healed and taught in Galilee, appointed twelve disciples . . . was arrested, tried, crucified—and appeared again, risen."[30] The gospels, then, are narratives that fix the identity of Jesus Christ. The identity of Jesus Christ is fundamentally articulated in terms of narrative. In other words, the definite description that fixes the identity of Jesus Christ is a description constituted by a narrative, a story. Hence, the identity of Jesus is irreducibly articulated in narrative terms. There are no 'metaphysical' categories more fundamental to identifying him, nothing that stands 'under' or 'over' the narrative itself. "Who is Jesus?" The answer is to tell a (true) story.

But furthermore, and central to an understanding of the baptist vision is the fact that the Gospels likewise identify the followers of Jesus. In Mark, the disciples are generally considered together: "it is 'the disciples' *as a group* who are rendered by the narrative."[31] Early they are portrayed as fairly clueless;

---

29 McClendon, *Ethics*, 335.

30 Ibid. What of the other Gospels? They provide "somewhat different definitive descriptions." (335). McClendon grants that the differences may be problematic with respect to truth, but not with respect to identification: "this will not defeat identification any more than it defeats identification of Shakespeare to find that, despite earlier claims, many now believe he never wrote the play named *Two Noble Kinsmen*." (335). Furthermore, without denying the issue of historical referent McClendon notes that the narrative issue is not simply identifiable with modern questions surrounding historiography.

31 Ibid., 336. Emphasis added.

later "it is they who receive the crucial call to follow the way of the cross," and yet they who flee. Their failures are still failures within the context of their response, their following after Jesus. This is born out in Acts, so that the definite description of the disciples, the fixing of their identity, is the narrative of their failures and faithfulness in response to Jesus's call. Like Jesus, then, their identity is given in terms of narrative: "Who are the disciples?" The answer is to tell a story.

Furthermore, it must not be overlooked that their stories cannot be told apart from Jesus. In the gospels, who they were before Jesus is the story of their coming *to* Jesus. Their stories are inextricably linked with Jesus's story. That the disciples' story cannot be told apart from Jesus appears to be a constitutive claim of the baptist vision. Says McClendon,

> Now note a vital feature of the Gospels understood as identity-documents: whereas the identity of Jesus is at once that of the risen Christ present in the readers' church *and* the central figure in the gospel, the identity of the "disciples" is by invitation the readers themselves as well as their originals in the story. . . . We are invited to become disciples, and thus to see ourselves figuring in this narrative.[32]

That is, what constitutes the self-understanding of the present church is precisely its narrative identification with the primitive church. *We* are those clueless disciples who flee in fear, and yet who nevertheless accept the invitation to follow the crucified and risen Jesus. To say that *we* are those disciples, to accept the full force of 'mystical' and 'immediate,' of the 'is' in this is that, is to say that their story is our story; that, our world is re-narrated in terms of the gospel so that we no longer have a story apart from it. As the disciples' story cannot be told apart from Jesus, neither can ours; and this simply means that the disciples' story *is* our story, the church now *is* the primitive church.

So, for McClendon, the narratives of Scripture as read by baptists serve the crucial purpose of identifying Jesus, the disciples, and the church; and this identification is made such that the baptist communities reading these narratives identify *themselves* as characters in the narrative. In this sense, the identities at issues are inextricably bound up with narratives. Because of the close relationship in McClendon's theology between narrative and identity, I will continue to speak explicitly of narrative identity. Of course, within McClendon's theology 'narrative identity' is strictly speaking a redundancy. Even so, it will be helpful to keep in view the role of narrative in making just these identity statements as I turn towards the end of the chapter to making explicit the role of narrative in ordering analogous uses of language.

---

32 McClendon, *Ethics,* 336.

Narrative Identity and the Church

Of course, this brings us back around to a central question: "How is [the church's] own story connected, how *must* it be connected, with the great story found in Scripture?"[33] McClendon claims that broadly speaking this sort of reading strategy has been the main one for Christians. Consequently, *that* the story of Scripture and the story of the church are connected is, as McClendon says, a common point of agreement among Christians. The creedal affirmation that the church is one, holy and apostolic is "the common property of the great Catholic and Protestant communions East and West."[34] The same Holy Spirit who "inspired the Scriptures **continues to constitute the inner life of the church through the ages, so that the Bible and church compose one story, one reality**. There is a strong link between **the plain sense of Scripture** and the church's self-understanding as a **continuation** of the biblical story."[35] The problem, of course, is that there is no general agreement on *how* it is that the church continues the biblical story. Is it (McClendon's examples) the Catholic emphasis on the sacraments of the church, a Lutheran proclamation of justification by faith alone, an Anglican mixture of the two, a Quaker emphasis on doing the work of God? McClendon suggests that the fragmentation comes just at the point of the spiritual sense of Scripture, the application of the plain sense to the contemporary church.[36]

However these other communions understand the link, McClendon's task is to articulate the baptist understanding, and this rounds us back yet again to the baptist vision: the reading strategy which appropriates the plain sense of Scripture in service to finding the point by means of seeing "past and present and future linked by a 'this is that' and 'then is now' vision, a trope of mystical identity binding the story now to the story then, and the story then and now to God's future yet to come."[37] McClendon's claim is that while baptists have no in principle objection to a (broadly understood) sacramental account of the

---

33 McClendon, *Doctrine*, 44.

34 Ibid.

35 Ibid. Bold in the original.

36 Ibid. In this context, McClendon follows Stephen Sykes's suggestion that "the *essence* of Christianity (or *real* or *authentic* Christianity) is itself 'an essentially contested concept,' one that by its very nature cannot be agreed on by all sides" (43), citing Stephen Sykes, *The Identity of Christianity: Theologians and the Essence of Christianity From Schleiermacher to Barth* (Philadelphia: Fortress, 1984), 251.

37 McClendon, *Doctrine*, 45. On Catholic and Protestant ways of linking the stories, McClendon says, "a Catholic answer is a theory of apostolic succession hierarchically maintained . . . , while a Protestant answer is inward and spiritually maintained . . . ." He contends that the baptist vision need not reject either of these, but that "neither of them can do the work demanded of it here." (45-46).

church; and while baptists have, historically, accepted the doctrine of justification by faith; and while many baptists have emphasized the importance of actively doing God's work in the world, none of these in themselves explain the link between the church's sacraments, the teaching of justification by faith, the doing of God's work, and Scripture.

McClendon thinks that for baptists, the 'this is that' reading strategy articulates the logic behind the various ways of practicing (or, in some cases rejecting) these Catholic, Protestant, Quaker (and other) models. So, for instance, if a particular baptist congregation or association articulates the practice of the church in broadly sacramental language (as some 17th century baptists did, and as some contemporary European baptists and American restorationist groups sometimes do), the 'why' and 'how' will be articulated in the framework of the baptist vision. The 'logic' explaining it will be in the pattern of 'this is that.' Hence, what is distinctive about *how* baptists link the primitive church and the contemporary church is the vision itself, not necessarily particular claims arising from the vision. Baptists are the ones whose congregational life (be it sacramental or non-sacramental) can be explained in terms of this vision.

But why call this vision "mystical and immediate,"[38] and a "trope of mystical identity" as McClendon does?[39] What does mystical and immediate have to do with narrative identity? Does the 'mystical' and 'immediate' that characterizes baptist readings of Scripture tend toward "simplistic;"[40] or does the mystical identity ignore wholesale the history of Christian life and theology?[41]

Both concerns voice the worry of SIS, that the baptist vision collapses 'this' church into 'that' church. We can get at these worries indirectly by returning to one of McClendon's "illuminating parallels," the Catholic identification of bread and body. Of course, this parallel is apt for my argument in other ways. In short, I want to suggest that the unexamined presence of what Hallett called the Strict Identity Supposition (SIS) confuses the illustration, directing attention away from the particular baptist 'is' in view. Noting the presence of SIS will prove useful for more clearly articulating the sort of identity in view in the baptist 'this is that;' and clarity on the baptist 'this is that' will, I argue later in the chapter, prove useful for Eucharistic identity.

---

38 McClendon, *Ethics*, 32.

39 Ibid., *Doctrine*, 45.

40 Robert Barron, "Considering the Systematic Theology of James William McClendon, Jr." *Modern Theology* 18 (April 2002): 271.

41 This is a central claim of David Wayne Layman about McClendon and John Howard Yoder. See Layman, "The Inner Ground of Christian Theology: Church, Faith, and Sectarianism," *Journal of Ecumenical Studies* 27 (Summer 1990): 480-504.

So, in what follows, I will suggest other illuminating parallels for the baptist vision, and then reverse the original parallel—now the baptist vision can serve as an illuminating parallel for the claim that this bread is that body. I will argue that the attention so far given to narrative, in particular to narrative identity, will be put to good use in considering these parallel identity claims, that attention to narrative will be the nimble tool appropriate to the baptist vision itself for teasing out the contours of the analogous uses of language that constitute the identities at issue.

Before doing so, however, it will be useful to summarize what has so far here been explored. First, I explicated McClendon's baptist vision, calling particular attention to its being constituted by a particular way of reading Scripture. Second, I showed that for McClendon, the way of reading Scripture that constitutes the baptist vision is fundamentally narrative shaped; that is, baptists read Scripture as an overarching narrative that makes intelligible all narratives, including baptists' own narratives. Furthermore, the way in which baptist readings of Scripture make intelligible those narratives is by means of baptists reading their own narratives in light of Scripture, so that 'this church is that church.' Finally, I argued that attention to narrative serves the particular purpose for McClendon of providing the conceptual framework for articulating the identity of Jesus, the disciples, the church, and the link between them. The emphasis on narrative up to this point is to set up the conceptual approach to McClendon's disciplined, though implicit, use of analogous uses of language to be explored later in the chapter.

Three Instances of The 'baptist' Vision at Work

In this section, I will first explore further the parallel to the baptist vision cited by McClendon, namely the Roman Catholic version of Eucharistic identity. While McClendon's purpose for using it is straightforward enough, the comparison is limited, and, I will suggest, potentially misleading. Even so, the comparison does illuminate further the narrative identity that constitutes the baptist vision. Furthermore, its limitedness is just the entrance required to helpfully illuminate the sort of identity in view. Second, I will turn to three instances of the baptist vision at work, instances which I will use to trace the contours of the identity claim of the baptist vision. Finally, I will make explicit the relation of the narrative reading strategy of baptists to analogous uses of language that constitute the identity claims at issue. In particular, I will show that, though McClendon makes no substantive use of the concept of analogous uses of language in his theology, his theology, like Hubmaier, is shot through with those uses; and, what disciplines those uses is precisely the baptist vision itself.

The 'baptist' Vision and Catholic Eucharistic Identity

McClendon, as we have seen, offers the Catholic understanding of 'this bread on the altar is the body of Christ' as a parallel for the baptist vision. The 'is' in 'this is my body' is an 'is' of real identity, not merely 'represents' or 'symbolizes': "No lesser word will do."[42] Real identity, and yet on all the ordinary ways of analyzing it, still bread: "For if we remark to the intelligent Catholic that the bread is still bread, can be analyzed in a laboratory as bread, etc., he will likely not quarrel with us. 'Yes, it is as you say, still bread, but . . .'"[43] As we noted, the aspect of this identity claim that McClendon explicitly brings to the fore is the unfalsifiability (at least according to ordinary criteria) of the claim.[44] The baker and the scientist would upon analyzing according to the criteria of bakers and scientists detect no difference between that which is on the altar before and after the consecration. McClendon is surely right that the intelligent Catholic understands that the conversion is not one that results in any chemical or material change of the stuff on the altar, and hence there is no ordinary way to prove the claim wrong.

This is all fine so far as it goes. However, it is worth articulating the limits of the parallel in order to bring to the fore the *kinds* of identity claims being made. Strictly speaking, if the Catholic understands the official version of transubstantiation, then that Catholic could only very loosely, and technically *incorrectly*, affirm that the bread is still bread. Of course, that Roman Catholic accepts that by every laboratory test of the scientist or by every taste test of the baker, that which is on the altar behaves just like bread. Still, it is *not* bread. It is Christ's body. What *was* bread is now body by the power of the Spirit.

---

42 McClendon, *Ethics*, 31.

43 Ibid.

44 Lest it look like I am making a mountain out of a mole hill given that McClendon only explicitly appeals to the link between the two with respect to unfalsifiability, note that Barry Harvey finds it "appropriate" that McClendon compares the baptist vision to Catholic Eucharistic theology because of the fact that "within the Roman Catholic Church and the churches of the magisterial Reformation there are communities that embody the baptist vision more faithfully than in most groups that claim the name of Baptist." Furthermore, "Some of the most insightful interpreters of this vision currently at work are Roman Catholic." So, what is appropriate is that McClendon "highlights certain affinities between the baptist vision and Roman Catholic eucharistic teaching." Harvey, "Following James McClendon's," 261. Also, in contrasting the baptist 'is' with a notion of succession or development, McClendon identifies the baptist vision as mystical and immediate in relation to the comparison with Catholic Eucharistic understanding (*Ethics,* 32). So, considering implications beyond only unfalsifiability is legitimate and relevant.

Hence, after the conversion, the Catholic can only say that that which is on the altar is bread in the loosest of senses.

In the Catholic claim (Thomistically understood) only one pole of the identity statement is actually present. Strictly speaking, bread is *not* there, only body. As Hallett suggested, on this version of Eucharistic identity there is no actual identity claim to be made between bread and body since there is only one thing after the consecration, namely body. As we saw in chapter 3, Hallett thinks that in transubstantiation, SIS is operative in a way it is not for other theological statements. Recall that SIS is the supposition (most often implicit) that any real identity is strict identity; that for one thing to be identified as another, it must share all the properties of the other. Identity entails indiscernibility else there really is no true identity.

Hallett, following Kilmartin thinks that the supposition becomes prominent in Eucharistic theology through Germanic influence, and because bread simply lacks 'ontological weight' to hold its own against body. Consequently, 'this bread is my body' comes to mean that this bread is converted into body in such a way that there really is no longer any bread remaining, only body (so, transubstantiation). The identity, to be real, must be strict, and strict identity entails that one of the ends of the relation must give way—it is bread or it is body, it cannot be both. Recall that Hallett notes that in this case, the acceptance of SIS and all that it entails in Eucharistic theology is actually at variance with other theological identity claims; for example the church is the body of Christ without losing either the humanity of the church or Christ; or Jesus is God without indistinguishably collapsing God into Jesus (or Jesus into God). Eucharistic theological identity appears to be odd man out.

Yet, it is just this claim that McClendon holds up as an illuminating parallel, and as the model for "mystical and immediate." As a result, one might fruitfully ask, is the identity of Jesus as God mystical and immediate? How about the identity of the church as the body of Christ? Perhaps both answer to mystical, insofar as both identities are spiritual and mysterious. But immediate appears problematic. Does immediate connote indiscernibility? If immediate indeed connotes indiscernibility, this may prove problematic for the baptist vision insofar as the 'this is that' hermeneutic in practice would *confuse* this with that.

However, McClendon's other illuminating parallel, Peter's appropriation of Joel's prophecy in Acts 2, appears straightforwardly to dispel any worry of confusion. In Acts 2, Peter understands the present activity of the Spirit in terms of Joel's prophecy—"this is that which was spoken by the prophet Joel." As we said, McClendon, following Napier contends that this is a real identification. Peter does not mean to say that Joel is an illustration of the Spirit's work, or that 'this' is merely metaphorically, or symbolically 'that.' McClendon would say of Peter's identification what he said of the Catholic:

"Not 'represents' or 'symbolizes', but *is*. No lesser word will do."[45] Yet this is plainly not *strict* identity as described by Hallett. The coming of the Spirit and the event Joel describes are not indiscernible. In fact, the claim that this event (the coming of the Spirit) is what Joel spoke about requires the integrity of both poles of the identity. If 'this' collapses without distinction into 'that,' then there is no identity to be made. If 'this' collapses into that, then the 'plain sense' of Joel's words are obliterated by the identification, rather than appropriated by the identification.

So, what to make of this identification? As it stands, the parallel with official Catholic accounts of transubstantiation appears problematic insofar as it would confuse the poles of the identity by collapsing one into the other. However, the parallel with Peter's appropriation of Joel appears straightforwardly to at least in form prevent the sort of confusion in view here.

To sort out the kind of identity embodied in the baptist vision, I turn now to three further illuminating parallels: McClendon's Christology, a baptist account of conversion, and McClendon's argument against priests. These illuminating parallels are especially helpful because they are actual instances of the baptist vision at work, identity claims that are generated by the reading strategy of baptists. Furthermore, they embody what I explicated above about the role of narrative in McClendon's theology. In particular, these three parallels will provide example cases bringing to the fore the role of narrative as the nimble tool in baptist theological articulations (usually implicit, though made explicit by McClendon) that allow for a plurality of kinds of identity claims, in particular real identity claims that do not collapse into strict identity. The immediate payoff will be to show how the baptist vision is constituted by a real identity claim, but a real identity that is not strict identity. The payoff later in the chapter will be to show how narrative provides the 'ordering' required for disciplined analogical uses of language that constitute the identity statements in view, in particular Eucharistic identity claims.

First, I will consider McClendon's two-narrative Christology. The goal will be to explicate how the identity of Jesus as both human and divine is facilitated by narrative, an identity that is real, but not strict. Following McClendon's narrative Christology, I will consider baptist conversion narratives as illuminating examples of an identity claim made by way of a change, though, unlike in transubstantiation, a change which results in an actual identification, rather than a collapse of one pole of the putative identity into the other. For McClendon, this sort of change is articulated in narrative terms. Finally, I will consider McClendon's argument against priests in light of an objection to his argument that raises just the issue of identity. There the goal will not be to evaluate McClendon's argument (either in defense of the objection or in support of it). Rather, the goal will be to call attention to the

---

45 McClendon, *Ethics*, 30.

form of the argument, in particular the use that McClendon's argument makes of the narrative of Scripture.

After considering these three parallels and the role that narrative plays in them, in a concluding section I will make explicit the promised fruit of this attention to narrative. There, I will make explicit the implicit ordering of analogous uses of language that constitute the various identities at issue, an ordering accomplished by the baptist hermeneutic of reading Scripture narratively, and the narrative identities generated by that reading strategy.

Two-Narratives Christology

McClendon's Christology, and his account of the history and development of past Christologies is an illuminating example of the baptist vision at work.[46] McClendon begins his Christology by identifying three underlying questions that have been behind Christological reflection throughout Christian history. These questions, he thinks, can serve the pedagogical role of organizing the concerns that were present as the church in the past considered Christology, and the concerns which continue to be present to us. These questions are useful because not only have they been implicit in Christian reflection, but they are occasioned by the biblical narrative itself. First, why ascribe the Lordship that Scripture reserves for God to Jesus? Second, how do we ascribe that Lordship to Jesus without violating the oneness of God (monotheism)? And third, what bearing does the life of Jesus as fully human have on our lives? How ought disciples of Jesus live?[47] These questions at once arose out of a reading of the biblical narrative and also governed that reading.

The Logos model of Christology was formulated in response to two Christological patterns that arose in the context of the early missionary efforts in the Roman Empire.[48] First, there was a pattern of emphasizing the humanity of Jesus, perhaps typified by the Ebionites. While the Ebionites were right to

---

[46] For McClendon's account of the development of Christology, and his constructive two-narratives proposal, see in particular *Doctrine*, 250-279. Thomas N. Finger offers a brief overview of McClendon's Narrative Christology in his *A Contemporary Anabaptist Theology: Biblical, Historical, Constructive* (Downers Grove, IL: IVP, 2004), 397-99.

[47] McClendon, *Doctrine*, 194-195.

[48] I follow McClendon's historical exposition and analysis (*Doctrine*, 251-257) in what comes below. For a brief theological and historical overview of the period in question see Veli-Matti Kärkkäinen, *Christology: A Global Introduction* (Grand Rapids: Baker Academic, 2003), 61-78. J.N.D. Kelly's *Early Christian Doctrines*, rev. ed. (New York: HarperSanFrancisco, 1978) is still a standard reference. See in particular pp. 138-142 for an overview of the Ebionites and Docetists (and their Gnostic influence), and chapters 9, and 11-12 for the developments that led to Chalcedon.

affirm Jesus's humanity, in practice the divinity of Jesus was overlooked. If the Ebionites affirmed the humanity of Jesus, Gnostics scorned it. Salvation was through knowledge. Jesus only appeared to be human. His real mission was to impart this secret, saving knowledge. Both of these patterns provided an answer to question three: both affirmed that following Jesus meant becoming more Christ-like, though of course becoming more Christ-like looked very different for the two. But neither pattern was able to satisfactorily answer the first and second questions since they were unable to hold together both the humanity of Jesus and the divinity of Jesus.

In response, the early apologists formulated the Logos model. God, impenetrable and inaccessible, sent his Logos to participate in humanity. The pagan logos, which was the organizing principle or the reason of the universe, became the Christian Logos—all things summed up in Christ (Col. 1:15-17). But a problem presented itself with the Logos model as well. The Logos model, while affirming the full divinity of Jesus, could not clearly articulate how Jesus was more than just *a* god, and hence could give only a problematic answer to question one. Still, the Logos model did better than either the Ebionites or the Gnostics did in answering why Jesus is Lord, and in protecting the oneness of God.

The Logos model had an important influence on Arius, who taught that the Word was created from nothing and hence of a different substance than the Father. In opposition to Arius, the council of Nicea affirmed instead that the Son was eternally of the same substance as the Father, but also fully human. For Nicea, the answer to the first question, then, was clear: Jesus is Lord because he is of the same substance as the Father. The answer to question two led to the formulation of the two-natures model at Chalcedon. How do we account for Jesus as one in substance with the Father, and also fully human? The answer was that Jesus was of two natures, one divine, one human. McClendon's concern is that this answer to the second question, while rightly embracing the full divinity of Jesus, overshadows the fully human Jesus as presented in the gospel narratives. By extension, then, the answer to question three is unsatisfying. How does a two-natures model inform the sort of life to be lived by disciples?

McClendon turns to narratives to articulate who Jesus is. Throughout *Doctrine*, McClendon speaks of the biblical story as a tale of two stories, one divine, one human. The distinction is important, for humans are not God, and God, though present to creation, cannot be simply identified with creation. Furthermore, the two stories narrate the reality both of the fallenness of creation and of the giftedness of redemption. The biblical narrative, then, is the story of humans reaching for God. As a story of grace, it is also a story of God reaching for humans, and making the human response to God possible at all. In these stories, God reaches for humans before humans even reach for God. The significance of Jesus is that these two stories are finally brought together as fully one story. In the story of Jesus, these two stories are indivisibly linked.

Recall that for McClendon, narrative or story fixes the identity of Jesus and his disciples; and likewise, the grand narrative of Scripture fixes the identity of God and the whole of creation. So, an appeal to narrative is a claim about who God is, and about how all that is is related to God.

To flesh out his narrative Christology, McClendon begins with a summarization of the Jesus story found in the early Christian hymn in Philippians 2:5-11. McClendon sees the emptying of the servant in Philippians not as the submission of the Divine to human flesh, but as the earthly Jesus's eschewing power in his rejection of the temptations. One line of evidence for this read is the comparison Paul makes between his own experience and the emptying of Jesus in chapter 3: though Paul was worthy of human admiration, he eschewed that to follow the way of Jesus. For both, their radical nonconformity cost them their lives. Here, then, is the story of Jesus the fully faithful human, the example for others who would follow him.[49]

But of course that Jesus's nonconformity cost him his life is not the end of the story. God raised Jesus from the dead. The resurrection is, first, the sign which characterizes all of Jesus's life. As the whole narrative thrust of the story makes clear, Jesus's resurrection was not the sign of 'adoption,' if by adoption one means that Jesus became God, or achieved godly status. Rather, God's intention was clear from the beginning. The "virginal conception," when properly read in light of the resurrection, makes this clear. There was never a time when the human Jesus was not united to God's story. In the resurrection, Jesus's earthly life is re-identified, re-narrated with the life of God so that the two lives, indivisible from the start, are now narratively linked.

Though the resurrection is the central feature of the story, it is not the chronological end of the story as told in Scripture. The apostolic church is the continuation of this Jesus story. The church practices baptism, publicly identifying those who follow Jesus. The church practices the Lord's Supper, a remembering meal of the salvation given by God. The church practices teaching, the handing on of the faith. The church also contributes its own early Christological reflection. For instance, the epistles identify Jesus as sinless, and this identification makes clear that Jesus's full faithfulness links his story to God's. The story of the truly human Jesus was indivisibly the story of God, and so links with the story of the church.

McClendon argues that this narrative Christology can answer the three questions that Christologies have sought to answer. First, what right does Jesus have to be called Lord? If Jesus's story is indivisibly linked with the story of God, then he has the right to be called Lord since we are confronted in this story "by an unimpeachable authority, with *God's own claim* upon our lives."[50]

---

[49] McClendon does not deny that the passage may also speak of divine kenosis, though he insists that the emphasis must be on the human emptying.

[50] McClendon, *Doctrine*, 277. Emphasis McClendon's.

Second, how can those who believe in one God tell the story of Jesus without violating the oneness of God? Here, McClendon argues that a narrative approach has distinct advantages over traditional Christologies, for the technical puzzles of *hypostasis*, *ousia*, and *persona* are bypassed.[51] These were "alien puzzles" anyway to the New Testament story. The question rather becomes, how can God be identified with just one of earth's many stories? This is a question of election. McClendon points readers to other parts of *Doctrine* that would take us too far astray here. But in short, the answer to this reformulated question is a call to service. Christ's divine election is justified because it is a call to servant-hood. This call to servant-hood is the clue to the answer to the third question. In Jesus, the human story is identified with God's story. Hence, the answer to the question of the relationship of Jesus's life to ours is in terms of our "concrete self-involvement in that story."[52] McClendon concludes,

> Absolute Lordship on Christ's part (question one) entails nothing less than perfect discipleship on our part (here John Wesley stands with the witness of Scripture) . . . . Discipleship meant (and means) commitment to the

---

51 There is nothing in McClendon's two-narrative Christology that compels a rejection of Chalcedon, though Terrence Tilley and Barry Harvey both worry that McClendon treats the traditional Christological formulations in too cursory a fashion. See Terrence Tilley's review of McClendon's *Doctrine* in *Pro Ecclesia* 6 (Summer 1997): 367, and Harvey "Following James McClendon's," 260. In a brief, but perceptive criticism of McClendon's dismissal of a two-natures Christology, J.A. DiNoia notes that the dismissal is ultimately without argument (more or less a blunt claim that it is not 'ours'), but also that the "intellectual sources of McClendon's procedure do not appear to be doctrinal (as if entailed by the baptist vision) or even theological (though perhaps connected with McClendon's narrative ontology)." DiNoia, review of McClendon's *Doctrine*, in *Modern Theology* 12 (January 1996), 119. Without mentioning McClendon (though influenced by him as his student), Terrence Tilley offers an account of narrative theology that suggests something of why McClendon treats Chalcedon the way he does. In his *Story Theology* (Collegeville, MN: Michael Glazier, 1985), Tilley contrasts the task of narrative theology and propositional theology, arguing that narrative theology is "more fundamental" than propositional theology, and that as a result narratives are necessary to contextualize the propositional claims given, 11-13. Perhaps what one might contribute to McClendon's narrative Christology, then, is more constructive reflection on *how* a two narratives Christology provides contextual 'support' for a two-natures Christology, without necessitating the replacement of the two-natures Christology. That is, even if a two-natures Christology is not 'ours' because of foreign concepts, perhaps a two-narrative Christology can help us 'rediscover' it by providing the storied 'flesh' that made it plausible in the first place.

52 McClendon, *Doctrine*, 278.

> social radicalism of a nonconformist Christ; it required (and requires) not inner torments . . . or guilty consciences but entire reorientation to a life with Jesus that will necessarily collide again and again with the powers, with the world's No, that is, with a cross (Mark 8:34f).[53]

For my purposes note that for McClendon naming Christ's divinity and humanity in narrative terms is no less 'real' or 'weighty' than doing so in terms of substance or nature. For the writers of the Old and New Testaments, God is not affirmed as real by appeal to substance or nature, but by retelling the stories of God's activity on behalf of the world.[54] 'Substance' and 'nature' are at best shorthand ways of referring to the narrative that shows Jesus to be very God and very man. Hence, if Jesus is the "exact representation of [God's] nature" (Heb 1:3) all of life finds its intelligibility in the story of Jesus's death and resurrection. The gospel story itself frames what is real. Narrative is not a category prior to the gospel, an external framework into which the gospel is made to fit. Rather, it is a way of confessing that 'reality' is not a category that is intelligible prior to the story of God revealed in Jesus Christ. In other words, the world is not a 'reality' to which the gospel of Jesus Christ is added on. The world is already 'gospelized' in the sense that "by [Christ] all things were created . . . . He is before all things, and in Him all things hold together" (Col. 1:16-17).[55] This is not to deny a relative narrative integrity to the world. All is not God. In fact, constitutive of the world's narrative identity is its creation by God, the generous gift of 'space' to *be* other than God. Even so, the world's 'space' to be other than God can only be identified as such 'space' insofar as it is identified as God's gift of creation.

This means, then, that 'narrative' is not a category prior to God's redemptive work. Hence, in his three volume systematic theology, McClendon spends little time articulating a theory of narrative or stories. He rather talks about the particular stories that make up the grand narrative of God's activity in and for the world. Even so, that narrative is not prior to gospel does not deny that, as Stanley Hauerwas has said, "the appeal to narrative is the primary expression of a theological metaphysics and is, therefore, an unembarrassed

---

53 McClendon, *Doctrine*, 278-9.

54 The New Testament does have a few references to the nature of God, but always within the framework of the narrative of what God has done in Israel and in Jesus of Nazareth. Even other passages of Scripture that are not narrative in form (epistles, for instance) depend upon the narrative structure of the gospel. See, for instance, Richard Hays, *The Faith of Jesus Christ: The Narrative Substructure of Galatians 3:1-4:11* (Grand Rapids: W.B. Eerdmans, 2002), and A. Katherin Grieb, *The Story of Romans: A Narrative Defense of God's Righteousness* (Louisville: Westminster John Knox Press, 2002).

55 Citation from the *New American Standard Bible*.

claim about the way things are."[56] If narrative is a "theological metaphysics," it is not because of anything about narratives in general, nor about the human need for myth or story. Neither is it because narrative is a category we can talk about when we cannot otherwise talk about God. It is rather because of a particular, true narrative—the story of Israel and the church as 'summed up' in the narrative of Jesus Christ, a narrative that sums up the way things are.

For my purposes, note then that for McClendon, a narrative identification of Jesus as human and divine, an identification constituted by the convergence of two stories, constitutes real identity. Yet, though real, it is not strict identity. It allows us to affirm in narrative terms the real identity of the humanity and divinity of Christ without collapsing one into the other. There is the story of the first century Jew, a story which would be intelligible if told by one who refused the second story. For the Christian, that this human story has its own relative integrity is necessary for the complete story. However, for the Christian, this first story is nevertheless incomplete, and as such though it has its own relative narrative integrity, it fails on its own to be the story of Jesus Christ, and hence fails to identify this Jesus. These two stories are one story in the incarnation, and yet not indiscernible. Hence, the narrative character of this identity claim does not run on SIS. In fact, it is suggestive of alternative ways of construing identity than strict identity.

I want to suggest, then, that this narrative identity of Jesus is a better model for grasping the baptist vision than Catholic Eucharistic identity. The 'is' in the baptist 'this is that' is illuminated by the 'is' in the narrative identity of Christ that the vision generates. This is because McClendon's narrative Christology, unlike transubstantiation, is able to hold together two stories in one real identity without confusing the two, or collapsing one into the other. Furthermore, the use of 'is' in these instances is best articulated in narrative terms. Finally, for the broader purposes of this chapter, the analogous uses of language that constitute this identity, in particular the analogous use of 'is,' is ordered by this appeal to narrative. I will spell this out more fully in the final section.

Conversion

For a second illuminating example of the vision at work, consider conversion stories, something central to most baptist traditions. While modern conversion stories may tend toward a kind of individualistic pietism, conversion stories nevertheless function to fix the identity of the convert—"this is the story of how I came to belong to Jesus." It will be useful to consider conversion stories in light of McClendon's account of a voluntary church because it brings to the

---

56 Stanley Hauerwas, *Performing the Faith: Bonhoeffer and the Practice of Nonviolence* (Grand Rapids: Brazos Press, 2004), 146.

fore that even overly individualistic conversion stories betray the corporate identity of the church.

For McClendon, "an intentional, or voluntary" church is partly defined in contrast to a hereditary or ethnic community, and to a national or civil religion.[57] It is a church of disciples, of followers of Jesus. Here, McClendon makes use of Jack Dean Kingsbury's analysis of the Gospel of Mathew's precise use of 'with' to identify the followers of Jesus. The disciples, Mary, tax collectors and even sinners are with Jesus, while the crowds surrounding him are not.[58] It is these sorts of people, those who have committed themselves to the way and person of Jesus, that constitute the church. McClendon says that "in the strict Troeltschian sense, then, the church Matthew addresses is 'sectarian,' composed of men and women of whatever age who have freely obeyed the 'follow me' of Christ."[59] The commitment to Jesus that identifies a disciple is expressed in obedience. One freely gives oneself over to obedience to her Lord, to a life of renunciation of self. Freedom that is exercised in commitment is completed, fulfilled in obedience. Obedience was a constitutive feature of that which made solidarity possible: disciples are one with their Lord and one another in mutual, shared obedience to their Lord.[60] This makes the person of Jesus central to the solidarity in obedience that is constitutive of discipleship: "Matthew would have his Syrian readers understand that by voluntarily linking their lives to Jesus, they have linked them to each other as well."[61] The solidarity that constitutes discipleship trumps other identifications

---

57 McClendon, *Ethics*, 217.

58 Ibid., 216-217. McClendon references Jack Dean Kingsbury, *Matthew*, Proclamation Commentaries (Philadelphia: Fortress Press, 1977), 80.

59 McClendon, *Ethics*, 217. Drawing on Wayne Meeks's analysis of early Christian communities, especially ones resulting from Paul's missionary journeys, McClendon contends that the biblical accounts of household conversions cannot be taken as evidence against a voluntary church as identified above. Says McClendon, "Whole households were converted (Acts 10:16), baptized (see also 1 Cor1:16), and sometimes *as households* commended for Christian service (1 Cor. 16:15ff). Meeks explains, though, that in such group conversions, 'not everyone who went along with the new practices would do so with the *same* understanding or inner participation' (1983:77, emphasis added). It is a case of modern practice shaping exegesis if we extrapolate from Meeks's cautious observation to the unwarranted conclusion that some new members perhaps had no faith at all, and were helpless infants or hapless slaves. For as Meeks correctly notes, Paul's letter to Philemon makes it clear that in Paul's understanding of the matter, 'not every member of a household always became a Christian when the head did' (Meeks, 1983:76)." See Wayne Meeks, *The First Urban Christians: The Social World of the Apostle Paul* (New Haven: Yale University Press, 1983), 76-77.

60 McClendon, *Ethics*, 218.

61 McClendon, *Ethics*, 218.

such as family or ethnic or national identity. Hence, for McClendon, the church is inherently and irreducibly social. Solidarity in obedience, not individual spirituality characterizes life in the church. Hence, conversion stories articulate this new identity, an identity that trumps past identities. While in contemporary Baptist churches, conversion stories tend toward individualism, even these individual conversion narratives implicitly fix the identity of the convert in the church of the disciples insofar as they relate the moment of pledge or trust, which issues in the obedience that characterizes discipleship.

Of course, for baptists who practice believers baptism, conversion accounts generally culminate in baptism. This is because, as McClendon articulates it, baptism is the liturgical act of initiation as a sign of salvation. Though spoken of in merely symbolic terms by many baptists, McClendon contends that baptism *does* something.[62] What it does is "to effect a turn in one life-story (the candidate's) on the basis of Jesus's crucified and risen life. Baptism brings those two lives together in the ongoing 'life-story' of the people of God."[63] Notice that the identity of these stories in form recalls (though of

---

62 McClendon, *Doctrine*, 390. Here, McClendon follows Austin's Speech-act theory. See McClendon and James M. Smith, *Convictions: Diffusing Religious Relativism*, rev. ed. (Valley Forge, PA: Trinity Press, 1994; originally published as *Understanding Religious Convictions* [Notre Dame: Notre Dame University Press, 1975]) chapter 3 for an account of Speech-act theory and its application to religious language.

In this context, McClendon cites the often used example of "I do" said in a marriage ceremony as a comparison to baptism. These words *do* something, not merely 'symbolize' something. Interestingly, John S. Hammett, a contemporary Southern Baptist theologian uses the example of marriage (though without Speech-act theory in view) as a comparison to baptism. He says that in baptism we are identified with Christ, suggesting that something is *done* in baptism. Yet, he then goes on to say that "A wedding ceremony does not create love between two people; they have already said 'yes' to each other well before the wedding. Yet at the wedding the couple's love is publicly confessed, celebrated, and confirmed. In the same way, baptism does not create faith or unite one with Christ, but it is the event by which faith is confessed, celebrated, and confirmed. It is the ordinance of commitment." Hammett, "Article VII: Baptism and the Lord's Supper," in *The Baptist Faith and Message 2000: Critical Issues in America's Largest Protestant Denomination*, ed. Douglas K. Blount and Joseph D. Wooddell (Lanham, MD: Rowman & Littlefield Publishers, 2007), 73-74. In Hammett's odd articulation, while confessing, celebrating and confirming are certainly things to be done at a wedding, the central thing is left out, namely *getting married*. This suggests the pervasiveness of a 'merely' symbolic approach to the sacraments in Southern Baptist life, despite Hammett's own desire to speak of God's blessings bestowed in the doing of them (72-73).

63 McClendon, *Doctrine*, 390.

course does not mimic) the incarnation—two stories, the convert's and Jesus's are brought together and converge in one story of the church. McClendon considers the "moral significance" of the various "metaphors" of baptism in the New Testament. The passage is worth quoting at length:

> First, *baptism points to, refers to, the life story of Jesus himself*. His own baptism had been his pledge and his ordination to the cause of the kingdom of God, his first deliberate step on that way. Confessing his sin, the sinless one had declared his identification with sinners and then set out on the way of redemption. Now, in his or her own baptism, each believer claims that story, appropriates it, accepts Jesus' story as this believer's identity-narrative. Second, however, *baptism focuses the candidate's own life story*: as a brother or sister takes this step the narrative of his or her life is brought out of obscurity, laid before God in repentance and faith, and decisively turned into God's new path in the company of the baptized community. In baptism, one's own conversion is confessed and oriented. Third, *baptism brings these two narratives,* Christ's and the candidate's, *together in the company of all the saints*. When one is baptized, the reference is both to Jesus' story and to one's own story—and these are in baptism confessed to be *one* with the church's story. Thus the identification with Jesus as the incarnate, obedient, crucified, and risen One is not merely legal or merely mystical—though it is those things; it is a *narrative* identification (just as in the resurrection, Jesus' identification with God consists in a narrative linking of his life with the life of God—Rom. 1:4). Here, then, the prophetic (or baptist) vision is at work: "this is that" and "then is now"—our baptisms recapitulate and claim as our own his resurrection.[64]

Here the link with Christology is clear: the identity of the convert baptized with Jesus "is a *narrative* identity."[65] Furthermore, in baptism the convert is made one with the church's story. All of the above about baptism suggests the narrative character of conversion itself, how in conversion one receives a new identity, fixed by and identified in a narrative mode on the pattern of the baptist vision.

Pressing the comparison with narrative Christology suggests the fundamental, *real* change in conversion—the identity of the believer with the resurrection of Jesus is no mere figure or symbol; it is an identification which results in a new life, a new identity. Things are not as they were. It is a real identity; and yet, it obviously is not the sort of identity which results in confusion of the two narratives—there is still a relative narrative integrity to the believer's pre-conversion story. Upon initiation into the reign of God the

---

64 Ibid., *Ethics*, 267. Emphases McClendon's.

65 Ibid.

narrative arrangement that identifies one's life prior to conversion does not change. No pieces are left out or shift in chronological order. The pre-conversion story has its own integrity as identifying narrative. But this integrity is indeed relative, for the convert led by wise and discerning members of the church begins to see that 'the facts' were never as simple as they seemed.[66] Post-conversion one begins to see hints of God's guidance where before one could not, so that the relative integrity of the storied identity of life before Jesus now finds its point in the new narrative identity. That is, though the narrative particulars remain the same, and though their chronological arrangement is unchanged, the narrative as a whole is different. Those same 'facts,' even in their relative integrity, are rendered anew in light of Jesus. Now their point, where the story aims, the context that makes sense of these particulars, is the story of Jesus and his disciples. The result is that the narrative identity of the believer in Christ both assumes the relative integrity of this pre-Christian narrative, and its fundamental re-narration in the life of Christ. The old is new without collapsing the old into the new; they are narratively distinguishable precisely because they are narratively inseparable. The narrative 'wedge' that distinguishes them (life before Jesus and life after Jesus) is also the ligament that joins them (life before Jesus leading to and bearing fruit in life after Jesus). In short, conversion constitutes a real identity claim between old life and new, without thereby necessitating strict identity.

This sort of identity is illuminating in light of transubstantiation, in which the conversion of bread to body entails the absence of bread after the change. Recall that in chapter 4 I suggested a way of reading Thomas such that the conversion of bread to body did not entail the eradication of the bread, that one can articulate a conversion in which the poles of the conversion both are present. Baptist accounts of conversion are like this sort of change. There is a real change from sinner to disciple; and yet it is a change that requires both pre- and post-conversion narratives in order to make the identification. Of course, conversion to following Jesus is not simply the same as conversion of bread to body. But both are conversions, and baptist conversion accounts disclose a kind of conversion that does not entail the collapse of one pole of the conversion into the other. Furthermore, as with narrative Christology, advertence to the way in which narrative makes possible a real identity that is not strict identity suggests the way in which the analogous uses of language in conversion stories are disciplined and ordered, a point to be spelled out further in the final section.

---

[66] I recognize, as Hans Frei says, that "the concept 'fact' is not theory-neutral." Frei, *Theology and Narrative: Selected Essays*, ed. by George Hunsinger and William C. Placher (New York: Oxford University Press, 1993), 211. Still, 'facts' is a good word and so I leave it blissfully undefined. If one is thinking of a theory of 'facts,' one should not, and then one will be close to how I mean to use it.

McClendon's Argument Against Priests

Consider one more illustrative example of the baptist vision at work, in this case occasioned by an objection to the baptist vision. The objection is the worry that the baptist vision generates a way of being church that is little more than a naïve primitivism, a kind of unreflective mimicry of the early church in the baptist 'this is that.' Robert Barron's criticism of McClendon's argument against the priesthood is an instance of this worry. Barron's claim is that McClendon is opposed to "a separate clerical class within certain Christian Churches on the grounds that the Scripture never speaks of priests but only of Christ the high priest and of the whole priestly people . . . ."[67] The criticism comes in a lengthy review essay that is otherwise supportive of McClendon's project.[68] Still, Barron's concern calls attention to a worry voiced more stridently by H. Wayne Layman, that despite McClendon's insistence otherwise the baptist vision constitutes a naïve restitutionism, a denial of church history, jumping straight back to the apostles.[69] The underlying concern voiced by both worries bears a family resemblance to SIS: 'this is that' appears to entail the collapsing of one pole into the other. In this case, to say that 'this church is that church' is to say that 'this' church is indistinguishably, indiscernibly 'that' church, as evidenced by the baptist vision's understanding of church leadership as simply the leadership of the New Testament church. As Barron's objection is really one particular instance of Layman's worry, for sake of space I will attend to Barron only.

My interest here is not defending McClendon's account of church leadership. Rather, I want to consider whether or not Barron's objection to McClendon's argument against priests fairly assesses the character of what in fact McClendon is doing. That is, I need not here make another argument against priests (maybe McClendon, even by the lights of his own baptist vision, turns out to be wrong about that; maybe not). Rather, all I mean to do is ask

---

67 Barron, 271.

68 Barron views McClendon's systematic theology as a constructive contribution to postliberal theology. For an overview of the issues and trajectories involved in postliberal theology, see the essays in John Webster and George P. Schner, eds. *Theology After Liberalism: A Reader*, Blackwell Readings In Modern Theology, ed. L. Gregory Jones and James Buckley (Oxford: Blackwell, 2000), in particular Webster's introductory essay, "Theology after Liberalism?" pp. 52-61.

69 Layman, 490. McClendon and John Howard Yoder respond to Layman's essay in McClendon and Yoder, "Christian Identity in Ecumenical Perspective: A Response to David Wayne Layman," *Journal of Ecumenical Studies* 27 (Summer 1990): 561-580. There, they address the baptist vision in terms of the issue of catholicity raised by Layman.

whether Barron has heard well the *form* of the argument. What I need to offer is an exposition of McClendon's narrative 'logic' at work in his argument against priests. In doing so, I mean to guide our attention once again along the contours of this vision in order to get at the sort of identity claim entailed by 'this is that.' McClendon's argument against a priestly class is another instance of the baptist vision generating an identity claim about 'this' church and 'that' church, and the identity claim is ordered by the baptist strategy of reading Scripture narratively.

So, to Barron's objection that McClendon denies a clerical class because "Scripture never speaks of priests," and that for Barron this denial constitutes a "simplistic" identification of this church with the apostolic church.[70] In short, this concern, stated by Barron misses the narrative character of the claim made by McClendon, a claim arising out of the link between this church and that church.[71]

McClendon thinks that the overarching narrative frame of Scripture suggests three pervasive and related themes which come to bear on the issue of priests (pervasive and prominent enough even to structure his *Doctrine* by them): the rule of God, the identity of Jesus Christ (in this context comes the three questions related to Christology), and the fellowship of the Spirit. The narrative theme of the rule of God encompasses much, but relevant to this issue is that it entails a politics, a community of a certain character.[72] Likewise, the identity of Jesus Christ encompasses much. Here two things in particular are important; first, the identity of Jesus is central to the identity of God, and hence to the God who rules; second, as indicated in McClendon's narrative Christology, the theme of the identity of Jesus entails much about the character of the community entailed by God's reign, the sort of politics that constitutes the community of disciples.[73] Finally, the fellowship of the Spirit draws together what is entailed about this community by the reign of God and the identity of Jesus into what the church teaches about the church itself.

McClendon's account of church leadership, included in his baptist ecclesiology, must be set in this narrative context. Says McClendon, "The rule of God requires church *members* subject to that very rule. The centrality of Jesus Christ demands church *leaders* led by Christ crucified and risen. The fellowship of the Spirit implies a *common life* whose practices suit, not the present age, but the age to come—a community at once redeemed and

---

70 Barron, 270.

71 This despite the fact that Barron notes the resemblance of McClendon's articulation of the baptist vision with "Lindbeck's call to draw our stories into the Biblical story rather than to affect some sort of correlation between them, as in the typically liberal approach." Barron, 270.

72 McClendon, *Doctrine*, 68.

73 Ibid., 194-195.

redemptive."[74] McClendon notes that Scripture does not present a "once-for-all-answer" to the question of the pattern of organized church life. What we do find are "long continuities of Christian teaching" developed along the three themes identified above:[75] membership by consent to God's rule; under the leadership of Christ, a leadership that "says No to social control shaped by the old aeon and Yes to a fellowship charged by that crucified and risen presence;" in the mode of a "vector of a community that lives between the times, adapting, adjusting, transforming, interpreting so that the church can be the church."[76]

To the question of church leadership, if the above themes constitute an accurate rendering of the narrative trajectory of Scripture, then they provide the frame for appropriating the narrative particulars relevant to leadership that constitute this trajectory. So, in the Old Testament we find God calling Israel to be his "priest-people, God's mediator nation, a people in the interest of all people and in that regard holy—not a nation with, but a nation of, priests."[77] In the New Testament we find Jesus instructing and embodying servant-leadership. So then, what of this fellowship of the Spirit? How did the disciples appropriate this trajectory? Says McClendon,

> While the primitive church felt free to borrow leadership names from Scripture (e.g., "prophet"), from Jewish practice ("elder"), and from the wider culture (*episkopos*, "overseer"), the readily available term "priest" is never applied in the New Testament to any Christian leader except Jesus the great high priest (Heb. 4:14ff; 6:13ff), but only (in echo of Exodus 19) to the new-chosen people of God (1 Pt. 2:9).[78]

This is because *all* disciples are priests insofar as all, and especially all *together* live "to become for others the bread of life."[79] In this sense, says McClendon, baptism is a sort of ordination to ministry. Of course, the New Testament epistles in particular make clear that there are different gifts, a variety of means of contributing to the corporate ministry of the life of the church. The special role of apostles, prophets and evangelists "is to equip God's people for work in his service."[80] In their own leadership roles, so also bishops and elders. Consequently, to say that all are ministers does not mean, as McClendon says, that there can no longer be itinerate 'apostles' or 'evangelists' or local 'bishops' or 'elders;' it does mean that "these must be seen as only part of the

---

74 McClendon, *Doctrine*, 366. McClendon gives an exposition of Hebrews 12-13 as a summary statement of these recurrent narrative themes in the church.

75 Ibid., 367.

76 Ibid.

77 Ibid., 368. McClendon cites Exodus 19:5f.

78 Ibid.

79 Ibid., 369.

80 McClendon, *Doctrine*, 369. McClendon cites Ephesians 4:11ff.

fullness of Christ. For on this view bishops are part of the laity; on this view every Christian is a cleric."[81]

Keeping in mind that my goal is not show why Barron is wrong to reject McClendon's account, but rather simply to suggest that McClendon's account does not reduce to a "simplistic" identification of this church with that church, we can now gather up this exposition and reflect on it appealing to the previous account of Christological identity as an illuminating paradigm. McClendon's argument against a priestly class within the church is as Barron rightly says, centered on Scripture rather than later "developments" in the life of the Church.[82] But the logic of the baptist vision, as should hopefully be clear, is not "Scripture does not speak of leaders in the church as priests, so we shouldn't have priests." McClendon's is no naïve biblicism in which a claim in Scripture is laid flatly and unreflectively over the contemporary church as an inflexible mold. Rather, the explicit appeal in McClendon's argument to the terms used in Scripture about church leaders is simply an acknowledgment of the pervasive logic of the narrative. The reason that the New Testament does not speak of church leaders as priests is because of the thematic narrative logic of all Scripture, the thread of narrative continuity from Old Testament to New Testament in which God's people are consistently a corporate priest people.[83] The narrative logic of a corporate priest-people, who in the Old Testament had

---

81 Ibid. McClendon's rejection of a clerical class is clearly aimed at the rejection of passive church congregations whose ministry is carried out almost solely by 'active' clergy. In fact, McClendon makes clear that this is intended to be a critique of any congregational pattern, be it Protestant, baptist, or otherwise, that fails to energize and engage all of God's people in the work of ministry. Still, McClendon clearly means the principle to apply to any distinction between lay and clergy, which is what Barron focuses on.

82 "Developments" is of course Barron's word, drawing on John Henry Newman. Barron, 270.

83 Veli-Matti Kärkkäinen summarizes McClendon's position in a way that though not incorrect, is misleading, and hence occasions the sort of worry Barron has. Though implicit in his situating of McClendon's claim about the New Testament in light of the Old, Kärkkäinen overlooks the role of narrative. He says of McClendon's claim, "the distinction between 'lay' and 'clerical' has no clear New Testament roots. Those churches that find such distinctions essential to the being of the church are not building on the testimony of the New Testament but rather on the emerging worldly standards of the postapostolic age." Kärkkäinen, *An Introduction to Ecclesiology: Ecumenical, Historical, and Global Perspectives* (Downers Grove, IL: IVP, 2002), 149. It is true that for McClendon 'lay' and 'clerical' have no clear New Testament roots. However, I am suggesting that this is an insufficient description of McClendon's argument, for it fails to attend to *why* the New Testament lacks those roots. The answer is because of the narrative trajectory identified between Old and New.

priests serving as go betweens between God and his people, is fulfilled in Christ the high priest, who opens up God and his people to one another in such a way that the eternal priesthood of Jesus pours out priestly, mediating, functions on all of God's people. Hence, that the New Testament never uses the word 'priest' of church leaders is simply a succinct and unsurprising indication of this narrative trajectory.

Now, it may be that the relative authorities of Scripture and church tradition for the Catholic (Barron) and the baptist (McClendon) remain a dividing line here. The baptist will insist that any pattern of church life, in order to be a 'development' must answer to the narrative trajectory of Scripture, and consequently any particular pattern of church life in Christian history must submit in this regard to Scripture. However, attention to the manner of Scripture's authority in the baptist vision, an authority in terms of the whole narrative trajectory of Scripture, not simply each individual imperative or pattern of speech, suggests again the contours of this vision.

For my purposes, I only mean to note this: McClendon's argument against a clerical class, an argument operating out of the baptist vision, acknowledges the relative integrity of both the New Testament church's story and ours, an integrity articulated for both in narrative terms. That all members are priests is to say that the identity of this church is fixed by *that* scriptural narrative, that the intelligibility of this church must be in terms of *that* story. Of course, this church has its own relatively distinct narrative—it is a church story that includes pre and post Constantinian stories and what those stories entail for leadership: its story includes reference, for example to modernity and modern science, Western individualism and autonomy, each of which has implications for church leadership and authority. None of these are strictly the apostles' stories; and in some respects the apostles' stories are not the contemporary church's stories. Yet, this relative sameness and difference is relative to the gospel itself, so that the narrative trajectory of Scripture frames both in their discernible identity. So, while there will no doubt be variety in church structure (as there apparently was in the New Testament church), for it to be intelligible to the gospel it must pattern the church such that leaders are servants who guide the whole congregation into the full priestly ministry of the church, because this is the narrative thread of Scripture. In this sense, this church is that church, and the identity is narrative in character—their two stories are rendered one. To repeat, this may not meet all the objections of the Roman Catholic (or the High Church Protestant or even some baptists), but it should make clear the pattern of reasoning that animates the baptist vision, and in doing so trace again the contours of the narrative identity effected by the vision as it reads Scripture.

The purpose of considering Barron's objection to McClendon's argument against priests has been to highlight what has been claimed all along, that the baptist vision is thoroughly and intrinsically a narrative vision, that the identity claim that constitutes the vision is ordered by a narrative reading of Scripture. Furthermore, as in incarnational identity and conversion considered through the baptist vision, the narrative reading strategy of baptists is able to hold both ends of the relation together in such a way as not to collapse them indiscernibly into one another. Hence, these three examples, as instances of the baptist vision at work, show the baptist vision itself to be constituted by an identity claim, narratively understood, which is not reducible to strict identity. As such, it ought to prove useful in turning to Eucharistic identity claims. In order to fruitfully bring them to bear on Eucharistic identity, I now make explicit the role that narrative plays in ordering analogous uses of language in McClendon's theology.

Analogous Uses of Language and Narrative Identities

Now, in the concluding section of this part of the chapter it is time to make explicit the relationship between narrative and analogous use. My claim is threefold. First, though never an explicit object of reflection in his theology, analogous uses of language are constitutive of McClendon's theology, archetypically so in the motto of the baptist vision itself, 'this is that.' Second, the analogous uses of language constitute claims that are real identifications, though not strict identity. Third, what orders or disciplines these analogous uses just is the narrative reading strategy of baptists. In other words, the contours of these analogous uses that constitute non-strict, but real identity claims are traced along narrative lines. All of these claims have been implicitly articulated already, but need to be gathered up explicitly.

I indicated in each of the sections above how an appeal to narrative brought to the surface the way in which real identities were claimed, without being strict identity. For McClendon, Jesus is God and human, and this identity claim is articulated in narrative terms. The identity claim is as real as any articulated in terms of natures. Furthermore, like the two natures model, it facilitated an identification of this one human as God that nevertheless retained the relative integrity of each. To say that two stories converge in the one story of Jesus Christ is to say that Jesus is God, but not indistinguishable from God. Likewise, conversion narratives articulate an identification of sinner and disciple in terms of Jesus's story and the church, but in such a way that the relative identities of each are preserved. I argued that the form of McClendon's argument against priests is inherently narrative, and that it reflected the discernibility of this church from that church within the baptist identification of this church as that church.

That these various identifications are real identities, but not strict identities, is sufficient to indicate that analogous uses of language are at work here. The 'is' in Jesus is God, this church is that church, I am a follower of Jesus, and the like is used analogously. The significance of this observation is along the same lines as the observation about Thomas and Hubmaier, namely that an affirmation of real identity need not demand an *explanation* of that identity, that strict identity is a supposition that need not be supposed. For

Christians, that identity claims central to the faith, like Jesus is God, conform neither to strict identity nor to merely 'symbolic' identity indicates the need for such uses.

Finally, in the case of McClendon, what orders these analogous uses is the baptist hermeneutic of reading Scripture narratively. In chapter 4, I argued that it was Thomas's advertence to God as first cause that allowed him to bring order to the varied uses of substance and accident. In chapter 5 I argued that it was a vestigial sensibility that allowed Hubmaier to test various ways of speaking of Christ. Here, I have shown how for McClendon it is appeal to the narrative of Scripture itself and the convergence of that narrative on the narratives of the contemporary church that discipline the analogous uses of language that constitute the identity statements. For example, the identity of Jesus as God and human is articulated in terms of the narratives that converge in the one narrative of Jesus Christ. The unity and the discernibility of the humanity and divinity of Jesus is traced along the narratives themselves. Of course, the narratives do not *justify* in an abstract theoretical way the claim made; nor do the narratives *explain* the relation so that the mystery of the relation is solved. Rather they *elucidate* the claim; that is, they take one by the hand and lead her along the narrative 'logic' that disciplines the analogous uses of 'is' that constitute the identity, without collapsing the poles of the identity. Hence, an appeal to narrative is no extrinsic theoretical justification of analogous usage, but rather the 'on the ground' grammar of those baptists making the claims.

So, for McClendon and baptists, at least insofar as McClendon has rightly identified the animating and orienting vision of baptists, analogous uses of language constitute identity claims that are real identities, though not strict identities; and appeal to the narrative reading habits of these baptists serves to trace the contours of these analogous uses of language. In what follows, I bring to bear on Eucharistic identity what has so far been gained.

The 'baptist' Vision and the Lord's Supper

In chapter 4 I argued that, owing to the fact that analogous uses of language are fitting for metaphysical discourse and required for affirmations about God, there was a way of construing Thomas's account of transubstantiation as a conversion of bread to body, but one that allowed both poles of the identity, 'this bread is Christ's body.' There we noted analogous uses of the terms 'substance' and 'accident,' and that their amenability to varied though related uses made them useful to Thomas's metaphysics, and suggested creative uses of them were fitting for Thomas's theological task. In chapter 5 I argued that Hubmaier's Eucharistic theology can be read as an exercise in disciplining what can be said about Christ's body for the purpose of instructing the church in how to suffer for the gospel. In particular, Hubmaier exploits the variety of *kinds* of identity statements available to shift the emphasis of Eucharistic identity claims from Christ's body in the bread to Christ's body in the church. Hubmaier traces the contours of these identity claims along the lines of analogous uses of 'is,' a theological task that facilitates his instruction to Christians on the life of a suffering church.

In this chapter, I have so far pursued the narrative character of the baptist vision's 'this is that.' The analogous uses of language that constitute the vision itself, as well as the various claims falling from the vision (doctrinal, ethical, and otherwise), are uses that are disciplined by the community practice of reading Scripture as itself an overarching narrative that incorporates these reading communities into its own story. We might say that baptists read their own stories into the stories of Scripture in such a way that 'this is *narratively* that,' where narrative serves as the framework for tracing the contours of the particular ways language is used analogously, ways that open up various sorts of identity claims that do not collapse 'this' into 'that' or vice versa. All of this has been in the service of showing how the baptist vision itself provides an illuminating parallel to the Eucharistic identity claim 'this bread is that body.' Now, it is time to see the baptist vision at work in a theology of the Lord's Supper in order to draw out the comparison.

So, in what follows I first describe McClendon's Eucharistic theology, paying particular attention to his setting of the Lord's Supper in the context of the church. McClendon understands the Lord's Supper ethically as a community-constituting practice, and doctrinally as corporate fellowship with Jesus. Then I turn to the more focused question of Jesus's body in the Lord's Supper. For McClendon, what is said about Christ's body in the Supper must be narratively related to the identity of the church, not only the bread and wine. It is this narrative context that facilitates analogous uses of language that constitute the various identity claims.

McClendon on the Lord's Supper

In explicating McClendon's account of the Lord's Supper, I will presume the account I gave in chapter 2 of McClendon's contribution to Baptist sacramentalism with respect to the Lord's Supper. To briefly recall the central points, first, for McClendon the Lord's Supper is a *community* practice. Its moral or ethical thrust is the formation of the church; its doctrinal explication is as a remembering sign of the church. This particular remembering sign "pledges and performs the *incorporation* of the lives of the gathered disciples not only into their crucified and risen Lord, but also into one another."[84] Second, the gathering performed by the Supper is focused on Jesus Christ, the "objective driving force" of worship. In worship, the church meets Christ; he is really present, which is to say "present *in a way that matters* . . . [which] is to

---

[84] McClendon, *Ethics*, 219.

say that the one of whom this story tells is present in such a way that *the story continues,* present in a way that makes no sense save for the story to this point, a way that shapes the story to follow."[85] Hence, the community practice is the occasion of incorporation into Christ by way of a genuine meeting with Jesus in the meal, where incorporation and meeting are traced out along narrative lines.

With this brief summary, and keeping in mind the longer exposition in chapter 2, it is appropriate to approach the Eucharistic identity statement from the perspective of *community*, the central location of the Supper for McClendon. Aside from being central to McClendon's own account, for McClendon, like Hubmaier, the relation of the Supper to the church is in the end an important indication of what to say about the bread and wine, and about Christ's body.

For McClendon, the Lord's Supper may be explicated both in terms of its ethical import and in terms of what the church teaches theologically about it. First, McClendon says that the Lord's Supper in the New Testament is one of two practices associated with community watchcare. In the Supper, participants "pledge anew the covenant with God and one another as they remember the exodus that set Israel free, drinking the proffered cup in anticipation of their Lord's return to 'drink it anew' in the kingdom of God."[86] McClendon says that the Lord's Super is the "*repeated* rite of renewal and pledge and hope for the men and women of Jesus' new kingdom."[87] McClendon says that the second practice of watchcare, "less often recalled by Christians today . . . is the practice of mutual admonition and forgiveness."[88] These two practices were means of facilitating life on the way, a life that stands as witness to God's visitation in Christ.

Though this was the New Testament practice, McClendon claims that the interiorization of the Christian life in later Christian history has sundered the Lord's Supper from its constitutive role as a *community* practice. In Roman Catholic Sacramental theology it became over time a means of dispensing grace in a "secret sacrament;" in Protestantism it became a "libertarian exaltation of primitive conscience that could neither endure common Christian scrutiny nor overcome the self-serving protection each of us erects around our private selves."[89] The problem with both Catholic and Protestant versions is that they fail to enact the Supper as a community constitutive practice.

---

85 Ibid., *Doctrine*, 378.

86 Ibid., *Ethics*, 52. McClendon cites Mark 14:22-25.

87 Ibid.

88 Ibid. McClendon cites Matthew 18:15ff, and 1 Thessalonians 5:14.

89 McClendon, *Ethics*, 77. In Protestant circles, one tires of hearing the repeated claim that the Supper hinges on its *meaningfulness*, which of course means the degree to

If the Lord's Supper is a community constitutive practice, then it must be approached in terms of the community itself, rather than the dynamics (be they psychological for Protestants or sacramental for Catholics) of individual conscience. This, then provides a useful entrance to the comparison I mean to make between the baptist vision and Eucharistic identity because it displays that for baptists the Eucharistic identity claim is not *merely* about the relation of bread and wine to Jesus, but about the identity of the community feasting on the bread.

For McClendon, the moral force of the Lords Supper does not exhaust what should be said about it, and as shown in chapter 2, he explicates it doctrinally in terms of community. There, I noted that for McClendon a doctrinal explication of the Lord's Supper presumes that Christian worship is a real meeting with God, because in worship Jesus has promised his presence; that the Lord's Supper is one of the remembering signs, remembering not as an inward calling to mind, but as a public memorial done in the church, through the Spirit, by which God remembers his promise in Christ to gather his followers into himself as one (in this sense these remembering signs are effectual signs); and that the identity of the Lord's Supper is directly related to the person of Jesus—the narrative that fixes the identity of Jesus constitutes the narrative frame of the liturgical performance of the sign, and hence fixes the identity of this sign. The narrative identity of the Supper is constituted by a "plurality of narratives" which converge in the narrative of Christ, and the convergence of Christ's narrative converges with the narrative of his disciples.

So, for McClendon, Jesus promises to be present, and by the gracious power of God is indeed present in Christian worship. With respect to the Lord's Supper, the issue of his presence is linked in some way (though not exhaustively) with the bread and wine. But the kind of identity is the question at hand. Given Jesus's presence in worship, McClendon says that "Jesus' 'real' presence is not limited to the Eucharist (far less to its food and drink)," but is instead the renewal of the presence of Jesus risen.[90] To say that this pervasive presence is 'real' is to say, as we have noted already, that Jesus is present "*in a way that matters* . . . [which] is to say that the one of whom this story tells is present in such a way that *the story continues*, present in a way that makes no sense save for the story to this point, a way that shapes the story still to follow."[91]

All of this sounds right to baptist ears. Whatever we say about Christ in the Lord's Supper must not override or contradict this: Jesus is really, truly present in worship, and we can fruitfully articulate that presence in Scripture's

---

which it engages the personal world of meaning of the participants. 'Personal world of meaning' is intentionally as vague as that which I use it to name.

90 Ibid., *Doctrine*, 378.

91 McClendon, *Doctrine*, 378.

own narrative terms rather than requiring traditionally metaphysical categories. This makes sense in light of the baptist vision—'that' Jesus meeting with 'those' disciples after the resurrection is 'this' Jesus meeting us; 'these' disciples, and the identity of all involved, as their identifications with each other, is narratively articulated. In other words, the analogous uses of is, presence, and the like falling from the baptist vision are uses that are elucidated by the practices of community reading of these baptists. The issue unaddressed seems to be this: not presence generally, or even personally, but Jesus's *embodied* presence.

Jesus's Body and the Lord's Supper

In the concluding section of this part of the chapter, I aim to make explicit the markers that McClendon implicitly employs to order the analogous uses of language that constitute a baptist articulation of Eucharistic identity. This ordering affirms a real identity between bread and body. Of course, no baptist would deny the presence of Jesus in the Lord's Supper (nor would any Roman Catholic or Protestant), but many baptists would deny, and indeed have denied, the presence of Jesus's *body* in the bread, that 'this is my body' constitutes anything more than a symbolic or figural identity of bread and body. That is the identity claim at issue.[92]

---

[92] In a description of McClendon's account of the Lord's Supper, Scott Bullard notes that McClendon does not speak of 'presence' with qualifiers indicating a relationship to the presence of Christ's *physical* body. Bullard suggests that McClendon is following the trajectory of his teacher, Walter Thomas Conner. Scott Bullard, "A Re-membering Sign: The Eucharist and Ecclesial Unity In Baptist Ecclesiologies" (PhD diss., Baylor University, 2009), 39-40. Conner said that an affirmation of symbolism with respect to the elements "does not deny the spiritual omnipresence of Christ, but it does deny that Christ is present in the bread and wine of the Supper any more than he is present in any other material substance." Conner, *Revelation and God: An Introduction to Christian Doctrine* (Nashville: Broadman Press, 1936), 287.

What does material substance have to do with presence? Robert Jenson, in reflecting on Paul's use of 'body,' argues that "someone's 'body' is simply the person him or herself insofar as this person is *available* to other persons and to him or herself, insofar as the person is an *object* for other persons and him or herself." Jenson goes on to say "for Paul, a 'spiritual' body, whatever that may be, is as much or more a body as is a biological body." Robert Jenson, *The Triune God*, vol. 1 of *Systematic Theology* (New York: Oxford Press, 1997), 205. Of course, Christ's 'historical' body was physical (it bled); but why think that Christ's 'historical,' bleeding body is only "*available* to other persons" *materially*? This is the gist of my suggestion to come, that narrative identity allows us to speak of the availability of Christ's body without presuming a simply 'physical' presence (though, of course, we *might* want to keep the label

So, what light does the baptist vision cast on the Eucharistic identity claim, this bread is Christ's *body*? McClendon argues that in the gospel narratives and Paul's letter, solidarity is an important theme. McClendon cites Austin M. Farrer who has argued that 'this is my body' would have been understood in Jesus's Jewish context as an invitation to communion with him as the host, a communion that takes place by means of the sharing of a meal.[93] So, presence is relevant to Eucharistic identity insofar as it is a meal of fellowship with Jesus. It is a remembering meal of solidarity, of *communion* with Jesus in sharing the bread he offers.

That in the gospel narrative it is Jesus who offers the bread by way of an identification with his body is indeed important for understanding the corporate communion of the church's celebration of the remembering signs. Says McClendon,

> At church we set bread and wine upon the table. Whose is it? Ours, but if we present it to the risen Lord, whom we trust to be there, is it not rather his? And if he returns it to us each in words first used long ago, "This is my body; this is for you" (cf. 1 Cor. 11:24) is it not rightfully his bread, his body, that we then receive? On this view, Christ does not lie slaughtered before us on the table to be eaten by hungry Christian cannibals; rather Christ risen is present in our eucharist to commune with us, to give us bread that is his, and so (by rights) his own body. When we have received it we can say with certain travelers to Emmaus, "He sat down with us at table, he took bread and said the blessing; he broke the bread, and offered it—to us." Afterward, perhaps we can tell "how he made himself known to us in the breaking of bread" (Luke 24:30-35). Such union with Jesus is re-membering, it is reconstitution, being made part of the whole. In it we are re-united, we are re-membered one to another as his members.[94]

On McClendon's read, the narrative trajectory entails that the bread is "rightfully his bread, his body," and the bread is "by rights his own body," and

---

'physical' so long as it is run through 'narrative '*ascesis*). In any case, Jenson's account of body allows him to make a strong claim about the church as Christ's body: that it is "the risen body of Christ," (*The Triune God*, 205). Yet, that identification does not entail the indiscernibility of the church and Christ's body: "In the New Testament, the church and risen Christ are one but can also be distinguished from each other; thus for example, the church is the risen Christ's bride [Eph. 5:31-32] so that Christ and the church are joined as *couple*. We may not so identify the risen Christ with the church as to be unable to refer distinctively to the one and then to the other." Jenson, *The Works Of God,* vol. 2 of *Systematic Theology* (New York: Oxford University Press, 1999), 213.

93 McClendon, *Doctrine*, 401-402.

94 McClendon, *Doctrine*, 402.

his bread is his communion with disciples that re-members disciples one to another.

But, what is this narrative trajectory? If, in the baptist vision, it is the narrative reading strategy itself that orders analogous uses of language, then what is the narrative elucidation of "rightfully," and "by rights" that McClendon employs to elucidate 'is' in 'this is my body'? McClendon suggests that the narrative trajectory in view is explicated in terms of the covenant. Reflecting on the theme of solidarity, McClendon notes that while Eucharistic theology has tended to focus on the mechanics of the presence of Christ's body and blood in the bread and wine (suggesting that McClendon means "by rights" something of an alternative to the debates surrounding 'substance' and the like), the notion of covenant is linked by Jesus with his blood in all three synoptic gospels and in 1 Corinthians. About this, McClendon says that we should

> concentrate first on covenant, reading the text not "this is my *blood* (of the covenant)," but with a better exegesis: "This is *my* blood-of-the-covenant"; that is, This rite we share tonight in the upper room is *my* reaffirmation of JWHW God's ancient pledge, linking us to that covenant and thereby to the ancient solidarity of God-and-Israel, and (as the reader knows with foreboding) linking it also to the ultimate blood-sacrifice, that of the Servant who will tomorrow witness to God's truth on a Roman cross.[95]

In this light, the identification of bread with body links with the theme of solidarity because the Supper is identified in the gospel narrative with God's prior promises to be in solidarity with Israel.

Because this meal is a meal of solidarity, the result is that the identity of the disciples "includes, rather than excludes, the broken chunks of nourishing bread as (prospectively) the rite pledges and performs the *incorporation* of the lives of the gathered disciples not only into their crucified and risen Lord, but also into one another."[96] That is, the identification of bread as Christ's body, understood in light of covenant, is the identification of the disciples as Christ's body, and as sharers of one another's bodies.

Still, what of the presence of Christ's body in bread? Have all the past and present Eucharistic debates simply missed the point? The above explication has already suggested the narrative direction of the answer: In the meal, by Jesus's own words and actions, the bread is his body broken for the world and made available in solidarity to those who worship him, and in its availability incorporates them into his own body. Covenant is the identification of this body as the fulfillment of God's promises. Consequently, negatively the baptist

---

95 Ibid., *Ethics,* 219.

96 Ibid.

vision simply does not allow a 'merely' symbolic read of this identity. If God is faithful to his promises, and if Jesus is available to his disciples in solidarity with them, then the identity claim about bread and body is real identity. Yet, the narrative contours of Scripture in the reading strategy of this community display that the analogous uses constitute a real, but not strict identity claim. Thus, it is precisely the reading strategy of these baptists that makes possible the claim of real, though not strict, identity.

McClendon's account of presence as a virtue is helpful if the issue is what to say about the presence of Jesus's body. McClendon claims that the virtue of presence is "the quality of *being there* for and with one another."[97] As embodied creatures, our bodies are integral to our living, and so McClendon claims, "*being there* is a function of our embodied existence; it is only by metaphor or analogy that we can speak of a disembodied presence."[98] In a similar trajectory, Robert Jenson, in reflecting on Paul's use of 'body,' argues that "someone's 'body' is simply the person him or herself insofar as this person is *available* to other persons and to him or herself, insofar as the person is an *object* for other persons and him or herself."[99] So, to speak of solidarity or the presence of Jesus is to say something about Jesus's body. Of course, there is no requirement here to think that speaking of Jesus's body in the Supper entails speaking of Jesus's body in just the same way we would speak of any other body, or even of the way we might speak of Jesus's crucified and risen body. Jesus's 'historical' body on the cross bled; Jesus's body in the bread does not bleed (at least according to Thomas and Hubmaier; and McClendon's own reading strategy supports this view), though of course Jesus's ecclesial body does bleed in martyrdom. Where Thomas might appeal to God's power as first cause to order the various senses of body and blood by way of 'substance' and 'accident,' the baptist vision orders the various senses in the narrative reading of Scripture itself. The identification of the narrative, the themes that arise from it, and the place of the readers themselves in the narrative discipline the identity claim, 'this is my body.'

For my purposes, recall what the series of linkages above discloses: The 'being one's self for someone else' of Jesus is intrinsically bodily. This is the thrust of the incarnation; not that God is with us (God is always with his people), but that God is with us '*in body*' in the humanity of Jesus. Hence, if bread is narratively linked with covenant, with Jesus's 'being one's self for someone else,' then it is narratively linked with the presence of Jesus's body. Furthermore, and crucial for McClendon, is that the narrative link between Jesus's body and the bread suggests the narrative link between Jesus's body and the church. Hence, the analogous uses of language constituting Eucharistic

97 McClendon, *Ethics*, 115.

98 Ibid.

99 Jenson, *The Triune God*, 205.

identity are traced out along narrative threads. As in Hubmaier, 'body' flickers back and forth between Jesus's body, the bread, and the church. What disciplines that flickering of language use, that is, what makes the uses analogous rather than spinning into equivocation is the narrative reading strategy of Scripture by these baptists and the identity claim that articulates their vision: this is that.

What a baptist will resist is what McClendon resists above, a *limiting* of Christ's body to the bread and the wine. Hubmaier proves to be a wise guide here to the degree that he implicitly sensed, if not explicitly articulated, that it is the narrative trajectory of Scripture itself that leads to the radical reformer's claim that the point of the Supper is the suffering church as Christ's suffering body. In fact, it is worth recalling that as a radical reformer, Hubmaier himself was a historical sharer in the baptist vision identified by McClendon. Operating implicitly on this vision, Hubmaier, like McClendon, displays that any account of the Lord's Supper that makes the conversion of bread to body the point to the exclusion of (or perhaps even merely to the oversight of) the 'conversion' of the church to Christ's body has missed the narrative trajectory of Scripture, and has thus failed to exploit the guideposts that make possible prolific and creative, though not unruly and confused, uses of language.

Even so, if a baptist joins Schmemann in lamenting the fact that Eucharistic debates in the West have focused so much attention on Christ's body in the bread to the detriment of the church as Christ's body, the prevalent modern baptist impulse to *exclude* Christ's body from the bread is equally mistaken; and it is mistaken on baptists' own grounds. The above account has attempted to show how the analogous uses of language that constitute Eucharistic identity claims articulate narrative linkages that must hold to be faithful to the narrative trajectory of Scripture, and one of those narrative linkages is indeed between bread and Christ's body. The link suggests that it is real identity, though not strict identity, and baptists' own vision is both illuminative of and generative of just such identity claims.

Conclusion: The 'baptist' Vision and Eucharistic Identity

I said in the introductory first chapter that I would show that there is an intrinsic relation between the baptist vision and catholic Eucharistic identity claims; and furthermore, that the baptist vision has something to offer broadly catholic Eucharistic theology. Both claims have been explored and defended, but now can be gathered up and stated more straightforwardly. Consequently, this conclusion to chapter 6 will serve as a fitting conclusion to the book as a whole.

I have claimed that what orders analogous uses of language that constitute Eucharistic identity claims in McClendon's theology of the Lord's Supper is the operation of the baptist vision itself embodied in the narrative reading strategy of baptists. Hence, the identity claims made by McClendon with respect to Jesus's body, bread, and the church, identity claims made by means of analogous uses of language, are traced along narrative lines. It is precisely these narrative lines that elucidate the identity as real, but not strict.

Furthermore, I showed how the baptist vision itself, a vision operating on the awareness of the identity of this church as that church, is likewise traced out along similar narrative lines. Tracing the narrative lines of the identity by means of the narrative reading strategy of Scripture displays the vision itself to be constituted by an identity claim that is real, yet not strict.

The result is that the baptist vision and Eucharistic identity are of a logical piece. Both employ analogous uses of language to constitute real, but not strict identity claims. Hence, the baptist vision itself is organically generative of such real, though not strict identity claims as 'this is my body.' If McClendon is right, baptists are promiscuous 'analogizers.' Baptists see *everything* under the aspect of the grand narrative of Scripture, and hence any identity claim of what something is (when the baptist vision is operative) is a narrative identification in light of Scripture. Any oppressive, authoritarian, slave-holding power is a biblical pharaoh and a Caesar; any present day martyr is Stephen seeing the Lord; any contemporary church is the disciples' following Jesus (and is perhaps *also* the teachers of the law failing to *see* Jesus). These identifications for the baptist are not merely figural; they constitute real identity claims. Of course, baptists do not thereby collapse every despot into the biblical Pharaoh. The vision that generates the identification likewise generates the narrative distinctions required to make the identifications unconfusedly.

Insofar as the vision is naturally generative of such real, but not strict Eucharistic identity claims, those claims ought not to be foreign to baptist life; in fact, it would be oddly out of place for the vision *not* to generate those sorts of claims. Consequently, the contribution my argument makes to the loose project of Baptist sacramentalism is simply that the project is in no way foreign to the baptist vision itself. If many Baptists think it is, then they have not understood their own form of life well. Attention to Hubmaier supports my claim, for insofar as Hubmaier was a baptist, my claim suggests that the 'sensibility' that allowed him to discipline his language about Christ's body was not only his reading of the patristic sources, but also his own animating baptist vision, though it was never articulated as such by Hubmaier himself.

I said in the introduction to chapter 1 that I would argue that what baptists have to offer broadly catholic Eucharistic theology is simply the baptist vision itself. Gathering up what has been said in this final chapter about the relationship between analogous uses of language, real identity, and narrative will make this claim clear. In sum, the narrative reading strategy of baptists that embodies the vision itself is a fruitful means of ordering the analogous uses of language at issue, and hence the vision itself is constructively engaged in catholic Eucharistic theological reflection.

First, as I showed throughout this final chapter, by the lights of the baptist vision, appeal to the narrative reading strategy of baptists occasions an appeal to real identity. For example, attention to a narrative Christology born of the baptist vision displayed the power of narrative to trace the contours of analogous uses of language that constitute the identity claim, showing the identity to be real, but not strict. In Christology, narrative identity can bear all the weight that 'nature' can in order to identify without confusion humanity and divinity in the one person of Christ.

Bringing such narrative readings to bear on Eucharistic identity suggested that, at least for baptists, there is no more fundamental way of explicating Eucharistic identities—the series of linkages between bread, Jesus's body, God, Israel, disciples, and us—than by the narrative reading strategy; that is, what disciplines the analogous uses of language that constitute the identity claims about Jesus's body, bread, and the church, just is the baptist vision's narrative reading of Scripture.

The reading strategy of these baptists disciplines Eucharistic identity claims such that the identity of Jesus's body, the bread, and the church flicker back and forth seamlessly one to another. Recall that for Hubmaier (as for Thomas, though coming from a different direction) though there is real identity between bread and body, one cannot simply say of the bread what one says of Christ's body, and vice versa. Narrative readings of Scripture by these baptists flesh out the contours of what can be said of each. Jesus offers himself to us in bread as a participation in his offering of himself for us on the cross. By participating in the meal of his body we are incorporated into his body and consequently are incorporated into one another. That we cannot say about the bread merely what we say about his body on the cross is indicative of the narrative that makes sense of the identification in the first place, in particular because that narrative has as its point the identification of the church as his body; and of course, that we cannot say of the church simply what we say of his body on the cross (or in the bread, for that matter) is indicative of the narrative that makes sense of that identity insofar as the point of the narrative is faithfulness, that is, following the one so crucified on the cross and given as gift in the bread. Hence, the identification of Jesus's body on the cross, his body in the bread, and the church as his body is traced along the narrative of Scripture. This reading of the grand narrative provides the linguistic 'ordering' necessary to keep analogous uses of 'is' from spinning into equivocation, an 'ordering' implicit in Hubmaier's 'sensibility' and evidenced in Hubmaier's theology of the Lord's Supper.

Furthermore, and immediately to the point of a baptist contribution to broadly catholic Eucharistic reflection, is the fact that the above narrative ordering of Hubmaier suggests why Thomas's neglect of the church from his account of transubstantiation is problematic. Thomas of course cites the standard theological affirmation that the Eucharist is the sacrament of unity. Yet, in his constructive reflections on Christ's body in the bread the church plays no substantive role. Even the reasonable response that Thomas is simply interested in a different, though related issue (namely, the change of bread to body) is shown to be inadequate by the narrative identifications above. If the identity of the bread as Christ's body is narratively linked with the identity of the church as Christ's body, then any account of the identity of the bread must intrinsically make room for the identity of the church. That is, even if Thomas's account of transubstantiation is not an explanation (Schmemann's objection) but instead metaphysical *ascesis*, he has not 'exercised' language enough to bend it toward its Eucharistic completion in the identification of the church as the body of Christ. In an odd sort of way, even in their usually overly pietistic-individualistic mode, baptist conversion stories are more Eucharistically appropriate than transubstantiation insofar as they articulate the convergence of these individual narratives into the narrative of the church. When brought in proximity to Eucharistic identity, the fit is natural, where for Thomas's account of Eucharistic identity, it is extrinsically relatable at best.

This further suggests why my attempted repair of Thomas, though better affirming the broadly catholic identity of bread and body than Thomas's actual account, is still inadequate. Even my repair leaves the account of change insulated from the church, an insulation that, by the baptist vision, is narratively out of place for these particular analogous uses of language.

Of course, the logic of the above criticisms of Thomas is a logic at home within the baptist vision. Though Schmemann, for instance, concurs with the claim that Thomas misconstrues the relation of the church to the bread and body, Schmemann's objection is motivated by, and ordered by, a logic different from baptists. In other words, for Schmemann what orders the analogous uses of language in Eucharistic identity statements is (obviously enough) not the baptist vision as it is embodied in baptist readings of Scripture. Given that baptists are a minority in the broad catholic tradition of the church, then, in what way is an appeal to the baptist vision a contribution to catholic Christianity? Just to the degree that, as I have claimed, the baptist vision itself is constituted by an awareness of an identity of this church as that church, an identity that is real, though not strict, and embodied in the baptist narrative hermeneutic, an identity claim in form shared by Eucharistic identity. Thus, if real, though not strict, identity characterizes catholic Eucharistic identity, and the sort of Eucharistic identity in view here is intrinsically related to the baptist vision, then the baptist vision itself shares a 'logic' that is, at least in this respect, broadly catholic.

Baptists claim many things by way of this vision that the church catholic has rejected. So, it would be too much to claim that the baptist vision is *the* catholic vision. Still, it is *in this respect* catholic; and insofar as it is, this dissenting peoples' own vision is what they can offer to the church catholic as a constructive participant in Eucharistic theology.

BIBLIOGRAPHY

Alter, Robert. *The Art of Biblical Narrative*. New York: Basic Books, 1981.

Armour, Rollin Stely. *Anabaptist Baptism: A Representative Study*. Studies in Anabaptist and Mennonite History, ed. John S. Oyer, *et al,* no. 11. Scottdale, PA: Herald Press, 1966.

Baker, G.P. and P.M.S. Hacker. *Wittgenstein, Understanding, and Meaning: An Analytical Commentary On the* Philosophical Investigations. Oxford: Basil Blackwell, 1980.

Ballie, John. *Our Knowledge of God*. London: Oxford University Press, 1939.

Barron, Robert. "Considering the Systematic Theology of James William McClendon, Jr." *Modern Theology* 18 (April 2002): 251-265.

Beachy, Alvin, J. *The Concept of Grace In the Radical Reformation*. Nieuwkoop: B. De Graaf, 1977.

Beckwith, Sarah. *Christ's Body: Identity, Culture and Society In Late Medieval Writings*. London: Routledge, 1993.

Bergsten, Torsten. *Balthasar Hubmaier: Anabaptist Theologian and Martyr*. Translated by Irwin J. Barnes and William R. Estep. Edited by William R. Estep. Valley Forge: Judson Press, 1978.

Black, Andrew D. "Kingdom of Priests or Democracy of Competent Souls? The 'Baptist Manifesto,' John Howard Yoder, and the Question of Baptist Identity." Master's Thesis, Baylor University, 2006

Bobik, Joseph. *Veritas Divina: Aquinas on Divine Truth: Some Philosophy of Religion*. South Bend: St. Augustine's Press, 2001.

Broadway, Mikael. "Is It Not Communion Of the Body Of Christ?" *Review and Expositor* 100 (Summer 2003): 403-447.

Budde, Michael. *The (Magic) Kingdom of God: Christianity and Global Cultural Industries*. Boulder, CO: Westview Press, 1997.

Budde, Michael, and Robert W. Brimlow. *Christianity Incorporated: How Big Business Is Buying the Church*. Grand Rapids: Brazos Press, 2002.

Bulgakov, Sergius. *The Holy Grail and the Eucharist*. Translated by Boris Jakim. Hudson, NY: Lindisfarne Books, 1997.

Bullard, Scott. "A Re-membering Sign: The Eucharist and Ecclesial Unity In Baptist Ecclesiologies." PhD diss., Baylor University, 2009.

Burrell, David. *Analogy and Philosophical Language*. New Haven: Yale University Press, 1973.

________. *Aquinas: God and Action.* 2nd ed. Scranton: University of Scranton, 2008.

________. "Aquinas on Naming God." *Theological Studies* 24 (June 1963): 183-212.

________. "Distinguishing God from the World." In *Language, Meaning and God: Essays in Honor of Herbert McCabe*, edited by Brian Davies, 75-92. Longdon: Geoffrey Chapman, 1987.

________. "Does Process Theology Rest on a Mistake?" *Theological Studies* 43 (March 1982): 125-135.

________. "From Analogy of 'Being' to Analogy of Being." In *Recovering Nature: essays in Natural Philosophy, Ethics, and Metaphysics in Honor of Ralph McInerny*, edited by Thomas Hibbs and John O'Callaghan, 253-266. Notre Dame: University of Notre Dame Press, 1999.

________. "Philosophy and Religion: Attention to Language and the Role of Reason." In *God, Reason and Religions: New Essays in the Philosophy of Religion*, edited by Eugene Thomas Long, 109-126. Dordrecth: Kluwer Academic Publishers, 1995.

________. "Religious Language and the Logic of Analogy: Apropos of McInerny's Book and Ross's Review." *International Philosophical Quarterly* 2 (December 1962): 643-658.

________. Review of *Rethinking Metaphysics*, edited by L. Gregory Jones and Stephen E. Fowl. *Modern Theology* 12 (January 1996), 109-112.

________. "Substance: A Performatory Account." In *Substances and Things: Aristotle's Doctrine of Physical Substance in Recent Essays*, edited by M.L. O'Hara, 226-249. Washington, D.C.: University Press of America, 1982.

_______. "Why Not Pursue the Metaphor of Artisan and View God's Knowledge as Practice?" In *Neoplatonism and Jewish Thought*, edited by Lenn E. Goodman, 207-217. Vol. 7 *Studies in Neoplatonism: Ancient and Modern*, edited by R. Bain Harris (Albany: State Univeristy of New York Press, 1992).

Carlton, John W. "Lord's Supper In Worship." *Review and Expositor* 66 (Winter 1969): 67-74.

Cavanaugh, William T. *Torture and Eucharist: Theology, Politics, and the Body of Christ*. Oxford: Blackwell Publishers, 1998.

Clark, Neville. *An Approach to the Theology of the Sacraments*. London: SCM Press, 1956.

Clarke, W. Norris. *The One and the Many: A Contemporary Thomistic Metaphysic*. Notre Dame: University of Notre Dame Press, 2001.

Colwell, John E. *Promise and Presence: An Exploration of Sacramental Theology*. Milton Keynes: Paternoster Press, 2005.

Cross, Anthony R. *Baptism and the Baptists: Theology and Practice in Twentieth-Century Britain*. Studies in Baptist History and Thought. Carlisle: Paternoster, 2000.

Cross, Anthony R., and Philip E. Thompson. "Introduction: Baptist Sacramentalism." In *Baptist Sacramentalism*, edited by Anthony R. Cross and Philip E. Thompson. Studies In Baptist History and Thought. Milton Keynes: Paternoster Press, 2003.

Davis, Kenneth Ronald. *Anabaptism and Asceticism: A Study in Intellectual Origins*. Studies in Anabaptist and Mennonite History. Scottdale: Herald Press, 1974.

________. "No Discipline, No Church: An Anabaptist Contribution To the Reformed Tradition." *The Sixteenth Century Journal* 13 (Winter, 1982): 43-58.

DiNoia, Joseph A. Review of *Systematic Theology, Volume II*, by James Wm. McClendon, Jr. *Modern Theology* 12 (January 1996): 117-119.

Dix, Gregory. *The Shape of the Liturgy.* With additional notes by Paul V. Marshall. New York: Seabury Press, 1982.

Dyck, Cornelius J. "The Suffering Church in Anabaptism," *Mennonite Quarterly Review* 59 (January 1985): 5-23.

Elders, Leo J. *The Metaphysics of Being of St. Thomas Aquinas In a Historical Perspective.* Translated by John Dudley. Studien Und Texte Zur Geistesgeschichte Des Mittelalters. Leiden: E.J.Brill, 1993.

Ellis, Christopher J. "Embodied Grace: Exploring the Sacraments and Sacramentality." In *Baptist Sacramentalism 2,* ed. Anthony R. Cross and Philip E. Thompson. Studies in Baptist History and Thought. Milton Keynes: Paternoster, 2008.

Estep, William R. *The Anabaptist Story: An Introduction to Sixteenth-Century Anabaptism,* 3rd ed. Grand Rapids: Eerdmans, 1996.

Fiddes, Paul. *Tracks and Traces: Baptist Identity in Church and Theology*. Studies in Baptist History and Thought. Milton Keynes: Paternoster, 2003.

Finger, Thomas N. *A Contemporary Anabaptist Theology: Biblical, Historical, Constructive*. Downers Grove, IL: IVP, 2004.

Fitzpatrick, P.J. *In Breaking of Bread: The Eucharist and Ritual*. Cambridge: Cambridge University Press, 2006.

________ [G. Egner]. "Some Thoughts On the Eucharistic Presence." In *God Matters*. Herbert McCabe, 130-145. London: Continuum, 1987.

________ [G. Egner], "More Thoughts On the Eucharistic Presence." In *God Matters*. Herbert McCabe, 155-164. London: Continuum, 1987.

Fowler, Stanley K. *More Than a Symbol: The British Baptist Recovery of Baptismal Sacramentalism.* Studies in Baptist History and Thought. Carslile: Paternoster Press, 2002.

Freeman, Curtis. "A Confession for Catholic Baptists." In *Ties that Bind: Life Together in the Baptist Vision*, edited by Gary A. Furr and Curtis W. Freeman. Macon, GA: Smyth and Helwys, 1994.

________."Can Baptist Theology be Revisioned?" *Perspectives In Religious Studies* 24 (Fall 1997): 273-310.

________."'To Feed Upon by Faith': Nourishment From the Lord's Table." In *Baptist Sacramentalism*, ed. Anthony R. Cross and Philip E. Thompson. Studies In Baptist History and Thought. Milton Keynes: Paternoster Press, 2003.

Frei, Hans. *The Eclipse of Biblical Narrative: A Study in Eighteenth and Nineteenth Century Hermeneutics*. New Haven: Yale University Press, 1974.

________. *The Identity of Jesus Christ: The Hermeneutical Bases Of Dogmatic Theology*. Philadelphia: Fortress Press, 1975.

________. "The 'Literal reading' of Biblical Narrative in the Christian Tradition: Does it Stretch or Will It Break?" In *The Bible and the Narrative Tradition*, edited by Frank McConnell, 36-77. New York: Oxford University Press, 1986.

________. *Theology and Narrative: Selected Essays*, edited by George Hunsinger and William C. Placher. New York: Oxford University Press, 1993.

Friedmann, Robert. *The Theology of Anabaptism: An Interpretation*. Studies in Anabaptist and Mennonite History. Scottdale, PA: Herald Press, 1973.

Fuller, Andrew. "Circular Letters." In *The Complete Works of the Rev. Andrew Fuller With a Memoir of His Life by Andrew Gunton Fuller*. Boston, MA: Lincoln, Edmans, & Co., 1833.

Goertz, Hans-Jurgen. *The Anabaptists*. Translated by Trevor Johnson. London: Routledge, 1996.

Gregory, Brad S. *Salvation at Stake: Christian Martyrdom in Early Modern Europe*. Cambridge, MA: Harvard University Press, 1999.

Grenz, Stanley and John Franke. *Beyond Foundationalism: Shaping Theology In a Postmodern Context*. Louisville: Westminster John Knox, 2001.

Grenze, Stanley J. "Baptism and the Lord's Supper as Community Acts: Toward a Sacramental Understanding of the Ordinances." In *Baptist Sacramentalism*, ed. Anthony R. Cross and Philip E. Thompson. Studies In Baptist History and Thought. Milton Keynes: Paternoster Press, 2003.

Grisez, Germain. "An Alternative Theology Of Jesus' Substantial Presence In the Eucharist." *Irish Theological Quarterly* 65 (June 2000): 111-131.

Gunton, Colin. "A Rose by Any Other Name? From 'Christian Doctrine' to 'Systematic Theology.'" *International Journal of Systematic Theology* 1 (March 1999): 4-23.

Hallett, Garth L. *A Companion to Wittgenstein's "Philosophical Investigations."* Ithaca: Cornell University Press, 1977.

________. *Essentialism: A Wittgensteinian Critique*. Albany: State University of New York Press, 1991.

________. *Identity and Mystery in Themes of Christian Faith: Late-Wittgensteinian Perspectives*. Aldershot: Ashgate, 2005.

________. *Language and Truth*. New Haven: Yale University Press, 1988.

________. *Logic For the Labyrinth: A Guide To Critical Thinking*. Lanham, MD: University Press of America, 1984.

Hammett, John S. "Article VII: Baptism and the Lord's Supper." In *The Baptist Faith and Message 2000: Critical Issues in America's Largest Protestant*

Denomination, ed. Douglas K. Blount and Joseph D. Wooddell, 71-88. Lanham, MD: Rowman & Littlefield Publishers, 2007.

Harmon, Steven R. *Towards Baptist Catholicity: Essays On Tradition and the Baptist Vision*. Studies In Baptist History and Thought. Milton Keynes: Paternoster, 2006.

Harris, R. Baine "The Anabaptist View of the Supper." *The Journal Of Religious Thought* 33 (Autumn/Winter 1976): 55-64.

Harvey, Barry. *Another City: An Ecclesiological Primer For a Post-Christian World*. Harrisburg, PA: Trinity Press International, 1999.

________. "Beginning in the Middle of Things: Following James McClendon's *Systematic Theology*." *Modern Theology* 18 (April 2002): 251-265.

________. *Can These Bones Live: A Catholic Baptist Engagement With Ecclesiology, Hermeneutics, and Social Theory*. Grand Rapids: Brazos Press, 2008.

________."The Eucharistic Idiom of the Gospel." *Pro Ecclesia* 9 (Summer 2000): 297-318.

________."Re-Membering the Body: Baptism, Eucharist and the Politics of Disestablishment." In *Baptist Sacramentalism*, ed. Anthony R. Cross and Philip E. Thompson. Studies In Baptist History and Thought. Milton Keynes: Paternoster Press, 2003.

Hauerwas, Stanley, and L. Gregory Jones, eds. *Why Narrative? Readings in Narrative Theology*. Grand Rapids: Eerdmans, 1989.

Hauerwas, Stanley. *Performing the Faith: Bonhoeffer and the Practice of Nonviolence*. Grand Rapids: Brazos Press, 2004.

Haykin, Michael A.G. "'His Soul-Refreshing Presence': The Lord's Supper in Calvinistic Baptist Thought and Experience in the 'Long' Eighteenth Century." In *Baptist Sacramentalism*, ed. Anthony R. Cross and Philip E. Thompson. Studies In Baptist History and Thought. Milton Keynes: Paternoster Press, 2003.

Hays, Richard. *The Faith of Jesus Christ: The Narrative Substructure of Galatians 3:1-4:11*. Grand Rapids: W.B. Eerdmans, 2002.

Hemming, Laurence Paul. "Transubstantiating Ourselves." *Heythrop Journal* 44 (October 2003): 418-439.

Hensley, Jeffrey. "Are Postliberals Necessarily Antirealists? Reexamining the Metaphysics of Lindbeck's Postliberal Theology." In *The Nature of Confession: Evangelicals and Postliberals in Conversation*, ed. Timothy R. Phillips and Dennis L. Okholm, 69-80. Downers Grove, IL: InterVarsity Press, 1996.

Higton, M. A. "Hans Frei and David Tracy on the Ordinary and the Extraordinary in Christianity." *The Journal of Religion* 79 (October 1999): 566-591.

Hobbs, Herschel H. *The Baptist Faith and Message*. Nashville: Convention Press, 1971.

________. *What Baptists Believe.* Nashville: Broadman Press, 1964.

Holmes, Stephen R. *Listening to the Past: The Place of Tradition in Theology*. Grand Rapids: Baker Academic, 2002.

Howard, Fred D. *Interpreting the Lord's Supper*. Nashville: Broadman Press, 1966.

Hubmaier, Balthasar. *Balthasar Hubmaier: Schriften*. Edited by Gunnar Westin and Torsten Bergsten. Heidelberg: Gutersloher Verlagshaus Gerd Mohn, 1962.

________. *Balthasar Hubmaier: Theologian of Anabaptism*. Translated and edited by H. Wane Pipkin and John H. Yoder. Scottdale, PA: Herald Press, 1989.

Incandela, Joseph M. "The Appropriation of Wittgenstein's Work by Philosopher's of Religion: Towards a Re-evaluation and an End." *Religious Studies* 21 (December 1985): 457-474.

Jenson, Robert. *The Triune God*. Vol. 1 of *Systematic Theology*. Oxford: Oxford University Press, 1997.

________. *The Works Of God*. Vol. 2 of *Systematic Theology*. New York: Oxford University Press, 1999.

Johnson, Todd E. "Initiation or Ordination? Balthasar Hubmaier's Rite of Baptism." *Studia Liturgica* 25 (1995): 68-85.

Jorgenson, Cameron. "Bapto-Catholicism: Recovering Tradition and Reconsidering the Baptist Identity." Ph.D. diss., Baylor University, 2008.

Kärkkäinen, Veli-Matti. *Christology: A Global Introduction*. Grand Rapids: Baker Academic, 2003.

________. *An Introduction to Ecclesiology: Ecumenical, Historical, and Global Perspectives*. Downers Grove, IL: IVP, 2002.

Kelly, J.N.D. *Early Christian Doctrines*. Rev. ed. New York: HarperCollins, 1978.

Kereszty, Roch. "On the Eucharistic Presence: Response To Germain Grisez." *Irish Theological Quarterly* 65 (Winter 2000): 347-352.

Kilmartin, Edward *The Eucharist In the West: History and Theology*. Edited by Robert J. Daley. Collegeville: Liturgical Press, 1998.

Klager, Andrew P. "Balthasar Hubmaier's Use of the Church Fathers: Availability, Access and Interaction," *Mennonite Quarterly Review* 84 (January 2010): 5-65.

Klauser, Theodor. *A Short History of the Liturgy*. Oxford: Oxford University Press, 1969.

Kuusela, Oskari. "Do the Concepts of Grammar and Use in Wittgenstein Articulate a Theory of Language or Meaning?" *Philosophical Investigations* 29 (October 2006): 309-341.

Layman, H. Wayne. "The Inner Ground of Christian Theology: Church, Faith, and Sectarianism." *Journal of Ecumenical Studies* 27 (Summer 1990): 480-504.

Leonard, Bill J. *Baptists In America*. Columbia Contemporary American Religion Series. New York: Columbia University Press, 2005.

Leth, Carl M. "Balthasar Hubmaier's 'Catholic' Exegesis: Matthew 16:18-19 and the Power of the Keys." In *Biblical Interpretation In the Era of the Reformation: Essays Presented to David C. Steinmetz In Honor of His Sixtieth Birthday*. Edited by Richard A. Muller and John L. Thompson, 103-117. Grand Rapids: Eerdmans, 1996.

Levering, Matthew. *Sacrifice and Community: Jewish Offering and the Christian Eucharist*. Illuminations: Theory and Religions. Malden: Blackwell, 2005.

________. *Scripture and Metaphysics: Aquinas and the Renewal of Trinitarian Theology*. Challenges in Contemporary Theology. Malden: Blackwell, 2004.

Lubac, Henri de. *Corpus Mysticum: The Eucharist and the Church In the Middle Ages*. Translated by Gemma Simmonds with Richard Price and Christopher Stephens. Edited by Laurence Paul Hemming and Susan Frank Parsons. London: SCM Press, 2006.

Lumpkin, William L. *Baptist Confessions of Faith*. Philadelphia: Judson Press, 1959.

Mabry, Eddie. *Balthasar Hubmaier's Doctrine Of the Church*. Lanham: University Press of America, 1994.

________. *Balthasar Hubmaier's Understanding Of Faith*. Lanham: University Press of America, 1998.

MacGregor, Kirk R. *A Central European Synthesis Of Radical and Magisterial Reform: The Sacramental Theology Of Balthasar Hubmaier*. Lanham: University Press of America, 2006.

Macquarrie, John. *A Guide To the Sacraments*. London: SCM Press, 1997.

Macy, Gary. *Treasures From the Storeroom: Medieval Religion and the Eucharist*. Collegeville, MN: The Liturgical Press, 1999.

Marshall, Bruce D. "The Disunity of the Church and the Credibility of the Gospel." *Theology Today* 50 (April 1993): 78-89.

McCabe, Herbert. *God Matters*. London: Continuum, 1987.

McInerny, Ralph. *Aquinas*. Cambridge: Polity Press, 2004.

________. *The Logic of Analogy: An Interpretation of St. Thomas*. The Hague: Nijhoff, 1961.

________. *Studies In Analogy*. The Hague: Mijhoff, 1968.

McClendon, Jr., James Wm. "Balthasar Hubmaier, Catholic Anabaptist." *Mennonite Quarterly Review* 65 (January 1991): 20-33.

________. *Biography as Theology: How Life Stories Can Remake Today's Theology*. Nashville: Abingdon Press, 1974.

________. *Ethics*. 2nd. ed. Vol. 1 of *Systematic Theology*. Nashville: Abingdon Press, 2002.

________. *Doctrine*. Vol. 2 of *Systematic Theology*. Nashville: Abingdon Press, 1994.

McClendon, Jr., James Wm and James M. Smith, *Convictions: Diffusing Religious Relativism*. Rev. ed. Valley Forge, PA: Trinity Press, 1994.

Originally published as *Understanding Religious Convictions*. Notre Dame: Notre Dame University Press, 1975.

Medley, Mark. "Catholics, Baptists, and the Normativity of Tradition: A Review Essay." *Perspectives in Religious Studies* 55 (Summer, 2001): 119-129.

Meeks, Wayne. *The First Urban Christians: The Social World of the Apostle Paul*. New Haven: Yale University Press, 1983.

Miller, Vince. *Consuming Religion: Christian Faith and Practice In a Consumer Culture*. New York: Continuum, 2003.

Newman, Elizabeth. "The Lord's Supper: Might Baptists Accept a Theory of Real Presence?" In *Baptist Sacramentalism*, ed. Anthony R. Cross and Philip E. Thompson. Studies In Baptist History and Thought. Milton Keynes: Paternoster Press, 2003.

________. "Rethinking the Eucharist: Towards a Unity of Word and Deed." *Ecumenical Review* 45 (October 1993): 454-462.

________. "Theology and Science Without Dualism." *Cross Currents* 48 (Spring 1998): 34-48.

________. *Untamed Hospitality: Welcoming God and Other Strangers*. Grand Rapids: Brazos Press, 2007.

O'Connor, James T. *The Hidden Manna: A Theology Of the Eucharist*. San Francisco: Ignatius Press, 1988.

Payne, Ernest A. *The Fellowship Of Believers: Baptist Thought and Practice Yesterday and Today.* Enlarged ed. London: The Carey Kingsgate Press, 1954.

Poteat, William H. *A Philosophical Daybook: Post-Critical Investigations*. Columbia, MO: University of Missouri Press, 1990.

Power, David N. *Sacrament: The Language Of God's Giving*. New York: Crossroad Publishers, 1999.

Rempel, John D. *The Lord's Supper In Anabaptism: A Study In the Christology Of Balthasar Hubmaier, Pilgram Marpeck, and Dirk Philips*. Studies in Anabaptist and Mennonite History. Waterloo, Ontario: Herald Press, 1993.

________. "The Lord's Supper in Mennonite Tradition." *Vision: A Journal Of Church and Theology* 2 (Spring 2001): 4-15.

Rhodes, Lewis E. "Sacrament of Wholeness." *Review and Expositor* 66 (Winter 1969): 59-65.

Rist, John M. "Augustine, Aristotelianism, and Aquinas." In *Aquinas the Augustinian*. Edited by Michael Dauphinais, Barry David, and Matthew Levering. Washington, D.C.: Catholic University of America Press, 2007.

Rust, Eric C. "Theology Of the Lord's Supper." *Review and Expositor* 66 (Winter 1969): 35-44.

Sachsse, Carl. *D. Balthasar Hubmaier Als Theologe*. Berlin: Trowitzsch & Sohn, 1914.

Schillebeeckx, Edward. *The Eucharist*. Translated by N. D. Smith. New York: Sheed and Ward, 1968.

Schmemann, Alexander. *The Eucharist: Sacrament Of the Kingdom*. Translated by Paul Kachur. Crestwood, NY: St. Vladimir's Seminary Press, 1987.

________. *Introduction To Liturgical Theology*. Translated by Asheleigh E. Moorehouse. Crestwood, NT: St. Vladimir's Seminary Press, 1966.

Shain, Barry Alan. *The Myth of American Individualism: The Protestant Origins of American Political Thought*. Princeton: Princeton University Press, 1994.

Sheerin, Daniel J. *The Eucharist*. Message of the Church Fathers. Wilmington, DE: Michael Glazier, 1986.

Snyder, Arnold C. *Anabaptist History and Theology: An Introduction*. Kitchener, Ontario: Pandora Press, 1995.

Sokolowski, Robert. *Eucharistic Presence: A Study in the Theology of Disclosure*. Washington, D.C.: The Catholic University of America Press, 1993.

Spurgeon, Charles H. "Mysterious Visions." In *Till He Come*. London: Passmore & Alabaster, 1894.

Stagg, Frank. "Lord's Supper In the New Testament." *Review and Expositor* 66 (Winter 1969): 5-14.

Stauffer, Ethelbert. "The Anabaptist Theology of Martyrdom." *Mennonite Quarterly Review* 19 (July 1945): 179-214.

Steinmetz, David C. *Reformers in the Wings: From Geiler von Kaysersberg To Theodore Beza*, 2nd. ed. Oxford: Oxford University press, 2001.

Stiver, Dan R. *The Philosophy Of Religious Language: Sign, Symbol, and Story*. Cambridge: Blackwell Publishers, 1996.

Stone, Darwell. *A History of the Doctrine Of the Holy Eucharist*. London: Longmans, Green, and Co., 1909.

Sykes, Stephen. *The Identity of Christianity: Theologians and the Essence of Christianity From Schleiermacher To Barth*. Philadelphia: Fortress, 1984.

Thomas Aquinas. *Summa Theologica*. Translated by Fathers of the English Dominican Province. New York: Benziger Bros, 1948.

Thompson, Philip E. "'As It Was In the Beginning'(?): The Myth of Changelessness In Baptist Life and Belief." In *Recycling the Past or Researching History: Studies in Baptist Historiography and Myths*. Edited by Anthony R. Cross and Philip E. Thompson. Studies In Baptist History and Thought. 184-206. Milton Keynes: Paternoster Press, 2005.

________. "Introduction: Practicing Sacramentality in Baptist Modality." In *Baptist Sacramentalism 2*. Edited by Anthony R. Cross and Philip E. Thompson. Studies In Baptist History and Thought. xvii-xxiv. Milton Keynes: Paternoster, 2008.

________. "A New Question in Baptist History: Seeking a Catholic Spirit Among Early Baptists." *Pro Ecclesia* 8 (Winter 1999): 51-72.

________. "Re-Envisioning Baptist Identity: Historical, Theological, and Liturgical Analysis." *Perspectives in Religious Studies* 27 (Fall 2000): 287-302.

________. "Sacraments and Religious Liberty: From Critical Practice to Rejected Infringement." In *Baptist Sacramentalism*. Edited by Anthony R. Cross and Philip E. Thompson. Studies In Baptist History and Thought. Milton Keynes: Paternoster Press, 2003.

Thurian, Max. *The Eucharistic Memorial.* Translated by J.G. Davies. Richmond: John Knox Press, 1961.

Tilley, Terrence. "Review Essay: Why American Catholic Theologians Should Read 'Baptist' Theology," *Horizons* 14 (Spring 1987): 129-137.

________. Review of *Systematic Theology*, vol. 2, *Doctrine*, by James Wm. McClendon, Jr. *Pro Ecclesia* 6 (Summer 1997): 366-368.

________. *Story Theology*. Collegeville, MN:Michael Glazier, 1985.

Tracy, David. "On Reading the Scriptures Theologically." In *Theology and Dialogue: Essays in Conversation with George Lindbeck*. Edited by Bruce D. Marshall, 35-68. Notre Dame: University of Notre Dame Press, 1990.

Vanhoozer, Kevin. "Systematic Theology." In *Dictionary For Theological Interpretation Of the Bible.* General editor Kevin Vanhoozer. Grand Rapids: Baker Academic, 2005.

Waltner, Erland. "The Anabaptist Conception of the Church." *Mennonite Quarterly Review* 25 (January 1951): 5-16.

Weaver, J. Denny. "Discipleship Redefined: Four Sixteenth Century Anabaptists." *Mennonite Quarterly Review* 54 (October 1980): 255-279.

Webster, John. "Theology After Liberalism?" In *Theology After Liberalism: A Reader*. Edited by John Webster and George P. Schner. Blackwell Readings In Modern Theology. Oxford: Blackwell Publishers, 2000.

Webster, John and George P. Schner, eds. *Theology After Liberalism: A Reader*. Blackwell Readings In Modern Theology. Oxford: Blackwell, 2000.

White, Sean A. "Southern Baptists, Sacramentalism, and Soul Competency." In *Baptist Sacramentalism 2*. Edited by Anthony R. Cross and Philip E. Thompson. Studies in Baptist History and Thought. Milton Keynes: Paternoster, 2008.

Williams, A.N. "Mystical Theology Redux: The Pattern of Aquinas' *Summa Theologiae." Modern Theology* 13 (January 1997): 53-74.

Williams, George Huntston. *The Radical Reformation.* 3rd rev. ed. Sixteenth Century Essays and Studies. Kirksville, MO: Sixteenth Century Journal Publishers, 1992.

Wippel, John F. *The Metaphysical Thought of Thomas Aquinas: From Finite Being to Uncreated Being*. Washington, D.C.: Catholic University of America Press, 2000.

Wittgenstein, Ludwig. *The Blue and Brown Books*. New York: Haper Colophon Books, 1958.

________. *Culture and Value*. Edited by G.H. Von Wright, with Heikki Numan. Translated by Peter Winch. Chicago: University of Chicago Press, 1980.

________. *Philosophical Grammar*. Edited by Rush Rhees. Translated by Anthony Kenny. Berkeley: University of California Press, 1974.

________. *Philosophical Investigations*. 3rd ed. Translated by G.E.M. Anscombe. New York: Macmillan Publishing, 1953.

York, Tripp. "Martyrdom and Eating Jesus: Two Neglected Practices?" *Conrad Grebel Review* 22 (Winter 2004): 71-86.

Index